S0-BRQ-267

Richard Strauss

A CRITICAL STUDY OF THE OPERAS

Richard Strauss outside Queen's Hall, June 26, 1914

Richard Strauss

A CRITICAL STUDY OF THE OPERAS

By
William Mann

NEW YORK
OXFORD UNIVERSITY PRESS
1966

MT
100
S84
M3

© *William Mann 1964*

52919

Printed and Bound in Great Britain by
Jarrold and Sons Ltd, Norwich
F.864

TO ERIKA

—*Der Strauss, den ich gepflücket, grüsse dich vieltausendmal!*

GOETHE

Der Anfang schon ist Verlegenheit
HUGO VON HOFMANNSTHAL

Contents

Illustrations

xi

Preface

Soon after the death of Richard Strauss I was invited by Eric Blom to contribute a volume on the composer to the *Master Musicians* series of which Blom was editor. In the years that followed I assembled a substantial quantity of information, but the book has until now proved difficult to shape satisfactorily if only because some portions of Strauss's later life are imperfectly documented, and await elucidation in Dr Willi Schuh's official biography.

This study of Strauss's operas is not a substitute for the book that I promised to write for Blom, nor does it attempt to rival the complete survey of Strauss's music on which Mr Norman Del Mar is currently engaged. It is an attempt to interpret Strauss's development through one branch of his music, the one which seems most significant and is the most substantial, his operas. To do this comprehensively would, I am aware, ideally involve a consideration of all his songs as well, and of his other stage-works including projected operas and adaptations. I have referred to some of these in passing, but for purposes of clarity and conciseness have preferred to concentrate on the fifteen completed operas, analysing each in some detail so as to show Strauss's approach to music-drama through collaboration with his various librettists, and the nature (very consistent) of his musical language. This is an extension of the method adopted so brilliantly by Ernest Newman in his several books of *Opera Nights*: I can only wish that my own application might be half as valuable.

I owe gratitude to many friends and colleagues who have, over the years, helped with the collection and deployment of material. For information and advice I am particularly grateful to Professor Dr Karl Böhm, Mr Walter Legge, Mr Peter Heyworth, Mr Harold Rosenthal, Mr Alan Jefferson, the late Dr E. M. von Asow, Miss Anne Ross, and Dr Ernst Roth. Mr Legge and Mr Harry L. Moon read and usefully criticized a number of chapters in typescript and Mr Noël Goodwin read the whole book in proof. Mr Jefferson was of tireless and invaluable assistance at all times.

Messrs Boosey & Hawkes placed orchestral material at my disposal. Generous assistance in locating photographic material came from the dramaturgical departments of the Weimar, Dresden, Munich, Zürich opera houses, from Mr Rosenthal and Dr Roth, and from the Wiener Philharmoniker Verlag; acknowledgement of photographic sources is made elsewhere. Mrs Wilfred Moulding drew the music examples. Mr Moon, Mrs Anthony Figgis, and my wife and daughter Domenique deciphered my manuscript and typed it. Miss Shirley Jowell took endless pains in the final preparation. I am delighted to record warm thanks to all these people, as well as to Mr David Ascoli who suggested the book and the title.

Some of the chapters incorporate material first published by *Opera*, by the Royal Opera House, Covent Garden and by the Decca Record Company, to all of whom acknowledgements are due.

Guntram

OPUS 25

Opera in Three Acts

LIBRETTO BY RICHARD STRAUSS

The old Duke	BASS
Freihild, his Daughter	SOPRANO
Duke Robert, her Husband	BARITONE
Guntram, a Singer	TENOR
Friedhold, a Singer	BASS
The Duke's Jester	TENOR
An Old Woman	ALTO
An Old Man	TENOR
Two Young Men	BASSES
Three Vassals	BASSES
A Messenger	BARITONE
Four Minnesingers	TWO TENORS
	TWO BASSES

I

There was never any doubt that Richard Strauss would become a professional musician. Both sides of his family were musical, on his father's side professionally so.* He began piano lessons at four with his mother (soon replaced by other teachers), violin lessons at seven, with his cousin Benno Walter. At five he composed his first pieces, a polka for piano and a Christmas carol, and thereafter went on composing until he took to his bed for the last time seventy-nine years later.

Franz Strauss, the finest horn-player in Germany, made sure that his son had a thorough academic education, crowned by a course of philosophy and the history of culture and aesthetics at Munich University. Piano-playing and composition were Richard's strong suits when in 1884 Hans von Bülow commissioned a suite for the wind ensemble of the Meiningen Court Orchestra, and sprang the surprise on young Strauss that he must conduct the first performance (at Munich) himself—without any rehearsal. Strauss had never held a baton in his hands before, but as a result Bülow obtained for him a post as assistant musical director at Meiningen.

Opera so far hardly entered his purview. His father had grounded him thoroughly in the classics, and these included standard operas given at the Munich Court Opera where Franz Strauss was principal horn. His first encounter with modern opera was not until 1878 when he saw *Tannhäuser* and *Siegfried*, and declared himself thoroughly bored, though he was no doubt echoing his father's deep-seated anti-Wagnerism. He studied Wagner scores nevertheless, rather as a student's duty (and perhaps because he knew how much Father would disapprove). When he came to Meiningen in October 1885 he and his parents may have suspected that conducting and composition would share his energies for the rest of his life, perhaps opera conducting (but Meiningen was a symphony orchestral appointment, though involving chorus-master's duties on the side), but by no means obviously the composition of operas.

It was at this point, however, that destiny stepped forward in the person of Alexander Ritter (1833–96), one of the first violins in the Meiningen Orchestra. Ritter's mother Julie and brother Karl were closely linked with Wagner (his mother had supported Wagner financially from 1851 to 1856, and had sung in the Munich first performances of *Das Rheingold* and *Die Walküre*). Alexander too had come into contact with Wagner, married his niece Franziska, and was a thorough-going apostle of the

* It may still be necessary to point out that Richard Strauss and his father's family (who came to Munich from the Upper Palatinate) were in no way related to the Waltz-Kings of Vienna.

Music of the Future. He took Strauss under his wing and made him acquainted with Wagnerian lore, with the Master's writings and those of Schopenhauer, with the music of Liszt and Berlioz, and taught him what to admire and love in scores by Wagner which young Strauss had looked at but not understood.

Ritter's relationship with Bülow was a nicely sharpened one: they had been school-friends, and both had married into the Wagner circle—though by divergent routes. After Cosima Bülow *née* Liszt became Wagner's choice for his second wife, Bülow began openly to espouse the cause of Brahms, who was of course regarded as Wagner's musical antipode. Yet he called Ritter, fanatical Wagnerian as he was, to Meiningen in 1882, and continued from time to time to conduct Wagner's music. Strauss had a story of a chance meeting on the hotel stairs when Bülow asked Ritter, 'How did you enjoy the *Tannhäuser* overture yesterday?' Ritter answered that 'it reminded me of a time when we both worshipped an ideal to which *I* have remained loyal'. Bülow's eyes filled with tears, he embraced his old friend, and rushed into his own room without another word. When news of Wagner's death reached Bülow, the conductor was prostrated with grief.

Ritter's zealous exposition of the Music of the Future turned his young friend's energies first towards symphonic poetry; Strauss completed the descriptive symphony *Aus Italien* in 1886, after a visit to that country (at Brahms's recommendation) and in the same year began his tone poem *Macbeth*. Meanwhile he had moved back to Munich as third conductor at the Royal Opera. It was during his engagement here, an unhappy and frustrating time for an ambitious conductor who had been pushed into prominence very early in his career, that Strauss began work on his first opera. Ritter had convinced him that opera must develop along Wagnerian lines as symphonic music drama expressing noble ideals. He was also of the opinion that the composer should be his own librettist, as Wagner had been, and as Ritter himself was in the operas *Der faule Hans* and *Wem die Krone?* Strauss was not much attracted to available librettists, and although he did not consider himself much of a poet he decided, at Ritter's urgent recommendation, to follow the Master's example.

Later in life Strauss declared that Wagner's operatic work so overawed him that he would never have attempted opera had not Ritter encouraged him to make the start. Even as a young man Strauss was not unduly slow to recognize his own talent, if we judge him by his letters to his parents, and we may take this reminiscence with a pillar or two of salt. It is, though, probably true that Ritter proposed the subject of Strauss's first opera; it was inspired by a remark thrown off in passing by the writer of an article printed in the *Neue freie Presse* of Vienna, about the medieval religious secret societies dedicated to art and good works, which were inspired by dissatisfaction with the secular ideals of the Minnesingers, and flourished for a time in Austria. Ritter, a pious Catholic, saw here a noble theme, or rather an ambience, suitable for post-Wagnerian treatment. One would suppose that he must have realized the close relationship to Wagner's *Tannhäuser*, and in certain respects *Parsifal*. Perhaps for that reason he did not appropriate it for himself, but hoped it would spur the imagination of a younger and as yet less selective Wagnerite. Far from questioning the suitability of the theme for treatment, Strauss elaborated an even more Wagnerian plot whose principal characters bear names directly associable with Wagner. The Wagnerisms in *Guntram* are its chief weakness, musical as well as dramatic. Yet it is not an opera that Wagner could conceivably have written himself. The atmosphere is of a quite independent order as I shall try to show, having summarized the plot.

2

The action is fixed in the mid-thirteenth century, and in Germany (though the Guilds were Austrian). We are to understand that the unspecified district is ruled, cruelly, by a ducal régime. The secret society of Love's Champions (*Streiter der Liebe*), referred to earlier, has determined to relieve suffering here, and to this end has sent hither a new recruit, Guntram. Minnesingers, whose restricted and non-political, even establishment-serving ideals have caused the founding of these religious secret societies, are attached to the ducal court.

Strauss begins with an orchestral Prelude in G major which proposes several principal themes of the opera. Thematic titles were attached to all of these by post-Wagnerian commentators, and one may think them justifiable only in so far as they illuminate the action at subsequent appearances. But it is noticeable that already they are applied less to people, as in Wagner, than to human qualities. Thus the expansive, idealistic initial phrase is identified with as many as four distinct emotional connotations: (a) represents love; (b) pity; (c) unselfishness; (d) the Cross.

I

The thematic surgery is justified by the extent to which Strauss breaks the melody up into separate, developable phrases, though he does expose the complex in one spontaneous melodic sweep. In a subsequent more fluent section, two more themes are added:

Here Ex. 2[1] portrays the Elders of the Guild; in Ex. 2[2] the phrase (a) represents Good Works and (b) the wretchedness which they are to relieve (cf. Ex. 1b). There shortly follows the theme of Minstrelsy.

The last section of the Prelude moves into double tempo and characterizes Guntram's youthful aspiring enthusiasm in a new theme:

It is quoted here in its second, tonic harmony version to show the characteristic pentatonic phrase that Strauss used on numerous other occasions, most memorably in *Arabella* (Ex. 7 there, also in F major). Ex. 4 unfolds in rather stiff phrases and is quickly dropped—it is more fully developed in Guntram's first monologue—for another thematic complex, later of some importance, concerned with Guntram's Guild, but also with his mission to the Duke, a Good Work (cf. Ex. 2[2]a and Ex. 5b).

It is perhaps worth recalling that the theme of Ex. 1 is familiar to concert audiences (many of them quite ignorant of *Guntram*) through its quotation in Strauss's *Ein Heldenleben*; and that two of the three Preludes to *Guntram* were popular for a time in the concert hall even though the opera as a whole was not enthusiastically received.

The scene reveals a forest clearing, with a fir-wood on the right, a thicket and a spring on the left, a lake at the back. Guntram and a party of poor refugees, their chattels on their backs, enter; the music is serene,

concerned with the Guild theme (Ex. 5b), and decidedly reminiscent of
Gurnemanz in *Parsifal*. With them, a little separate, is a mysterious
fellow, Friedhold, whose role is not made clear until much later. Guntram
shares his midday sandwiches with the crowd, and asks what has caused
their humiliation. A new theme, connected with suffering, runs through
the reply.

6
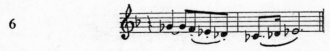

They tell him of persecution by the local aristocracy (and here the alto
role of the Old Woman offers great possibilities to an ambitious dramatic
voice with a lively top register). Their only consolation is the old Duke's
daughter, Freihild, herself prevented from performing the good works she
would do. At the first mention of Freihild's name, we hear the themes
associated with her goodness.

7

The mysterious Friedhold now offers a few words of encouragement to
the crowd, and to Guntram whom he calls *Streiter der Liebe*—Love's
Champion; and then departs. Later we are to discover that he is Guntram's
mentor in the ways of the Guild; but on visible evidence he is so unhelpful
that we cannot be surprised if Guntram later rejects his advice, though
now he is aware that he must have reached the spot where his help is
required.

The crowd fades away (the Old Woman delivering a tremendous
Wagnerian curse) and Guntram takes the farewell greeting of an old
man as the exordium of an extended monologue, *Ein glückliches Los*,
beginning with echoes of the suffering motif, Ex. 6, passing through a
perhaps too self-conscious quotation of the Reverie of Childhood theme
from *Tod und Verklärung*, and developing material already exposed in the
Prelude to the opera and the first scene, notably Ex. 4. The monologue is
well designed and full of musical invention, leading from the initial slow
meditation on nature to a dramatic fast section in which Guntram muses
on the horrors of human cruelty and hatred, and bursting at last into an
impassioned prayer for strength in the ordeal to come—we are reminded
a little of *Parsifal*, but more of *Tannhäuser*. Guntram's last words (to
Ex. 5) *Auf, ans Werk, Streiter der Liebe!* seem destined to introduce an
extended orchestral epilogue on his own theme, Ex. 4, but this is broken
off with a rapid descending scale, as he turns and observes the precipitous

entry of a young, beautiful woman, dressed in mourning and clearly at her wits' end as she hurries out of the forest towards the lake. Clear, buoyant F major has moved into a misty B minor with an extra note (the sharpened fourth) in its scale and a quantity of narrow chromatic intervals harmonized in bare fifths; the stylistic effect is astonishing, even in retrospect.

8

The lady is Freihild and she intends, literally, to drown her sorrows in the depths of the lake. How curious, comments Guntram with masterly understatement, and he is only just in time to restrain her, by clasping her in his arms, in which she faints as he draws her away from the lake. He revives her with spring water* (all this is very reminiscent of Siegmund and Sieglinde in *Die Walküre*, Acts 1 and 2—it was surely somewhere in Strauss's mind, for Ex. 8 shows a half-conscious allusion to the Valkyrie Ride, and even the first chromatic theme faintly suggests Wagner's Fate motif). Freihild is by no means grateful for these ministrations; she yearns for kindly death, and when her father's hunting horns are heard in the distance she begs Guntram to release her. The long ensuing lyrical dialogue, in which she rejects each new appeal to her finer feelings, allowed Strauss's invention to expand short themes into broad, flexible melodious paragraphs, and shows how clearly he already understood Wagner's symphonic technique in opera. Elements of Ex. 1 are involved, and also Exs. 6 and 7, to which are added two important new themes: Ex. 9 (unsuitably akin to one of the noblest themes in *Tristan*) refers to her detestation of a loveless marriage and so to her husband, the vile Robert.

9

Ver- hass - ter Minne   schreck-li- cher Zwang!

Ex. 10, which is enthusiastically developed (slipping effortlessly into 7/4 metre at one point), seems connected with protective love, here that of Freihild for the persecuted peasantry.

10

* The B flat major music here, deriving from Ex. 5, is linked by *NDM* with the quiet antithetical D major theme at the beginning of *Don Quixote*, though to me there seems a much closer connexion, especially through the rhythms of Ex. 5, with the Composer's theme which opens the Prologue to *Ariadne auf Naxos*.

This duet scene brings us face to face with the Strauss who had served his apprenticeship in *Lieder* (had by now, indeed, composed many of his most celebrated songs) and was henceforth to triumph as a composer *par excellence* of impassioned lyrico-dramatic music, above all for the soprano voice; here in fact is the beginning of the road which ends with the closing scene of *Capriccio*.*

The expansive mood of this section is broken when Guntram proudly introduces himself as a *kühner Sänger* (bold singer). Freihild, remembering the toady minstrels at court, rounds on him scornfully, struggles to release herself as the hunting calls draw nearer, and finally freeing one arm slaps his face so that he lets go of her, and she can, in his momentary shock, make for the lake once more. In this very moment the old Duke calls to her from the distance and the name 'Freihild' pulls Guntram together; this is the woman of whom the peasants spoke, the woman he most wished to meet. He rushes to her, as the name echoes again, and clasps her feet. The theme of her goodness, Ex. 7, rings out again and again as he sings her praises—much to her astonishment. Guntram has time only to beg for her confidence before the Duke and his Jester, followed in due course by the ducal retinue, discover them, and Ex. 10, matched with a festive triplet counterpoint, underlines the father's joyful reunion with his daughter. Guntram introduces himself and diplomatically adds that his goal is the ducal court which is so well spoken of by his fellow singers. Of course he is invited there and offered any favour he cares to name. At this moment we hear the voice of Duke Robert, Freihild's detested husband, shouting gall and venom at Guntram's peasant friends whom he has hunted down and is driving to dungeons or worse. Robert's brutal music here, involving Ex. 9 naturally enough, adds a new texture and density to the score. Freihild, Guntram, and the old Duke react in character, Guntram with a new theme that will later have to do with Freihild's discovery of true love.

11

Guntram promptly asks the old Duke, as his promised favour, for the freedom of these persecuted wretches. Robert protests, while the peasants call for mercy (to Ex. 6 and, with it, a figure which we may associate with the *Tanz und Musik* fugue in *Capriccio*, though Strauss was thinking, if anything, of the theme which opens the second act of *Tristan*). The Duke is fairly cross with Guntram, but agrees to let the peasants go. Now he turns to Freihild and the assembled huntsmen, suggesting that they all

* Curiously enough it was one of the sections which Strauss abbreviated in his 1940 version of the opera.

return to court; this cheerful B flat solo brings strong echoes of Wagner's Nuremberg.* Freihild accepts the invitation, to Ex. 11, i.e. because Guntram will be there.

The Jester breaks into a jubilant summons, which will be repeated at the beginning of Act 2, and this inaugurates a grand ensemble to close the act. It is quite short, and crowned with the chorus, who have till now been silent (Strauss was careful to respect the technical limitations of the average opera house chorus in his time, if not of our own). But the spotlight falls all the more brightly on this stupid character of the Jester, so beloved of the romantics (including modern Soviet choreographers, alas) and so profoundly embarrassing. The Fool in *King Lear* is a marvellously ambivalent figure, and Verdi's *Rigoletto*, inspired of course by Victor Hugo's character, makes something of the contrast figure (which Gilbert and Sullivan more or less echoed purposefully in Jack Point). But Jesters at court are, for a modern audience, neither gay nor piquant and this one in *Guntram* is a pain in the neck. Strauss very sensibly reduced his part considerably in the revised version, but failed to excise this deplorable *Hi diddle dum di* episode.

In a commentary on this act it must be added that Robert, with most unconvincing gaiety, reclaims Freihild; that the Guild theme makes a strong reappearance, as does Guntram's; and that the closing bars look forward strongly to *Till Eulenspiegel.*†

3

The Prelude to Act 2 is entitled *The Triumphal Feast at the Ducal Court.* It is in D major and begins with the pompous court theme of *Hi diddle dum di*, moving to other courtly themes. There is a short middle section based on Ex. 7, and a reprise in which one of the Jester themes turns prophetically into Sancho Panza's music.‡

We are in a grand ducal setting populated by the whole court; luxury rules undisputed, and the Jester, crouched at the old Duke's feet, sings a lute song, to a thin but busy orchestral background. His solo is provocative and pathetic; it describes a sort of feudal tyranny which young Robert has easily shown himself adept in—the peasant ejected by the landlord. Robert pretends to be angry, but is obviously rather flattered by what he takes as a tribute to his authority—the ambivalence is nicely judged, a testimony to Strauss's native dramatic sense. It gives a tone of irony to the flatulent and pompous Minnesinger chorus which

---

* It was much shortened in 1940.
† *NDM* traces a link with *Arabella*. This is inherent in the Guntram theme as I have indicated.
‡ See *NDM* p. 153.

follows (we may here appreciate the rhythmic figure as a derivative of the
Guild theme—the other, more active Guild of which Guntram, a by-
stander here, is a member) and to which the Jester adds archly sarcastic
comments.* Three of the courtiers (obviously borrowed from *Lohengrin*,
Act 2)† express seditious opinions, and these are overheard by Guntram,
who laments the frustrations of this task to which he has been assigned.
He is convinced that he will be able to have no effect on this discontented
and divided court. He gets up and is on the point of leaving the palace
for ever when his eye catches Freihild, and love wells up, to a theme
Wagner might not have disdained.

12

It tells us that Guntram is enchained by love for Freihild and all the
humanity that she represents. His action of getting to his feet catches the
attention of Robert who orders him to sing for Freihild; the old Duke
confirms this command, and Freihild mutters Guntram's last words to
her. So with a reference to her love theme (Ex. 11) he strikes the appropriate chords, *à la Tannhäuser* and begins his big set-piece, a *tour de force*
for the robustest tenor. The first half (*Ich schaue ein glänzend prunkendes
Fest*) discourses exhaustively on a populace's peace under a kindly ruler
(the old Duke). After a brief intermezzo ensemble in character, dominated
by Freihild's rapturous acclaim, Guntram turns to the second half of his
Bar, and here he moves his listeners to horror and fear by his vivid
description of war and its attendant cruelties and devastation. The old
Duke and Robert attempt to make light of the subject by insisting that
such things belonged only to the past—they could never happen now in
times of peace and festal joy. Guntram would like to contradict and he
continues to dwell on the misery of war, to Robert's noisy indignation.
Even the old Duke orders Guntram to moderate his language, and so the
minstrel begins his *Nachgesang* with an apostrophe of his host, a ruler with
a German crown whose kindly yet strict paternal protection (Ex. 10) calls
forth the loyalty of all his subjects. He contrasts this with the seditious
discontent of peoples ruled by cruelty and suppression (Ex. 9); in such
places revolution is the child of despair—here again Robert interrupts
scornfully after each phrase from Guntram, and the Duke confesses aside
that he himself is not guiltless. Guntram closes with a grand passionate
appeal in spacious C major to all that is noblest and most benevolent in
the ruler of this land.

* Much of this was removed in the 1940 version.
† This episode was cut in the 1940 version together with Guntram's lament.

Guntram's *Meisterlied* has occupied almost thirty pages of vocal score with very few interruptions; small wonder that even at the time of its original performances Strauss felt obliged to sanction several cuts (though he pointed out that they should only be made in cases of absolute necessity). Form and content are clear and coherent, the *Nachgesang* acting as a sort of reprise, and its outer sections being thematically connected; but the vocal writing is rather stiffly conceived and ineffectively placed in the middle and lower registers against a welling orchestral foreground. And considered as a whole the length of the solo seems an unnecessary luxury. At all events Strauss, when he revised *Guntram* in 1940, reduced it to no more than a verse and a half, removing not only the formal interrelations but also the inspiring close (the second verse thus became part of the scene following the Messenger's entry, since the episode now to be described was also cut).

Guntram's entire audience is visibly moved, excepting Robert, who laughs at the idea that he should minister to the poor as Freihild does. The Vassals support Guntram's advice, until Robert accuses him of inspiring sedition and orders him to be whipped and imprisoned. The Vassals rise to Guntram's defence, but mutiny is checked by the arrival of a Messenger announcing an invasion of the land by a neighbouring army which Robert had thought defeated, and the uprising of many Vassals against the Duke. While Ex. 12 bursts forth gloriously, Guntram steps out and denounces Robert as the foe of peace; he calls on the Vassals at court to arrest Robert and set the people free from tyranny. Robert lunges out with his sword but Guntram strikes back, and the tyrant drops lifeless, to the despairing cries of Freihild and the Duke, and the horror of everyone.

A long orchestral Interlude dominated by a descending figure (derived from Ex. 1b via Ex. 2b, itself prominent in the latter part of Guntram's long solo*) expresses the stunned reaction of all as they stand motionless round the corpse. One might expect jubilation to reign at the removal of the nigger from the woodpile, but this is a drama of ethics in which violence is not to be quelled by violence. They all know it, and the old Duke is the most disheartened of them all. Slowly he regains his voice and orders Guntram, in tones of bitterness, to slay him too and so complete his wretched work. He chides himself for being duped by flattery and soft words of hypocritical meekness; he mocks Guntram's tardy repentance for his fatal act. Then asserting his dignity he calls on the Vassals to follow him into battle. He himself arrests Guntram and commands the imprisonment of this murderer to await torture and death, as Robert's body must await burial after the battle's successful conclusion. The Duke and his now loyal Vassals depart to the strains of a rather tawdry march, while Robert's corpse is carried out by monks to lie in

* But therefore in the 1940 version no longer quite so significant.

state. Freihild is left alone, watched from the shadows by the Jester. The extended monologue, in which her feelings are transformed from wretched perplexity to thankfulness and overwhelming love for Guntram, contains probably the finest, most intensely characteristic music in the whole opera, and as the complement of the duet in Act 1 proclaims Strauss's transcendent sympathy for the soprano voice and understanding of its highest emotive possibilities. In later operas his treatment of the voice seems altogether *sui generis*, but in this monologue we can trace its ancestry in Wagner's heroines, above all Elisabeth and Brünnhilde. Her ecstatic cry *Guntram, Guntram* (rising to top B) *Ich liebe dich* is crowned by an extension of Ex. 11.

In the 1940 version the act ends with Ex. 11 as Freihild rushes away to rescue her beloved. The original version showed how this was to be achieved. She hears the military march in the distance, turns and sees the Jester, who offers his life for her happiness. Quickly she asks him to liberate Guntram. He promises to drug the guards, slip away, and never see her again. She bids him farewell and once again gives expression to her new-found love. On the whole all this is poorly motivated and elaborated, and Freihild's closing phrases sound anticlimactic after the earlier monologue. The cut was surely a sensible one; as far as plausibility goes, it could easily be Freihild who drugs the guards.

4

The Prelude to Act 3 is fairly short but intense, a résumé of Guntram's recent history: the Guild's Elders and their work (Ex. 2); Guntram himself (Ex. 4); Wretchedness (Ex. 2b); the ideal of the Guild (Ex. 5); Guntram's love ending in tragedy (Exs. 12 plus 2b as above); spiritual love (Ex. 1a); Freihild's goodness (Ex. 7a). An accelerando climax is cut off by the rise of the curtain to disclose night-time in the dungeon where Guntram lies motionless, while in the chapel nearby the monks sing Requiems for Robert's soul. Their unison chanting (Aeolian mode with occasional Phrygian seconds, i.e. 'creative' Gregorian) continues out of step with the resumed orchestral commentary; Ex. 2b's mood in this transformation rather looks forward to *Die Frau ohne Schatten* and especially the Prelude to its third act, a similar context. Guntram jumps up crying for silence and calling imprecations on these 'miserable heralds of cruel certainty'. The chant begins again,* with it Guntram's anguished questions to his own conscience and knocking heart as much as to the invisible, unhearing monks. Curse you! he yells; it is himself he is

---

* Not in the 1940 edition, which cuts to the vision of Robert's ghost, rather suggesting that the monks hear and obey!

cursing. The chant goes on and fades away. But even now Guntram knows no rest; he still hears the knocking of his heart, and seems to see Robert's accusing ghost; a phantom theme dominates the texture.

13

Guntram tries to banish the vision: You had to die that thousands might live, he cries. My hands are clean! Another figure stands in the doorway as Ex. 12 thunders out: Freihild, whom Guntram takes for another hallucination even when she calls his name and stretches out her arms while themes of her love pour forth continuously from the orchestra pit. Incredulous, he becomes aware of her reality and her readiness to be his wife; the full realization is too much and he sinks to the ground in a swoon. She covers his face with kisses, calling him to awake,* in long spacious phrases often tied over the bar-line in a manner that we associate particularly with the later Strauss—for example:

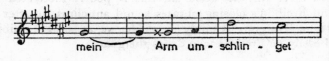

14

It is a glorious outburst and as soon as Guntram revives, to Ex. 12, she continues to pour out her love in glowing phrases borrowed, many of them, from the first verse of his big solo in Act 2, recalling their first encounter, her first realization of love as he sang, her gratitude at his victory over Robert, and her decision to set him free. Her confusion is punctuated by Guntram, who calls her name in tones of increasing urgency and anxiety and finally of certain decision. Come away, she ends, to eternal glorious bliss! A grand affirmation theme in C thunders out.

15

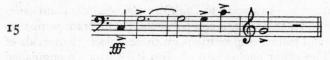

Yes, away, far away from you for ever, he replies, to her complete consternation. And he tears himself from her clutches. Freihild sees this as mere selfish ingratitude; with all her goodness she does not comprehend

* *Siegfried* Act 3 in reverse!

the moral issues. Guntram will explain them in due course, and explain
the victorious rightness of his decision to depart alone. Meanwhile he
does not get farther than the door, for standing there is Friedhold, the
Elder of the Guild who came and went so mysteriously at the start of the
opera. He has returned to conduct Guntram before the other Elders of
the Guild, there to be tried for his crime. Guntram, who has already
accepted his own sentence (Ex. 15 in questioning diminution), is non-
plussed. He hardly recognizes Friedhold and asks in wonderment what
this deed has to do with the Guild. Friedhold reminds him of the responsibilities he undertook when, too early alas, he was initiated into full
membership; of the harp and sword lent him by the Guild; and of the
Cross given him to preach God's word. Guntram's riposte is to break his
harp, forswear his sword, but (Ex. 1d) clasp to his breast the Cross whose
true meaning he has now recognized for himself. With this he proposes
to depart, but Friedhold holds him back; Guntram cannot go free without
first undergoing trial. Let him first listen to the voice of duty. Freihild,
who has been left on one side during all this, registers puzzlement and
anxiety. Guntram insists that his decision is not to be changed, but agrees
to hear Friedhold out.

The Elder offers a silent prayer, while the orchestra recalls the Prelude
to the first act (Ex. 1, Ex. 2), then he begins his narrative in sub-
Wagnerian *Stabreim*, of the Guild's foundation and aim (Ex. 3 joins the
smoothly flowering texture), minstrelsy in God's service. Guntram enthusiastically agrees to all this. Friedhold patiently continues to explain about
the Guild's strict rules, but Guntram interrupts impatiently; what have
rules and restrictions to do with high idealism? Even so, idealism is a
dream annihilated by the pressures of daily life, to which Friedhold
replies that one failure is no cause for despair. The obscure passage
summarized in this sentence must seem to weaken Guntram's case and
confuse the argument.* Guntram is bound to the Guild by its laws, and
he must accept its curative sentence, says Friedhold. Not so, comes
Guntram's rejoinder: the Guild punishes the deed which in itself was
good; his sin was in his heart and this can only be atoned by his own act
of will. The hopeful young man who took the oath to obey the Guild's
rules truly believed in them; but Guntram is no longer that man. He has
grown up and learned to trust only himself, obey only his own spirit,
accept only the punishment of his own choice; God, for Guntram, can
only speak to him through himself.

These are the crucial sentences of the opera, an expression of Strauss's
most earnest belief: that they run completely counter to Catholic doctrine
was the cause of a quarrel later to be described.

Friedhold is appalled, but also convinced of Guntram's sincerity, and
of the impossibility of bringing him back within the Guild. With a prayer

* Strauss very sensibly removed it in 1940.

to God, who moves in mysterious ways and may forgive this heresy, he takes his leave so that Guntram may explain to Freihild in private the nature of his decision. She is still somehow sure that his victory over the Guild leaves him free to share and return her love as man and wife (Ex. 12 takes over from Ex. 1a). Guntram, on the other hand, does not prize that victory at all; he has still to win a harder fight, with himself; and she must share this fight by sharing the decision he knows he must take. The curse of life is that the man who strives after heaven (Ex. 1d) is still tied to earth (Ex. 12, new developments); he cannot preach redemption until he is himself redeemed (Ex. 4 together with Ex. 1a). Guntram's sin was that he preached freedom while yet a slave to love, and killed Robert not because he was a tyrant but because he was Freihild's husband. Guntram admits that his despair in prison was only lifted from him when she embraced him and roused his longing for her. This was the moment when God spoke to him (Ex. 15), and when he knew that redemption demanded a severance from his last and dearest link with the world; only so can his guilt be expiated. By living out his life in solitude he may hope to be accepted among the blessed after death (Ex. 1, variants).

Freihild has been weeping bitterly, of course, and now Guntram, with the utmost tenderness, tells her how she who is guiltless has still a lofty mission to fulfil, as his inspiration afar off. A new and wonderfully beautiful theme accompanies his words in D flat major, Strauss's favourite tonality for the great, generous moment.*

16

The Jester runs in upon this lofty moment, to his 'Sancho Panza' theme (see p. 10), alternating with the military march, and announces that Freihild's father has been slain in battle, and the aristocracy vanquished; however, the rebels at once proclaimed Freihild their ruler, and are on their way to greet her with jubilation. He hurries away, and Guntram (Ex. 1, also the military march, and Ex. 7a) hails the new Princess, bidding her dry her tears over vain love, and rejoice in the glorious destiny that has fulfilled his prophecy. Let her wear her crown, even in sorrow, for the salvation of her people.

Guntram's last words have brought home to Freihild that splendour of her 'lofty mission', and she raises her head, now gently smiling, to him as Ex. 16 returns and the morning sun beams on them through the dungeon

---

* Cf. *Rosenkavalier* trio and tenor aria; *Ariadne* final duet; *Frau ohne Schatten*, Barak's *Mir anvertraut*; *Capriccio*, closing scene. It was not a key he used idly.

In the 1940 version Strauss cut from here to the reappearance of Ex. 16, so as to eliminate the entrance of the Jester, which was at once a good idea and a pity.

window. Guntram foretells the happiness she will experience through her subjects' love and trust. He begs her for a parting favour, the acceptance of renunciation. Ex. 1, in its most human and loving transformation, gently steals out in warm G flat major as Freihild, speechless with emotion, inclines her head in affirmation. Solemnly and with great dignity Guntram bids her farewell and, while Ex. 15 thunders forth, slowly departs. Womanly feelings master her for a moment after his departure (Ex. 11 in B minor) and she breaks down in tears, then pulls herself together (Ex. 16 moving from B minor to G flat major merging into Ex. 1a) and remains proudly erect as the curtain falls.

5

Guntram was Strauss's child of sorrow; things kept going wrong with it; perhaps that is why Strauss loved it so dearly. Perhaps also because one thing went right: while Strauss was tearing his hair over the libretto a critic called Max Steinitzer (later the first and one of the best of Strauss's biographers) sent him a pupil to coach. She was Pauline, the daughter of General de Ahna; she had a marvellous soprano voice and Strauss fell in love with her. There have been those who reckoned this a disaster too —Pauline dominated Strauss for the next sixty-two years—but he knew otherwise. 'I need to be kept in order,' he once admitted. The very last songs he wrote pay tribute to her lifelong companionship, and almost all his music for the soprano voice was inspired by her own vocal method, timbre, and musicianship; this is particularly true of Freihild, the first part specifically written with Pauline in mind. Freihild has all the finest music in *Guntram*.

It must have seemed to Strauss a heaven-sent opportunity for this first opera of his when, in 1889, after a miserable period of subsidiary office at the Munich Opera, he was appointed director at Weimar, where Liszt had done such valiant work for modern music. The première production of *Guntram* did indeed occur there; it was, so to speak, Strauss's leaving present in 1894, before getting married to Pauline and assuming a new, more responsible post in Munich. But the Weimar chorus was small and modest in accomplishment, which restricted opportunities that *Guntram* must have inspired; great things could well have been made of the Peasants, the Mastersingers, the Vassals, and finally the assembled populace in *Guntram*, an opera which lays so much stress on the conflict of the individual and society. And then there was the Weimar orchestra, good and willing but small (only three double basses). Strauss was perhaps the more ready to promise his father that his music would henceforth be for double wind only, and much simpler. That of *Guntram* is considerably more simple, not to say unoriginal, than the scores of *Don Juan* and *Tod und Verklärung* which were completed in the meanwhile. Perhaps the Weimar orchestra was to blame—but Strauss made no bones, promise or no promise, about using triple wind with four bassoons—perhaps merely his inexperience as a musician of the theatre (but his performing edition of Gluck's *Iphigénie en Tauride* and his rebalanced version of *Tristan und Isolde* for a small orchestra in an uncovered pit were both acclaimed at the time and were clearly not a tyro's work).

At all events things went wrong. Strauss got pneumonia and then pleurisy and bronchitis during the composition of *Guntram* (he blamed it all on the triads in an opera by Hans Sommer called *Lorelei* which he was conducting), though he was lucky enough to be given a convalescent trip to the Mediterranean, where the inspiration of the countries he visited left its mark on his music in after years. *Guntram* was completed during this holiday, the first act at Luxor, the second at Blandine Bülow's villa in Ramacca near Catania, the third in Athens, and the whole in Shepheard's Hotel, Cairo.

But then Strauss had to show *Guntram* to Ritter, the 'onlie begetter'. Ritter, a sincere Catholic, was appalled by the dénouement of Act 3, which preaches that the individual conscience is more important than the religious establishment. He begged Strauss to alter this deplorable turn of action which stemmed from a whole series of disreputable authors such as Nietzsche and Max Stirner (whose *Der Einzige und sein Eigentum* Strauss claimed not to have finished reading, though elsewhere he admitted it had influenced his thinking), not to mention Schopenhauer's *Die Welt als Wille und Vorstellung*. Strauss was not an orthodox Christian, though he held ethical beliefs as a result of his philosophical reading; the dénouement of *Guntram* reflected, as I have indicated, his deepest and most sincere convictions; Guntram here is Strauss, as Friedhold (he must at the time have sensed) is Ritter. The break was inevitable, and Strauss could not have altered the outcome of *Guntram* without destroying the idea that gives it strength and individuality, and an independence from Wagnerism such as a young composer needed. Guntram's concept of salvation by renouncing a pure and noble love was exactly contrary to the *idée fixe* of Wagner's operas (whence Siegfried Wagner's denunciation of the piece), but it was and remains an idea of real force and idiosyncrasy, the mainstay of the drama's validity. Ritter, like Friedhold, could appreciate but never forgive this.

Then there was the role of Guntram, quite exceptionally strenuous—he is on the stage all the time except at the end of Act 2—yet has many long solos to sing, and a musical tessitura that is ungrateful, falling in ineffective registers except at the end of a long marathon where top notes are expected to materialize like a conjuror's magical rabbit out of an unlined and hollow hat. Julius Patzak once lamented that Strauss wrote no really strong and positive tenor role. It is true; even the Kaiser in *Die Frau ohne Schatten* (of which Patzak has been the greatest exponent) is ungrateful to a singer, though he has more character than say Apollo in *Daphne* or Bacchus in *Ariadne auf Naxos*, or even Flamand in *Capriccio*. And a role of Guntram's length taxed every German tenor in existence: Heinrich Zeller, who created it, grew more hoarse with each rehearsal. The Guntram of a Munich fiasco production demanded the equivalent of danger money. After the first performance Mahler and Mottl both promised performances which, for reasons little known but quite inferable, fell through. Strauss noticed how many enemies *Guntram* had given him, and when, after other successes, he saw that revivals would not be forthcoming, he erected a tombstone in his garden to Guntram 'slain by his own father's symphony orchestra'. This Lazarus was resurrected in 1933 when Berlin Radio gave a broadcast performance under Rosbaud which revived good impressions of the piece; resulting from this Strauss cut and partly modified the scoring into a version given at Weimar in 1940 under Paul Sixt, and in Berlin under Robert Heger. But the phoenix never flew clear of the flames.

With all its Wagnerisms* *Guntram* remains an utterly un-Wagnerian conception that fails because there is too much compromising with practicability. Wagner's ghosts, and Strauss's own intentions too, demand a higher degree of tension and attack than Strauss could allow himself at this stage. The real creator thinks first of what must be done, and afterwards of how performers can accomplish it. The working out of the drama too is full of woolliness and weak tension that make the score sag; some examples have been noted. But the characters themselves are no more than symbols, however much we may identify them with real persons in Strauss's life. Guntram's problems of repentance and responsibility, the old Duke's swivelling from benevolence to strictness, are conveyed in generalized terms. And the diction of the libretto falls much too often into a mannerism of impacted vague generalizations (*vide* Guntram's first monologue, for example) that he did not even escape in *Capriccio* when he extended what his librettist Clemens Krauss gave him.

Wagner would have rejected the moral implications of *Guntram*; he would have invented stronger themes for metamorphosis and development; he would have rejected the blacker-than-black character of Robert, and the want of intriguing contrast in other characters. But he could not have written lyrical outpourings of this kind, nor that sumptuous, spacious orchestral music; Wagner would have thought it, despite all the thematic working, unsuitably diffuse. And so it is—for Wagner, though it is Strauss's way and manner of musical speech. An opera composer has to begin

---

* There is a nice story of a 'cellist who, reproved by the composer at rehearsal for playing a passage inaccurately, answered, 'But Maestro, we never get this passage right in *Tristan* either.'

somewhere. *Guntram* is no *Peter Grimes*, but its good qualities are worth reviving if only as gramophone highlights; it is not ripe for the waste-paper basket, technically or emotionally. One might even say that *Guntram* commands respect for its manifest sincerity, which encompasses long scenes even if, on occasion, practicability takes control of convincing intention. Perhaps in 1964 and afterwards some of us will change our minds and find more in *Guntram* to enjoy and admire.

Feuersnot

OPUS 50

Poem for Singing in One Act

LIBRETTO BY ERNST VON WOLZOGEN

Schweiker von Gundelfingen, the Bailiff	TENOR
Ortolf Sentlinger, the Burgomaster	BASS
Diemut, his Daughter	SOPRANO
Elsbeth	MEZZO-SOPRANO
Wigelis } *Friends of Diemut*	ALTO
Margret	SOPRANO
Kunrad (Der Ebner), an Alchemist	BARITONE
Jörg Pöschel, the Innkeeper	BASS
Hämerlein, the Haberdasher	BARITONE
Kofel, the Smith	BASS
Kunz Gilgenstock, the Baker and Brewer	BASS
Ortlieb Tulbeck, the Cooper	TENOR
Ursula, his Wife	ALTO
Ruger Aspeck, the Potter	TENOR
Walpurg, his Wife	SOPRANO

I

The failure of *Guntram* was a wound both raw and deep to Strauss. When in 1942 he wrote some reminiscences of his operas and their premières,* he declared that 'after the fiasco of *Guntram* I rather lost the courage to write for the theatre'. But this is not strictly true since in 1896, the year following the disastrous and, to Strauss, exceptionally painful Munich production (November 1895), he was seriously contemplating a comic opera, with Count Ferdinand von Spork as librettist, on *The Forsaken Women of Schilda*. This had grown out of an abandoned libretto for a *Till Eulenspiegel* opera that Strauss had considered in 1893, and of which he completed the text for one act. Strauss made a few preliminary sketches for *Schilda*—from which by this time the character of Till had been omitted, since Strauss had already completed his immortal characterization in purely orchestral terms—and then dropped it for *Don Quixote* and *Ein Heldenleben*, which were conceived more or less simultaneously. Perhaps Count Spork's libretto displeased him, perhaps he really was too disheartened by *Guntram* to try again. He did not have to wait long.

During 1898 he became more and more discouraged by working conditions in Munich where, to crown everything, his wages had been cut. Just when all seemed black he was offered Weingartner's post at Berlin as first conductor of the Prussian Royal Orchestra, and though the Munich authorities suddenly became affectionate and generous, Strauss gladly packed his bags and left home for the capital. Shortly before his departure he made the acquaintance of another discontented Municher, Ernst von Wolzogen,† who had tried without success to translate the French satirical cabaret to Munich, though with his Berlin *Überbrettl* he was to succeed and make his name. Strauss and Wolzogen shared their sorrows and concocted a plan of revenge in the form of a theatrical diatribe against Munich which had rejected them and Wagner before them (not to mention Bülow).

Strauss had found a suitable subject in a book edited by Johann Wilhelm Wolf entitled *Sagas of the Netherlands* (published 1843); this was an account, taken wholesale from the *Oudenaarde Gazette*, of an incident portrayed in fresco on one of the old houses of Oudenaarde (situated west of Brussels and the scene of Marlborough's famous victory in 1708). It described how a young man was played a practical

---

* *BUE*, p. 179 (Eng. ed. p. 149).

† Trenner (*RSJB*, 1954, p. 110) dates this meeting at the turn of the year. Wolzogen specifies 'during my last week's stay in Munich'; but Strauss was in Berlin by then. *Ein Heldenleben* was completed in Berlin–Charlottenburg on 27 December. It is possible that they did meet at Christmas, but it would have been in Berlin, not Munich. I incline to August or September.

joke by the proud girl with whom he was hopelessly in love. She offered
to let him into her house at night if he would ascend by the basket
on the house-front.* The boy prepared to make the ascent, but half-way
up to the girl's window the basket stopped, the window remained shut,
and the young man had to swing there all night, and suffer the jeers of the
crowd next morning. Escaping from the town, ablaze with hatred for
the cruel girl, he met a kindly wizard who offered to help him obtain
revenge. The wizard cast a spell on every fire in the town: lamp, hearth
and all. He then informed the terrified citizens who were gathered in the
market-place that the curse could only be exorcized by one way, and that
not easily. Of course the citizens agreed to anything. Then the wizard
sent for the proud and cruel girl who was made to undress completely and
kneel on a table. Hardly had she done so when a flame sprang magically
out of her back-passage, and the townsfolk had to line up with their
candles and light them from this unusual source. 'It took many hours
before all the inhabitants had fire, but there was no other way, no candle
would light from another, but only from the maiden's backside, which
was not done without great laughter.'

Wolzogen thought kindly of the plot, though the closing scene was
hardly stageable as it stood. It might have remained only a pleasant idea,
but in March 1900† he happened to attend a concert in Munich at which
Strauss's *Also sprach Zarathustra* was received with whistles (the equivalent of booing) by part of the audience. Wolzogen's disgust was sufficient
to determine him to proceed at once with *Feuersnot*, as the projected opera
was already named. In a letter to Strauss he outlined his projected
scenario for the one-acter; the old wizard never appears (the authors had
evidently already decided to identify him with Wagner); the proud girl
now exorcizes the spell by sacrificing her maidenhead to the boy.
Wolzogen adds, 'When love is united with the magic of genius, light
must dawn on even the dullest Philistine.' He added, 'I think the diction
will be satirical (*derb-lustig*), rather archaic in style with local dialect.'

Wolzogen's libretto departs from the *Oudenaarde* source-material in
one other respect. The poet married the theme of magic fire to the age-old
custom of Fire-Festivals which were celebrated at given seasons all over
Europe (taking slightly different forms in other lands as well). Sir James
Frazer collated an enormous quantity of information about these Fire-
Festivals, and their probable significance, in *The Golden Bough*.‡ His

---

* These baskets, let up and down from the balcony, are still used by Sicilian house-
wives as a convenient means of traffic with itinerant salesmen in the street below. The
principle is clearly shown in Plate 5.

† Wolzogen dated his letter 1899, but this was clearly a slip of the pen. *Zarathustra*
was first given in Munich in 1900. The 1899 date always did make it seem odd that
Wolzogen should express determination to start work at once and then wait precisely a
year and a day! (I am indebted to Erich Müller von Asow for help in solving this mystery.)

‡ Vols. 10 and 11: *Balder the Beautiful; The Fire-Festivals of Europe and the Doctrine
of the External Soul*. Macmillan, 1913.

researches included the Midsummer or St John's Eve Solstice Fires in Bavaria, and he specifically mentions that 'the children collected firewood from door to door on the eve of the festival, singing their request for fuel at every house in doggerel verse. . . . Many a householder on that day put out the fire on the domestic hearth and rekindled it by means of a brand taken from the midsummer bonfire [this practice links up with Kunrad's ban in the opera, and also with the Oudenaarde legend]. . . . But it was especially the practice for lovers to spring over the fire hand in hand, and the way in which each couple made the leap was the subject of many a jest and many a superstition.' These superstitions, Frazer shows, involved the harvest, freedom from illness, and marital fertility (though in Bavaria the girl who leaped successfully through the fire with her lover would *not* become a mother in the ensuing twelve-month). Frazer's source for these observations was *Bavaria, Landes und Volkskunde des Königreichs Bayern* (Munich, 1860–67), which Wolzogen could doubtless have read. The Fire-Festivals were originally purificatory by intention, and the lovers' leap was often a relic of earlier human sacrifice.

Strauss had by this time settled down in Berlin and was toying with the libretto for a comic opera called *Ekke und Schnittlein*. After *Guntram* he clearly recognized an inner need for a comic or light opera; he was to spend the rest of his life plaguing his collaborators for specimens. Wolzogen soon settled down to write the text of *Feuersnot*; he repaired to the Island of Rügen, and under the stimulus of a blissful love affair completed the poem in a few days.

Like a true satirist he took *Feuersnot* seriously. In his autobiography (1922) he declares: 'All creative power stems from sensuality. The creative spirit possesses the magical power to mould something living out of nothing. If then this magic is only effected through the fire of the senses, I have the right to clasp this fire to me wherever I find it. Not a single person grasped the hidden meaning of this allegory. For cultured people at least, art alone gives to life its light, colour, warmth, deeper meaning. Each true artist is a Prometheus who creates men in the image of God. But for his creations he has no need to steal the light of distant heaven, he can take the fire from the earth, since,

> All warmth comes from woman,
> all light from love springs. . . .

This is in fact the moral of this little poem.'

By October 1900 Strauss was at work on *Feuersnot*: he told his parents it would be very simple and tuneful too, pure Lortzing; the Leitmotifs were Munich popular songs. By New Year's Day 1901 the sketch was complete and he began the scoring: 'these days one can hardly orchestrate without triple woodwind' (so much for his promises at the time of *Guntram*). He worked ten hours a day, apart from his conducting jobs, at the score and completed it on 22 May of the same year, as he noted at the time: 'on the birthday and to the greater glory of the Almighty'!*

By this time Strauss was famous and his works in demand. Berlin, Vienna, and Dresden all wanted the première of *Feuersnot*—until they read the libretto, and then eyebrows were raised and blushes sprang to cheeks, and Berlin at least insisted upon numerous alterations and substitutions for the bawdy Bavarian phrases that Wolzogen had used, and the frankly indelicate dénouement. The authors stood firm ('an opera libretto', insisted Wolzogen, 'is not a nursery fairy-story') and Berlin was out of the running. Gustav Mahler in Vienna ran into difficulties too, but offered to produce the opera later. And so the first of many Strauss premières went to Ernst von Schuch in Dresden, even so not without some textual modifications which, Strauss insisted, must be made known not to be the original work of the authors.

The first performance on 21 November 1901 (hardly a year after Strauss had started composing it) was generally acknowledged to be very fine indeed, particularly as regards chorus, orchestra, the anti-heroine Diemut (Annie Krull, later the first Electra), and the hero Kunrad (Karl Scheidemantel, one of the outstanding and most popular baritones of his day, though Faninal was the only part that he subsequently created for Strauss). The opera was not, evidently, an outstanding success; some attributed this to the excess of Munich local references in the music as well as the text. However, in Frankfurt the following month, when the composer conducted, the reception was very warm indeed; likewise in Vienna under Mahler, with Leopold Demuth as Kunrad. Berlin felt obliged, after this, to accept the work, and Strauss conducted the local première in 1902, with Emmy Destinn as Diemut (Strauss found her acting 'coarse and ungraceful'!); however, the work was withdrawn after seven performances by order of the Kaiser, to whom it had been denounced by prudish gossips. There was an almighty scandal, and the Intendant of the Royal Opera resigned in protest. Munich did not see *Feuersnot* until 1905, when Strauss conducted it. Many years later when he was given the freedom of his native city he made a present of the autograph scores to Munich. Beecham conducted the London première in 1910, in Wallace's English version. *Feuersnot* was given in French at Brussels in 1911; and in Italian at La Scala, Milan, under Tullio Serafin, in 1912. It has continued to hold a modest place in German repertory. The Swiss première took place as recently as 1953 during a selective Strauss cycle. In Munich *Feuersnot* has figured in several recent festivals, partly out of belated local pride (unfavourable publicity is better than none at all), partly because of the copious local colour—heightened perhaps by the rubicund blush of local shame at old intolerances and

---

* Almighty Wagner was not, however, the dedicatee; that honour was reserved for another loyal and discontented Municher, Friedrich Rösch, one of Strauss's best friends.

1
Alexander Ritter

2
Heinrich Zeller and
Pauline de Ahna in the
Weimar première of
Guntram, 1894

3 Franz Völker and Hilde Scheppan in the Berlin
Staatsoper revival of *Guntram*, 1941

4 Ernst von Wolzogen, the librettist of *Feuersnot*

5 A scene from the Munich revival of *Feuersnot*, 1958

misjudgements which may be forgiven but, for our present and future health, ought not to be forgotten.

2

The action of the *Singgedicht* (or 'poem for singing') takes place not in Oudenaarde of course but in Munich (and to be exact, in Sendlingerstrasse near the gate where the modern visitor can still see a house very like that specified in the libretto as the Burgomaster's, though without block and tackle); the stage directions specify the twelfth century for scenery and costumes, though elsewhere the period is simply 'legendary' (*fabelhafte Unzeit*). The time is Solstice Day, Midsummer Day, as in the second act of *Die Meistersinger* which the effervescent orchestral trills strongly recall at the opening of the opera. Almost at once they trace an outline of some thematic importance:

1

'Solstice Fire' (*Subendfeuer*) sings the children's choir soon after curtain-rise to Ex. 1; and later, at a tremendous high-point of emotion, Kunrad puts the title-name *Feuersnot* to it (in a slightly different harmonic context).

Having captivated attention and suggested a certain emotional pretension, the orchestral introduction (which is short and leads straight into the action) collapses cheerfully into the racy traditional idiom (Germans would call it *volkstümlich*) which is to be characteristic of the opera as a whole:

2

Strauss uses sundry melodies from Munich in the course of the opera, and this one, but for its second note, could be one of them, but it is not. Its volatile rhythms and static harmony might connect it with some of the *Bourgeois Gentilhomme* music, but to admit this is to fault the delightful later work rather than the suggestive mood of this one. While Ex. 2 unfolds, the curtain rises to show an intersection of the street, with an alley receding in the distance. On one corner stands the Burgomaster's house, with a block and tackle attached to the gable, and with a balcony at an upper window. Next door is the inn. There are other houses and, farther away, a park with trees. It is late afternoon and the local children are importuning for wood to make a Midsummer bonfire. The street is full of citizens promenading or standing in front of their houses. The children do not have to beg. They order; it is a privilege of old customs. As soon as they sing we are reminded not of *Die Meistersinger* but rather of *Hänsel und Gretel*; which is appreciable in so similar an ambience—we may recall that in Weimar a few years earlier Strauss had conducted the première of Humperdinck's work. The music of *Feuersnot* even here is harmonically rather more intricate, and therefore more difficult for a children's choir, as Beecham remarked in his autobiography.* The counting refrain is a good example of the chromatic alteration involved.

The children have paused to sing their song outside the Burgomaster's house, and threaten that, if no wood is forthcoming, his daughter Diemut will not find a husband. Down comes the basket full of wood. The Burgomaster, Ortolf Sentlinger—presumably related to the man who gave this street and this gate their name—greets the children from a window, and Diemut, with her three playmates, comes from the house to distribute cake and mead to the children. The Burgomaster calls out that they have enough wood to baptize the Evil One (*den Schwarzen*) with fire; a pattern of rapidly falling sextuplets may suggest the crackling of fire here, but later it is specifically connected with the menace of Evil. Diemut, as she showers out sweets, sings a captivating tune of popular character.

* *A Mingled Chime* (1944), p. 96: 'The chief features of this gay and audacious work are the number and difficulty of the choruses and the indelicacy of the story.'

bend.Imma Ursel,Li sa -weth, al-le Mä deln mö-gen Meth.

It will return significantly at the end of the opera, where its last line
'Every girl likes her honey' (*Alle Mädeln mögen Meth*) acquires a fresh
and piquant connotation.

One of the children prophesies that Diemut will soon wed, and with
talk of husbands and babies the children's playful songs become more
and more impudent until the grown-ups turn on them, to Ex. 2, and tell
them to look for wood elsewhere. So they turn their attention to the house
on the other corner (*Heilinga Veit, schenk uns Scheit*), knocking furiously
and calling farmyard noises. Jörg Pöschel, the Innkeeper, comes out of
his inn, to a slower version of Ex. 6[2], and advises the children to leave
that house alone; the man who lives there is a recluse and an unknown
quantity (flickering sextuplets suggest he may well be a bad man). Pöschel
is characterized as narrow-minded and self-important. The cheerful
baker and brewer (these jobs were often combined, until quite recently),
Kunz Gilgenstock, stands up for the stranger as a nobleman who proved
his claim to the house; Strauss here introduces the first of his traditional
melodies, *Der alte Peter*:

5

The Haberdasher, Hämerlein, a lively elegant man, supports the kindly
view of the stranger and gives a more ingratiating theme to portray him.

6

The first of these is to be the main theme of Kunrad as others see him;
though, as for Pöschel above, it is subject to numerous transformations
such as Ex. 6[2]. One of them is promptly heard when the fanatical old cooper
Ortlieb Tulbeck screams out a warning that the house stinks and the Evil
One should be warded off (sextuplets); Tulbeck could tell them all something. And of course he does, in an extensive ballad about the Crusader
Duke Henry who brought back a Moorish giant called Onuphrius
as his prisoner. The giant begat children and grandchildren; they were
deformed and sorcerers (sextuplets). Strauss couples the references to
giants with the traditional *Mir san net von Pasing*, set in such a way as to

recall Wagner's Fasolt and Fafner.* Another old man, Kofel the Smith, dismisses all this as rubbish; Onuphrius was a worthy magician who did a lot of good. Tulbeck's curiosity, he says, is very much that of a sniffing dog. Loud laughter, and the children resume their Humperdinckian songs which this time do arouse the house owner. Kunrad answers from within; Ex. 6² collapses hastily, and its subject stands before them, a pale, long-haired young man of about twenty-five. This moment marks the end of the first section, a continuous web of popular and traditional melody, and the start of a fresh paragraph in the score.

Kunrad's own theme proclaims seriousness.

7

He greets the children gently and asks what they want. Shyly at first, then with growing confidence, they remind him of Solstice Day (*Subend* or *Sonnwend*). Ex. 6² accompanies their puzzled explanations. The *Meistersinger* trills from the introduction return, as the penny drops for Kunrad, together with Ex. 1. In the equivalent of a cavatina with fast cabaletta he chides himself for poring over books on this great day. As well as Exs. 6 and 7 we hear a new theme, connected with sensual love.

8

Then he shakes off his brown study and proceeds, much to the delight of the children and the vexed astonishment of the respectable burghers, to break up his house for firewood, inviting the children to help him. Accordingly Ex. 7 is transformed into a rapid energetic phrase, and an immensely spirited ensemble with chorus gathers weight under its momentum. The young people know, instinctively, what their grotesque elders have forgotten: that the Solstice Fire is not merely a superstitious rite of propitiation. As Wolzogen intimates in the passage cited earlier, it is the creative fire through which Kunrad, as the artist, must jump with his muse before he may accomplish anything.† *Sonnwend* is the time for these bonfires through which lovers were accustomed to leap together. (Frazer found that, in neighbouring Baden, such a leap was tantamount to

* I wonder if this was not a standard Munich joke about Wagner's theme.
† The point of the drama is a little blunted by the apparent obscurity of Kunrad's overt status. We are told he is of noble stock; he seems to have spent all his time in study, presumably the study of magic. Yet he is described as Kunrad the Ebner, the cabinet-maker (literally and symbolically the 'leveller'). These inconsistencies do not help to establish him as a person.

official betrothal.) And the muse, as Wolzogen's couplet reminds us, is not to be found in any book, but walking in the street—'warmth comes from women'. Hence Kunrad's delight at being reminded of *Subend*, and the zeal with which he is breaking up the home for firewood.

Diemut's friends find him handsome too, and wonder who will dare pass through the flames with him. In a quasi-Rhinemaiden trio (Strauss tapped the barrel again in *Ariadne auf Naxos*) they suggest that Diemut fancies her chances (Ex. 8), and when she answers coolly they begin to tease her more insistently—not without reason, since her answer carries Kunrad (Ex. 7) and love (Ex. 8) in its wake. Diemut becomes very angry indeed and turns her back on them. She is facing Kunrad when, in answer to the Burgomaster's protests, he comes gaily to the threshold, his arms full of wood, and gazing ardently at her bursts into an arioso with an early Wagner repeated woodwind accompaniment. He declares that he has broken up his dwelling because the true magician needs the elements about him. Good sense depends on the senses, he announces, and an important new love theme underlines Wolzogen's philosophy (Strauss had already written it for an uncompleted ballet called *Cytherea*).

9

Take all the wood I gave you, he ends, I will leap through the flames. And jumping down to where Diemut stands, he asks her if she will leap after him, and kisses her fairly and squarely on the lips.

Some scream, some chuckle; Diemut runs away in terror and embarrassment from the sex maniac—though not completely out of sight, we observe. Her father is quick to reprove Kunrad for his impudence; he has the vocal support of his fellow-citizens (*Pfuch! der Schande*), though Diemut's playmates secretly envy her good luck. Important to the musical texture, as well as development of Exs. 7 and 8, is what sounds like a new idea, representing Diemut's shame and anger:

10

ff appassionato

Fundamentally and deliberately this derives from an inversion of Ex. 7, because Diemut's feelings about Kunrad are turned topsy-turvy. Ex. 10, and the quick version of Ex. 7, underlie the ensemble in which Diemut voices her indignation, while her friends try to console and reconcile her to this desirable suitor. She is fixed on revenge, and secretly shares her intentions with them, while the boys and girls resume Exs. 2 and 3 and their fire-songs, dancing first round Kunrad, then round Diemut, in a quick waltz of the kind that Strauss was later to use copiously in his work —the present example gives, in particular, a foretaste of Baron Ochs's discomfiture in the third act of *Der Rosenkavalier*. It swings easily into what sounds like the waltz from Tchaikovsky's *Eugene Onegin*, but is actually a Munich drinking song, *Guten Morgen, Herr Fischer*.* The Burgo-master does his best to shoo the children away but without success until the Bailiff, Schweiker von Gundelfingen, looms in sight with his con-stables, a stupid-looking body of men. He had heard the uproar and has come to investigate. A fire perhaps? Only in one or two hearts, answers the Burgomaster, with a hint that Kunrad, who is standing deep in thought on what remains of his threshold, might explain further. The Bailiff does not trouble; he knows that Kunrad would not hurt a fly. Diemut, almost in tears, begs leave to remain indoors during the Mid-summer bonfire (the children are heard afar off, singing Exs. 3 and 4); she retires, locking her bedroom door. Kunrad's theme, Ex. 6^2, follows her. The Bailiff is much perplexed; there is an attractive depiction of his surprise, reminiscent of a moment in *Heldenleben*. Sentlinger, off to the bonfire, points again to Kunrad as the cause of the girl's down-heartedness.

Light dawns on the dim Bailiff (Ex. 10, comically fragmented), and he tries a question or two on Kunrad, who still is deep in thought (Ex. 7) and hears nothing, unless perhaps the children's Ex. 3. Suddenly beyond the Gate the Midsummer bonfire is seen blazing up to the sky; there is a distant cry of *Subendfeuer* in close E flat triad harmony (rather similar to the shout in the final scene of *Hänsel und Gretel*). Fire-music seethes within the orchestra (incorporating Ex. 8), and atop it Kunrad intones the title of the opera to an intensely impressive statement of Ex. 1. Fire, herald of love (*Feuersnot, Minnegebot*), he sings, and Ex. 9 smoulders uneasily in the bass, and begins to unfold much as it will in the closing scene. Much of Kunrad's vocal line accompanies the long orchestral melody with arching counterpoint, as he voices his thoughts of fire and love and magic, in heavy Wagnerian language. The Bailiff, who has watched open-mouthed, concludes that the fellow is mad and goes off through the great gate to watch the bonfire. Who, Kunrad finally asks, can control the enchantment?

Diemut has lit the lamp in her room and now steps softly on to the balcony. Is she the answer to his question? At first the music, gentle in A flat major, with a new lulling figure in thirds, suggests that she is as enchanted as he.

---

* Tchaikovsky had paid numerous visits to Germany, including one to Nuremberg and Bayreuth in 1876, before composing *Onegin*. It is possible that he passed through Munich and heard this tune somewhere.

But her touching song 'Midsummer Night' is all of sadness and complaint. When she mentions the man who mistakenly thought to woo her, Kunrad steps out from beneath the balcony and, with Ex. 9, begs her boldly to receive him as suitor. She answers him shortly, to a peremptory diminution of Ex. 10, and begins to plait her long hair. The exchanges continue; one is reminded of the lovers in Wolf's *Italian Songbook*. Kunrad grows more insistent, Diemut more scornful, throwing off Salomesque arpeggios and even a double-octave drop worthy of Boulez. The pace quickens until she seems to be echoing and approving his ardent appeals, which lead back to the *Feuersnot, Minnegebot* confession that started this scene (this time it brings the second act of *Tristan* even more vividly to mind). Their apparent love duet is now in full developmental cry and involves Ex. 7, Ex. 8, and Ex. 10 contrapuntally combined, until rapturously they bridge the distance between them with the thirds and sixths of Ex. 11, and hurl Tristanesque endearments at one another to Ex. 6 and Ex. 9—these indicated to be sung with extremely exaggerated expression, for both are overplaying their hands absurdly in the hope of ensnaring each other, but to very different ends. So that the audience, while transported by sumptuous love-music, recognizes the hollowness of the sham. The symbolic fire flares higher than before, and the children's Ex. 3 is heard again.

Kunrad is emboldened to ask Diemut to let him into her room and she feigns willingness, though Ex. 10 should show her true intention. She indicates the basket and offers to pull him up. Ex. 7 makes the journey; but will he? At any rate he climbs in. Diemut's playmates draw closer (evidently they have been eavesdropping) to watch, giggling Rhine-maidenly to one another as the block and tackle begin laboriously to pull Kunrad up the façade of the house (Ex. 7 repeatedly in quick tempo). And then it stops beneath the balcony. Kunrad is good-humoured at this breakdown, even when he hears the titters from below; he is a true optimist. Diemut complains of the strain; this is a man's job. She offers a sleeve, then an arm, but not very far. Kunrad is still enthusiastic (Exs. 8 and 9) even in failure. Her hair is too painful a ladder. Finally she tells him to use his magical powers and fly. Now he sees the plot and loses his temper; she admits that he is to pay for his insult to her. Gaily she calls her friends to admire the bird she caught and caged, and a crowd is quick to collect and laugh at poor Kunrad. It includes the Bailiff, astonished as ever, the children still dancing to Ex. 3, the Burgomaster who fancies that his daughter (Ex. 4 returns) has gone too far ('Sentlingers don't do that sort of thing'), and of course the gleeful, giggling girls, and the populace

52919

('He's swinging like a bell'). They are all creased with laughter when
Kunrad, from this absurd position, calls with a terrible voice on his absent
Master, over a boiling orchestral tremolo, invoking aid in a spell which
shall rob the city of all light, since the inhabitants have laughed at love.
His imperious invocation of course involves Ex. 1 and the love theme
Ex. 8. He stretches out both arms and the whole of Munich is plunged,
in a trice, into total darkness. Shrieks all round. Hesitant attempts at
Ex. 7. Choral interjections in unaccompanied four-part chords. The
sextuplets of Evil, and the *Feuersnot* theme. A whining nursery song for
the children (it links Humperdinck with the Carl Orff—another Municher
—of *Der Mond*). Fragments of choral and solo dialogue, held together
by a reprise of Ex. 5 and, here and there, Ex. 8. Some of the young
couples find this darkness congenial for courting (*Sollen wir im Dunkel
streichen*). Bit by bit the music swings into a not too cheerless 6/8 which
puts the grousing solo burghers (Tulbeck and the rest) in their places.
They are gaining righteous indignation, though, and are finding individual
voices of combined protest to this malefactor (nobody is more indignant
than the victim who has just done his best to break your arm). This they
do in an ensemble that builds up gradually into fifteen vocal parts before
uniting in a hysterical repetition, at a quick tempo, of the theme noted as
Ex. 1, the *Feuersnot* theme.

But, unseen by them, Kunrad has somehow managed to climb on to the
balcony. Did he fly? Did Diemut get help or recant? Did the Master lend
his magic? We are not told how he arrived where he wanted, unobserved
by the crowd. He is leaning on a column, a smile of supercilious superiority
on his lips (Ex. 7, quick). And now he addresses the good citizens who
laughed at him, and failed to understand the meaning of their bonfire, or
the bonfire within the creative artist. Kunrad now explains (*O weh, Herr
Schweiker von Gundelfing*) what brought him to perform this drastic
action. His is the house in which once dwelt Reichhart the Master
(=Wagner), the Ruler of the Spirits; at this point we expect Weber's
overture, but in fact we get Wagner's Valhalla motif, loud and clear.
Weber is not in question. There are other references, perhaps intended,
to the Rhinemaidens' song. The point is that Munich drove Master
Reichhart out of town, for all his benevolent intentions. He wanted to
bring the town up to date; but the townsfolk preferred to crawl along in
the old way. And here, contrary to all rhetorical rules, Strauss drops
happily, without a trace of polemic, into a lazy sensuous slow waltz that
even he must have thought captivating. It is a special effect. Kunrad
resumes his diatribe with a quotation from *The Flying Dutchman*: 'He
gave you his Wagon and you drove the Wagoner (=Wagner) away!' But
the enemy came back fighting (the obsolete word here is *Strauss*,* accom-

---

* *Strauss* also means an ostrich. One hopes Wolzogen forgot this, though cartoonists
did not: a nice specimen was reproduced in *Tempo* magazine, June 1964.

panied by the fighting Robert theme out of *Guntram*, and the next
sentence begins with a pun on the librettist's name, *Wohl zogen*, rather
far fetched). Kunrad's narration begins to get out of hand here, and
Strauss falls cheerfully, once again, into a slow waltz which robs the
speech of its bite but sustains interest or at least docility in the audience;
he has the motivation of sentences describing the obsession of Munich
with relaxation and pleasure. It is a good waltz too, strongly prophetic of
Rosenkavalier; but when Kunrad should, by the implications of the
libretto (and the original intention of the authors), be teaching Munich
a stern lesson, he is in the event encouraging them into a heady daze when
not a word will sink in. Perhaps that is why *Feuersnot* is now a favourite
repertory piece in its own town. In his own time Kunrad returns to 4/4
and Ex. 7, also Ex. 8; it was for the honour of his master as well as his own
authority that he doused the light in Munich. Even the moon wanes in his
defence. And he concludes with the motto of the piece, as quoted earlier:
'all warmth springs from women,' etc., ending

> from maiden body inflamed
> alone your fire flames anew.

Kunrad's oration is over. The moonlight has left the balcony. In the
dark Diemut quietly opens her balcony door and draws him inside—one
hopes out of love and self-understanding, one fears out of unthinking
small-town weakness that knows when defeat may be a certainty.

The music has dropped into semi-traditional tunes, a come-down, and
this is no doubt why Strauss carefully specified, in a letter, that from this
point onward it must be interpreted in an audacious, shameless, parodistic
manner. There is nothing in the invention, beyond the individual characterization specified by Wolzogen, to indicate anything of the kind. There
is a fairly obvious joke when the citizens agree that individually they had
all remarked his excellent characteristics; their phraseology is a close
mimic of Goethe's *Gretchen at the Spinning Wheel*.

> *Sein hoher Gang*
> *seine edle Gestalt.*

And Strauss himself maliciously inserted the punch-line, set for the three
playmates:

> *Und ach sein Kuss!**

In the course of discussion they all agree, for one completely selfish
reason, that Diemut must give herself to Kunrad and end this black-out.
The young men and maidens burst out in unison with a ribald verse that
may roughly be rendered:

---

* Strauss asked, in vain, that this addition, his own clinching contribution, should be
omitted from the printed textbook.

> The psalms they will not fetch the price,
> nor any clerical sets,
> until, my girl, you sacrifice
> your . . . sweet violets.*

There is a pause of suspense before the nonsense here translated in terms of a famous Rugger Club refrain, which is gradually taken up by others in counterpoint with even less decorous sentiments. The extremely cheerful effect does not in performance rise above the vulgarest Palm Court drivel, in the tradition of Heykens's *Serenade*. Fortunately for Diemut's critical prestige she has already anticipated the valuable elements in this proffered advice. And it switches, by a cross-fade technique, first into a long melody in which Diemut is urged to give herself to the Master (the hypocritical motivation is quite repellent, deliberately so, there is no doubt), then into a reprise of Kunrad-Wolzogen's 'All warmth comes from woman' passage (Ex. 8), finally a cry to help them from '*Feuersnot*' (voices in twenty parts). An infinity of diminished sevenths slowly detumesces. A pause. The closing scene (the only part of this opera to achieve international acceptance so far) begins quietly and mysteriously, out of silence, with Kunrad's Ex. 7, newly extended. Diemut's Ex. 4 answers, on woodwind and harp. Ex. 8 resumes the dialogue, soft and passionate on strings, at quicker tempo. Again Ex. 4 answers with an offstage band, in support, which leads the Burgomaster to imagine light coming from his daughter's room. Now, on low woodwind, Ex. 9 rises again, as before in Kunrad's monologue, joined by Diemut's Ex. 10. In this way Strauss gradually reproduces, as later in *Der Rosenkavalier* and *Arabella*, a graphic, scrupulous, and artistically uplifted musical depiction of the act of love. It cannot worthily, decorously, be followed in words; the themes involved are those already cited. At the moment of climax there is complete silence, and then every light in Munich flames once more, from the tiniest candle to the enormous midsummer bonfire outside the city. Ex. 4 wells triumphantly for the initiation and salvation of Diemut, and we hear her Ex. 11 sung by both lovers in their bedroom. The chorus of burghers hails their union with glad shouts to the trilling harmonies of the introduction and Ex. 1. And the young people pointedly acknowledge that, in Diemut's own innocent words of not two hours ago, 'every girl likes her honey'.

Feuersnot is, in terms of compositional technique, a very accomplished piece of work indeed. It moves well, is intricately but not obscurely constructed in terms of episode and scene, dialogue, and meditation (i.e. recitative and aria), contains a number of set-pieces whose mastery of

---

* *Da hilft nun kein Psallieren*
noch auch die Klerisei;
das Mädlein muss verlieren
sein Lirum larum lei.

texture and counterpoint any composer must admire, carries its sense of humour and comedy unusually well poised on the scales (perhaps better poised than *Die Meistersinger*, its distinguished parent), contains no role that is less than acutely characterized, and two roles at least that are good to sing, those of the lovers—perhaps Diemut is catered for less generously than Kunrad. The instrumentation is as masterful and as diversified as we expect from the hero of *Ein Heldenleben* and the portrayer of *Don Quixote*. The closing scene is popular among concert audiences. The opera as a whole conveys a flavour of knowing simplicity that is unique among Strauss's fifteen operas, and though here and there it may remind us of its predecessors, particularly *Die Meistersinger* and *Hänsel und Gretel*, but also *Tristan und Isolde*, the finger of Strauss is dipped in the ink that wrote every bar. In a decent performance it sits quite securely.

Why then is it not a staple item in the slender repertory of twentieth-century comic operas? Beecham maintained that the choruses were excessively difficult, but not for any chorus that has sung subsequent operas of progressive persuasion. He avowed too that Kunrad is a great bore; that is a matter of opinion—I would stoutly defend the honeyed or authoritative music of the part when sung by a fine baritone with (as Strauss admitted) a fluent top register. *Feuersnot* used to be considered too local in its appeal; but Britten's *Albert Herring*, a more parochial opera, has spanned the western world without difficulty.

Feuersnot, however, bears the burden of a forgotten topicality; the sharp satirical tone of the original cannot, however brilliantly the conductor does his work, be revived at full strength, because the references are now mostly obsolete. And those that remain identifiable sound unnecessary to the captivating of an audience for which *The Flying Dutchman* or *Das Rheingold* are classics, not talking-points, and for whom a quotation from *Guntram* is a blank book. Much in *Feuersnot* has dated, especially the once provocative bits. There remains the kernel of the drama, which Wolzogen isolated from the element of temporary indignation and longing for revenge (if he and Strauss identified themselves with Kunrad, their object in making the opera was close to Diemut with her basket—and Munich would not be wheedled into it). This is the allegory of creative force and its inspiration. Perhaps scientific preoccupation has taken modern audiences beyond Wolzogen's creed, but I do not think so. Indeed it is a deed less daring than of old, more obviously sensible, to accept the truth of his thesis.

Feuersnot is simply not as sharp and pointfully communicative as its authors hoped; and the weaknesses are not topical or temporary by cause. The Wagnerisms of the libretto were never either funny or convincing; the characters, from Kunrad to the Minnie Bannister-figure of Frau Tulbeck, do not really, even negatively, endear themselves and stick in the memory, as do Beckmesser and the Nightwatchman in *Meistersinger*, or even the Shepherd in Act 3 of *Tristan*. If we love *Feuersnot* and their place in it, it is for the music given to them.

Even then, it is music that one welcomes, when it is there. Those who know and enjoy *Feuersnot* would surely cross the town on a wet night for Kunrad's 'Feuersnot' aria, or the insincere love duet—some of us for the volatile, amiably popular music that can be found nowhere else so positively innocent in Strauss until his last instrumental works. But most of us, having heard *Feuersnot*, probably believe that its transitional qualities are the most striking, and that the best bits are those which reappeared later in stronger form. That may be true, but the individuality could not be repeated; nothing else in Strauss gives us quite this atmosphere of ambivalent geniality, of private seriousness kept in subservience to urban sociability, now swayed, now swinging, and finally mutually content. Not even *Ariadne auf Naxos*, which treats a related theme, has quite the same unsophisticated lightness and brilliance. Who would reject *The Flying Dutchman* because it is all done more magisterially in *Tristan*?

Salome

OPUS 54

Music Drama in One Act
After Oscar Wilde's Drama
GERMAN TRANSLATION BY HEDWIG LACHMANN

Herod	TENOR
Herodias, Wife of Herod	MEZZO-SOPRANO
Salome, daughter of Herodias	SOPRANO
Jokanaan (John the Baptist)	BARITONE
Narraboth, a young Syrian, Captain of the Guard	TENOR
The Page of Herodias	ALTO
Five Jews	FOUR TENORS, ONE BASS
Two Nazarenes	TENOR, BASS
Two Soldiers	BASSES
A Cappadocian	BASS
A Slave	SOPRANO or TENOR (unspecified)

I

The success of *Feuersnot* effectively established Strauss as one of Germany's principal composers and it was not long before he began contemplating new subjects. Wolzogen gave him a new libretto in 1903 entitled *The Wicked Boys of Seville*, based on a tale by Cervantes, and Strauss considered it seriously for a time. But he had in fact already found the theme for his next opera; in April 1902 he wrote to his parents that he 'projected another one-act opera (as a pendant to *Feuersnot*), if the text proposed by the librettist, Anton Lindner in Vienna, is successful'. Lindner had suggested a new adaptation of Oscar Wilde's *Salome* (1891) which, after years of censorship troubles, had enjoyed its first triumph in Breslau shortly before. Strauss liked the idea and Lindner accordingly prepared some sample scenes. During the rest of 1902 Strauss was busy with the cantata *Taillefer* and the Domestic Symphony, as well as with travel and tours. When he came to look at Lindner's verses he found them 'cleverly versified' but not truly inspiring; so he compared them with Wilde, in the new translation of Hedwig Lachmann, and the very first line, *Wie schön ist die Prinzessin Salome* struck him at once as marvellously apt for music. So that when early in 1903, to confirm his intentions, he visited Max Reinhardt's Kleines Theater in Berlin, where Lachmann's translation was being performed with Gertrud Eysoldt, he could truthfully answer to the friend who suggested *Salome* as a good operatic subject, that he was already at work on it.

In fact, he did not seriously begin the composition until August 1903, when the Domestic Symphony was almost complete—and it is odd to think how dissimilar these two simultaneous projects were and how hair-raising the mutual implications (exemplified in the protests when I wrote that *Salome* warns parents how their teenage daughters might behave). Strauss had reduced the German text of Wilde's drama by about one-third, so as to allow for the slower pace at which literature moves when it is set to music. Some subsidiary or elucidatory episodes were removed, the exposition of the play was cut down by two substantial episodes, and in general Wilde's sentences were shorn wherever possible of their subordinate or elaborate clauses—a characteristic of the literary style, but one that Strauss always found unsuitable for musical setting because it overloads a cantabile phrase with too many words.*

---

* One example from the very first scene may show Strauss's typical method of cutting:

Le jeune Syrien *Elle a l'air très étrange. Elle ressemble à une petite princesse qui porte un voile jaune, et a des pieds d'argent. Elle ressemble à une petite princesse qui a des pieds comme des petites colombes blanches. . . . On dirait qu'elle danse*

Narraboth *Sie ist sehr seltsam. Wie eine kleine Prinzessin, deren Füsse weisse Tauben sind. Man könnte meinen, sie tanzt.*

The sketch of *Salome* occupied Strauss for just over a year (it must be remembered that conducting occupied a good part of his time—he toured America during this period)* and was completed in September 1904. The writing of the full score—one of the most masterly and original composed in this century—took another nine months. During this time Strauss played it to Mahler who remarked with surprise that Salome's Dance was not yet composed; Strauss, quite unperturbed, declared that he would get it done later. He also played parts to his father, who commented, 'God, what nervous music! Like having a cockchafer crawling about in your trousers.' This redoubtable old reactionary did not live to attend a performance: he died at the age of eighty-four on 31 May 1905, less than a month before his son completed the full score, which was on 20 June. The opera was dedicated to Sir Edgar Speyer, a London banker of German extraction who, like the rest of his musical family, were famous benefactors of music in Britain at the turn of the century. Edgar Speyer had befriended Strauss during the composer's visit to London in 1899. The autograph score is unfortunately (one hopes only temporarily) lost.

Strauss had again decided that the première should go to Dresden, and before even the short score was completed he began negotiation and preparation with Schuch, promising the material by the autumn of 1905. He warned Schuch that despite the exclusion of full choruses, the orchestral and solo parts would be twice as difficult as *Feuersnot*; and having decided that, for the title role, a big voice, accustomed to Wagnerian dramatic soprano music, was more important than a petite figure, and that for this reason Marie Wittich was the only possible choice in the Dresden company, he warned Schuch that Wittich, a slow learner, must begin studying the part at least three months before the première. Herod and Jokanaan should have their parts at this time also; the others would need no more than three weeks to prepare the music. Strauss kept his part of the bargain, and counted on a première in mid-November. Schuch does not seem to have taken all this very seriously. It was not until the last week of October that he asked Strauss for a score. Frau Wittich had high-handedly left herself no more than a month to learn her part. What she saw, when she saw it, made her hair stand on end. She complained to Cosima Wagner who asked Strauss, much against his will, to play part of *Salome* on the piano. Frau Wagner, who was not only the widow of Richard but the mother of Siegfried Wagner, an industrious opera composer, pronounced it sheer lunacy. At the first piano rehearsal Mme Wittich marched up to Schuch and handed back the music, followed by all her colleagues except Carl Burrian (Herod) who, when asked his opinion, announced that he knew his role by heart already. This was

---

* Strauss also found time to revise and bring up to date Berlioz's treatise on instrumentation. A letter to his father indicates that he completed this task in November 1904.

a body-blow to the prestige of the others, and they felt obliged to try again. This, I take it, was where Schuch got cold feet,* and asked for a postponement of the première. The composer mounted his high horse and gave Schuch a deadline of 9 December for the première, declaring that Artur Nikisch was hard at work on *Salome* in Leipzig; likewise Mahler, who proposed to introduce the work to Vienna on that date and who had four sopranos lined up for the name-part. This may or may not have been bluff: in the event neither of these great men conducted the work, as we shall see. But Schuch did what he was told. He managed to quell the strikes threatened by Frau Wittich, who as the highly respectable wife of the Burgomaster took the strongest moral objection to the stage business devised for her by Willi Wirk, a producer much stimulated in imagination by the perversity and impiety of the piece. He managed to get past the censor, who was rumoured in the Press to be looming— though the Wilde *Salome* had been performed uncut in almost every theatre in Germany. He contrived to teach this unprecedentedly exacting and novel score to his orchestra in just over a month. All this was a challenge to Schuch's pride—particularly as rumour ran wild in Dresden that *Salome* was impossibly difficult and the première would have to be put off. Schuch was a conductor noted as much for the refinement of his readings as for his championship of advanced contemporary music. Strauss once remarked that there was no higher praise than to talk about 'carrying pianissimi to Dresden', and he told an orchestra to play *Salome* as if it were fairy music by Mendelssohn. At the first rehearsal he announced, 'Gentlemen, there are no difficulties or problems. This opera is a scherzo with a fatal conclusion!' *Salome*, despite its grand tutti climaxes, and despite the hugeness of the orchestra, chiefly abounds in orchestral music of coruscating lightness and delicacy; it was made for Schuch (as also for Nikisch and Mahler who had similar gifts, it must be admitted). Not that difficulties were not experienced during rehearsals; one dispute between Schuch and Strauss ended when the composer asked, 'Who wrote this opera—you or I?' Back came Schuch's answer: 'You, thank God!'

It is difficult to establish from anybody who really knew the score just how good the first performance, on the ultimatum day 9 December, really was. Strauss congratulated Schuch in the most fulsome terms (but partly, his letter suggests, because he wanted to persuade Schuch to perform *Salome* as often as possible immediately after the première), but later he admitted to Hofmannsthal that '*Salome* succeeded in spite of Auntie Wittich'. It was phenomenally successful with the public, who demanded thirty-eight curtain-calls at the conclusion. Almost all German

---

* The sequence of events, as narrated below, makes sense and is internally supported by Strauss's letters to Schuch. Unfortunately Schuch's letters are not preserved, and some of the known facts are not dated.

music critics of the day were hidebound academics, and devoted their notices to abuse.* The less unregenerate had to admit that nothing so exciting had occurred in opera since the première of Verdi's *Falstaff*, indeed since Wagner's last works were introduced to Dresden. One or two bluntly proclaimed the advent of a masterpiece, as Mahler did in a private letter to his wife after he saw it at Berlin in 1907. Breslau, where Wilde's play had its first success in 1901, was the second company to produce Strauss's *Salome*. Other towns followed without delay, fifty of them within two years. By 1911 it had been given in almost every country in Europe. Strauss first conducted it in the Austrian première at Graz on 16 May 1906; he also directed the Italian première at Turin. Four days later Toscanini followed suit at La Scala.

Schuch was luckier with the Dresden censor than some of his colleagues. Strauss, who had suffered enough from interfering quasi-moralists at the time of *Feuersnot*, took it for granted that he would have no trouble with *Salome*: first since Wilde's drama, as he reminded Schuch, was regularly given in the theatre; secondly since he had carefully removed all precise historical references. One of his expected obstacles, the Kaiser in Berlin (who was known to dislike Biblical subjects on stage), had actually suggested that Strauss should write an opera about Herod, and so had to show interest when Strauss confessed he was already doing so. But the Kaiser experienced new qualms when *Salome* came up for a Berlin première, and was only pacified by the promise that the Star of Bethlehem would be seen to twinkle on the backcloth at the end of the opera! This worked so effectively that Berlin notched up fifty performances in eleven months. Mahler in Vienna, where the première was to have been ready at the same time as in Dresden, was point-blank refused permission by the church; a guest production by the Breslau company was allowed, by some curious act of conscience-squaring, to be seen in Vienna at the German Volkstheater in May 1907, but the ban on home performance was only lifted in 1911, after Mahler's death alas. In New York two productions were quashed by influential private patrons. In London the Lord Chamberlain banned the opera in 1907, and four years later still insisted on modifications memorably recalled, in hilarious detail, by the conductor of this British première, Sir Thomas Beecham.† London critics quickly pointed out that Maud Allan had danced the story of *Salome* in unblushing detail, for Londoners—without interference from his Lordship.‡ Many critics, in many countries, echoed the Kaiser's remark

* Many are quoted verbatim in *Steinitzer* (Vol. 1, p. 259 ff.) and in *Gregor* (p. 76 ff.). It is curious to find that one major obstacle to acceptance was the use of a libretto in prose.

† *A Mingled Chime*, Chapter 21, p. 102 ff.

‡ Allan's *The Vision of Salome*, with music by Marcel Rémy (not Strauss, as is sometimes stated), was first performed in Vienna in 1904, then throughout the continent until in 1908 she reached the Palace Theatre, London, where her *Salome* ran for 250 consecutive performances. This ballet was based, it should be added, on Flaubert, not Wilde (see p. 60) though of course it included the famous head on a silver charger.

that *Salome* would do Strauss no good in the end; Strauss later commented that the proceeds of *Salome* had enabled him to build his villa at Garmisch.

2

Strauss, we have seen, called *Salome* 'a scherzo with a fatal conclusion'; without belittling the brilliant virtuosity of the score, we might more accurately describe the opera as a dream that turns into a nightmare. The first scene of *Salome*, in reduced Strauss as in complete Wilde, has a strong flavour of the dream landscape. The curtain rises with a scale on the clarinet and discloses first the moon full, over-full and brightly shining, then a terrace in Herod's palace at Tiberias on the sea of Galilee, abutting, via an entrance up a flight of steps, on to the dining hall. In the courtyard of the terrace stands an old cistern, a kind of well with an iron grille over the top.* A young captain of the guard, Syrian by birth, named Narraboth, gazes through the portal into the hall. The clarinet tells us, even before he sings, at whom he is gazing. This is Salome, daughter of Herodias, princess of Judaea.

I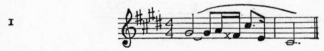

Narraboth's first phrase tells us that the Princess's name is accented on the first, not as in English on the second syllable (in French there is no strong accentuation).

2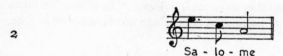

Sa - lo - me

Curiously enough Strauss adopted our pronunciation when he came, in *Die Ägyptische Helena*, to Aithra's sister, another Salome. When Narraboth speaks Salome's name, a theme of swinging major sixths rises on the cellos; it is his theme of infatuation for Salome—his *idée fixe*.

3

* Strauss followed Wilde's stage directions in placing the staircase stage R. and the cistern stage L. In every production or photograph that I have seen these are reversed, save in the Dresden half-centenary production of 1955.

The change of mode from C sharp minor to major, just as Narraboth speaks, is like a sudden emergence of the moon. Above Ex. 1 hovers a violin tremolo that floats languidly upward and downward, and clearly portrays the pale orb. Beside Narraboth stands Herodias's Page, devoted to the Syrian captain; the Page (a contralto trouser-role, or should one here say tunic-role?) is gazing indolently at the moon, which he compares to a woman rising from the grave (the slow scale, pungently supported by cor anglais, continues to rise). Narraboth continues the simile, but since he is looking at Salome, not the moon at all, he compares it to a little princess, with feet like doves, like a dancer; there is a flicker of rhythmic interest in woodwind and celesta (oddly like Electra's dance of triumph). Everything is still, frozen in dreamland like the divided cello harmonics as the moon soars upward, the Page's voice downwards.

There is a sudden hubbub of chatter and dispute in the banquet hall—a characteristic piece of expressionist tone-painting, eight or nine distinct themes impacted into two bars, and orchestrated with brilliant precision (not for individual audibility but for total effect). The most important are quoted here, though Ex. 4a will not be properly heard until the big ensemble later in the opera, and then in the minor mode.

4

These and their concomitant motifs portray the contentious Jews at Herod's table. Two soldiers, standing at ease on the ramparts, remark scornfully that they are fighting over their religion. Narraboth resumes his ecstatic contemplation of Salome, and the Page warns him not to gaze too long:

5

Du siehst sie   im - mer an.

a phrase, softly underlined by horn, that seems to refer to animal lust (it is related to Ex. 20 and has frequent isolated entries on drums). A very soft and slithering extended diminution of Ex. 1, on violas, gives further expression to the Page's fears; something terrible could happen (*Schreckliches kann geschehen*) is his constant refrain. But Narraboth is not listening, and this quasi-rondo exposition returns to Ex. 1. The soldiers comment on Herod's sombre face; the patterns on plucked strings tell us what is in his mind—

—since pattern (a) is the source of Salome's Ex. 10, while the sliding chromatic scale of (b) is typical of Herod's unrest (cf. Ex. 21).*

Narraboth remarks on the paleness of the Princess:

and the motif marked x, piercingly echoed on clarinet, is thematically of some importance, a symbol of Salome's tense mood. The Page repeats his warning and, omitting two pages of dialogue, Strauss at once signals whence the *Schreckliches* will come. From inside the cistern the voice of the prophet Jokanaan (or John the Baptist as we know him) is heard announcing the arrival of the Messiah (as in Mark i, vii, and substantially in all four Gospels), in solemn and dignified A flat major. Ex. 8 is heard in some form or other whenever Jesus is spoken of; it is not specifically one of Jokanaan's own themes.

* Even if we try to associate the main themes with particular states of mind, or more rarely with particular characters, we should remember that they are primarily symphonic materials which may and often do appear to change their precise meaning according to the symphonic context. This is true of all Strauss's operas.

A soft brass chord, with an awesome stroke of the tam-tam, sets a halo, as it were, upon Jokanaan's pronouncement. Almost at once the cellos introduce John's own theme, to which may be appended one of his thematic phrases (it should be compared with Ex. 5 and their compendium Ex. 20).

9

John was imprisoned by Herod not for preaching or baptizing in the name of Jesus, but for his fearless denunciation of Herodias's immorality in marrying her husband's brother. The two soldiers discuss this prophet, his provenance, the obscurity of his *dicta*, and his strict solitary confinement at the Tetrarch's orders. (Strauss here omitted the soldiers' further discussion of the cistern where Salome's father was imprisoned for twelve years, and finally strangled—Herod's order being given by the delivery of his ring to the Executioner Naaman. This last piece of information is relevant to the plot later on, but not indispensable. This central section of the exposition is long enough already, and we are ready for the entry of the protagonist.)

Ex. 1 now returns fortissimo, impacted with Narraboth's Ex. 3, as he observes Salome rise and leave the hall. The second scene of the opera begins in A major, as she sweeps excitedly on to the terrace, and Ex. 1 now obtains a new opening, characteristic of the Princess.

10

Ex. 7 is added to the flickering, nervous texture as Salome complains of her discomfort within the palace, where her own mother's husband gazes with mole-like eyes continuously at her. The mole-eyes evoke a tiny but important new phrase:

11
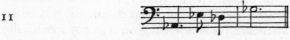

Salome contrasts that oppressive atmosphere with the gentle fresh air outside, where one can at last breathe. The accompanying motif is not concerned with balmy breezes, though, but with Salome herself.

12

Later this theme, often with a chromatically altered third note as shown, will seem to denote Salome's relationship to her mother Herodias, or her own dawning sexuality.

Ex. 12 is at once followed by Ex. 10, set down an octave even though its second note falls a third below the lowest open string of the second violins (who nevertheless find it written in their part, as do some first violins a few pages later). Salome detests the company of the squabbling Jews (Ex. 4), and taciturn Egyptians and coarse Romans (who are Herod's guests of honour, Wilde tells us). She gazes blissfully at the moon (Ex. 1 and Ex. 10, and the high, floating violin tremolo) which is like a chaste virgin. For of course the moon, as a vehicle of reflected light, resembles to every character what is in his or her mind; and this tells us a little of Salome's self-centred personality.

3

We may perhaps pause a moment to consider what Salome herself is like, in voice as well as person. Confusion and dispute have arisen throughout the almost sixty years of the opera's history—understandably. Strauss told Marie Wittich that she should impersonate a sixteen-year-old princess with an Isolde voice, to which she sensibly replied that one doesn't do that sort of thing, Herr Strauss; it's Either—Or. A glance at the photograph of this first Salome will confirm the force of her argument. At the time Strauss, being a musician, was chiefly concerned with the musical effect, and in discussing the cast with Schuch he declared firmly that 'experiments with little worms are absolutely out of the question'— the main necessity was to get the voice across the orchestra. I suspect that famous order to a *Salome* orchestra, 'Louder, louder, I can still hear the singers!' was either apocryphal or wishful pleonasm.*

The first Salomes were all amply built, and content to send a deputy when it came to the famous Dance; Wittich once essayed it herself, much to Strauss's distress. The first to look and dance as well as sing like a Salome was Aïno Ackté, who took the part in the London première, and remained unexcelled for many years (she also had a love-affair with the composer). In time, however, Strauss became greatly attracted to a lighter, more silvery timbre of voice—his concert tours with Elisabeth Schumann (again attended by romance, though unsuccessfully) contributed signifi- cantly here. Strauss suggested that Schumann should undertake the role,

---

* During the rehearsal for another *Salome* Strauss told the first clarinets, 'Gentlemen, if I can hear the passage, it's too loud.' There is a similar remark about the brass in *Hints to a Young Conductor* (*BUE*, Eng. trans., p. 38). Strauss's pessimistic aim was a forty per cent word audibility in operatic performances.

promising to retouch the scoring for her benefit. This plan came to nothing, though it left behind some traces in several of Strauss's later soprano roles, and of course in the *Brentano Lieder*, Op. 68, where Strauss was specifically writing for Schumann's voice. Strauss did not, however, abandon his new ideal of a lyric-soprano Salome, and when in 1930 Otto Erhardt devised a new silver jubilee production of *Salome* for Dresden, the title role was allotted to Maria Rajdl (the first Aithra in *Die Ägyptische Helena*), for whose *leggiero* voice Strauss expressly reduced the orchestration at dangerously noisy moments, above all lightening the woodwind parts; these alterations are now regularly used in smaller orchestra pits, and the newer conception of the part has given us such memorable Salomes as Ljuba Welitsch, Maria Cebotari, Lisa Della Casa, and Anja Silja.*

Two factors caused Strauss to alter his vocal conception of the role. One was his collaboration with Hugo von Hofmannsthal, an artist dedicated to dignity and poise, for whom what he called 'Wagnerian bawling' was the very nadir of good taste. Hofmannsthal waged merciless war upon Strauss's inborn Teutonic heaviness, encouraging him always to lighten and ingratiate his music. In due course we shall examine how successful he was, or even how beneficial; but Strauss did come to realize that, in *Salome* at least, Wagnerian declamation could be significantly alleviated. Executive technique is obliged, sooner or later, to catch up with creative audacity: the solo part in Tchaikovsky's violin concerto is no longer 'unplayable' as Leopold Auer at first maintained; *Tristan* no longer reduces its interpreters to lunacy or voicelessness. And *Salome*, having quickly shown that the ardours of the name-part were feasible to an Isolde, inevitably progressed towards the point at which the credible if not actual voice as well as the figure of a sixteen-year-old girl could carry across the tempest in the orchestra pit and round a large auditorium.

Strauss was, as the circumstances became more propitious, artistically obliged to use the moment in order to bring his ideal *Salome* closer to realization. He was the more obliged because, ever since Willi Wirk's first production, the name-part in *Salome* had become increasingly a vehicle for demonstration of the most blatant exhibitionism by sex-cats if not sex-kittens; and commentators had not hesitated to accept Depravity as Salome's second name.† The key to Salome's character is to be found in her comparison of the moon (viz. herself) with a chaste virgin. Strauss eventually set down on paper his view of Salome:‡ 'Anyone who has been in the Orient and has observed the decorum of its women, will appreciate

---

* Though in the early 1960s the outstanding Salome of the day is an Isolde-type Salome, Birgit Nilsson who, incidentally, does not attempt the Dance—and in this connexion we may observe that the Dance does tempt a singer into taking a welcome rest in a part which offers no other respite from her first entry until the end of the opera.
† Kobbé's *Complete Opera Guide* is lamentably misleading in this respect.
BUE, p. 182.

that Salome should be played as a chaste virgin, an oriental princess, with but the simplest, most dignified gestures, if her shipwreck on encountering the miracle of a brave new world is to arouse compassion and not horror and disgust.' Salome is a spoiled nymphet, at the age of maximum antagonism towards her mother and stepfather and indeed the whole atmosphere of the court where she has grown up. Her father, whom she needs at this age, was immured in this cistern and then killed; what more natural than that she should seek the father-substitute who is incarcerated in the very same place, is quite unlike any of the courtiers she so detests, and who, so far from sharing their wolfish attention to her physical person, behaves in a remote, austerely *noli me tangere* fashion towards her? The need for paternal influence coincides with the dawn of sexual instinct, and this is how Salome goes astray, making the unnatural, impure decision for the instinctively natural, pure reason, and knowing quite well that she will get her desire, as she always has done. There is no Aristotelian 'purging by pity and terror' (Strauss was not an ardent Hellenist for nothing) if Salome is presented, from the word Go, as a kinky Strip Queen from a Sex-Bar.

4

As Salome contemplates the moon, so chaste and clean and unlike everybody at court except herself, Jokanaan's voice is again uplifted to announce the advent of the Lord (Ex. 8). Salome's Ex. 10 plus 1 is plunged into C minor at the sound, and the information of the voice's identity (she has never heard him before) increases her inner tension, and brings back Ex. 7. Narraboth senses awkwardness and suggests a tour of the garden (Ex. 3); but a fragmented, staccato version of Ex. 1, always associated with the flute, has already answered the invitation in the negative as its later reappearances also do. Salome's mind is on the Prophet who says dreadful things about her mother (Ex. 12, later in diminution with specific reference to Herodias, after Ex. 10). A Slave (whose quality of voice is curiously nowhere specified, though the part is notated in the treble clef—it is usually sung by a soprano, sometimes by a tenor) brings Herod's message that Salome should return to the banquet; Salome's reply is firm and abrupt (Ex. 10 variant), and she discovers, by questioning the guards, that the Prophet is quite young—we appreciate Narraboth's growing concern. Jokanaan prophesies again (Ex. 8), foretelling the basilisk born of serpent (Ex. 11, stretched out, Procrustes fashion) that will devour the birds of the air (frenzied flutter-tonguing on three flutes, very evocative).

Salome, fascinated, asks to see the prisoner and is told of the Tetrarch's ban (Ex. 9b—prophecy, the cause of the ban). She grows more insistent

(Ex. 1 plus 10 again), but to no avail, and she is therefore obliged to seek a different tactic, though while she is cudgelling her brains she passes her time with a digression, gazing through the grille into the black ugly cistern (low horns and tuba):

13

It is like a tomb, she remarks in her lowest register extending down to a low G flat. One more peremptory command to the guards fails (Ex. 10, again falling outside the violin compass), and so, to the Page's horror, she turns and wheedles Narraboth, using her knowledge of his devotion (Ex. 3) and her own girlish charm (Ex. 1, staccato augmented variant, destined not to succeed, *vide supra*). Narraboth's refusals only provoke her powers of persuasion and Strauss's most translucent, alluring instrumental textures. She is almost tripping over her words in excited urgency; and at last she succeeds. Horns and low strings call out a desperate warning of Ex. 9b (soon to be Ex. 20) as he orders the Prisoner to be brought out for the Princess's scrutiny.

The soldiers remove the grille from the cistern and descend to fetch Jokanaan. Salome's heart is fluttering madly, partly with apprehension (wind trills and string arpeggios) and partly with elation (Ex. 10), frequently involving the violins in non-existent notes. The extended orchestral interlude makes reference to Ex. 9a, Ex. 13, and two new vital themes, one applied to Jokanaan's ascetic remoteness:

14

the other to the passions that are welling inside Salome's untutored heart.

15

This last phrase will only later achieve its full length (cf. *Elektra*, Ex. 9ˣ).

Ex. 9a resounds sonorously in E flat minor (one expects organ and harmonium here; Strauss does not need them at this moment) while Jokanaan climbs out of the cistern and looks around him (soft, emaciated woodwind on Ex. 14). Salome moves away, horrified (dense violin tremolo). John begins a denunciation of Herod, which moves from C to D major. Here we may remark that portly booming baritones are out of place: Jokanaan is young, handsome, ascetic in his way of life and therefore slender if not ill-nourished. It is the forthrightness of his pronouncements that has excited Salome's interest, and it is his un-worldly dedicated fanaticism that she finds extraordinary and, in the context of her experience so far, attractive. Strauss, anti-Christian and anti-evangelical, intended at one time to present Jokanaan as a grotesque figure; fortunately he realized that, with so many grotesques among the Herodian entourage, no point would be gained, and the purpose of the dramatic conflict decidedly weakened. Jokanaan's music is stiff and square, betraying Strauss's lack of sympathy; it was not until he met Barak in *Die Frau ohne Schatten* that he learned to write convincing music for a simple, idealistic man.

After a puzzled question from Salome, Jokanaan resumes his diatribe, turning to the monstrous courtesan Herodias. His denunciations extend Ex. 9a so that the second bar continues upwards, colliding either with a descending chromatic scale, or with a new cadential figure:

16

Both ideas are associated with Herodias. Salome is aware of this, though Narraboth claims incomprehension. When this lucid case for the prosecution has rested, the clarinet timidly voices a new Salome theme.

17

Salome, to Narraboth's (and Ex. 3's) grave concern, is transfixed by the
Prophet's terrible look; by his terrible hollow eyes (Ex. 1 in diminution
and staccato augmentation) like dark seas; by his emaciated body (Ex. 14)
like cool ivory—the poise of the vocal line here is among the opera's chief
beauties; and by her desire to see him at closer quarters. John hears rather
than sees the frivolous fascinated girl, and orders her to withdraw. She
announces her name and rank, trusting in their prestige. She did not
expect the venomous verbal assault on her as daughter of the pandemic
strumpet (Ex. 16). But she is drawn by what she hears, and asks the
Prophet what she must do. Sackcloth and ashes are his advice, and a
Quest for the Son of Man for whom he has a striking phrase:

18

Salome's innocent answer is another question: 'Is this Son of Man as
beautiful as you?' (Ex. 17 and Ex. 16). The sound of the orchestra at this
point is of a wonderful tranquillity. Narraboth joins the Baptist in advising
her to go somewhere else. But something too big for them has occurred.
This is a monumental point of repose in the score at which the music
sinks into a timeless B major while Salome cries the Prophet's name, and
first horn with oboes and clarinets drag out Ex. 1 as from a sluggish chest
of drawers. After what seems an eternal *tenuto* she begins her song of love,
to Ex. 17: Jokanaan, I am in love with your body—and she expatiates
rapturously on its charms to a version of Ex. 15; her sincerity is such that
we should never, for a moment, question her propriety. Only, as she ends,
her cadence, *Lass mich ihn berühren, deinen Leib* ('Let me touch your
body') squashes together, like the rotten centre of a toothsome-looking
apple, with the Ex. 16 that referred to Herodias.

Firmly, without hesitation, Jokanaan brings out Ex. 9a and his total
rejection of her advances. Ex. 14 in diminution marks Salome's change of
instinct: his body is vile (a slithery descending scale, as for Herodias).
Ex. 10 resumes; it is his hair that she loves. It is like black grapes, like
cedar trees, voluptuous (Exs. 10 and 12), like lions (a trombone roar), like
starless nights. Again the violent riposte with a percussive monotone, on
trombones, of Ex. 5. Salome disowns his hair (Ex. 16) with many a vile
comparison. It is his mouth that she desires, the mouth that has given
expression to Ex. 9 and its denunciations of her loathsome mother. Her
third panegyric is about Jokanaan's mouth, like scarlet, or trumpets, or
grapes stamped in the wine-press; she longs to kiss it.

Jokanaan has not deigned to look at Salome, but he has heard, and is
properly appalled. Narraboth intercedes more plaintively than ever (Ex. 3).

Salome is completely preoccupied with the Baptist's mouth. Narraboth might be miles away for all the effect his pleas have on her. She cries anew for her heart's desire:

Ich will dei-nen Mund küs - sen, Jo - cha - na - an.

Narraboth stabs himself (to Ex. 3, Ex. 1, and Ex. 16) and, according to a stage tradition, rolls from far upstage to a prominent point between Jokanaan and the now hysterical nymphet. She sees nothing but the mouth she desires; nor does she comprehend the Baptist's shocked reproaches, and his advice to seek out Jesus (Ex. 8) in a boat on Galilee. As John speaks, the orchestra repeats her Ex. 19, conveying her unhearing passion. This is a stalemate; neither listens to the other. Jokanaan, desperate, curses her (noisy Ex. 17), now and for ever; and, with Ex. 14 on the drums, he descends into his cell. Their individual themes resound again (Ex. 15 is now in C sharp minor). At the climax of this tremendous orchestral interlude another squashed cadence deriving from Ex. 17 depicts the frustration which Salome is experiencing, for the first time in her life, and the contrabassoon plunges Ex. 1 into the depths, giving it a peremptory appendix:

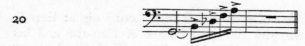

This musical idea represents command, as yet denied to Salome, but increased, by her will, from one to three *fagotto* voices. Terribly we hear Salome's plan for getting her way, though it has yet to be put into words.

Ich will den Kopf des Jo - cha - na - an

The fourth scene now begins with quarrelling Jews (Ex. 4), and an uneasy Herodian scale in whole tones, mercurial but dull. The Tetrarch has finished supper, and now seeks his stepdaughter. His discovery of her is all wide-eyed wonder.

Herodias follows, pouring cold water on everything he says.

23

Herod sees the moon which, for him, is like Herodias, a mad woman in search of lovers. Herodias has a special interest in seeing the moon as no more than the moon. Herod, ill at ease, upset, excited (a virtuoso orchestral portrait based on Ex. 23), slips on the blood around Narraboth's corpse, and sees an evil omen; he recognizes the body, is bewildered because he has not ordered the Syrian's death (Ex. 3), and has him transported hence ('Do you think I am like the King of Egypt,' he says in Wilde's original, 'who never gives a banquet without showing a corpse?'). The slippery scales prolong Herod's disquiet; he senses cold wind (Ex. 9b then Ex. 9a), is hardly to be calmed, and now he calls for wine (there is an uncomfortable cut of Wilde's text here). His purpose is to recall Salome to the circle; she must drink with him. But (fragmented Ex. 1) she is not thirsty. He offers her fruit to eat with him. Strauss gives voluptuous expression to the action of biting.

24

She is not hungry. And her mother injects a cruel dig at Herod's humble birth, compared with the royal lineage of Herodias and her daughter. Here we may remark that, although Herodias's frigid, almost statuesque behaviour, throughout this second half of the opera, is to contrast violently with the impetuous, unconsidered actions of Herod, yet the Tetrarch is, as Strauss pointed out, a *parvenu* who is seeking all the time to impress his guests from Rome. He is vulgar, but must not appear deliberately so.

Herod's next tactic, partly provoked by his wife, is to offer Salome the throne of the Queen. She rejects this too. The contrabassoon offers Ex. 1 prefixed to the truculent Ex. 20, which itself has some altercation with Ex. 10—but this is interrupted by the voice from the cistern, prophesying unnamed doom. Herodias advises her husband to yield this prophet to the Jews, which Herod is unwilling to do since the man is an accredited holy one, an intimate of God. This is enough to start a theological discussion among the Jews, in the form of a contrapuntal fugato with Ex. 4a as its theme. Its course, and concomitant countersubjects, are in Strauss's brilliant, expressionistic vein; they build to a climax which may seem too protracted for ignorant listeners who have not appreciated or cannot hear the animated counterpoints of the argument—they are worthy of the wildest schisms indulged by Christians of a later epoch. Herodias calls for silence, in vain; she is less effective than the voice from the cistern proclaiming the Saviour of the world. This shuts them all up, and Herod is able to hear and ask who this Saviour may be. Two Nazarenes, followers of Jesus, explain Jesus's miracles. But the miracle of resurrection is too dangerous for Herod (his brother might testify against him), and he categorically forbids anyone to raise the dead. When John prophesies the death of Salome neither the Tetrarch nor his wife listens seriously (Ex. 9a); Herodias regards this purely as a personal slander. Herod, wishing to change the subject, suggests a dance by Salome, who at first demurs. Herod's persistent entreaties cover the prophecy, by Jokanaan, of the Tetrarch's own terrible death. Salome suddenly changes her mind when Herod promises to reward her with whatever her heart desires. Herodias advises her not to dance, but Salome's mind is on a particular wish. Herod swears, with a solemn oath, to fulfil it, even though a hallucination of cold wind sweeps through the palace. As Jokanaan prophesies (for the last time), the couple dispute, and Salome, who has changed her garments, prepares to dance her famous Dance. There is by the way no artistic necessity for Salome to send a deputy to the dance floor; Herod, to say the least, is not expecting a display of choreographic virtuosity, but something along the lines of a belly-dance, for his sexual stimulation. At the beginning Salome remains motionless in a pose, while the stage musicians set up a furious drumming. When trumpets and trombones throw out the essence of Ex. 21, she signals to the musicians, who make the transition to a more seductive mood, in slow waltz time. And now she dances the Dance of the Seven Veils. Musically this is largely a potpourri of familiar themes, Ex. 21, Ex. 1, Ex. 17, Ex. 10, Ex. 15, Ex. 14, Ex. 19, Ex. 3 (strangely, since Narraboth meant nothing to Salome, in death or life—until we remember that it was he whose order brought Jokanaan out of the cistern), Ex. 12, and the 'squashed cadence'. There is one brand-new tune in the melody.

It will be remembered that Strauss, according to Alma Mahler, wrote the Dance after the rest of the opera was complete, and the internal evidence of the scoring and textures supports her account. It is harder and more blatant in sound than the rest of the opera and the thematic references sometimes seem meaningless and automatic. This may be remarked if one listens to the whole opera on the radio or on gramophone records. In the opera house there is always the visual diversion of the dance to keep the attention from wandering; and in the concert hall, as a separate orchestral item, the virtuoso music can be appreciated out of context.

The score does not indicate at which points Salome removes the veils; just before the fast coda, she is to appear weary for a moment, and then to summon her strength anew. And towards the end of the Dance Salome remains poised over the cistern before bursting into Herod's embrace. She demands her reward for the Dance—and Herod keeps interrupting in his delight until he hears that John's head is the price, and then he is thunderstruck with horror, though Herodias is pleased. Salome insists on her right, invoking Herod's oath. He tries to reason with her.

26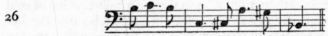

He tempts her with other trophies—jewels, peacocks, sacred relics, even the veil of the Jewish temple (the Jews vanish, aghast). But to each offer Salome stubbornly counters her original wish—the head of the Prophet—set to Ex. 21. Her demand is finally confirmed, incontrovertibly, with a virtuoso cadenza on the drums. Herod, exhausted, accedes. His command is reflected in a wide-ranging trumpet theme:

27

(perversely enough it was first heard when he spoke of an order that he had *not* given). Herodias quickly takes advantage of his exhaustion to remove his ring and dispatch it to the executioner. Herod revives, and at once regrets his decision; Ex. 9a is stretched out with a sinister menace. Salome is listening by the cistern. Her heart pants horribly (high double-bass pinched sounds—these are *not*, the composer said, anything but the cries of her innermost self). Her self-control has vanished, she is wrought up, and stammers impatient commands to all the servants; they must expedite the gift that is hers by promise. The percussion continually hammers out the beginning of Ex. 21, alias Ex. 9b. At last in the silence a huge black arm, that of Naaman, lifts Jokanaan's head, on a silver dish, out of the cistern. Salome grasps it in ecstasy, and begins her terrible song of love, as virtually every theme remotely connected with herself and Jokanaan floods back.* This is the head that refused her love, and now

---

* Ernest Newman had a theory, based on thematic references, that the closing scene was composed before the rest of the opera.

must accept it. Jokanaan never looked at her; had he done so, he would
have loved her. He despised her; now his head is for her to throw to the
dogs or vultures. His body was infinitely desirable (Ex. 15, grandiosely
extended). Now she may feast herself inexhaustibly upon his mouth. He
would have loved her, and the secret of love is greater than the secret of
death.

The moon is shrouded. The drums pound gently at Ex. 17 as she
falls upon her prey in the darkness. Herod shudders at what he sees.
Herodias is icily approving; she would doubtless claim that Salome has
grown to woman's status. Herod moves away. In the blackness Salome is
heard crooning blissfully to the object that has fulfilled her first longings;
has she tasted blood or love? The demand of Ex. 21 has now been transformed into rapturous acceptance of a death's-head love. Ex. 15 thunders
forth as she cries: I have kissed your mouth, Jokanaan. The theme finds
its cadence on a chord that plumbs the depths of horror—almost every
constituent note is further complicated by a trill somewhere in the
orchestra:

28

Ex. 17 calls out of the darkness, but the moon shines out and illuminates
this loathsome scene. Herod, on the stairs, sees it and calls to his guards:
Kill that woman. Ex. 26 confirms the order, as before. The soldiers
batter Salome to death with their shields.

5

As an achievement of musical composition, considered in terms of
thematic sculpture and colouring, symphonic structure and musical
characterization, *Salome* is the most brilliant and far-reaching of all
Strauss's works, not excepting *Don Quixote* and—his most 'advanced'
composition—*Elektra*. The foregoing account, though doubtless overloaded with thematic references, gives no more than the most superficial
estimate of the inventive riches that are to be found in this treasure-house

of a score. And yet, when credit is given to its extraordinary accomplishment, we are likely to judge *Salome*, in the cold light of day, as the nastiest opera in existence—much more unpleasant because, through its music, much more explicit than Wilde's drama.

Whatever possessed Strauss to choose such a subject? He has told us, with blandest *naïveté*, that he merely wanted to surpass the cheapjack pseudo-exoticism of existing operas with Oriental settings; 'they lacked the colour and the sunlight of the East'. He was drawn to the story of *Salome*, as artists have been for nineteen hundred years, by the brutal contrast of the young innocent girl and her power to order the murder of a holy man; the problems of guilt and responsibility; at its simplest level, the confrontation of life and death. Gustave Flaubert (whose short story on the subject was used as the basis of Massenet's opera *Hérodiade*, 1881) had suggested that Herodias's motive in ordering John's death was frustrated love—and in this version Salome, who is also in love with the Baptist, has no part in the execution, indeed stabs herself when she hears the news. Wilde simply carried this interpretation a step further, out of that fascination with Eastern ways of thought, and particularly Oriental cruelty, which was in the French cultural air at the time. Wilde may also have had a private interest in demonstrating what *he* regarded as sexual perversity.

For Strauss the stimulus was partly, no doubt, a provocative one—to make his listeners sit up and attune their ears to a new wave-length; provocation is part of the progressive artist's stock in trade. But, even more than this, *Salome* was a technical challenge to the composer who had been for more than a decade investigating the power of music to express verbal and psychological concepts with absolute precision: sheep, windmills, Don Quixote's hallucinations, the diatribes of music critics, the mercurial whims of a woman, the humdrum details of domestic life. His first two operas had not given him the opportunity to carry these investigations significantly further; they are less adventurous in language than the orchestral works written immediately before them. *Salome* gave Strauss every opportunity to demonstrate his thesis, expounded to Romain Rolland, apropos of literary censorship,* that 'in music one can say anything; people won't understand it'.

Strauss grasped these opportunities; *Salome* was the most adventurous of all his works to date, and today remains one of the great monuments of twentieth-century music. He himself was particularly proud of his 'shot-silk cadences' (as in Exs. 16 and 25). We may point with special interest to his introduction of the heckelphone into an orchestra; his highly individual usage of the E flat clarinet, particularly in high, tense trills; the extraordinary string effects (double bass glissandi, multiple harmonics,

---

* The censor in Berlin had attempted to ban *Die Walküre* because of the incest of Siegmund and Sieglinde; it was suggested that they should be declared cousins!

and of course the pinched high B on the bass during the execution scene); the highly imaginative blends of woodwind, and the rich variety obtained from a huge percussion department—Strauss at first prescribed ten players, but later reduced this number to six or seven. This amazing virtuosity is applied hardly ever for purposes of titillating colour, but almost entirely in the interest of dramatic characterization at its most precise and articulate, telling us in close detail what this or that character is thinking or doing (e.g. the network of themes for the Jews' dispute, as in our Ex. 4). From this point of view orchestra and voices are hardly to be considered apart; they work together to create these extraordinarily vivid characters, vivid not only in themselves, but in relation to one another (e.g. Narraboth with the Page and with Salome). Salome herself, and the Tetrarch, are of course the most brilliantly portrayed, Jokanaan much more impressively in denunciation than in gentleness. But the haughty, cynical figure of Herodias, with her ambivalent themes and strained vocal delivery, is hardly less deserving of study; and the smaller parts, down to each individual Jew, are very sharply delineated.

Much of the most imaginative and original invention was inspired by the grotesquerie of the personages in this drama, and so it is remarkable that the long line of the music is so predominantly lyrical. It is the melodic richness of Salome's part, not merely the psychological collapse of the girl, that has attracted so many fine singers to it. The quantity of accomplished singing demanded of Herod is perhaps less obvious, but a moment's recollection of his three invitations to Salome, to drink, to eat, to dance, will perhaps remind the reader that the role should not be given to an actor with a poor vocal technique or a worn-out voice; the first Herod, Carl Burrian, was thirty-five and an admired Wagner *Heldentenor* who sang *Parsifal* at Bayreuth. Phrases like *Tanze, Salome tanz, für mich* need to ring out strongly.

Music has travelled such a way since 1905, and the score of *Salome* now seems so finely and scrupulously calculated that it is salutary to remember how wild and incomprehensible it once sounded to ordinary opera-goers. As an epilogue to this chapter, it may be helpful to quote some lines of verse published in the New York *World* at the time of the Manhattan production of *Salome* with Mary Garden in the title role:

> Hark! from the pit a fearsome sound
> that makes your blood run cold.
> Symphonic cyclones rush around—
> and the worst is yet untold.

> The muted tuba's dismal groan
> uprising from the gloom,
> and answered by the heckelphone,
> suggest the crack of doom.

Mama! is this the earthquake zone?
What ho, there! stand from under!
or is that the tonitruone
Just imitating thunder?

Nay, fear not, little one, because
of this sublime rough-house;
'tis modern opera by the laws
of Master Richard Strauss.

Singers? they're scarcely heard nor seen—
in yon back seat they sit,
the day of Song is past, I ween;
the orchestra is it.

Elektra

OPUS 58

Tragedy in One Act

LIBRETTO BY HUGO VON HOFMANNSTHAL

Clytemnestra, Widow of Agamemnon	MEZZO-SOPRANO
Electra ⎫	SOPRANO
Chrysothemis ⎬ *her daughters*	SOPRANO
Aegisthus, Clytemnestra's Paramour	TENOR
Orestes, Son of Clytemnestra and Agamemnon	BARITONE
Tutor of Orestes	BASS
The Confidante of Clytemnestra	SOPRANO
The Trainbearer of Clytemnestra	SOPRANO
A Young Servant	TENOR
An Old Servant	BASS
The Overseer	SOPRANO
Five Maidservants	FIRST, CONTRALTO
	SECOND, THIRD, MEZZO-SOPRANOS
	FOURTH, FIFTH, SOPRANOS

I

After the lurid psychopath melodramatics of *Salome*, Strauss felt a strong necessity to return to comic or light opera, to equal and perhaps surpass the witty comedy of *Till Eulenspiegel*, to improve on the gay, satirical, burlesque characters of *Feuersnot*, or the cheerful home-life scenes of the Domestic Symphony. He was fairly sure in his mind that he did not want to prolong the catalogue of orchestral symphonic poems: he could say more, and say it more explicitly, and since *Salome* with more mastery, in opera. At the same time his imagination, as well as his technique, needed to rove freely from one type of subject to another, and a natural, *homme moyen sensuel* cheerfulness, fanned by a love of unstinted popularity (better a riot than a polite success), determined him to pick something closer to *Figaro* than to *Tristan und Isolde*. He was close to achieving this ambition, but not quite close enough.

Max Reinhardt had pushed *Salome* in Strauss's direction with his 1902 production at the Kleines Theater in Berlin. A year later he presented the same actress Gertrud Eysoldt in another one-act play, also of morbid psychological context and recognizably similar in treatment to *Salome*, a new treatment of the Sophocles *Electra** by the Austrian poet and dramatist Hugo von Hofmannsthal. Strauss saw it, and likewise earmarked it as a promising operatic theme. He had no intention, at the moment, of doing anything about it; he was already busy, and he wanted to write a comic opera first, in any case. But fate does not always comply with an artist's superficial desires. Fate decreed that Strauss had to create an *Elektra* opera before he would find his *Figaro*, that he would therein collaborate with as distinguished an author as any composer of opera in history was ever granted, and that afterwards it would have been impossible for him to do justice to the *Electra* theme. Strauss, in his early forties already Germany's outstanding progressive composer, was destined to be influenced for the rest of his life by his work with Hofmannsthal—influenced, it may be argued, detrimentally: since Hofmannsthal dragged Strauss away from the vanguard of influential musical thought towards a product less provocative and, not only less admired, but curiously less popular. Strauss's later operas made less impact on musicians than those up to and possibly including *Ariadne auf Naxos*; nor has the non-professional musical public shown itself as fond of these later works. Yet

* In this chapter I distinguish between Hofmannsthal's German play (therefore Strauss's opera) *Elektra* and the Greek dramas which are spelt *Electra* after the English fashion. I have retained English spellings for all the characters, in whichever version. Orestes means more to an English reader than Orest (which may only suggest a famous oratorio solo by Mendelssohn). Oddly enough the Hofmannsthal–Strauss character does, at a crucial moment, refer to himself in German as 'Orestes'.

it can also be maintained that Strauss's creative temperament had, by this
time, had enough of exploration and provocation, and that Hofmannsthal
merely recalled him to his own true creative self as a 'first-class second-
rate composer' (his own phrase) who wanted, not to write brand-new
operas for remote posterity, but far more to match the masterworks he had
revered since boyhood—to write a 'new' *Figaro*, *Zauberflöte*, *Fidelio*.
Perhaps he achieved his wish in *Rosenkavalier*, *Frau ohne Schatten*,
Friedenstag; but his achievement as far as *Elektra* warranted much more,
and for his failure to do so we have to blame Hofmannsthal as much as
Strauss. In the course of these chapters we shall try to determine the truth
and, if necessary, the pity. But at this moment, when Strauss had seen
Hofmannsthal's *Elektra* and taken a composer's fancy to it, we must take
an initial look at the poet who was, for almost a quarter of a century, to
determine Strauss's development.

2

Hugo von Hofmannsthal was born in Vienna on 1 February 1874; his
ancestry was part Jewish, part northern Italian, half Austrian. He grew
up in a well-to-do banker's home and while still at school began to write
poems and essays that were accepted for publication under the pseudonym
'Loris', and admired for their apparent maturity of form and content, as
well as for remarkable imaginative perception. These, in fact, form the
bulk of his published poetry. Hofmannsthal studied law and philology, and
intended an academic career; but his continued success as a writer, after
he left school, decided him upon a literary life. Like many a *Wunderkind*
he found it difficult to pass from the intuitive understanding of the
precocious youth to the self-determined, intellectually reasoning perception of the adult artist. But his more mature work conveyed, at a deeper
level, the same care for form, the same spiritual uncovering as his youthful
poems. Some of his finest works of adult life were *Das kleine Welttheater*
(1897) and *Das grosse Salzburger Welttheater* (1922), *Das Bergwerk zu
Falun* (1899—eventually made into an opera by Wagner-Regeny), *Cristinas Heimreise* (1910), *Der Schwierige* (1921), *Der Turm* (1925), and the
posthumous fragment *Andreas* (assigned to 1910).

Hofmannsthal was a thinking writer of a power and sensibility that
approach genius; and he had a command of words and literary style that,
coupled with his intellectual self-criticism, clarified the most elaborate
ideas and conveyed them with maximum impact:

> *Viele Geschicke weben neben dem Meinen,*
> *Durcheinander spielt sie alle das Dasein,*
> *Und mein Teil ist mehr als dieses Lebens*
> *schlanke Flamme oder schmale Leier.*

Many destinies weave alongside mine; existence throws the shuttle through them all, and my share is more than this life's slender flame or paltry lyre.

How many poets would have wrapped up this attractive poetic image in sonorities like cotton wool? Yet in Hofmannsthal's quatrain there is not a single word that a child in primary school might not use every day. This simplicity of language, coupled with such penetrating reflection upon real and difficult problems in life, go far to explain the success of Hofmannsthal's collaboration with Strauss. His poetry is expressed in a diction that invites, and is not hurt by music—a composer can rephrase or, with melismas, prolong its cadences without disguising the run of the line or the purpose of the sentence. After listening to musical settings of Mallarmé and Rilke and Dylan Thomas (all poets popular among composers, and all writing poetry full already with its own inherent music) I have sometimes wondered that the poems of 'Loris' are still so ignored in music.

Hofmannsthal had yet another gift as a writer that marked him out for the stage and so, when the above is considered, also for opera: his extraordinary ability to assume other personalities and make his impersonation completely, vividly convincing. He regarded every literary project in this light—it was part of a characteristic anxiety not to repeat himself, and part too of his life-long preoccupation with looking-glasses and reflections. There is perhaps a connexion here with a trait noticed by Bruno Walter: 'On his desk he kept a small box filled with coloured glass balls [marbles?] that the play of his imagination caused him to let slide through his fingers.' We shall find evidence, again and again, of this poetic concern with mutually reflecting antitheses (in this chapter, for instance, the contrast of Electra and Chrysothemis). The link between creation and auto-metamorphosis is illuminated in one remark that Hofmannsthal let fall to Strauss: 'Start work again—that's easily said, but it means carefully translating one's whole personality into another world, children and father, house and household and writing materials. The inexpressibly uplifting identity of inward and outward things, of oneself and the world, without this I would not live.' It was this capacity for identification that took Hofmannsthal to *Jedermann*, the *Everyman* play (1911), *Venice Preserved* (1905), and the *Oedipus* legend (1906). And to many of the operatic subjects that he elaborated for Strauss, but particularly to *Elektra*, which was the prime cause of their splendid collaboration.

Splendid, I write, and earlier I implied that it had a disastrous effect upon Strauss's development. It was a peculiarly ambivalent relationship: Hofmannsthal the recluse, the painfully sensitive man of exquisite taste; Strauss the practical musician and man of the theatre, blunt in his utterance, Bavarian *bourgeois* to the last drop in the *Mass*. But Strauss was also a man of culture, astonishingly well-versed in literature and deeply appreciative of travel. And Hofmannsthal felt the inner need to communicate with every human creature, however different from himself. Each of the two contained within himself somewhere a reflection of everything that made the other an artist. And each admired the other for the artistic compensation he afforded, the weaknesses he would spontaneously fortify. That they met very seldom was Strauss's loss, but was Hofmannsthal's intention (so he confessed privately to his closest friends); each meeting intensified his distaste for Strauss the man as opposed to the artist. But because each recognized this valuable disparity, it was the more easy for them to ask one another for alterations at the most practical level; to criticize one another's work, to edge one another into taking another track that might better suit their dual artistic capacity. Besides, and of importance to us rather than to their work, this curious reluctance to meet and work together face to face meant that their collaboration was carried on through the post; and this has left posterity a unique insight into operatic creation, through the large volume of their letters to one another. One other fruit of their collaboration was the influence that both had on the Salzburg Festival which Hofmannsthal was instrumental in founding and guiding.

3

Hofmannsthal's abiding fascination with the assumption of other personalities in different periods or civilizations began with his boyhood poems; the compulsion is a romantic one, but in his case unusual because so vividly carried out. He first applied it to a pre-existing dramatic subject in his version of *Elektra*, written quite quickly in 1903 during a trip to Italy, under the inspiration of Sophocles's *Electra*, but also the stimulus of a conversation with Max Reinhardt. Hofmannsthal, perhaps impelled by Reinhardt's production of Wilde's *Salome*, suggested that the producer should turn his hand to Greek drama, whereupon Reinhardt expressed his complete antipathy to the lifeless, statuesque style of the period. Hofmannsthal went away, read Rohde's *Psyche* and *Studies in Hysteria* by Breuer and Freud, examined the diction of the Old Testament for a medium between fifth-century Greece and twentieth-century Germany, and came home with his version of *Elektra*, which Reinhardt promptly put on in Berlin, with Gertrud Eysoldt again in the title-role. What Hofmannsthal read in these books can only have intensified what Sophocles intended to put into his version of the Electra story.

The *Electra* of Sophocles is a single re-interpretation of a classical myth known in detail to all its contemporaries. The story of Orestes's return and matricide in revenge for his father's murder forms only one part of the huge saga of the house of Atreus, a saga embracing nine generations from Chronos, who begat the female Pluto who, with Zeus, begat Tantalus, who begat Pelops, who begat Atreus, who begat Agamemnon, who begat Orestes (and his sisters). Orestes begat Penthilos, who begat Gras and Archelaus, and these, no doubt, had descendants of their own. The house of Atreus ruled in Mycenae (Orestes and his descendants enlarged the empire) and for Greek audiences a potent fascination of the story, as expounded by Aeschylus in his *Oresteia* trilogy, was the inheritance of *hubris* or wrong, or deviation from normal social behaviour, which from generation to generation called for the expiation of one crime by the next, itself needing revenge or expiation. Sophocles left only one complete play on the subject, his *Electra*, but he is known also to have written dramas about Pelops and the curse which Myrtilus laid on the house of Pelops, about the strife between Pelops's sons Atreus and Thyestes, and about the exile of Thyestes in Sicyon where, having laid another curse on the family (Atreus had made soup of his little nephews and given their unsuspecting father the dish for supper), he ravished his own daughter and begat Aegisthus.

Robert Graves* has unfolded this monumental horse-opera (the term is particularly applicable to the descendants of Oenomaus and his daughter Hippodamia) in comprehensive detail, and explained every deviation in terms of some ancient ritual tradition; but the fact remains that, for us as well as for the ancient Greeks, the tale of the house of Atreus is on its own terms a hair-raisingly eventful one, which involves pederasty, cannibalism, incest, rape, matricide and every other variety of inter-familial murder. Every dramatist who treated the central drama of Orestes's return gave his own special interpretation to the fact and personalities already known. For Aeschylus the emphasis lay upon objective hereditary responsibility, for Sophocles upon individual idiosyncrasy, for Euripides upon democratic humanity. Each of these three dramas reflects its own climate of thought. Today a re-interpreter might find Aeschylus's Brechtian treatment or Euripides's emphasis on socialistic values particularly suitable as a starting-point. For Hofmannsthal's temperament in 1903 the analytic psychological method of Sophocles was clearly the most appropriate point of departure—though he borrowed certain glosses of his own from other versions of the tale.

And this psychological probing captured Strauss's interest, coupled with that economy of words which suited him so well (cf. his technique of abbreviation in *Salome*), and which seemed to him, in the climaxes of *Elektra* (entrance of Clytemnestra, Recognition), dangerously under-emphatic on their own but made for enhancement by music.

Early in 1906 Strauss got in touch with Hofmannsthal and asked permission to set *Elektra*. A sentence in one of Hofmannsthal's later letters

* *Greek Myths*, Cassell, 1958.

suggests that they met in Berlin. Strauss must have been fairly vague in his expressed intentions, for Hofmannsthal's first *Elektra* letter asks 'whether this hope may remain alive or is to be buried' (7 March 1906)—a gentle reminder of Hofmannsthal's disappointment over their first joint project. The two had originally met in Paris during March 1900, and had corresponded briefly with a view to collaboration in a ballet entitled *The Triumph of Time*—it came to a scenario which Strauss returned with a fulsomely polite rejection letter. Hofmannsthal need not have been fearful. Strauss had begun abridging the text of the play and was set on starting the opera during the summer when he would at last have time to compose. His only doubt was whether *Elektra* was not too similar to *Salome*. Besides, as we have seen, he wanted to compose a cheerful opera: could not Hofmannsthal offer him another subject, something from the Renaissance period perhaps (Caesar Borgia or Savonarola)? He left Hofmannsthal in no doubt of his desire to collaborate: 'We were born for one another and are certain to do fine things together if you remain faithful to me.'

Hofmannsthal made light of the similarities between *Salome* and *Elektra*: boiled down, they amounted to no more than that both were one-act pieces, both had a woman's name for title, both played in ancient time, and Eysoldt had created both title-roles in Berlin. In fact, he countered, *Elektra* with its colour scheme of night and day, dark and light, was completely different from the purple and violet, the stifling atmosphere of *Salome*. The Renaissance was out of the question, a detestable, antipathetic era which had roused all the least felicitous painters and the most unfortunate poets. Strauss made a last attempt to side-track his collaborator with a piece about Saul and David, and then meekly capitulated and began work on *Elektra* in June 1906. Hofmannsthal approved the textual and structural emendations, offered to remove the scene of the cook and servant, and suggested that Orestes should be recognized by several old servants and not just one. Strauss fell in with this plan, but decided, wisely, against omitting the character of Aegisthus; the sound of the music in his ears told him there was already such a predominance of female voices that he could not afford to drop any of the three or four remaining male solo entries. He even suggested that both Clytemnestra and Aegisthus should be killed on stage, in defiance of Aristotelian canon. But he may, as a student of the classics, in maturity as well as youth,* have had in mind Sophocles's own momentous disregard for this canon in the *Electra* where the text clearly implies that Aegisthus is struck down *coram populo*. He thought better of it at once, though, and the murders were agreed to take place behind the scenes. More problematic was the structure of these final scenes in which Strauss found the line of action dangerously broken up by the frequent to-ing and fro-ing of the

---

* In his schooldays Strauss had set one of the choruses from Sophocles's *Electra* to music, no doubt as a result of studying the play in class.

servants' chorus; much discussion of this ensued, but we may think that the final plan is still dramatically uncomfortable. Some obscurities of topography in the text prompted Hofmannsthal to draw a ground-plan of the palace at Mycenae, as the author imagined it; and this is of the utmost value to all designers and producers of the opera.

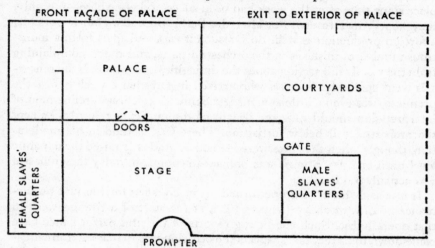

Throughout 1907 and the first half of 1908 Strauss was fully occupied with conducting; when not busy with his orchestra and opera in Berlin, he found himself obliged to follow *Salome* on her triumphant European tour. *Elektra* was of course part of his baggage, but it was not until June 1908 that he was able to settle down to more or less uninterrupted work on the opera, in his newly completed villa at Garmisch, and one of his first requests from there was for extra text at the great point of repose immediately after the recognition: the moving address to Orestes which begins at *Es rührt sich niemand*. In October 1908 Strauss was promoted from Royal Kapellmeister* to general music director. Simultaneously he was generously awarded a year's leave of absence so that he could complete *Elektra*. As it turned out he did not need so long a leave; despite interruption for a conducting engagement or so and other hold-ups (he had twice to rewrite the great central scene for Clytemnestra and Electra) he finished the score on 22 September. Strauss had again chosen Dresden as the place for the première, and begged Schuch to give the title-role to the most dramatic soprano he could lay hands on. Rather to the composer's relief Marie Wittich, his first Salome, was out of the running. Strauss visited Dresden in October, auditioned the possible Electras, and selected

---

* The Kaiser, who detested modern music, referred to Strauss as 'that viper which I have nourished in my bosom', and Strauss was thereafter known privately as the Royal Bosom-viper (*Hofbusenschlange*).

Annie Krull (who had created Diemut in *Feuersnot*). Weingartner, who had succeeded Mahler in Vienna, would have liked to give the world première, and was hoping that Anna Bahr-Mildenburg would be able to sing Electra. But Hofmannsthal insisted that, Viennese audiences being so conservative and fashion-swayed, a Viennese première should take place some time after the work had been successful elsewhere—not only, they hoped, in Dresden, but after the Berlin première and, if possible, a foreign production as well. So Dresden it was, and apart from a monstrous number of mistakes in the orchestral parts, and much complaining from the woodwind section about the difficulties encountered, the rehearsals went smoothly. Strauss, who arrived in Dresden a week before the première, was even a little anxious lest Schuch's celebrated refinement of interpretation should miss the weight of the music; at rehearsal he kept the orchestra well below fortissimo. There was method in his moderation, though; when the notes were learned he gradually raised the dynamic level until one day Strauss was obliged to complain 'today the orchestra was actually too loud'.

It was said that all Europe turned up in Dresden for the first performance of *Elektra* on 25 January 1909, at the start of a Strauss week in that opera house. Such conflicting reports of the first performance have come down to us that one suspects the occasion was to blame. Hofmannsthal recorded 'painful recollections both of the performance and of the production', which was by Georg Toller. Strauss himself called it 'One of the most beautiful and pure artistic experiences of my life', though later he had unkind words to say about the guest Clytemnestra, old Ernestine Schumann-Heink who called the opera a 'fearful din' (*furchtbares Gebrüll*) and sang it as though it were Wagner. But other observers spoke with high enthusiasm of Schumann-Heink's acting and singing. Krull seems to have been generally admired in the name-part, though it was later admitted that, by comparison with other Electras, her interpretation was small-scaled. In other roles were Margarethe Siems (Chrysothemis), previously type-cast in coloratura parts but destined to be the first Marschallin; and Carl Perron (Orestes), later, and less successfully, the first Ochs.

This first performance was, if not the 'disaster' that Angelo Neumann reported to Prague, a *succès d'estime* rather than a riot or a triumph—according to contemporary opinion (but the most of the sensational possibilities was made in the delightful cartoons in Plates 9 and 10). Subsequent Dresden performances were received with much stronger enthusiasm, and the Munich, Berlin, and Vienna local premières were all considered extremely fine; Bahr-Mildenburg, in Vienna, did *not* in the end agree to sing Electra, but triumphed as Clytemnestra—and in this production the opera at last had décor worthy of it, by Alfred Roller, henceforth to be closely associated with Strauss operas. As with *Salome*,

Elektra was quickly taken up everywhere: Milan in April 1909, with Salomea Kruszelnicka ('perfect', wrote Strauss, 'as both Salome and Electra', a rare achievement); Manhattan in February 1910, in French (it had been banned from the Metropolitan—can it be that the language of *oo-la-la* was thought the only suitable one for such an indecorous piece?). In the same month Strauss conducted a performance for the first time,* at the Hague première, and from there he went to London for the British première under Beecham; Strauss conducted the last rehearsal and two performances. The American Edyth Walker shared the title-role with Zdenka Fassbender from Munich and Krull from Dresden. Willi Wirk (who had produced the first *Salome* in Dresden) produced and, to judge from contemporary notices, managed here too to emphasize the sensational aspects of the drama. *Elektra* was the first Strauss opera to be heard in Britain and was received with such admiration that Beecham extended his season, took *Elektra* on tour and followed it quickly with *Feuersnot*, *Salome*, *Der Rosenkavalier*, and the first version of *Ariadne auf Naxos*, all within three years. It was this production of *Elektra* which detonated a monumental public correspondence between Bernard Shaw and Ernest Newman in the columns of *The Nation*; it continued on and off for four years, and may still be read today, if with more entertainment than edification.†

4

Newman, who subsequently modified his view that *Elektra* is needlessly ugly and often clumsily composed, was by no means alone in his disapproval. In Germany most critics veered between scorn for Strauss's role as the 'Barnum of German music' and indignant exposure of the opera's 'immorality and perversity'. The *Wiener Fremdenblatt* dryly remarked: '*Wie schön war die Prinzessin Salome.*'

The Viennese critic Hermann Bahr was almost alone among his colleagues in declaring roundly 'it was a glorious evening', and did so in an enormous notice, superbly and delightfully written.‡ Not all the admirers were helpful: Richard Specht, in his monumental study, likens the composer of *Elektra* to 'a Rodin who models in gold and ivory'. Specht must have had in mind the extraordinary richness of the score, with its three sections of violins (expanded to four towards the end of the opera), its Wagner tubas and its basset-horns, the startling array of timbres

---

* He had taken the baton during one of the Dresden rehearsals, but quickly returned it to Schuch saying, 'I was able to compose it but I can't conduct it yet.'

† It is reprinted complete in Newman's posthumously published *Testament of Music* (p. 115).

‡ *Neue freie Presse*, 29 January 1909, reprinted in *ATV*, pp. 426–32. Bahr (see Plate 20) later worked with Strauss in the initial stages of *Intermezzo*.

and special effects, and the masterly complexity of the harmonic vocabulary, which took Strauss as far as he was ever to penetrate the jungle of advanced tonality. If we contrast Electra's promise to Chrysothemis, *Von jetzt an will ich deine Schwester sein*, its scrupulously economical wind and richly divided *molto vibrato* strings, with the adamantine hardness of the harmony and scoring almost immediately afterwards, at *Dir führt kein Weg hinaus*, Specht's chryselephantine sculpture becomes credible. But the former passage is exceptional; the passages of deep expressive feeling have a harder, less voluptuous sound; to continue Specht's metaphor, Strauss was surely modelling in granite, in megaliths. Strauss had visited Greece, and was acquainted with Greek art; he knew the difference between the Lion Gate at Mycenae and the Parthenon, and he knew which form and proportions and colours were appropriate to the saga of the Atrides. It might be argued that he approached chryselephantine textures in *Die Liebe der Danae*. If, however, one were to see *Salome* and *Elektra* in a double bill (it has been done, though Strauss detested the notion), one would appreciate clearly the special atmosphere of *Elektra*. The orchestra is bigger, the range of effects wider, the dissonances harsher—he made much more of bitonal harmony in *Elektra*. And yet the musical climate of *Elektra* is less sophisticated because the music is rooted more firmly in diatonicism, in tonic and dominant chords and diatonic or bitonally diatonic dissonance.

It is partly a matter of subject, of pre-classical Greece rather than the Near East under the Roman Empire, and of vengeance, not voluptuousness (compare Salome, even at her most virginal, with Chrysothemis —the only remotely sex-appealing character in *Elektra*—and this distinction is clear; and then compare the 'good' characters, Jokanaan and Orestes). But largely the individuality of the *Elektra* sound does, as that parenthesis suggests, depend on the musical ideas with which Strauss clothes the characters of the drama, and although the language is clearly that of the composer of *Salome*, the characters of *Elektra* here demanded sharper musical outlines, and Strauss has responded. This can be appreciated if we compare the *Elektra* themes that most strongly recall the language of *Salome*: the rising-sixth themes of Narraboth (Ex. 3 in *Salome*) and, much more temperamental and outspoken, of Chrysothemis in Ex.11; the imperious, very impetuous, and diatonic Salome theme (Ex. 10 in *Salome*) with Electra's triumph theme, Ex. 26, which follows a similar contour with more complex harmonic implications, but also with greater impressive weight; or the heavy, flabby Herod themes (Exs. 11 and 22 in *Salome*) with the equivalent Clytemnestra themes, Exs. 12 and 16 in *Elektra*. The likenesses are apparent; to admit that we distinguish them because they belong to different characters is only to admit that Strauss had penetrated each of the two dramas and caught the tonal mirror-reflection of each.

6 *In einem silbernen Schüssel* . . . Salome tells Herod the price of her dance.
A scene from the Dresden première, 1905

7   Salome with the head of Jokanaan:
Annelies Kupper in the Munich revival, 1950

8 Christel Goltz in *Elektra*
at La Scala, Milan, 1954

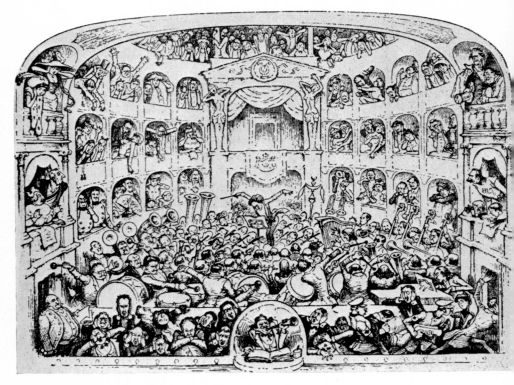

9 Strauss raises pandemonium at Dresden: a contemporary cartoon

10
The Elektric Chair:
another contemporary
cartoon

And the characters are personifications of the theme that they act out before us. Strauss was right to protest the similarity of situation: both operas are about a female protagonist consumed with lust and destroyed by its fulfilment (the fact of destruction, viz. the final bars of both operas, evoked the closest similarity of response from Strauss—a rhythmic pattern that unites Salome's Ex. 17 with Electra's, or rather Agamemnon's, Ex. 1; and in the difference of implication lies the identity of each ending). But the themes and situations are altogether distinct, indeed they are opposites. *Salome* is about a highly sexed, amoral anti-heroine consumed by a lust for physical possession and in a social position to expect to achieve it. *Elektra* is about an unsexed, fanatically moral heroine, consumed by a lust for physical restoration of the *status quo ante*, and in no social position at all even to hope for what she desires. It was through this fundamental contrast that Strauss was able to turn what promised to be a sequel into another, independent masterpiece.

5

When Agamemnon set sail for Troy with the men of Argos, he left behind him in Mycenae his wife Clytemnestra and four children, the boy Orestes and three daughters, Electra, Iphigenia, and Chrysothemis. Agamemnon was not much loved by Clytemnestra because he had won her by force, having first slaughtered her husband, his own first cousin once removed, Tantalus II,* as well as the babe at her own breast. Furthermore, in order to dispel the inclement weather, which was preventing the Argive ships from reaching Troy, Agamemnon had sacrificed his daughter Iphigenia (though some say she was spirited away to become a priestess of Artemis at Tauris—as in Gluck's opera). When therefore Aegisthus arrived at Mycenae, his arms full of rich gifts and his heart set on further revenge for the vile murder of his stepbrothers (he had already, as a boy, taken the first step by killing Atreus), he had little difficulty in persuading Clytemnestra to join his plot; indeed he quickly became her paramour. The Trojan War ended. Agamemnon returned home and had just stepped from a refreshing bath when Clytemnestra threw a tight-fitting net over him so that he could not escape, whereupon Aegisthus stabbed him twice with a two-edged sword, and Clytemnestra finished the deed by beheading him with an axe. Strictly speaking, Aegisthus's revenge was complete when he killed Atreus, and Hermes had warned him against attempting Agamemnon's life, since Orestes would be in duty bound to revenge his father. At the time of Agamemnon's murder the boy Orestes

---

* Not to be confused with Pelops's father, the first Tantalus, who earned an eternity's gastronomic frustration, and thereby his proverbial immortality, as the penalty for stealing ambrosia from the gods.

was hustled away from Mycenae with a tutor who led him to Crisa, where King Strophius was married to Agamemnon's sister Anaxibia. It was here that Orestes met his lifelong friend, Strophius's son, Pylades (who figures in Gluck's *Iphigenia in Tauris*, but not in Hofmannsthal's *Elektra*).*

Clytemnestra now ruled over Argos, with Aegisthus as her puppet-consort; on the 13th of every month they celebrated Agamemnon's death (he was killed on 13 January) with sacrifices and dancing, overtly in triumph, but really out of anxiety to obtain divine protection against the dreaded return of Orestes as avenging angel. Chrysothemis accepted this régime: outside Sophocles's version she is no more than a name, the only one of Agamemnon's children who did nothing worth recording. Sophocles may have raised her from this obscurity because he needed a gentle foil to his grand tragic heroine—as Hofmannsthal and Strauss also did. But Electra took every opportunity to insult Clytemnestra and Aegisthus, before their faces and in public, as adulterous murderers. She was accordingly kept under strict watch and made to live in the most squalid conditions. Princes and nobles sought her hand in marriage, but Clytemnestra sent them all away, fearing that Electra would bear a son who would grow up to revenge Agamemnon's death.† Electra meanwhile sent many messages to Orestes, entreating him to return. He, however, was in an awkward dilemma: if he failed to exact retribution for his father's death, the gods would visit him with foul disease and he would be a social outcast into the bargain; on the other hand he would be hounded by the Furies if he were so unfilial as to kill his mother. She, it seems, was spared the attentions of these rapacious creatures, who were only interested in the murder of blood-relations (but the gods forgot that Agamemnon and Clytemnestra were third cousins, both being descended from their great-great-grandfather Zeus, he through the union of Zeus and the nymph Pluto who gave birth to Tantalus I, she through her mother Leda who was the granddaughter of Zeus's son Ares, the god of war).

Sophocles could assume that his audiences knew all this before his version of the *Electra* began. Hofmannsthal and Strauss, and their audiences in Germany during the first decade of this century, were more familiar with the doings of the house of Atreus than most audiences of the 1960s. Some of the above details are relevant to the opera in that they seem to have given Hofmannsthal ideas for his treatment of the drama. It must, however, be emphasized that his version is closely based, in structure and characterization, on Sophocles. Hofmannsthal begins and

---

* In the *Electra* plays of Sophocles and Euripides, Pylades is a mute character. In Aeschylus's *Choephorae* he opens his mouth only to deliver three lines—but they are of historic importance because this was the first occasion in which a third speaker was introduced into dramatic dialogue.

† In Euripides's version Electra has been married, by Aegisthus, to a farmer, and Clytemnestra is lured to her doom with an invitation to inspect her first grandchild. Hofmannsthal may have had this in mind when he makes Chrysothemis long for a husband 'even if he were only a farmer'.

ends in his own way, and he does without the traditional chorus; but in other respects his version now seems more faithful to the spirit of Sophocles than does the milder and more genteel English translation of Gilbert Murray which reflects the conventional view of classicists, in Britain at least, at the time of Strauss's *Elektra*.

6

Sophocles began his play with the return of Orestes, Pylades, and the Tutor. Hofmannsthal omitted this scene in order to reserve Orestes's first entrance for the Recognition scene. His play and Strauss's opera begin with an ensemble for six maidservants; we may regard them as a substitute for a Greek chorus, though in fact they only appear at the beginning and towards the end of the opera. The whole opera takes place through the protagonist, Electra. Like Salome, she remains on stage from her entry in Scene 2 until her death; but even in the servants' opening exchanges (which may be regarded as a Prelude) she makes a fleeting appearance that heightens and intensifies their remarks.

The opera falls into two parts, divided very firmly by a pause and a double bar-line (and as if to emphasize the break, Strauss's rehearsal cues revert at this point from 274 to 1a). We may identify the scenes as follows:

1 Prelude: the Servants
2 Electra
3 Chrysothemis
4 Clytemnestra
5 Chrysothemis rejected
6 Orestes
7 The Murders
8 Dance and Finale

The Prelude has its own epigrammatic overture, short but immensely impressive and of vital importance throughout the opera. Perhaps it is a text rather than an epigram. It represents the dead but spiritually omnipresent Agamemnon, King of Kings.

I

I

In the same quotation I also give two important and almost independent derivatives. The curtain rises during the third syllable of the theme, and the last low D is sustained on bass clarinet and bass drum, giving an impression of fear and furtive conspiracy to the scene, which represents the rear courtyard of Agamemnon's palace. There is a large brass-bound double door, and to either side a window. For a fuller conspectus of the setting, see Hofmannsthal's plan (p. 71).

The servants are drawing water from a well, and we overhear their chatter from the moment Electra is mentioned. Is it not now the hour (woodwind shudder at the thought) when every day she howls for her father? Sure enough the door opens and the ragged, wasted, besmirched figure of Electra stands on the threshold, blinded by the afternoon light. Her wild, menacing expression and rough, bestial gestures are vividly suggested in the first (Ex. 2a) of three Electra themes now presented one after another. Ex. 2b mimics the motion of the axe which dominates her thoughts, the instrument of her father's death which she has kept hidden for revenge on her abhorred mother. Ex. 2c will be associated with her implacable hatred of all about her, and with her pride even in degradation.

2

I have said that *Elektra* is, harmonically, rooted in diatonicism, yet I must point out that the dissonant chord underlying Ex. 2c assumes, throughout the opera, the function of a tonic, a point of departure and return, of repose and momentousness. It is in fact created by throwing together the tonic triads of D flat major and E major a third apart, and this interval of a third unites almost every theme connected in the opera with the family of Agamemnon (principal exceptions, for particularly strong, independent effect, are Exs. 8, 15, and 25). The violent, hostile effect of Ex. 2b is caused by the juxtaposition of two triads a tritone apart, as far as is possible in music.

Electra rushes quickly back into the darkness of the palace. The servants compare her to a poisonous wild cat, yowling at sundown (here Ex. 1² appears, the sorrow of the Atrides). Once, they recall, they approached her while she was wailing, and she swatted at them like flies (appropriate noises from the percussive *Rute* or birch spray struck on wood), mocking their simple domestic pleasures (sensuous thirds). And when one servant answered her back Electra cried that she fed a vulture in her body (Ex. 2c, infinitely wild and wretched), to which the maid-servant threw back an insult about corpse-scavenging (tritone-related triads with snarling strings, a horrifying effect) which rendered Electra speechless. The maids agree that Electra is a disgrace to the household, and should be locked up; and this tight-lipped pronouncement is accompanied ironically by the proud and dignified theme of the Argive royal family, the house of Agamemnon.

3

Ex. 3 consists, it will be seen, of three steps each of a third; the falling third is like an echo of Agamemnon's Ex. 1¹; the diminished third similarly echoes Electra's green memories of the axe (Ex. 2b) while the rising minor third connects with Ex. 5, Ex. 10³, Ex. 19, Ex. 27, and others here unquoted, including Electra's recognition cry of 'Orest!'

One of the maidservants asks if they are not unfeeling towards this pitiable creature; a gentle, compassionate melody hints at her feelings—

4

—and is expanded as another very young maid confesses her abject devotion to this noble mistress of theirs, downtrodden, though of royal birth. Signal for another royalty theme related to Ex. 2c.

5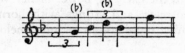

When the forewoman of the servants orders her inside, this plucky girl berates her fellows for their cruelty and wishes them all hanged for disloyalty. She is hustled off into the servants' quarters and can be heard crying under the lash (*Sie schlagen mich*) while the others toss their heads and voice moral indignation at their memories of Electra's taunts. There are pitiful after-echoes of the compassionate Ex. 4 tune which reaches a Quixotic surprise cadence as they return to their quarters.

They thus leave the stage empty for Ex. 2c and Electra's return for what the servants call her Howling Hour, though it is a grand scena in ternary form. First she laments her loneliness (Ex. 1^2, Ex. 2c, Ex. 3) and calls solemnly (Ex. 5 in the minor) on her father to appear before her—this is where she links his name explicitly with Ex. 1^1—at the hour when he was vilely assassinated by his wife and her paramour. We are given lightning portraits of the murderers, Clytemnestra:

6

and almost at once Aegisthus, whom Electra cannot bring herself to name.

7
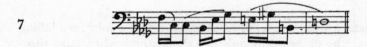

Electra recalls the murder of Agamemnon, how he was dragged from the bath, soaked in blood (slippery chromatic scales harmonized in glutinous dominant sevenths), his wide eyes staring round at his own home. So he must gaze when he returns stigmatized with his blood but victorious. A new, overpowering motif of rising octaves, which eventually swamps the compass of the listening ear like an overpowering presence, surges through the orchestra, not the name of Agamemnon but his sensed presence.

8

Electra continues to call Agamemnon's name through these shattering orchestral challenges to the carrying power of her voice. Show yourself to your child, she entreats; and strings with horn reflect her wish-fulfilment of the family reunited, in a long melody of bitter-sweet yearning.

In a worthwhile performance, as Electra stumbles childlike towards her vision of Agamemnon restored to his family, this is a moment of blinding poignancy; the whirlwind Maenad is dispelled to become once again a dignified and beautiful princess. But Strauss, the symphonic craftsman, took care to fix this glorious revelation with a lyrical invention that would yield symphonic elaboration, and accordingly Ex. 9 contains three ideas that can be referred to, or developed, with instantaneous communication of their provenance and purport, as the square brackets show.

This vision inspires a central section of the monologue in which Electra foresees the wholesale slaughter at Agamemnon's moment of revenge (wild variant of Ex. 9, and much slippery blood, as well as Ex. 1^2 and Ex. 3). The expiation will involve animals too, and this for her is the point at which destruction will break into triumphal, hieratic dancing. Her imagination envisages the strong, stamping rhythm of the dance, and during this final section of her soliloquy several themes emerge, all united by their rhythm. I quote three of them.

Exs. 1^2 and 9 and even 8 are pressed into choreographic service as Electra's mind imagines this sacred, rapturous ritual (and it should be

merely imagined; an Electra who breaks into ballet at this point ruins the
impact of the closing scene where, in any case, her corybantics are liable
to strain an audience's capacity for preserving straight faces).

Her vision is interrupted, the dream broken; Chrysothemis, her
younger sister, has found her and is calling her name from the house
door. Electra's return to reality is abrupt, her reaction brusque and
unwelcoming: Say what you must and then go. Chrysothemis is speechless, and can only wring her hands.

11

The gesture at once reminds Electra, terribly, of their father when he
was struck down with the axe (Ex. 2a, not the Axe theme), and this in
turn recalls the mother to whom Chrysothemis is loyal—tormented,
sleepless, weighed down with talismans and superstitions: Clytemnestra.

12

What does Clytemnestra's daughter (Ex. 6 is added) want with Electra?
A dreadful deed? Was it hatched by those two women, their mother
(Ex. 6) and that other cowardly creature (Ex. 7), heroic only in bed?†
Chrysothemis has overheard that Electra is to be locked away in a tower.
Electra does not share her sister's anxiety, but Chrysothemis bursts into
a passionate solo (3/4, molto vivace, E flat major, *Ich hab's wie Feuer in
der Brust*), absolutely characteristic of an uncontrolled animal longing for freedom, marriage, children—all withheld through Electra's
stubborn antagonism to their ruler-guardians. The radiant personality (*Lichtgestalt*) identified by Strauss, finds expression in

* Strauss has even remembered to link this motif with Ex. 9! See the first four notes
† This is Sophocles's own jibe, and seems to have been a standard characterization in
the fifth century B.C., which is odd, since earlier accounts of the myth made Aegisthus
a fairly redoubtable villain and his name, after all, means 'goat-strength'.

Chrysothemis's impetuous, euphonious, passively sensual music, exemplified here:

Electra comments with no more than summary sympathy (Ex. 4), while Chrysothemis pours out her lonely, frustrated soul. Ex. 13² becomes the most important of her phrases, though the plaintive Ex. 11 manages to find a place in this apparently contrary context (the reason is that Ex. 11 presents Chrysothemis as she sees herself). Better dead, she wails finally (and the basses remind her of Ex. 1²), than alive without living. Electra jeers (Ex. 2c) that her place is in the palace (Strauss has here cut some vital lines: If only I were away from here, Chrysothemis moans, I should forget. And Electra answers—I cannot forget). But from inside there comes the approaching sound of a crowd in hurried procession, and this scares Chrysothemis. It is certainly a scarifying piece of orchestral music —whipcracks, metallic jangling, shrill cries, and groans, stealthy scales and sliding chromatic figures and twilit orchestral colours suggesting fear and menace behind those great doors. The whole palace is there, says Chrysothemis, and slaughter is afoot. This, we presume, will be one of the monthly sacrifices made by Clytemnestra, as mentioned in Sophocles; and the orchestra confirms the presumption with a succinct conjunction of two motifs, Ex. 12¹ coupled with the grim procession motif shown below it here:

Chrysothemis advises her sister to steer clear of their mother today: she is in venomous mood after a nightmare. We know from Aeschylus that she dreamed she had given birth to a serpent, and when she held it to her breast it sucked out blood instead of milk. Strauss's trumpet tells us who the serpent is: the ever-present menace of vengeful Orestes.

After this dream Clytemnestra and all her entourage are on their way to the altar to propitiate the gods. Through the window-opening we can dimly glimpse a sea of faces lit up here and there by torch-flares. Chrysothemis describes the procession of maids and torchbearers and animals and sacrificial knives; she urges Electra (Ex. 11 joins the unholy march) to remain out of sight. But Electra is determined to converse with her mother on this day of all days, and unlike Chrysothemis she stands and watches the passing of the tumultuous cortège; as Ex. 12^1 gives way to 12^2, we catch sight at last of Clytemnestra and Ex. 12^2 lurches and lunges upwards and back.

Hofmannsthal's description of Clytemnestra is graphic: 'Her sallow, bloated face appears, in the lurid glare of the torches, all the more pale above her scarlet robe. She is leaning on her Confidante (dressed in dark violet) and also on an ivory stick decked with jewels and talismans. Her arms are hung with bangles, her fingers glisten with rings. Her eyelids appear unnaturally large, and it seems to cost her a fearful effort to keep them open.' Strauss, after many performances' experience, thought it well to point out that she is not an ancient hag, but a proud and beautiful woman of about fifty whose ruin is primarily spiritual. She lives in terror, and cannot sleep without at once falling into the most terrible nightmares. Hofmannsthal borrowed this idea from Euripides. With all her good-luck charms and careful religious observances, her mind is eaten up with terror and guilty conscience; the Furies never leave her, whatever Apollo may have told Orestes, but they are inside, not around her.

True to her word Electra does not hide but raises herself to her full height, through three octaves worth of Ex. 5 in the minor. Clytemnestra points scornfully at the bedraggled creature (Ex. 2c), asking why she allows it to pollute the palace. A new version of Ex. 5, in which the last three notes of the first bar are prolonged into a tremolo, becomes prominent here (I have always taken it for a portrayal of the rattling and clinking talismans hung round the form of the Queen, but most commentators apply it to the cunning double-talk which Electra adopts in her presence.) Clytemnestra chides the gods for allowing her strength and vigour to waste away so that she is too weak to uproot the nettle that has grown out of her fallow body. Her tiredness is expressed in another rearing theme.

16

Electra asks: Why chide the gods? Are you not also a goddess? (which is true, as I explained above in tracing the genealogy of the Atrides). Clytemnestra's attendants try to persuade her that the remark was sarcastically intended (a clear double reference here to Ex. 15 and to Ex. 5 with its third newly diminished as in the middle of Ex. 3, and therefore in Ex. 2b). But Clytemnestra has taken the compliment to heart, and above Ex. 12² floats a placid oboe solo, rather reminiscent of the red-headed lady in *Don Juan*. She has been reminded of a half-forgotten past when the family was together in peace and amity (Ex. 9), and she is inclined to treat Electra kindly, as a daughter (other Atrides family themes). Electra warns her against the corrupting influence of her malicious attendants, even now concocting slander. You are not yourself when they are there, she sings to a new melody full of wheedling thirds:

17

Clytemnestra decides to leave the palace and converse with Electra, who seems more amenable than usual—though the attendants warn their mistress of Electra's duplicity; she dismisses them as minions of Aegisthus (a hint of Ex. 7 with a burlesque glissando for violin tacked on to the end) who can never agree in their advice, except to continue slaughtering for sacrifice. They talk of truth and falsehood, but what mortal knows one from the other? (Flutes and oboes exchange major and minor thirds in a quizzical passage prompted by Ex. 10³.) What Electra says at the moment gives Clytemnestra solace, and so she intends to hear some more, since it may leave her more serene of mind (this section, chiefly concerned with Ex. 17, is full of fascinating colours and textures and fleeting touches of word-painting—a vision of the serenity for which Clytemnestra hankers).

The attendants are dismissed and flutter away like sulky moths. Clytemnestra descends to her daughter in the courtyard, her talismans jangling lightly at each step.

18

What she wants is a cure for bad dreams; dreams, so the music tells us, of the family and particularly of Agamemnon and Orestes and their royal line. These dreams, she says, are part of growing old, but there must be some recognized cure for them—Strauss shows us Ex. 15 quietly disappearing, as it were, down the plug-hole on the double bassoon. But she cannot banish the omnipresent shadow of Agamemnon, Ex. 8, with all the talismans of Ex. 18, and so she seeks advice from resourceful Electra whose venomous Ex. 2c is now mated with the placatory Ex. 17. One helpful word from Electra might drive away the dreadful agony that she now describes (to a transient figure very closely connected with the Empress's nightmare music in *Die Frau ohne Schatten*; see Ex. 19, p. 180), a nameless horror that will not kill her and give her the peace of death, but keeps her in a deathly sickness of the spirit, a living death, like a garment eaten up by moths. Out of the stillness a monstrous fortissimo looms up, the memory of countless nightmares that she must endure if ever sleep takes her, drawing the marrow from her very bones (here the bassoons, very curiously, seem to quote Ex. 20 from the previous chapter!). An evil spectre joins her in the darkness when she starts from tortured sleep. Such dreams must have an end; every evil spirit can be exorcized if one knows what sort of victim must be slaughtered to placate it. This whole fantastically inventive passage resembles a gruesome development section using the Agamemnon family themes. To cap the recital comes the truth-falsehood version of Ex. 10^3 on trumpet and horn, when Clytemnestra speaks of the right sacrificial victim; Electra indicates that she knows the answer, and in wildest desperation Clytemnestra offers to bathe the whole palace in blood if only she may sleep peacefully. Electra promises that when the chosen victim falls beneath the axe, she need dream no more (appropriate motifs, including a contrapuntal combination of Ex. 1^2, and two versions of Ex. 10^3). As she answers her mother's urgent questions with enigmatical answers, Ex. 6 gives us the name over and over again, and Ex. 10^3 also repeatedly tells what will happen afterwards. The victim is a woman (Ex. 18), not a virgin (Ex. 13^1) —Clytemnestra is past caring which of her family is to die next—but a wedded wife; any time or place will serve—Electra is swinging into her triumphal waltz gradually—and the deed is to be done, not this time by the Queen, with net and axe, but by a man, no, not Aegisthus; it must be a man (Ex. 15, of course, with copious echoes), a stranger, but of their kin. Clytemnestra is sick of these riddles and wants some straight answers.

Ex. 9 introduces the answer that sounds like a digression. When will Orestes come home? Bassoons introduce a tiny new motif, the actuality, rather than Ex. 15's hopes and fears, of Orestes as sacrificial death-dealer.

19
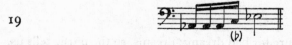

Clytemnestra answers that he is a forbidden topic of conversation; not that she fears him, for he is weak-brained and stammers (an impedimental extremely graphic Ex. 3c), and was ill-nurtured. Electra starts up vituperatively: Orestes is well, though his mother tried to have him murdered, since she fears him, day and night (Exs. 15 and 19); he will return. Clytemnestra, almost but not quite coolly, promises Electra that she has enough servants to guard her (a blandly diatonic version of Ex. 12¹, which underlines its kinship with Ex. 9, and also with the Queen's so-called protector, Ex. 7—what a master of suggestive thematic meta-morphoses Strauss was!). And she warns Electra, in a waltz of her own, based on Ex. 18, that if she does not reveal the nature of the necessary sacrifice here and now, she will be locked up and starved until she does.* Clytemnestra intends at all costs to sleep (a long-held stentorian top G sharp).

Out thunders Ex. 19 and out springs Electra like a caged lion suddenly faced with a Christian. Whose blood? Yours, when the hunter captures you! She describes in vivid detail the hunt for the chosen victim, from bedroom to bathroom, downstairs and through the vaults. Electra will hound her this way and that until Clytemnestra's flight is blocked by a wall where, in the darkness, she is pressed at the feet of Agamemnon (Ex. 8). But she does not die yet; the rites are not fulfilled. She must first know the eternity of waiting for doom (reprise of Ex. 1³), unable to cry, unable to escape, imprisoned within herself and at the mercy of her executioners, waiting until with a swish the axe falls. She must, the orchestra specifies, suffer what Agamemnon suffered.† And when the blow falls, she will never dream again, but those who live will rejoice (a triumphant top C, the first in the opera) at her demise. The horns ecstatically leap with her in Ex. 15. The proud Ex. 5 confronts the maniac terror of Ex. 12 as these women face one another, Electra glaring defiantly, Clytemnestra tottering with fear. Something must burst.

It is a diversion from within the palace. Lights flicker. The Confidante‡ hurries out to Clytemnestra and whispers in her ear. After a moment's incomprehension the Queen calls for lights; the feathery and mercurial scherzando music of this scene looks forward strongly to the opening of the third act in *Der Rosenkavalier* (another case of *Schadenfreude*!). One very fetching theme that accompanies the torchbearers will reappear later with ironic effect.

20

* A short cut, and a longer one later, is often made here. Strauss deplored these, and the cuts in the following Electra–Clytemnestra duet, and went into print on the subject, so that one gasps when his protégé, Karl Böhm, consents to introduce his recording of *Elektra* as 'complete', calmly declaring that the composer always made these cuts in later life! But see p. 344n. for Dr Böhm's report to me on Strauss's view of cuts.

† Believe it or not, this vitally important passage of musical and textual narrative (described in the foregoing three sentences) is one of the standard mutilations for which Strauss's blessing is claimed.

‡ In Sophocles it is the Tutor in disguise. Hofmannsthal's dramatic instinct rejected this for modern theatrical effect.

Gradually Clytemnestra moves away from terror to triumph. Ex. 15 tells us the cause of her fearful joy. Ex. 4 makes an unexpected and rather obscure reappearance too; but the jubilant transformation of Ex. 12² is clearly Clytemnestra's own equivalent of Electra's Ex. 10. She points scornfully and with mocking delight at Electra and hurries unceremoniously into the palace. From the twittering suspense emerges, on the oboe, the rhythm of Ex. 19 applied to the notes of Ex. 10¹; in fact, a dance of victory for the downfall of Orestes as killer. Electra is mystified, but not yet downhearted: he that is down need fear no fall.

Here the halves of the opera divide, and we start again with a brand-new theme that had been mooted at the moment of Electra's greatest triumph, though at the time without specific reference. Now it specifically refers to the reported death of Orestes.

21

It is a poignant lamentation in E flat minor. The voice of lamentation issues from Chrysothemis, who runs like an animal out of the palace, accompanied mournfully by her Ex. 11 (in the minor), howling that Orestes is dead. Ex. 9 turns into an elegy out of sympathy. Electra ignores the news, insisting that it cannot be true; Ex. 15 is as real to her as ever. Hope like hers cannot perish, and for her Ex. 9 is solidly, persistently geared to her own bitonal chord of *credo quia impossibile*, two triads a tritone apart as in the Axe theme, Ex. 2b. Chrysothemis reports that two messengers have arrived with the news. A powerful thematic interlude does its best to bring the report home to Electra. She gazes darkly, as unwilling as ever to believe. At this moment a young male servant of Aegisthus (part of Ex. 7), runs from the house, calling for a horse to take him to his master. This is, we may suddenly realize, the first time that a male voice has been heard in this opera of, so far, hysterical females. But the slave does not delay. He gets his horse and departs at top speed (drum-beats raise the dust behind him).

It is this positive happening that brings home the truth to Electra. Even while those drums are pounding, Ex. 5 reappears urgently and interrupted. It means that the great deed of revenge has devolved upon Agamemnon's daughters, and must be done as soon as possible, by them both. For a minute Chrysothemis does not understand what deed must be done, and Electra has to explain that their mother, and then her paramour, or vice versa, have to be killed, as they sleep, each daughter claiming one victim. The axe at least is to hand. Chrysothemis, stupefied, is apprised of her importance in this great, necessary work—for she is strong. Electra embarks on a tribute to Chrysothemis's muscular power, developed through virginal nights (—odd phrase: were Electra's nights less chaste?). Here again is a recapitulation of the earlier Chrysothemis themes, now with energetically positive implication; this is Electra's greatest sacrifice to the humanity she has long since abjured, in favour of the sister she so urgently needs to claim as helper, a strong and devoted young girl—there is a hint here from the mythology of Aegisthus who, as a boy, killed his uncle to revenge his father.* Electra is too weak to perform the deed unaided. Chrysothemis entreats her for help —in escape rather than slaughter. But Electra is now quite determined on her task. In a passage scored and imagined with wonderful complexity she swears to serve Chrysothemis abjectly and for ever; it is like a declaration of love, even after the expected eventuality of Chrysothemis's marriage (Ex. 13^2, marvellously developed). The deed has to be done (Ex. 19 shows that Orestes does not have to be involved, Ex. 2c that Electra must be the power behind the murder). But Chrysothemis was never courageous enough to defy authority. She refuses and Electra summarily curses her. She does so to Ex. 5, in a restatement of maximum impressiveness which is structural as well as dramatic. For at this point the music reaches its symphonic recapitulation, and the themes from the first two scenes (excluding Ex. 4) return in logical and also structurally appropriate order, as if to indicate the existence of a larger sonata-form shape governing the architecture of the whole work. Chrysothemis flees in terror. Then, says Electra, I must do it alone, and a confused but strongly exhilaratory pattern of anxious energy accompanies her frenzied search for the murderous axe that she has kept hidden. Does Agamemnon approach (Ex. 8)? No, the axe is still hidden. She goes on digging and, almost unnoticed, the violins begin to descend a scale, which would not count as a theme did it not by its rhythmic character assume melodic proportions. It is a lament for Orestes.

22

As she digs feverishly a man takes his place at a side entrance of the courtyard. The last rays of sunshine illuminate his form. Electra sees him and brusquely asks his business. Since it will not be with her, she would rather be left in peace.

A deathly calm descends as, with the utmost solemnity, Wagner tubas and trombones give an answer that carries more than transitory meaning.

23

* Alas, here is another standard and regrettable cut.

The stranger is waiting for his summons. Meanwhile he has time for conversation. He discovers that she is of the household (Ex. 22), and tells her that he must confirm the tidings of Orestes's death (Ex. 21). She rebukes him for intruding on her lonely mourning, herald of misfortune, that he is to be alive and talking while Orestes (Ex. 22 grows to monumental poignancy) is departed for ever. The man gently suggests that Orestes loved life too much and therefore had to die. But what of me? Electra's question expresses not merely her own self-pity but the loss of the whole family (Ex. 9, especially segment x), little though the self-seeking folk in the palace may appreciate this. Who are you? he asks, and simultaneously Ex. 5 on the horn and Ex. 9 on solo cello give answer, though her reply is non-committal—her real answer is a plaintive oboe recollection of Ex. 15. He senses her kinship with Agamemnon: Kinship, she protests, I am of the same blood. Pace and tension quicken with the stranger's heartbeat as, to his shocked amazement, she tells her name and laments her degradation. Now it is his turn to pour out pity and sorrow at her estate (Exs. 22 and 1b). She tries to turn him away, to pretend indifference. But knowing her identity he can afford, in haste and stealth, to breathe the vital words: Orestes lives! He does so to Ex. 1, in the major, and a trumpet jumps the gun with a variant of the same theme, henceforth the thematic signal of what must be capitalized as the Deed.

24

In a tempo of the utmost excitement Electra exchanges hurried, vital questions (therefore thinly scored) with her interlocutor. Save Orestes, she cries, before they massacre him. By my father's body I have come for that, the stranger answers. For the first time Electra is moved to ask who he is, though the music is proclaiming the reunification of the family, with Ex. 9, and we in the audience are amazed that she too does not hear it. It is left to four elderly servants, who choose this moment to enter the courtyard, to recognize their master, and fall down before him, kissing his feet, hands, and the hem of his garment. They know him, as Electra does not yet; their recognition precedes hers, and the inexpressibly moving Recognition theme now makes itself heard.

25

Who are you? asks Electra fearfully. He answers (and everyone who loves Homer will remember Odysseus and his dog Argos): The dogs in the yard know me, but not my sister. Whether spectators have read the *Odyssey* or not, this moment of recognition must bring tears to the eyes and a strangling lump to the throat, for the tension, built up so long, reaches its climax here, with the pounding of two hearts and the release of every fear and sorrow that a greatly courageous and proud woman has, for seven years, lived with minute for minute. Strauss knew the weaknesses of the human heart as well as any of us, but in this blinding instant he touched them as cogently and as profoundly as at any time in his long and magisterial career. The descent from this gigantic climax is contrived with marvellous gradualness, the emotional tension let down ever so subtly, so that the emerging themes seem like familiar signs glimpsed through tear-dimmed eyes. As the eyes (or, rather, the ears) grow clearer, the rising third of Ex. 3c, which I have associated throughout with Orestes, dominates the music, reiterated like a locket pressed to a lover's heart again and again. At length Electra is ready to speak again, and with great delicacy she calls his name on a rising fourth. Ex. 25 finds its natural level and unrolls quite naturally into the makings of an extended and unforgettable solo for Electra, powerfully assisted by the strongly associative Ex. 9x. (We connect it with Electra's sorrowful 'He'll come no more'—*Nie wieder kommt*.)* The profoundly stirring sound of her solo is enhanced by the richness of the string-writing; strings are heavily subdivided, and for greater luminosity some of the violas have enabled the violins to divide into no less than four sections.† But the entire orchestra is deployed with extraordinary delicacy and richness of sonority. The whole passage ranks with the greatest moments in the music of this century.

It is an intermezzo in the recapitulation section; what follows, her deprecation of her estate, though emotionally a heavy anticlimax, does structurally resume the recapitulation of themes. Conductors who make cuts here remove Electra's touching reminiscences of the time, when, a daughter of the royal line (Ex. 5), she could pride herself on what she saw in the mirror (the passage is imagined with wonderful pictorial perception), though now it is sadly gone to waste (Ex. 1³), because she has sacrificed her beauty to hopes of family loyalty, and reduced herself to prophecy of objuration and despair. Orestes rouses her pride by his promise to do what must be done (Ex. 24, and also Ex. 23). It is his task to lead the way. The music tells us whither—to the dance of triumph. I cite the theme in its later, fully elaborated form.

26
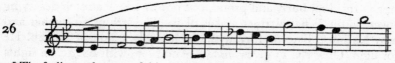

* The feeling and nature of this passage must have been clear in Strauss's mind when, very late in the stage of composition, he asked Hofmannsthal for the extra sentences to go with it.

† Strauss later decided that this was a precedent to be followed with caution, and advised composers not to over-divide their violins in vocal music: 'The more divided the strings are, the more they eat up the human voice.'

The final section of their duet takes the form of Electra's benediction upon him, bland, confident, and C-majorish; and it is not less stirring for the terrible brutality which she takes so firmly for granted. She is, after all, telling her brother how glorious it will be for him to assassinate their own mother.

She does not achieve all this without raising the decibels, and reasonably enough she rouses Orestes's tutor who storms in, to thunderous affirmations of Ex. 24, and reminds them that secrecy is essential to the success of the operation, especially now when all the men are away from court. His firmness and wisdom are portrayed in a new theme:

27

Brother and sister take note, just in time, since after a noisy reprise of Ex. 1³, joined by Ex. 25, they have no sooner resumed the stillness of Ex. 23 when the palace doors open and attendants emerge to light the way (here is the return of Ex. 20) of the messengers who, Clytemnestra is still sure, will prove the demise of Orestes. Orestes thinks of his mother (a diatonic, i.e. undistorted view of Ex. 12²) and apprehensively closes his eyes before the two messengers enter the house.

Drums pound, like Electra's heart, and her thoughts pound too with visions of what Orestes must do (Ex. 19). The suspense edges her like a caged beast, and at last she knows why: I did not give him the axe. For her mind, bent on sacrificial ritual, the omission is appalling. As she bristles with horror, Ex. 2c cuts through the agitated musical texture. Scarifying scales, endlessly protracted. At last a gruesome cry from Clytemnestra. Strike again, Electra yells, and again comes the mortal screech; it brings with it the pacified ghost of Ex. 8, a father revenged.

Electra is standing pressed against the doors of the palace when Chrysothemis and the maidservants throng from their quarters towards her. Antipathy is now converted all too suddenly into loyalty, and Ex. 4 hastily diminished, accompanies them, though we are not shown why the fifth and most loyal servant is not among them. Someone sights Aegisthus who has received the first message. Fearful, the maids retreat. The amiable, complacent sounds of Ex. 7, now extended to a sentence or so, accompany this fop, burly and proud, but not by a long stretch deserving of respect, as the E flat clarinet makes plain. The strings go further and prophesy his immediate destiny at the ineluctable action of Ex. 2b. He calls for light. Only Ex. 15 gives answer. And then, with Ex. 2c, he sights Electra, smiling, inviting, offering her services, unprecedentedly, as his torchbearer. Much to his surprise she leads him carefully across the yard, warning him against steps where he might hurt himself. Her Ex. 2c has become as gentle as any sacrificial lamb—but the sacrificial victim, she knows, is not herself. She dances curiously, as she walks—again we are reminded of *Rosenkavalier*, though the woodwind scoring is unique in its satirical character. What, he asks, has possessed her? Nothing, she answers, but an access of common sense. Who are these strangers on the threshold? They bring news, and confirm their words with the most cogent evidence. It is a fantastic and hair-raising scene. We note that when Aegisthus's person passes through the fatal gate his bland F major theme is repeated in the much darker E flat. There is a vast harp-glissando, and then sounds of dismay and agitation. To Ex. 27 Aegisthus appears at a window yelling for help against his murderers. Does nobody hear his orders? Electra knows her moment, and answers: Agamemnon hears you (Ex. 1). With a last cry Aegisthus is dragged away to death.

The deed, long recognized as inevitable, has been done. Electra, her breast heaving with the rise and fall of Ex. 25, stands pressed against the doors of the palace, as Chrysothemis and the maidservants run in again (Strauss was right, this is inefficient dramatic planning and can hardly look other than clumsy). They wish to greet Orestes—Chrysothemis's Ex. 11 has at last turned gratefully into the major. Electra, for the moment, shows no reaction. The tremendous activity in the orchestra describes the civil war going on indoors, and its eventual victory for Orestes. Chrysothemis reports the joyful triumph of her brother, and asks if Electra does not hear it. As if from a trance Electra responds that of course she hears this triumph since she is its source and inspiration. A waltz, based on Ex. 25, lends force to her words. All are waiting until she begins her dance of triumph. In a daze of profoundest jubilation, and in most solemn triumphant C major, while Ex. 24 pounds against Ex. 5, Electra begins her panegyric, to Ex. 26, joined by Chrysothemis (this is the only true duet in the opera, and marvellously stirring for the effect of two voices in consort). Eventually Chrysothemis runs to find Orestes. But Electra, head thrown back like some Maenad, knees bent, arms outstretched, embarks at last on the nameless dance that she has promised herself all these years. It ought to look galumphing and ungainly; we may not admire it—but we should not be invited to laugh at something so marvellous and pathetic. When Chrysothemis returns and calls to her, Electra answers that all must be silent and dance with her. She galumphs a couple of paces further. Agamemnon's Ex. 8 stalks monumentally with her. Suddenly low woodwind and Wagner tubas collapse on to a chord of doom-laden E flat minor, and Electra drops dead as a megalith. Chrysothemis runs to her; the corpse does not move. The living sister batters importunately at the door, calling her brother. Within too is silence. The harmony twists, like a stabbing knife, into C major, and Ex. 24 hammers home the end of the drama with fierce C major chords.

The penultimate chord is not a C major triad. Its E flat minor refers explicitly to Electra's death, implicitly to a story uncompleted. To revert to history, the mythological Electra did not die. She lived to marry her first cousin Pylades. And Orestes, whom we left inside the palace, dumbstruck by the tortures of the Furies, expiated his crime and married another first cousin, Hermione (who will reappear in *Die Ägyptische Helena*). As for Chrysothemis, nobody knows. If Euripides had anything to to with it, she surely married a peasant, had countless children, and lived far happier than anyone ever after. She deserved it.

Der Rosenkavalier

OPUS 59

Comedy for Music in Three Acts

LIBRETTO BY HUGO VON HOFMANNSTHAL

Marie Thérèse, Princess of Werdenberg (The Feldmarschallin)	SOPRANO
Baron Ochs auf Lerchenau	BASS
Octavian Rofrano, a young Nobleman	MEZZO-SOPRANO
Herr von Faninal, a wealthy parvenu	BARITONE
Sophie, his Daughter	SOPRANO
Mistress Marianne Leitmetzerin, her Duenna	SOPRANO
Valzacchi, an Italian Intriguer	TENOR
Annina, his Niece and Partner	CONTRALTO
The Inspector of Police	BASS
Struhan, the Major-domo of the Marschallin	TENOR
The Major-domo of Faninal	TENOR
A Notary	BASS
An Innkeeper	TENOR
A Singer	TENOR
A Flute-player	
A Hairdresser	SILENT
A Scholar	
A Noble Widow	
Three Noble Orphans	SOPRANO, MEZZO-SOPRANO, CONTRALTO
A Dressmaker	SOPRANO
A Pet-Seller	TENOR
Four Servants of the Marschallin	TWO TENORS, TWO BASSES
Four Waiters	ONE TENOR, THREE BASSES
Mohammed, a little Negro Page SILENT	

I

After the first performance of *Elektra* Strauss is reported to have said 'Next time I shall write a Mozart opera'. This was more than the wishful thinking that had prompted similar remarks after *Salome*; the experience of working with Hofmannsthal had convinced him, from the very first of his letters to the poet about *Elektra*, that he had found an ideal collaborator, and that he would be unwise to seek librettos elsewhere. Hofmannsthal, for his part, saw in the prospect of regular collaboration with Germany's most eminent and discussed living opera composer an opportunity to 'regenerate' the status of the opera libretto, setting new standards of imagination and literary excellence. At first he took it for granted that he would continue to write and first present his dramas as plays for the spoken theatre, afterwards adapting them for music; this method had in the case of *Elektra* allowed his poetic text to be absorbed and appreciated on its own without lessening its attraction when it reappeared as an opera (and when, as the poet never ceased to lament, most of the words were rendered inaudible by the music). And so, before Strauss had finished composing *Elektra*, Hofmannsthal had begun a comedy about Casanova, eventually entitled *Cristinas Heimreise*, and offered it to Strauss as their next opera, the *Figaro* of Strauss's dreams. Strauss understandably expressed some disappointment that the libretto for a comic opera should first be given to the stages of the world as yet unclothed with music. But by this time Hofmannsthal had begun to realize that words suitable for musical setting had to be of a particular kind; *Cristinas* would need to be substantially altered before it would be of any use for Strauss (particularly for his idiosyncratic technique of lyrical conversation). On the other hand, it had been necessary for Hofmannsthal first to elaborate the subject as a psychological comedy in prose. 'I am so much in awe of the difficulties of producing a really good libretto that to write one out of the blue would seem to me almost impossible.' He therefore felt obliged to let Max Reinhardt produce *Cristinas Heimreise* as a play, which he proposed to reshape boldly for the lyric stage and Strauss.

This then was the 'Mozart opera' that Strauss imagined was to be the immediate successor to *Elektra*. But if he had reservations so it seemed had Hofmannsthal, since *Cristinas Heimreise* was never adapted for the opera house, and Hofmannsthal never again attempted to draft a libretto in the form of a play. In February 1909 after the première of *Elektra* he went to stay in Weimar with his friend Count Henry von Kessler, and while on a walk together in Tiefurt Park these two elaborated the basis for a new comic opera 'thoroughly comic in characters and situation', Hofmannsthal wrote to his composer, 'with action bright, transparent and almost pantomime-like. There are opportunities in it for lyricism, for wit and humour, even for a small ballet. There are two major roles, one for a baritone and another for a graceful girl dressed as a man.' He thought of Lucien Fugère for the first of these, Geraldine Farrar or Mary Garden for the second.

At first Hofmannsthal and Kessler thought simply in terms of comedy types, 'the buffo, the old man, the young girl, the lady, the Cherubino'. But during the three peaceful afternoons at Kessler's home when Hofmannsthal worked out his sketch on paper, they did acquire names, and these are able to lead us to the sources for the opera we now know as *Der Rosenkavalier*. Hofmannsthal dedicated the final libretto (as distinct from the finished opera)* to Kessler, in terms which point to real collaboration, and we cannot tell which of them remembered Molière's *Monsieur de Pourceaugnac* and *Les Fourberies de Scapin*, and *Les Amours du Chevalier de Faublas* by Beaumarchais's contemporary Louvet de Couvray. For these three works give us the names, and in part the actions, of the characters outlined in the sketch which Hofmannsthal made at Weimar, and which was discovered after his death. Here is a translation of the document (it will be seen that Hofmannsthal very soon reversed the position of Acts 1 and 2):

1. The house of Geronte. Geronte awaits son-in-law from good country nobility. Sophie with pretty Faublas talks about marriage. She is surprised that it angers him. Arrival of Pourceaugnac and elderly aunts, pets and marvellous luggage (double bed). Conspirators sent for. Marquise. Rendezvous for the night with Faublas, at which Faublas not so unreservedly delighted. Sophie begs for rescue. The conspirators.

2. Bedroom of the Marquise. Love-making by night. Morning. Thanks. Pourceaugnac announced. Faublas remains in woman's clothes. Faublas so similar: yes, all noblemen's natural children. Hairdresser, servants, etc., importuning Pourceaugnac. He departs. While Marquise is having hair dressed, Pourceaugnac invites the maid to supper. Pourceaugnac parsimonious (meticulous discussion where supper). Pourceaugnac departs. Conspirator comes and tells how to do it.

3. Tavern room. Rehearsal of supernumeraries. Faublas's boots under frock. The supper. Arrest. Geronte compromised in front of courtiers. Enter Marquise. Geronte wants enter bridal chamber. Faublas appears in travesty. Marquise announces he is a man.

The plot is, in essence, that of *Der Rosenkavalier* but the locale is clearly French (by 11 February it had been transposed decisively to the Vienna of the Empress Maria Theresa) and, Sophie apart, the characters have

---

* The opera's dedicatees are Strauss's maternal relations, the Pschorr family.

different names. Molière's type-names supply Geronte, the old man
(Greek γερών), later Faninal.* Pourceaugnac, Molière's provincial lawyer,
a fat old man brought to Paris to marry a pretty young girl, and scared
away by the ingenious and degrading machinations of her young lover,
supplied the idea of Baron Ochs; and the play also suggested the conspiratorial figures of Annina and Valzacchi—who assume, in Molière,
such a variety of hilarious French regional disguises and accents that one
wishes Hofmannsthal had been able to transfer more fully to Austria;
in *Der Rosenkavalier* we simply have their Italianate German and
Annina's Bohemian mimicry in Act 3 as a reminder, though the pseudo-
wife and her 'Papa'-screaming children also hail from *Pourceaugnac*.

Couvray's novel gave Hofmannsthal the prototype of Octavian and his
transvestist escapades; the name and nature of Sophie; the Marquise,
later Feldmarschallin; and numerous smaller points such as the rendezvous during a ride in the Prater, the episode of the sword left lying in the
Feldmarschallin's bedroom while its owner is concealed, and the allusion
to a *Qui pro quo*. The *schadenfreudig* pantomime in the inn derives from
a Viennese rococo comedy by Philipp Haffner, the frustrated Ochs–Sophie
betrothal from *Don Pasquale* and many similar *commedia dell'arte* plots.
The hairdresser, the black page-boy, and the singer with flute obbligato
have been traced to Goethe's *Wilhelm Meister* and Hogarth's *Marriage à
la mode*, the Marschallin's clock-stopping ploy to Alfred de Musset, the
Presentation of the Silver Rose to a Papal custom of giving a *golden* rose
to virtuous and noble ladies. We even know that Octavian's pet-name,
Quinquin, came from a Count Esterhazy (I suppose his real name was
Quintus, or something of the kind—surely not Harlequin?). A little further
research may in time reveal the provenance of the names Rofrano† and
Faninal. Hofmannsthal cast his net wide and then, so to say, made a
bouillabaisse of the catch to his own recipe. Like Handel, he paid back
his borrowings with interest. Certainly he himself invented the anachronistic prominence of the slow Viennese waltz throughout the third act,
and the largely imaginary diction of the characters, based on Viennese
and other dialects at several different social levels, which somehow
contrives to convince even a Viennese audience—indeed, many of the
phrases and whole lines have passed into common parlance. Strauss, on
the other hand, was responsible for the duel in the second act, as well as
for the shape of the third act. *Der Rosenkavalier* is in the best and fullest
sense the result of a collaboration; perhaps that is why it has the inimitable
finality of an end-product.

For a while, as the sketch transformed itself into a libretto, Strauss was

---

* Incidentally *Les Fourberies de Scapin* also handed Zerbinetta to Hofmannsthal, on
the same plate.
† Alan Jefferson tells me that Rofrano is a small town between Como and Erba in
Lombardy; Hofmannsthal is likely to have passed through it on one of his many drives
through Italy.

content to report delight, inspiration, inexpressible gratitude; it set itself to music, the ideas flooded on to paper like the Loisach torrent through his garden at Garmisch. And then when he reached Act 2, the weather-cock swung round and Strauss discovered that the plot was not running fluently. From the moment at which Annina and Valzacchi catch the young lovers *in flagrante delicto*, the shape and action were going badly and would not set well to music. Strauss's literary collaborators came to know this moment and these complaints all too well. In this case at least Strauss, whose sense of shape was more reliable than his creative literary faculty (some of his ideas for plot would not have satisfied an intelligent schoolboy), contrived to see the run of events in a manageable order and to twist what Hofmannsthal had proposed into a workable design which the poet was willing to accept gracefully.

Strauss was still employed at the Berlin Court Opera, and had antici-pated that his duties would prevent him from attempting the third act before the summer of 1910. Imagine Hofmannsthal's dismay when, in April of that year, Strauss wrote that the full score of Act 2 was already with the printer, and he was sitting at Garmisch on tenterhooks for the last act. He had finished the first act in December 1909, the second one on 3 April 1910, while still in Berlin. Furthermore, he had already written the tune for the closing Sophie–Octavian duet (*Ist ein Traum*) before Hofmannsthal had begun the text, so that the poet was ordered to supply words made to musical measure. When the third act text did begin to reach Garmisch, Strauss again found fault with it. It was not simply that he was upset by the death of his mother on 16 May; he was able to analyse the defects and point firmly to the character of the Police Inspector who was holding up the development of the final climax and dénouement. Hofmannsthal obliged, though he never managed to raise this scene to a point of positive dramatic quality—it is still, even with music, only a mark-time before the arrival of the Marschallin, after which Strauss persuaded his co-author to get rid of the official at top speed.

Strauss was able to finish the opera on 26 September 1910, after only seventeen months' work: he noted that the music was 'Mozartian but true to myself; the orchestra is by no means small, but Mozart was delighted to hear one of his own symphonies played by an orchestra with a hundred violins.' During his work on the third act he had given an interview to a correspondent of the *Daily Mail*, and among the remarks reported were some sentences about Strauss's composing methods: 'Before I improvise even the smallest sketch for an opera I allow the text to permeate my thoughts and mature in me for at least six months, so that the situations and characters may be thoroughly assimilated. Then only do I let the musical thought enter my brain. At that time the sub-sketches become sketches. They are copied out, elaborated, arranged for piano, and rearranged as often as four times. That is the hard part of the work; the part-scores [does this mean *Particell* or short score?], the symphonic colouring, which follow, are my recreation. The score I write in my study straight away, without trouble, working at it for twelve hours on end. Thus I make the work a homogeneous whole, and that is the main thing.' Strauss's remarks are the more interesting when one considers that, a few weeks later, he received the final libretto of the third act on 2 July, and had the whole composition complete by 26 September! Nevertheless this article, printed on 26 May, does tell us (as the published correspondence does not) that the opera which, on 2 May, was still called *Ochs auf Lerchenau*,* had, just over three weeks later, found its ultimate title of *Der Rosenkavalier*.

2

The authors might well have turned to Vienna, scene of the action, for their première, but Hofmannsthal's mistrust of the conservative and fashion-swayed Viennese inclined him and Strauss to Dresden and Schuch. Vienna was the only company that could provide a satisfactory Ochs, Richard Mayr (Strauss told him 'I thought of you all the time, Herr Mayr, while I was writing the part', to which Mayr replied that he did not know whether to take this as a compliment or an insult); but by the time the authors had settled for Dresden, Vienna, in the person of the conductor Franz Schalk, had decided, perhaps out of pique, that Mayr could accept no guest engagements until February. And the première was fixed for 26 January 1911. Schuch could offer only Carl Perron (the Orestes in the first *Elektra*) as Baron Ochs, but Perron was a baritone— Ochs's voice had now become a buffo bass—and he was tall and thin and rather refined in presence, quite un-Falstaffian (it is clear that Hofmannsthal had taken Shakespeare's fat knight as his inspiration); moreover, Perron disliked the part.

For the rest, Dresden could provide eminently suitable singers, particularly since Strauss had this time avoided excessive vocal demands—we tend, after all these years, to forget how sympathetically *Der Rosenkavalier* is designed for the singing voice because we connect it automatically with the operas that followed, not with *Salome* and *Elektra*. The Chrysothemis of *Elektra*, Margarethe Siems, was cast as the Feldmarschallin. If this seems strange in a role that we associate with dramatic sopranos of at least Sieglinde calibre, we may remember that Berlin chose Frieda Hempel, the Sutherland of her day. It was in Vienna that a Brünnhilde, Lucy

* The Baron's title is so given in the printed German libretto, the printed full score, and the programme of the first performance. Many modern cast lists call him Ochs *von* Lerchenau, but I am sure this is a thoughtless slip perpetuated by a succession of incautious scribes; there is no authoritative source for such a styling. The title 'von' indicates the owner of the land, 'auf' being the life tenant of a small part of the district named.

Weidt, first essayed and triumphed in the part; and the greatest of all Marschallins, Lotte Lehmann, began as Sophie and graduated to Octavian before attempting Marie Thérèse. Minnie Nast, who had taken small soprano parts in *Feuersnot* and *Elektra*, now stepped forward as Sophie. Eva von der Osten was chosen for Octavian and, in view of the controversy which has continued ever since about the timbre most suited to this part, we may recall that her Covent Garden roles in 1914 were Strauss's Ariadne and Wagner's Isolde, Kundry and Sieglinde—soprano with contralto associations. The admirable Karl Scheidemantel, Strauss's first Kunrad, took Faninal; and we may note that the roles of the Italian tenor and Faninal's major-domo were doubled by the *Heldentenor*, Fritz Soot.

These were all good singers, but Strauss had already observed that *Der Rosenkavalier* would above all demand quite exceptional acting talent from the cast, and both he and Hofmannsthal were well aware that Georg Toller, the resident producer, had not, in *Elektra*, shown any sign of appreciating the new and more realistic, psychologically true style of acting implicit in modern opera. The producer who did understand it was, they both knew, Max Reinhardt. Their initial negotiations had, very carefully, included a stipulation of Alfred Roller as scenic designer, and Roller had prepared a production book for *Der Rosenkavalier* which is still commonly regarded by producers as vital source-material—designers likewise revere his sets which are based on Galli-Bibiena and the brothers Fischer von Erlach. Yet even with the availability of this book Hofmannsthal and Strauss knew that somehow Reinhardt would have to be imported if the *Rosenkavalier* première was to represent their work at its most attractive. By cajoling first Reinhardt, then the Dresden staff, and finally the singers, they attained their objective and eventually the production was largely Reinhardt's work, though Toller's name alone was mentioned on the programme for the first performance. Schuch, for whom the southern elegance and sophistication of *Der Rosenkavalier* might have been expressly designed, gave the score thirty-three full orchestral rehearsals, and this may well have been the insurance policy, so to say, of the success which all concerned were determined must be the reward of the new opera. And so it was. The Press could grimace at the 'prolix and humourless libretto', at the 'superficial, thin music' and the unsavouriness of the plot; but the audience responded rapturously to the new opera, demanding ten curtain-calls after the second act, and twenty after the conclusion of the piece. Sir George Stuart Robertson, then already a seasoned opera-goer, who represented *The Times* for the occasion, recalled fifty years later that there had been nothing like it in his experience and probably never would be; he reported after the première to his newspaper, 'If this work does not achieve universal acclaim, one surely must despair at the audience's taste.'

Local premières of *Der Rosenkavalier* followed thick and fast: Nuremberg on the following evening, 27 January 1911, Munich and Basle and Hamburg (where Elisabeth Schumann created the part of Sophie under the nose of Lotte Lehmann) within the next four weeks. The Italian première* at La Scala on 1 March, under Serafin and with Lucrezia Bori as Octavian, was almost shouted off the stage because the Viennese waltzes were thought degrading; but the final reception was loudly enthusiastic. The Prague première in Czech followed four days later, and on 8 April the piece reached Vienna at last, and its finest performance. Hungary in May, Holland in November (when the composer conducted it for the first time). A fortnight earlier *Der Rosenkavalier* had tardily arrived in Berlin (where Strauss had resigned his post the previous November). During the Dresden première weeks the demand in Prussia's capital had been so great that special box-offices had been set up, and special *Rosenkavalier* trains run from Berlin to Dresden; but the court censor would not allow the new piece on to the Kaiser's stage until the numerous indelicacies had been removed. Berlin's own bowdlerized version remained current there until 1924. The authors had already agreed, most unwillingly, to the publication of a tame libretto which could be shown without qualms to sensitive Intendants—the printed scores retained the libretto as set by Strauss. Hofmannsthal asserted his literary individuality by publishing his play, excised of Strauss's subsequent demands for extra lines, though the poet was good enough to admit in a postscript that 'a work is a whole, and even two men's work can be a whole. . . . Whoever separates will do an injustice. Whoever lifts anything out forgets that, unwittingly, the entity always ceases to exert itself. The music must not be torn from the text, nor the word from the living image. This is made for the stage, not for a book nor for any individual at his piano.'

Strauss had, in his enthusiasm, set the whole of Hofmannsthal's text to music, including one stage direction (*diskret, vertraulich*). Nevertheless, and aware as he was of Schuch's cannibalistic appetite for cuts ('His happiest moment', said Strauss, 'was when he found a new opera from which he could remove a whole act'), Strauss had to write a blunt and rude letter to Schuch when he found that these cuts, which had been introduced in Dresden after the première, amounted to some fifteen or twenty minutes, and were being passed on as though authoritative to conductors in other theatres. We do well to remember Strauss's harsh words when we hear festival performances, heavily cut under the excuse that Strauss in his old age did so himself. As well expect a veteran sportsman to clear a six-foot-high jump—it does not mean he disapproves of athletic achievement if he will not attempt more than two foot six.

* It is amusing to note that, in the Italian version, the Italian intriguers Annina and her uncle Valzacchi become '*Rys-Galla, levanto intrigante e Zephyra, sua compagna*'.

3

The scene is Vienna in the first years of Maria Theresa's sovereignty, i.e. about 1745. The first act takes place in the bedroom of another Marie Thérèse, a princess, the wife of Field-Marshal Werdenberg. She is one of the great ladies of Vienna, with an extensive castle; like Rosina Almaviva who partly inspired her existence, she has married young and been disappointed early, and so has taken lovers to refresh and add to the boredom of days and nights when her husband is absent. The Marschallin (as everybody knows her) talks a good deal about growing old—and indeed the theme of the opera is time with its transitory, irrepressible flow, and the changes which time effects upon our minds if not our bodies, without our remarking them. We have noticed that this most important role in the opera has been assigned to sopranos of very different timbre and dramatic experience. Many opera-goers regard the Marschallin as a mother-figure, and therefore a woman of forty or more. But Strauss carefully stipulated, very soon after the première (during the La Scala rehearsals), that she must be a young woman who has had lovers before, and will have many others; at thirty-two or thereabouts she has been married for sixteen years, half her life, and she feels herself precociously aged, not least because her husband leaves her so often. Lotte Lehmann's portrayal was unique and immensely moving, but the part makes equally good sense and stronger drama if we regard the Marschallin not as a pseudo-mother but as the young lover that every young man would count himself lucky to acquire. This view of the role, given a singer in her vocal prime (as Siems surely was), accords best of all with the music that Strauss has given her.

Her current lover is Count Octavian Maria Ehrenreich Bonaventura Fernand Hyacinth Rofrano, a seventeen-year-old boy of very noble family indeed. By a nice stroke of aesthetic imagination, designed to bring home his immaturity, he is presented as a trouser-role in the tradition of Cherubino and Urbain and Oscar. The musical results are marvellous throughout every scene of the opera; but it seems distasteful that Hofmannsthal should have cast so sexually virile a figure as a female role, particularly in the opening scene which demands overt demonstrations of the most passionate love—it is seldom that the two actresses involved manage to avoid suggesting a repellent sort of Lesbianism as they hug and caress one another, crooning torrid endearments. As if to atone for this disastrous miscalculation, Strauss leaves no doubt in the introduction to the first act that Octavian is a proper man. The opera begins with an unrestrained and highly suggestive musical description of the act of love. Strauss had written similar music in *Feuersnot* and was to repeat the dose in the Prelude to the third act of *Arabella*. But the Prelude to *Rosenkavalier* is musically the most memorable of all these erotic descriptions. Nobody who understands the language of music can misunderstand the meaning of the initial rising horn-call.

The answer to it is undeniably feminine, yielding, flexible, and rapturous. With this (Ex. 2¹) I quote two more Octavian themes, the piercing and receding arpeggio which rises higher than expected (Ex. 2²), and the more considerate, gently but firmly active sixths theme of Ex. 2³.

The progress of the orchestral introduction is so graphic as to leave us in no doubt that this ardent boy, in his inexperience, reaches his climax (whooping horns) much too soon, and that Ex. 2³ has to resume activity, rather less inspiredly, until Ex. 2¹ is ready to subside with the 'second subject'.* This is a melody of the utmost subsequent importance (the principal expression of the Marschallin's enduring love for Octavian), accompanied by sighing and aspiring figures and attempts at Exs. 2² and 2³. I quote two versions.

* Though it is possible to sustain the tension right through from the beginning until the appearance of this second subject, as Antal Dorati showed in a performance given after this chapter was written.

The Prelude finds serenity at last in two long-drawn-out and infinitely endearing feminine themes, both associated with the Marschallin.

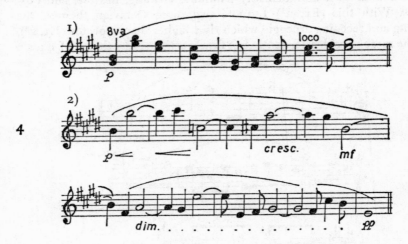

It is in this atmosphere of loving contentment that the curtain rises to disclose, thanks to the censorship, Octavian fully dressed, kneeling before the Marschallin who is wearing a *négligée* and still in bed (unless the Lord Chamberlain decrees that she must by now be reclining upon a sofa). Distant sound of bird-calls in the woodwind, and a theme of aching passion (Ex. 5) precede his first words.

He praises that womanly response which he of all men knows. The music slips away, by a semitone, as she asks part ironically if he wants every woman to know it. So of course he glories in his unique revelation (or so he thinks, to her amusement); Strauss carefully uses adjacent keys to indicate their different attitudes, and we may notice that whereas Octavian addresses her with the intimate *Du*, she adopts the more formal

Er at this moment; at other times he will rather distantly call her *Sie* and she adopts *Du* when wanting to demonstrate her love.*

His hymn of praise is an elaborate fantasy on the love themes quoted above, and Hofmannsthal was evidently intending gentle mockery of Wagner's love language in *Tristan* (*Was heisst das Du?* etc. and a great deal of philosophizing about *der Tag*). At Octavian's ingenuous attempt to postpone daytime, when the Marschallin is no longer his alone, by drawing the window-curtains, she is unable to repress a discreet laugh. Perhaps she has heard the tinkle of bells which announces her breakfast, while her lover was confidently excluding all such intrusions. She turns aside, with an endearment, his accusation that she does not take him seriously, but she also warns him of the tinkling. He tries not to listen, but trombones, then drums, then horns put her on the alert with an inescapable rhythm, associated primarily with her husband.

6
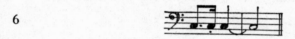

Not that her husband is yet at hand. No sooner has Octavian insisted that he is master here, and no one may enter the room, than a grotesque but graceful march announces the unopposed intrusion of the least person in the household—Mohammed, the Marschallin's little negro page, who has brought her breakfast of chocolate. Although he is so ignominious and never opens his mouth he has two themes.

7

Mohammed appears three times in the opera, and each time is significant, each time he betrays his awareness of the whole situation, including the bits which the Marschallin is sure are secrets. Now, for example, his entry is the signal for a tremendous performance while the Marschallin gets Octavian out of sight behind a screen, including the sword which he

* Hofmannsthal's use of the *Er* and *Sie* is idiosyncratic in this respect, an example of the make-believe language that he invented for the world of *Rosenkavalier*. In conventional German *Er* and *Sie* indicate the speaker's social superiority; the inferior person would use the second person plural *Ihr*, *Euer Gnaden* (Your Grace) as Ochs does, for example in conversation with the Marschallin. But the characters in *Rosenkavalier* use *Er* and *Sie* much more indiscriminately.

has left in full view. Ex. 6 as well as Ex. 7 is involved in the page's
pantomime, and also a quick diminution of Ex. 2¹ to show whose page
he is, as well as a slower version of this theme while the Marschallin lies
back in bed, pretending that she is still only half-awake. Mohammed puts
sofa, table, and tray in convenient proximity, bows to the bed, and skips
out. He keeps looking back at his mistress, for he knows perfectly well
that she has a companion, and who he is as well as where he is.

He leaves the room, and the Marschallin rebukes Octavian for leaving
his sword lying about. Ex. 1 becomes disconsolate as he complains that, if
he is so foolish, how can she see anything in him? Don't philosophize,
sweetheart, come to breakfast, is her enchanting reply. And as he shares
her chocolate, a delicate minuet in A major, scored like a Mozart serenade
(no, this is an *Aubade*), accompanies their exchange of endearments,
including pet-names. She is Bichette, he Quinquin.* The second strain
of the minuet is thematically even more important than the first.

We may regard this as the end of the idyll that opens the opera; from
now on events will begin, very, very gradually, to motivate the unwilling
but inevitable fracture of this love-affair, culminating in the Marschallin's
great-hearted act of self-sacrifice towards the end of Act 3.

At this point we may appropriately wonder how long the love-affair of
Quinquin and Bichette has been going on, and how he made his way into
her bedroom—how indeed he proposed to leave it, if he or she considered
the matter. In Hofmannsthal's film-script of 1926 Octavian is shown
climbing up the façade of her palace, over the statues beneath her bedroom balcony. He will hardly have walked into the room through either
of the main doors, attended by servants as they would be (in any case the
Marschallin particularly asks him to return by the front door this time);

---

* The origin of Quinquin has already been mentioned. Bichette in French is 'Little
Doe'; *ma biche* is still a common French endearment.

if he used a secret door on the previous night, one would expect him to leave by it. The natural inference to be taken from the opening scene is that Octavian and the Marschallin had slept together on numerous occasions—she is unlikely to talk of the affair's end when it has only just started—and on the evidence of the orchestral Prelude successfully. On the other hand, if he had slept with her on previous occasions he would hardly need to be informed which door led in which direction, nor would he be likely to hide without taking his sword with him. There is also the orchestral hint in the Overture that he is sexually inexperienced. . . . The question remains open.

Octavian, still in lover's bliss, compares his lot favourably with that of Bichette's husband, the Field-Marshal (Ex. 6) who is hunting big game, whereas Octavian is hunting—what? For the Marschallin this is a bad moment to be reminded of her husband; she confesses, quite innocently, that she dreamed of him last night. And, for Octavian, this is something like an insult; how could she dream of anyone but the lover in her arms (Ex. 5)? She dreamed, she continues, that the Field-Marshal suddenly returned home—and indeed she still hears the noise (Ex. 6). She becomes increasingly convinced that he really has come home. After all, even when far away, she has known him to travel very quickly—there was one occasion . . . she stops, out of tactful consideration for the boy who believes himself the first and last of all Marie Thérèse's lovers. And of course he pesters her to finish the narrative (*Was war einmal?*). She would not in any case do so, least of all when the drumming figure of Ex. 6 has turned into a melody; she is quite certain her husband is on his way into the room, and that the boy must lose no time in hiding. But none of the ready exits is empty and people are everywhere, waiting for the Marschallin's official levee. Octavian makes a token resistance and then jumps once more, completely degraded, behind the screen; now it is Marie Thérèse who stands up for herself (I am, she insists, no Neapolitan General—of the armies that retreated hastily when the Austrian troops entered Naples in 1744). Noises off begin to become very obvious, and she recognizes that the importunate male voice is not her husband's; the servants call him Baron; he is a visitor. A pattern already mooted now turns effervescently into a new and captivating waltz tune, which lightens the Marschallin's spirits no end.

9

And almost at once she realizes that this noisy stranger must be her country cousin, Baron Ochs auf Lerchenau. A firm, bluff arpeggio figure identifies his blustering in the antechamber.

10

What is Ochs doing here? All the time the enchanting waltz of Ex. 9 goes on and soon it is joined in waltz time by Ex. 1. Of course, she remembers, Ochs sent her a letter a week ago. Octavian brought it to her and (nice flattery) of course she has no idea of the contents. It is Quinquin's fault. The Baron's voice has arrived just outside the door. He is being asked to wait, and is refusing—Lerchenaus do not wait in ante-rooms. Octavian now presents himself again; he has disguised himself as a chambermaid—we must not ask which of the Marschallin's clothes can conceivably have supplied the disguise (the realistic logical tone of the whole drama at this instant vanishes, most curiously, into charades)—and pays his/her respects in a rustic Austrian accent. Bichette is enchanted, as Ex. 8² makes plain. Alas, one kiss is all she can reward him with. But Strauss has misunderstood the libretto and, Freud-wise, made her say that she has no time to give him more than a *kiss*—instead of what? Octavian's escape is now assured, and he is told to return by the front door when he has changed into his own clothes. He goes to escape through the bedroom door just as it is violently flung open by Baron Ochs who, surrounded by the Marschallin's faithful and appalled servants, walks blandly into the room, declaring that Her Grace will of course be overjoyed to receive him. He is on his best, most courtly behaviour, bowing and scraping like any lackey, and his elaborate reverences are depicted in detail.

II

Leopold Anton, Baron Ochs auf Lerchenau, is going to be the buffoon of the piece. In the country, where he has been raised, he is a great man and since he is well connected, being the Marschallin's cousin, he imagines that he cannot put a foot wrong. Alas, he is the original clown who puts his foot into it every time he opens his mouth. He is a gentleman farmer, with the emphasis on farming; his manners are superficially good enough to pass in his cousin's palace—just, and eventually not quite—and in the household of Faninal, his parvenu, very snobbish old father-in-law to be, for whom the baronial title excuses every sin in or out of the Etiquette Book. If Ochs lived in town he would be called a lecher, but he comes from the country, and so his preoccupation with sex is only a natural example of humanity copying its own animal surroundings. Ochs's insensibility to atmosphere is appalling, but his frankness is delightful—even his cattle-market approach to Sophie is so funny that one laughs with him, not against him—and his ultimate degradation in the tavern is so brutally *schadenfreudig* that sympathy is actually deflected towards him. Hofmannsthal may well have intended Ochs as a cruel portrait of Strauss's least refined side; he made his point so thoroughly that, in the end, one turns against Hofmannsthal. Strauss never admitted the likeness, in music or words, but he let it be known that Ochs should be played as a rustic Don Juan in his early thirties, whose manners must be adequate for urban society. As with Clytemnestra, the corruption must be seen to come from within. Ochs is greedy and mean, unscrupulous, and lacking modesty;* that is why in the end he is punished. But his sublime assumption that there is no difference between town and country manners so long as you are noble enough is charming as well as very funny.

One aspect of his greed is at once demonstrated. Having bumped into this pretty chambermaid, as he thinks, he at once proceeds to make up to her. The footmen, observing that they have failed to keep Ochs from the Marschallin's presence, now attempt to direct his attention towards her, and away from her domestic staff. The Marschallin, who has been doing her best to sip her chocolate as if all were well, rises to greet her country cousin with a polite comment on his good health. Ochs approaches, still bowing elaborately and pointing out to the lackeys, as he moves forward, that of course Her Grace is delighted to receive him (though as he speaks the woodwind contradict him with pale, nondescript block harmony of the least enthusiastic sort). After all, he warms to his self-justification, persons of rank are quite accustomed to early morning calls, and he instances a princess known as 'Brioche' whom he was in the habit of visiting daily while she was in the bath (a ludicrous low F), and he no farther away than the other side of a screen. Now that he has made his reverences, his cheerful composure is quite restored.

Indeed he is inclined to complain of the lackeys' presumption. The Marschallin waves him to an arm-chair (which the servants have brought forward before withdrawing), resumes her seat on the sofa, and confesses

---

* He is usually assumed to be virtually penniless as well, but I find no evidence of this, except that of the 1926 film which explores his ramshackle castle in detail. But the film deviates in many other respects from the opera, and is complementary rather than parallel to it.

that they were only acting upon her orders: she had been suffering from a migraine—the score discreetly tells us that her 'migraine' was in fact Ex. 5—and is not quite recovered even now (Ex. 4^2, rather wistfully on the basset-horn); perhaps her cousin will therefore be so kind. . . . Quite, quite, answers the cousin absently; he is fidgeting with the arm-chair so as to keep his eye on the pretty chambermaid who has violently excited his interest.

13

The Marschallin, observing this, asks if the servant's presence incommodes her cousin—perhaps this will allow Octavian to escape. But Ochs has no intention of letting the delightful morsel of girlhood out of his sight; indeed he is almost splitting himself in two to hold her and the Marschallin's attention at the same time, as the brilliant scherzando music, compounded of Exs. 9, 11, 12, and 13, makes clear behind his rapid patter. For the prime purpose of Ochs's call is to enlist the Marschallin's advice on a matter touching his forthcoming marriage, as explained in his letter to her. And now she has to pick up the contents of the letter which she is supposed to have read—all this is carried on in brilliant, mercurial dialogue, musical as well as verbal—but this is made easier for her by the Baron's absorption in the pretty chambermaid. The name of the bride? She is, as Ochs had told her in his letter, Fräulein Faninal, whose father has recently been ennobled for supplying the army in the Netherlands. At mention of her name, a solo cello introduces a new theme associated with Sophie Faninal's wide-eyed innocent charm. It is not unconnected with Ex. 5.

14

The Marschallin wrinkles her brow at Octavian, indicating that he should take the breakfast tray and withdraw. Ochs takes the grimace for an expression of disapproval at his choice of bride, and hastens to enumerate her charms, which include not only youth and beauty, but considerable wealth and an aged, ailing father. As for blue blood, Ochs is confident that he owns enough for two, and their children, if not vouchsafed the golden key of nobility (which Ochs will be seen, in a good production of Act 2, to be wearing on his hip), will doubtless rest content with the twelve iron keys to the family mansions in Vienna.* Catching

* The Marschallin's obscure reply, that Ochs's children will surely be no Don Quixotes, may be taken as a reference to their father's complete lack of false illusions.

sight of Octavian on his way out with the chocolate, Ochs frustrates the Marschallin's orders by pleading hunger, so that she is obliged to order Mariandel (we now learn the name under which Octavian is masquerading—not for the last time) to serve chocolate to His Lordship. Ochs is now able to embark on another double conversation with mistress and maid, to Exs. 12 and 10, making advances to Mariandel while simultaneously explaining that he and his retinue are staying two nights at the White Horse before moving to Chez Faninal after the customary presentation of the Silver Rose (Ex. 14 complete with celesta, a portmanteau of two striking features to be connected with the ceremony). It is to seek Her Highness's advice on a choice of Rose-Bearer from among their kinsmen that Ochs has ventured to attend her morning levee. The Marschallin, after a moment's consideration, invites Ochs to take dinner with her on the following day when she will suggest a Rose-Bearer. If she hoped that this would dispose of her cousin, she is mistaken; he has not finished with Mariandel and therefore begs Her Grace to let him consult her Notary about the marriage settlement. The Notary has his own theme.

He is, says the Marschallin, usually at the morning levee; Mariandel can go and look. But Ochs has no hesitation in countermanding this order, so great is his concern for the protection of this exquisite child—a new theme dripping with intimate confidences.

Fortunately Struhan, the Marschallin's Major-domo, enters at this moment to receive instructions about the levee, and is able to assure her that the Notary is in attendance, together with numerous others. A new waltz theme begins and develops almost at once with the melody which is particularly concerned with Ochs's attempted seduction of Mariandel.

To this waltz theme Ochs invites Mariandel, point-blank, to have supper with him, taking advantage of the Marschallin's preoccupation with Struhan. Mariandel plays up, sly but agog. And when Marie Thérèse has dismissed the Major-domo with instructions to let the company wait a little, she observes that her cousin is by no means a slave of convention, even conventions attending a betrothed fiancée. Ochs now launches, with highest spirits, into a brilliant presto exposition of his amorous philosophy, outrageous, uproarious, and entirely spontaneous. Man, he says, has the advantage of all animal creation in enjoying the same instincts without being confined to periods of heat. Every month is good for love-making, and every girl requires a different approach and gives a different pleasure. He gives sundry examples, based on the bevy of girls around him at his country estate. He could wish himself 'like the late Jupiter', in a thousand disguises, each good for its own purpose.* The Marschallin is at first amused by this recital, and comments gaily on her cousin's credo, to a spirited theme.

But eventually she grows weary of it (how could she ever begin to accept so crude and inhuman a declaration?) and the credo ends with a nicely differentiated vocal trio in which Mariandel contributes suitably peasant-girlish comments of shocked surprise. Ochs begs the Marschallin to give this angelic creature to his future wife as body-servant; he can see that Mariandel must be a nobleman's love-child—such as he himself has in his own retinue, his own bastard son. The mention gives the Marschallin an idea; she asks Mariandel to bring her the locket—Octavian's portrait. Mariandel-Octavian warns her of danger, but the Marschallin, to strains of the voluptuous Ex. 16, invites Ochs to inspect the likeness of this young cousin, Count Octavian, an ideal Rose-Bearer (Ex. 1). And naturally Ochs remarks the resemblance—a Rofrano is something special even out of the servants' entrance! The Marschallin, admitting that this special servant is always about her person (Ex. 8²), carefully uses this diversion as a moment when Mariandel, pursued by the Baron's lustful protests, can summon the levee and escape. The Baron tries to follow her out of the door but is foiled by the sudden substitution of a hideous old waiting-woman who has come to wash and dress the Marschallin. Suddenly the room is thronged with people, a Scholar with a studious volume of research, the Cook, and others who lend vocal assistance to the proceedings. First come a soldier's Widow and three orphaned daughters with an absurd trio number about the heroism of their deceased father, then a Milliner hawking hats and face-powder, and a Pet-seller with tiny,

---

* This superb musical texture is brutally and unmusically foreshortened in many performances, though Strauss objected violently to the cuts in question—they place two carefully judged climaxes much too close together.

house-trained puppies, a monkey and some parrots, each with descriptively characterized music of the most finely imagined sort.* The Marschallin, who has retired behind the screen to be washed and dressed (the height of luxury, remember, though probably with tepid water and that evil-smelling soap which was until recently still the norm in Austria), now steps forward in day-dress, greets her suppliants, and introduces Ochs (who has dispatched a footman in search of Mariandel) to her Notary. The Scholar now advances to apply for his Marschallin scholarship, but he is pushed out of the way by a seedy-looking man and woman, speaking heavily Italian-accented German, and hawking the local scandal sheet. The man, Valzacchi, attempts to sell it, quite unsuccessfully, to the Marschallin. But since he has a vital role to play in the drama, and his themes return significantly, we must quote two of them, fast, sinister, and suspicious:

19

The Widow and her Orphans, who have been given a purse during the foregoing, now take their leave in equally extravagant terms, and the Marschallin's Hairdresser, with his assistant, hustle in to a minuet that looks forward to *Le Bourgeois Gentilhomme*. At the same time, and with specially felicitous musical effect, a flautist steps forward and begins to describe a Prelude, above the Hairdresser's music, to the song which he is about to accompany. At this moment one of the lackeys brings the Marschallin a note (from Octavian, reporting his successful exit and intention to return, presumably) and this, with the Marschallin's approval, the Hairdresser uses to cool his tongs. It is merely a sign that she no longer keeps Octavian's missives next to her heart. The flautist is accompanied by an Italian tenor, sent to claim the Marschallin's patronage, who now delivers himself of an aria in Italian. It has yet to be established if Hofmannsthal wrote the text for this himself or borrowed

* It is in such a scene as this that one is thankful for Strauss's adventures in the wonderland of romantic programme music, and his development of the thesis that anything in existence can be set accurately to music. In quite adjacent Moravia, Janáček was working on similar lines, and though this is another story, I suggest that it would be an interesting one.

There is, incidentally, a delightful tale of a performance in which Elisabeth Schumann tied a pink ribbon round the neck of her pekinese Happy, and gave it to the impersonator of the dog-seller who was to exhibit his wares to the Marschallin. Happy, recognizing his old friend, Lotte Lehmann, yapped loudly and wagged his tail, much to the consternation of Lehmann, and the delight of Schumann who was standing in the wings.

it from some unknown source, and if Strauss here intended to mimic or caricature the music of some composer popular in Vienna around 1745. The aria, in D flat major, certainly sounds like nothing that Strauss or any other composer ever wrote, though it does sound attractive and reaches to a gratifying top C flat. One's main comment here is that, in the 1740s, such a singer would certainly have been a castrato, but that Strauss knew perfectly well the impossibility of bringing on another trouser-role part. The first exponent of the part, Fritz Soot, was a well-known *Heldentenor*, but this only begs the unassumed question whether the song is for a robust tenor, who will ruin it, or a lyric tenor; the accompaniment, mainly dark in colour, suggests the former, but on stage the light tenors are the more successful (Tauber, Roswänge). For the Hamburg première Strauss was anxious that this part should be sung by Caruso, who was touring Germany at the time. Alas, the great tenor demanded 3,000 marks, and was not engaged. As a result, Strauss did not attend this production.

The tenor solo ends, and the music turns coarse and graceless for the entry of Ochs's appalling retinue, led of course by his bastard son.

cor anglais

20

They look a fearsome gang: the bastard Ochs, an impudent lout, carrying the Silver Rose case; the Almoner, a dwarf Priest, the third member of the party clearly a dung-spreader in his Sunday best (Hofmannsthal's directions are vitriolic). They take up positions next to Ochs, who is in conference with the Notary and is endeavouring to explain that his marriage must be attended by the cession to him of property that had passed from his family into that of his forthcoming bride. He is told that the law makes no provision for a bride's present to a bridegroom, but he maintains that his marriage is socially exceptional. He is marrying beneath his station, and expects something in return, even if the law disapproves. His attitude is severely practical and commercial; we even suspect that he has picked Sophie solely in order to get the property returned. Strauss's music, however, suggests something altogether more sympathetic—because we see the marriage from the bride's idealistic point of view.

21

The Baron continues to press his case, and the tenor, a bit impatiently, bides his time for the second verse of his song, now a semitone higher— according to Puccini's practice. This time it has Ex. 21 as a flowing countersubject, since during the verse Ochs continues to haggle for his settlement and eventually, just as the tenor reaches the climax of his song, Ochs loses his temper and yells out petulantly that there must be a bridal present, or else. Everything stops; the company is scandalized, and the Marschallin accuses her coiffeur Hippolyte of turning her into an old woman. Hippolyte tries to improve his work, and the Marschallin orders the closure of the levee. This precipitates a general exodus, though the Scholar remains behind, quietly talking to the Marschallin. This is where the Intriguers, Annina and Valzacchi, try to interest Ochs in their work.* Several more Valzacchi themes are brought in for this brilliant mercurial scherzo.

22

As proof of their capabilities they instance their customer's young wife of whom he is perhaps jealous; they will make her their business, *affare nostro*, and wherever she may go Annina and Valzacchi will be there.

23

As a test case Ochs asks for a dossier on Mariandel, and though neither has ever heard of her, they promise immediate results, though they are clearly disappointed to receive no tip.

The Marschallin has risen and Ochs now presents what he discreetly calls the counterpart of her chambermaid,† viz. Leopold the valet, who steps forward to hand over the Silver Rose in its casket (Ex. 14 has now become attached to the object itself). Ochs would really like Mariandel to receive it herself, but the Marschallin promises to give it herself to the *Rosenkavalier*, Count Rofrano. Ex. 4² returns here, gently and royally,

---

* Their unashamed flattery of Ochs's god-like features, and his warm appreciation of Valzacchi's perception, were surely borrowed from a parallel scene in *M. de Pourceaugnac*.

† Strauss originally set the stage directions 'Discreetly, confidentially' as part of Ochs's vocal line. Subsequently he re-composed the bars in question and restored the direction to its proper place!

more for structural than characteristic purposes. We are reaching the end of the second scene. She bids adieu to her cousin; she has to make ready for church. He solemnly expresses formal thanks and withdraws with his retinue, including the Italian intriguers.

But Ex. 11 remains behind, alone with Marie Thérèse, who is at last free to express some of her disgust at the odious conceited fellow who believes himself to be the loser by this marriage (*Da geht er hin*). Sophie's poor prospects in marriage remind the Marschallin of the time when she too was ordered straight from the convent into holy wedlock, and she reminisces in a semi-arioso that is almost a Mozartian separate number —for the orchestral part recalls Mozart in its line and textures, but the vocal part is in Strauss's expressive melodious recitative, what he called his conversation style. Nor is Strauss to be blamed for eschewing cantilena; he gives the Marschallin an aria of transcendental melodiousness hardly five minutes later, and if he does not do so here it is partly so as not to rob the lustre from *Die Zeit, die ist ein sonderbar Ding*, and perhaps because he regarded intense, uplifted melody as unsuitable for a woman alone and determined to regard her feelings dispassionately. The monologue is attended by a host of memorable musical phrases, most of them destined not to recur in the score; yet they are derived, with a concentration worthy of a good Mozartian, from the first violin's opening phrase and from the pattern repeated at the climax of the tune.

24

This last pattern will continue to yield fresh designs.

The Marschallin's recollections set her musing upon the mystery of time passing, of the little girl Resi that she still feels herself to be, and the old Princess Resi that she will one day find herself to have become. It is the cross that we were all born to carry—the oboe very softly and poignantly interjects a version of Ex. 3—and the vital point of life is how we carry it.

This pattern is, as we have already noted, the underlying theme of the opera; it is not pure chance that Sophie Faninal brought it into the Marschallin's mind, nor is it the first time that she has worried about it. It is deep inside her and cannot, hard as she may try, be shaken off by the cheerful reappearance of Octavian, to Ex. 5 in lively tempo. She excuses her melancholy on grounds of her uncontrollably volatile temperament, and he pardons it on the grounds of her anxiety for him, in case the Field-Marshal (Ex. 6) had really returned. But as he speaks Ex. 5 turns into Ex. 24, and we know that this structural recapitulation of the opening scene is not quite an emotional recapitulation, because something has changed in her. When Octavian begins to woo her with words of fiery devotion Ex. 9b, with its overtones of Ochs and Mariandel, stands between them, and she wards off his embrace, calling him not Quinquin but Taverl (diminutive of Octavian), and to an elusive but firmly stated new theme which completely alters the atmosphere of this lover's meeting, for Octavian no less a matter for joy than the previous one—but for Marie Thérèse infinitely pregnant with farewell.

25

The wild passion of the boy, and the deprecating gentle conciliation of the woman (summed up in her quasi-proverb 'whoever embraces too tightly, holds nothing fast') create, for the first time in the opera, a real tension of characters at any deeper level; the exposition of the drama is completed and the development has begun. And in this gradually achieved, suddenly experienced tension, we are made aware how unequal are the forces. Octavian, not really appreciating the delicacy of the situation—a mood on the point of becoming a habit, such as middle age—renews his protests of passion. And Marie Thérèse, a little impatient, tells him not to be as all other men are; Ex. 25 is joined to her own quintessentially feminine Ex. 3 and to an impaction of Exs. 6 and 11 (upper and lower voices simultaneously). At this insulting equation of self and the whole sex, his passion turns into tearful pleading. For a minute Bichette is minded to yield, with the gentle waltz of Ex. 8²; but then as he renews his pleas for love, she sees him, through Ex. 25, as a child seeking his mother's protection, and she knows that she is not ready yet to play the mother-substitute, and that he has to grow out of mother-love and discover the more positive, developing love of coeval man and woman. This is why, eventually, she will give him to another girl; and it is also why the Marschallin should on no account be played as a *femme d'une certaine âge*, if the full implications of this scene, and of the last act, are to be conveyed.

Ex. 4¹ wells up magnificently, over and together with Ex. 25, as the Marschallin calls him again by his pet-name Quinquin, and explains her deeply felt perception that nothing on earth seems to be permanent, nothing can be held with a hug, everything slips away. Her conviction is expressed, with the utmost sensibility, in a mysterious phrase for clarinet and violas, a theme of transience.

26

At this point (*Bis in mein Herz hinein*) the Marschallin is really on the verge of arioso melodic music exquisitely matched to Hofmannsthal's haunting lines. The tension is prolonged by Octavian's accusations of cruel infidelity, and by her half-amused riposte that: See, she must comfort him for leaving her sooner or later.* He asks what puts these words into her mouth. Time, she answers (*Die Zeit im Grunde*), and her Ex. 3 is transformed and reborn as she begins the touching aria, referred to earlier, in which she reflects to Octavian on the omnipresence and ineluctability of passing time, long unnoticed and then suddenly ubiquitous—there are moments when one can even hear it flowing past inexorably. It wakes her in the middle of the night till she must get out of bed and stop the ticking of the clocks (celesta and harps striking thirteen; Strauss knew that eighteenth-century clocks strike the hour, and then the appropriate quarter—one for the full hour, two for fifteen minutes past, and so on; the quarter strokes are louder than the hour ones, but he does not differentiate the thirteenth stroke dynamically). Yet time is not to be feared; it is, like all of us, one of God's creations.

This is among the most beautiful and meaning-filled vocal solos that Strauss ever wrote; it reflects the very best aspect of Hofmannsthal's constant advice that the music should not always bawl at us, that we should hear the words and sense the finer feelings. Octavian is certainly sobered, and perhaps matured a little by this sermon; his appeals are now more detailed, more insinuating, and musically full of allusions to motifs of love, only the last motif comes from Ex. 24² and the Marschallin's awareness of what will happen, today or tomorrow (*Heut oder Morgen*) when he leaves her for a girl younger and/or prettier than she.†

These words, Today and Tomorrow, are vile phantoms to a boy in love, and he fights them away with all the eloquence he can muster, including Ex. 4². But Marie Thérèse knows better, or more profoundly, and as Ex. 4² is repeated, she repeats the same words, *Heut oder Morgen*, to the melodic line which will accompany them momentously at a decisive point in the third act, and which already marks the climax of this first act.

27

Heut   o-der Mor-gen   o   der den ü-ber nächsten Tag

* This is surely a perfect example of the mood in which Strauss declared the Marschallin must play this scene, 'with one eye wet and the other dry'. It is the self-imposed, self-disciplining irony that makes the scene so moving, and the Marschallin so impressive a character.

† Hofmannsthal, tactfully, wanted *jünger oder schöner*. Strauss, rather unchivalrously, set Isolde's *liebe Wörtlein und* instead of the much kinder *oder*.

With infinite tenderness she explains that holding and releasing must be, for them both, hands and hearts, something easy and natural if God is to have mercy on them and their lives; it is at this moment that one of many interconnecting thematic references in this marvellously integrated score becomes particularly clear, the link between Marie Thérèse's Ex. 3 and Sophie's Ex. 21—sensed long before it may be noted. Octavian remains still optimistic though his theme is the farewell one of Ex. 25, and he addresses her rather frigidly as *Sie*. And with an almost ironic counterploy, it is to the yielding, selfishly loving Ex. 2¹ that the Marschallin tells him to go now, because she is bound for church, thence to lunch with her crippled old uncle Greifenklau,* and afterwards to the Prater where perhaps Octavian will ride beside her carriage. This whole passage is suffused with kindly but firm farewell, a moving epilogue to the scene—it will return significantly for the last words sung by the Marschallin in the opera. A certain distance, verbally symbolized by their mutual abandonment of *Du* as a form of address, can be sensed in the new appendix of extensive glissando thirds to Ex. 3, almost three-dimensional in effect.

Octavian obeys her command, quietly and unemotionally. As he leaves, we hear a resentful reference to the lower voice of Ochs's Ex. 11, a gentle hint of what is to follow. As soon as he is gone the Marschallin experiences pangs of loving conscience. She did not kiss him good-bye (he might not ride in the Prater that afternoon). She rings the bell and orders her lackeys to recall him. In vain. They return almost at once with the report that Count Rofrano has already ridden away out of earshot. She calls Mohammed who trips in to Ex. 7¹, and is ordered: Take this! He picks up the Silver Rose casket automatically and moves away. He has not been told *what* to take, or where to; but one suspects that he already knows. Nevertheless the Marschallin gives precise instructions, to Exs. 3 and 4 at their most gentle and wistful. It is Bichette, and young Resi, not the Princess Feldmarschallin, who leans her head on her hand in thought as the act ends; the thoughts are too deep for words—but not for music. She is thinking along the lines of Ex. 24² and Ex. 1. Hofmannsthal thought this whole final duologue too long. Perhaps he was right, but it added a new dimension to opera, and none of us would wish it a moment shorter.

4

Two days later we are ushered straight into the drawing-room of the palatial and doubtless rather too ostentatiously decorated mansion of

---

* A character so real to Vienna, though he is nowhere else mentioned, that Viennese shops not long ago had on sale a dinnerplate bearing his portrait and quoting the sentence which refers to him.

Herr von Faninal, which has been a-flutter since dawn, and probably for days before, with preparation for the arrival of Sophie's nobly born bridegroom Baron Ochs, preceded according to custom by his kinsman the Rose-Bearer. The drawing-room has doors left and right, and at the back in the centre a large double door opening on the entrance hall. The orchestral Prelude, quick, short, and very animated, but full of associative thematic material, depends largely on a not quite new theme.

28

Later in the opera this becomes associated with Faninal himself, but it clearly has nothing in common with this anxious old invalid. The link with the Field-Marshal of Werdenberg (Ex. 6) is even more tenuous, though musically obvious. Since Ex. 28 was obviously intended, in the first place, merely to convey intense excitement about an important forthcoming event, we may the more easily connect it with Ex. 6 and the to-ings and fro-ings in the Marschallin's bedroom at the start of Act 1. Ex. 28 is a good example of Strauss's thematic technique, primarily symphonic and structural, secondarily general or qualitative, rather than personal in reference. Presently a rhythmic pattern, derived from the bass of Ex. 11, joins the hubbub, and will eventually unfold itself in Ex. 29 as a symbol of the absurdly undignified bridegroom Ochs. For the moment it becomes the punctuating bass of a vivacious chatterbox figuration (not unlike the quarrel motif for the Jews in *Salome*, Ex. 4) associated with the empty loquacity of Mistress Marianne Leitmetzerin, Sophie Faninal's chaperone or ex-nanny, who is to be found stationed at a window, excitedly describing the scene in the street outside. The second main theme of the introduction, preceded by a nondescript idea that crops up quite often in all three acts for purely structural purpose, is the rapturous Ex. 21, and for the moment we associate this with Sophie, the heroine of the occasion now imminent. As the curtain goes up Ex. 29 is thundered forth, untypically but ominously in the minor, and attended by a dignified rhythmic pattern connected with Octavian as the Rose Cavalier.

29

Faninal is solemnly taking leave of Sophie, rather needlessly impressing on her the importance of the occasion. She is already doing her best to subdue her high spirits.

11
Der Neurosenkavalier:
a caricature
of the composer

12
Ernst von Schuch

13
Kann mich auch an ein Mädel erinnern . . .
Lotte Lehmann as the Marschallin
at Covent Garden, 1938

halt aso . . .
senkavalier at
-bourne, 1959

15
Elisabeth Schwarzkopf
and Sena Jurinač in
the first act of *Der
Rosenkavalier*, Covent
Garden, 1959

16 Hugo von Hofmannsthal

The Major-domo of the household, a walking etiquette book, is nagging Faninal to get himself out of the house and away to meet the bride-groom before the Rose Cavalier approaches; protocol requires it.

Sophie Faninal is therefore left alone to compose herself for 'this solemn hour of trial' as she describes it, a time for pious self-abasement and self-dedication to the Almighty. She is not entirely successful in this exercise, partly because her chaperone Marianne keeps disturbing her with titbits of running commentary, but also because she does not really believe in the lessons of humility that she has been taught in the convent. She has been fed opinions there and at home, and the two sets are mutually exclusive, for Faninal's life is that of an ambitious social climber. She has furthermore grown up without a mother's guidance, Frau Faninal having died some time earlier; and so she has never learned to think for herself. But she is a girl of some spirit, and this will eventually prove her salvation.

At the moment her spirit is sorely tried by her natural curiosity, and when the cries of 'Rofrano' reach the house-door, and Marianne likens the Cavalier to an angel from heaven (Ex. 1 has turned into a sort of solemn chorale, much extended), Sophie discovers that pious humility cannot possibly compete against a girl's natural happiness in a moment of such nobility and splendour. The Rofrano cries, on the orchestra, grow louder and louder until the centre doors are opened on a full orchestral chord of F sharp major and, attended by his retinue in white and pale green uniforms (these are the Rofrano family colours), Octavian steps solemnly into the room, dressed from head to foot in silver and carrying the famous Silver Rose in his right hand. He, as well as Sophie, is a little overcome by the occasion; they are both very young and very good-looking, and are meeting for the first time in these very formal and public circumstances. Something of their bashful confusion, as well as the Rose's silver sparkle, is reflected in the tonal divagations of a new pendant to Sophie's Ex. 14; set for flutes, celesta, harps, and high muted violins, it makes a curiously blank shimmering effect.

When Octavian opens his mouth to deliver his formal greeting as Rose-Bearer, the words come with some difficulty to him. He, after all, has seen Baron Ochs, and knows better than Herr von Faninal what sort of a bridegroom has been chosen. And now he is also seeing what sort of a bride Ochs has won for himself. The contrast upsets his native poise, and there is a perceptible pause before he can utter the words 'my cousin' and 'Lerchenau'; these of course introduce Ex. 29. Sophie takes the Rose from him, stammers her empty phrases of thanks, and after a pause of confusion smells the Rose and remarks very tactfully on the vividness of the scent. The ice is broken with Octavian's equally tactful explanation —the scent is due to attar of roses. Sophie's ecstatic utterance, that it is like a heavenly, not an earthly rose, must however be taken as an inward comment, of course, not by any possible standard of conduct a public one. Her gloriously expansive, high-flying phrases are of a confidential rapture that we overhear rather than hear, and they are justly the most famous in her role, if not in the whole opera. They inspire, as it seems, a new trumpet phrase (also succeeded by the mixed triads of Ex. 31, representing the Rose).

I have quoted it with the words sung to it, almost at once, by Octavian as well as Sophie. The dramatic action has stopped for the moment, while we and the two young people savour the magical revelation of this instant in phrases of the utmost lyrical beauty that weave in and out of one another in a manner that leaves no doubt of their sudden, unavowed mutual infatuation. Hofmannsthal was at pains to convince Strauss that these dear children must on no account bawl like Tristan and Isolde, or even Walther and Evchen. Perhaps that is why he removed Octavian from the reality of sexual love by making his a travesty role—the reality of this love is something precious and virginal which must not, in this unspoken moment, be spoiled by animal mating-calls. Sophie's first phrase (*Wie himmlische, nicht irdische*) could well have been assigned to an Isolde voice, and would have sounded marvellous, but absolutely wrong. Strauss recognized the intense but immaculate quality of the required soprano voice, and he scored the whole section very gently and intricately so as to suggest the dawning of a first love between a boy and a girl who, only a few minutes before, had been emotionally children (and had been revealed as such before our eyes and ears). Hofmannsthal went out of his way to stress that Octavian, after the Marschallin's words of advice at the end of Act 1, falls for the first pretty young girl that he meets—however much he may tell himself that his love is already given to Bichette. Before the end of the opera we may find Sophie a more desirable and estimable character than her literary creator intended. For the present, as their voices blend and soar together, we are supposed chiefly to recognize that this is the *clou* of the drama, the moment of meeting which, for Hofmannsthal, was the most sensual and spiritual of any in human life, when the attractions of body and intellect are at their maximum because no faults have been discovered, and therefore there is no equivocation nor any calculated justification or disappointment to be recorded by either party. It is not the only great *coup de théâtre* in *Der Rosenkavalier*; many people would give the palm to other moments in these three acts. But I have to record that Hofmannsthal placed greatest weight on this one.

Sophie and Octavian express their wonder and *empressement* in different words, realistically enough (since they are talking to themselves), but end with the same phrase—'not to be forgotten till my death'. The E flat clarinet squeals out a sarcastic phrase, a broken arpeggio connecting Ex. 5 and Ex. 14 with the waltz music to which Sophie and Octavian, now seated but still observed by the chaperone (the two households having just withdrawn), begin to converse. Sophie first volunteers her knowledge, through the Viennese Debrett, of Octavian's ancestry, his complete tally of Christian names, and even his pet-name Quinquin. This last inspires a new idea, still connected with Octavian's Ex. 1 through the rising sixth, and with Exs. 5 and 14, but marked with a new, adult intensity that will dominate his later actions on her behalf.

33

Quinquin, Sophie knows, is the name given to her new cousin by the beautiful ladies who are his intimates (Ex. 8², very attractive). Sophie thaws sufficiently to express her pleasurable anticipation of marriage—it is so different from celibacy (Ex. 8², again significantly, together with the bridegroom Ochs motif Ex. 29, and the new Octavian idea Ex. 33)—and to confess that she is determined to uphold her rank even if she has to box any upstart's ears (Hofmannsthal wondered if this phrase was too violent for such a girl, but it is perfectly in character, and indeed makes this entrancing child even more lovable, if only because we are sure she would never go so far—we shall shortly see the full extent of her active independence). Hofmannsthal speaks through Octavian (and Strauss through Mozart's wind serenades) in protesting that Sophie need never fear lack of respect, since she is so much more beautiful than anyone with whom she will ever have dealings. She twits him with mockery, adding that she accepts anything from so delightful a young cavalier. And this is the decisive moment, for the centre doors open to admit Faninal with Ochs and the Lerchenau retinue, in D flat major, very solemn, and to the rather un-awe-inspiring Ex. 29.

Faninal introduces bride and bridegroom, and Ochs at once compliments his new father-in-law on Sophie's dainty wrist, a rare distinction in any middle-class person. He completely ignores the chaperone who is introduced next, because he cannot wait to meet Mariandel's foster-brother (he loses no time in telling Faninal of the *sub rosa* relationship). Octavian's distaste is quiet and predictable. Sophie has seen at once what an uncouth bridegroom she is collecting, pock-marked as well, and she is unassured by Marianne's indication of the Chamberlain's golden key which hangs on Ochs's frog—Marianne, like Faninal, is enchanted by this easy-speaking nobleman, who drops condescending approval of the Tokay that Faninal now offers, and loudly informs Rofrano that these *nouveaux riches* have to be kept in their places, completely insensitive to Octavian's highly sarcastic compliments on his Lordship's brilliantly diplomatic manners. Now, thinks Ochs, it is time to draw the young lady out; but his ideas of wooing, ironically conveyed in not quite graceful rococo music, are brutally direct and boorish. One of these rococo phrases plays an important part in the dénouement of Act 3.

34

He pulls Sophie on to his knee and asks what she most looks forward to in marriage—which shocks her the more, because her secret longings in this respect are directed towards the handsomeness and exquisite manners of Ex. 1. Faninal is transported by the honour of such a status symbol—his own daughter on the knee of a Lerchenau, with a Rofrano in attendance. But the Rofrano mutters murderous violences to himself, and the daughter resists indignantly and energetically—all of which only inflames the old lecher's passion. Octavian, in his rage, crushes the Tokay glass into smithereens and flings them away; the only result is that Marianne runs to pick them up, commenting to him on the delightful familiarity of his cousin's amusing manners.

The Notary from Act 1 makes his appearance to preside over the civil marriage; and in this diversion Sophie bluntly asks Ochs how he dares behave in this fashion. Ochs's mind reacts like clockwork: Sophie, himself, Notary, contract, bed. You'll learn overnight just how, he answers, and very quietly his optimism is reflected in saucy phrases which will soon turn into Ex. 35; his philosophy of love is contained in the words of a popular song, and promptly he sings it—'happy with me, wretched without me'. The strings give us the first taste of the most famous waltz *not* written by a Viennese composer (though it is very close to Josef Strauss's *Dynamiden*, Op. 173, as Roland Tenschert has conclusively shown).

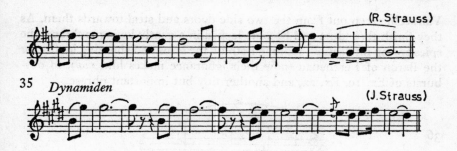

It has never, throughout all this scene, occurred to Ochs for one second that Sophie's recalcitrance is more than hypocritical modesty—he has never before tried to seduce a carefully brought-up town girl of good family (parvenu and peasant are equivalent to him). And so when he sees the Notary he drops Sophie like a stone, convinced that she is enchanted, and informs her, as one might a child, that business is to be done, so he must go, and Cousin Tavy will entertain her—perhaps he will warm her up a bit for her forthcoming husband. As he, with Faninal several paces behind, and the legal staff move into the adjoining room, the orchestra plays dilatorily with Ex. 21, Ex. 29, and Ex. 35. Quickly Octavian looks to see who is left (only the chaperone) and in greatest anxiety asks Sophie if she wants to marry this specimen. Sophie's motif for dejection now comes to the fore (Ex. 30), but she answers shyly that she can hardly pass an opinion on one who is Octavian's own cousin. Thank God, answers Octavian, I never saw him until yesterday; he is only a courtesy relation. Their further conversation on the subject is obviously restricted so long as the chaperone is in attendance; but fortunately she is got out of the way, very sharply, by a commotion provoked through the violent and lecherous drunkenness of the Lerchenau household who can be seen doing a latter-day Rape of the Sabine Women on the Faninal maidservants. (The musical representation is carefully connected with Sophie's remark about looking forward to marriage.) Marianne is fetched away to deal with this dreadful problem, and so both young people can speak freely, which they do via Ex. 1 and Exs. 30 and 32. Sophie begs for help, and this Octavian promises her if only she will take the first step. This clearly involves a firm refusal on her part to marry Cousin Ochs, though Octavian does not say so. He only asks her to remain as she is, kisses her quickly on the lips, and holds her in his arms while they confide in one another, very softly and *sotto voce*, during a beautiful duet (*Mit Ihren Augen voll Tränen*), largely accompanied by heavily divided strings.*

While they sing this exquisite quasi-separate number, Annina and

---

* To begin with, they use the *Er* and *Sie* form of address. Soon they adopt *Du*, presumably because they have kissed.

Valzacchi creep out from the two side doors and steal towards them. As
they finish their duet and become locked in a gently loving embrace, the
spies spring into action, pinning both by the arms and shouting loudly for
the Baron of Lerchenau (now their ignorance makes him *von*), to out-
bursts of Ex. 19, Ex. 22, and another tiny but important phrase.

36

The words quoted appear later. Neither of the Italians dares leave the
captives, but fortunately for them Baron Ochs's attention is roused, and
he leaves the adjoining room to see what is going on. The Italians acclaim
his entry in Ex. 37, and he exhibits his man-of-the-world acceptance of the
situation (which after all he provoked in his last words to Cousin Tavy)
in the second half of this quotation, the demisemiquavers of which link up
with those of Ex. 11, perhaps suggesting the slippery absurdity of Ochs's
most would-be-dignified moments.

37

Ochs's reactions are unsurprised but quizzical. He is inclined to con-
gratulate Rofrano, even when the boy tries unsuccessfully to convey
Sophie's distaste for her intended. She cannot find tongue to utter her
refusal of marriage; he, on the other hand, is interrupted every time that
he mentions *die Fräulein*.* Ochs is not interested; now is the time, interruption or not, for Sophie to go and sign the marriage contract herself.
She doesn't care for him? She will! He begins to pull Sophie towards the
middle door (the wrong one, in his confusion), ignoring or brushing aside
Octavian's threats and imprecations (Ex. 2^2 now makes a delayed reappearance). Octavian's language grows more and more insulting and
challenging and finally he draws his sword, defying the sozzle-eyed
Lerchenau servants called by Ochs's cabman-style whistle to attendance,

* *Fräulein* is neuter in conventional German.

and makes towards this thick-skinned seducer. The Baron, trusting to his retinue and holding Sophie firm in his grasp, has ignored every threat, and the approach of cold steel catches him unawares. He attempts too late to fetch out his sword, lunges forward, and is wounded in the arm by Octavian.

Chaos now takes over. Ochs yells blue, pink, and every other colour of murder, as his servants, crying revenge, lead him to a sofa. Octavian and Sophie stand well apart; he holds the Lerchenau servants away at sword-point. Ochs's cries are sung to Sophie's Ex. 30 and her *Ich freu mich auf Heiraten*; we cannot see him, as he is surrounded completely by his servants, including the Italian spies. A sizeable ensemble in waltz rhythm now begins, closely worked in terms of appropriate themes. Marianne rushes in to join the crowd round Ochs (which includes a doctor), and last of all comes Faninal with the Notary. Sophie's father, who is swiftly put into the picture by Annina, is dumbfounded; and here Strauss brings out one of his best tunes, which I quote in a later, more clearly defined form.

38

This is usually called 'Luck of the Lerchenaus', but every appearance has to do with Annina and Ochs, and she is certainly *not* lucky for the Lerchenaus. After a little, Faninal finds his voice for demonstrations of the utmost apology and deploration—worst of all is the sight of blue blood poured on the floor as if in any knacker's yard. Faninal does not know whether most to deplore Ochs's parlous condition, or Rofrano's un-chivalrous behaviour, or Sophie's gentle but resolute refusal to marry this appalling suitor. Nevertheless he does his best, at the lively tempo still in progress, to keep in touch with them all (and here it must be added that Faninal is, at this moment, completely estranged from our sympathies, unless a Fischer-Dieskau is in charge of the role—or, doubtless, a Scheidemantel, as at the première; it is a tricky part for even the best singing-actor). Sophie, with tender diplomacy, attempts to explain her antagonistic feelings, but Faninal only sees dishonour in them. His depression is transformed into tearing rage as his own theme, Ex. 28, joins the optimistic betrothal tune of Ex. 21 and the dogmatic Ex. 36. He insists that, dead or alive, Sophie shall marry this nice gentleman. And he indicates that Octavian would do better to leave the house. Every bow, every sentence, is returned formally by Octavian. Marianne manages to get first Sophie then Octavian out of the room, but not before they have exchanged loving messages. Faninal still yells that she will go back to a convent for life *auf Lebenszeit*, if she will not marry Ochs. The whole scene, if properly produced, goes on oiled wheels and is funny.

There are fewer people in the room, and we can now see Baron Ochs sitting complacently on several chairs put together in the shape of a sofa, and beginning to relax, though when Faninal shows his appreciation with an embrace, Ochs's self-pity bursts out noisily from his slow-march transformation of Ex. 11 (and Ex. 34). The doctor forbids potions of wine, beer, or even cinnamon with ginger ale. Faninal continues to pour imprecations on his terrible, ungrateful daughter, and takes his leave together with all the Faninal entourage, including the Italians who, we are left to assume, have already made some tentative arrangements with Octavian before his departure.

Ochs now begins the monologue of self-pity which, with one interruption, constitutes the coda of this richly inventive and brilliantly paced act. The tempo of the music becomes more tranquil as he decides quite calmly to annihilate this Dago boy (the Italian-surnamed Rofrano), as his servants confirm in a unison chorus of profoundest and most devoted dreariness.* At the appearance of a Faninal maidservant with a jug of wine for him Ochs cheers up (have doctor's orders been ignored?) to a gentle march that has gradually been marking his convalescence, and goes so far as to ask the doctor to make a feather bed ready for him so that he can go and lie down when he is recovered from his injury, after having fortified himself with a glass or two (Strauss so far forgot himself at this point as to drag Ex. 1, for symphonic but otherwise meaningless purposes, into the pretty march tune). He dismisses most of his entourage, sips a draught or two, and thinks back to his favourite waltz, Ex. 35, 'Without me, with me' . . . and the next preposition, 'for me', comes pat to hand with a letter which the Italian Annina has silently brought him. It is private and highly confidential (Ex. 38 makes its reappearance), so he sends even his bastard son and yes-men packing. But he cannot read it; he says he has not got his glasses, and so Annina must oblige. She reads a love- and rendezvous-letter from Mariandel, to the cheeky waltz made out of Ex. 1 with its chorale-like succeeding phrases. The rest of the act, in which Ochs orders Annina to help him prepare an answer later, and then glories in the family good luck, is a chain of the most exhilarating waltzes. After the Ex. 1 specimen comes Ex. 38. Once again Ochs fails to tip Annina, though she importunes him through two whole octaves in the hope. Finally, as she departs, shaking her fist at this parsimonious old fellow, his favourite waltz, Ex. 35, makes its grandest and most famous appearance, with full orchestra and swooning Viennese violin glissandi. It fades towards the distance as Baron Ochs, his sickness forgotten, waltzes contentedly round the drawing-room (not so long ago the scene of a grand and solemn ceremony, we may not be inclined to remember) singing his own song, and taking the tune down to low E, whereupon the

* Hofmannsthal later told Strauss that he had intended it to go in quick musical tempo.

orchestra brings the act to an end with three softish repetitions of Ex. 35's first phrase.*

5

Hofmannsthal summed up the third act of *Der Rosenkavalier* very succinctly: 'a little spicy to begin with, then broadly comic, only to end on a note of tenderness'. A few weeks earlier he had asked Strauss to 'try and think of an old-fashioned Viennese waltz, sweet and yet saucy, which must pervade the whole of the last act'. As we have seen, Strauss put some delightful waltzes of this sort into the first and second acts, but he respected the spirit of his collaborator's request. A large part of the third act is like a chain of waltzes *à la* Johann Strauss, some of them taken over from earlier acts, and all of them recapitulated towards the end of the opera in a feat of astounding virtuosity.

The act begins with a display of virtuosity too in the introduction and pantomime describing the further conspiracies of Valzacchi and Annina on behalf of their new employer Octavian. This is an electrifying *vivace possibile* in C minor based on themes already cited as Ex. 19 and Exs. 22 and 23, often in new forms (it is a characteristic feature of Strauss's thematic technique that important identifying ideas very often arrive at a typical form quite unlike that of their first appearance—rather as great men look quite unlike their childhood photographs) but also on two new ideas, both concerned with underhand intrigue, disguise, and concealment.

39

Ex. 1 rings out in the middle, and then Ex. 29 to let us know who else is involved. The Italians' *Wir sind da* of Ex. 23 closes the introduction very softly. And then Valzacchi's Ex. 22[1] storms back again, for the

* The earliest record of the scene accompanies each of these with crescendo chuckles from Annina. Later it became customary for the stage manager to press the button for curtain-fall on the first, so that the drops would be halfway down by the second, and closed by the third. When Strauss saw this for the first time, he commented: 'Very neat, but not what I originally meant.' Since Annina is offstage by this time, and since Ex. 35 belongs primarily to Ochs, perhaps these are Ochs's three chuckles of anticipatory pleasure.

curtain has risen upon a private room in the sleazy pub which Ochs has parsimoniously selected for his seduction rendezvous with the supposed chambermaid Mariandel. A table is laid for two, by candlelight, and there is an alcove with a big double bed, at present concealed by curtains. A fire is burning in the hearth, and the doors lead to the main part of the tavern and the front hall. Pictures, a false window as well as a real one opening on the street, a mirror over the mantelpiece, another door into an adjoining room, and numerous spyholes and trapdoors at present invisible,* will play their part in the events of the act. There are various candelabra about the room, but only a few of them here and there are lit at present, and by these we see Valzacchi engaged in approving the widow's costume with veil worn by Annina, and in making her up. Annina's disguise as a widow, and her eventual role, are described in a short but striking, not to say spectacular new theme:

40

With great circumspection the little side door is now opened and an old woman scurries across the room to the main door and admits Octavian with his Mariandel disguise over his own clothes (Ex. 1 in waltz time, as in the first act, and indeed as in Annina's letter scene with Ochs). Mariandel at once strides over to Valzacchi and Annina (who takes a moment to recognize Count Rofrano beneath the disguise) and pays them. Five sinister-looking characters enter the room furtively. A clock strikes the half-hour (its chime is not musically notated, but it should presumably strike three times, not twice), and Ex. 17, the rendezvous waltz, tells Octavian that it is time he went to meet Ochs. Valzacchi now disposes the five supernumeraries in their hiding-places, through side doors and a trapdoor. He conducts Annina, who seems to be studying a speaking part, through one of these doors—all with noiseless stealth, on tiptoe, finger to lips, and to the conspiratorial introductory music. On his return Valzacchi steps into the middle of the room and claps his hands, whereupon there is a tremendous uproar in the orchestra and faces appear at every hiding-place, then disappear as quickly and quietly at another signal. Valzacchi, evidently content with the dress rehearsal, is now ready to open the centre doors, and snatches of Ex. 17 tell us that the masquerade is ready to begin. Valzacchi strikes a tinder and begins to light all the candles in the room (woodwind vividly match the flaring of each flame), helped by two waiters who have come with tapers from the main restaurant where a sizeable orchestra can now be heard playing Viennese waltzes (the band, which includes harmonium and piano as well as wind, brass, and strings,

---

* We must wonder if they were a standard installation in Viennese pubs (like secret mikes in totalitarian countries), or whether peculiar to this tavern.

is of course disposed backstage, and makes magical antiphonal effects with the pit orchestra during the ensuing scene). This is where Richard Strauss's splendid chain of waltzes begins, and I quote the eight melodies in sequence—or rather such of them as are not already familiar.

The flaring of candles goes on in the orchestra. Valzacchi moves to the centre door, and while Ex. 41[1] continues backstage, the pit orchestra combines it as if by magic with Ex. 2[2] and a suggestion of Ex. 29, because here through the door come Ochs, his arm in a sling, and Mariandel, together with the bastard Ochs junior. Mariandel runs to the looking-glass and combs 'her' hair. Ochs takes exception to the bright lights, pulls the waiters from their work at lighting more, and takes a napkin to douse those that are already lit (a real Ochs would regard fingers as a quicker way of snuffing them—I have never seen a countryman snuff candles in any other way). Valzacchi discreetly draws Ochs's attention to the furnishings of the room, particularly those behind the curtained alcove. Ex. 41² begins in the pit orchestra, and the Landlord together with a posse of waiters crowds round the distinguished guest, offering further amenities and service. Ochs, of course, wants as little as he can get away with, and he sends them all packing, protests about the café band which he didn't order, suspects a draught in the dummy window, refuses the attention of the waiters, since his body-servant will dish out and he himself will pour the wine. Ex. 17 provides the third waltz, less adequately than it could have done—it is restricted to coda noises instead of the real tune. Ochs is typically promising a cut to Valzacchi if he can obtain a reduction on the bill, which is sure to cost a packet (the rough characteristic touches are very nicely judged). Is it so smart a pub?

Mariandel and the Baron now sit down to supper (Valzacchi having departed), while young Leopold busies himself (Ex. 6) with the carafe of wine (for once do not let us blame Baron Ochs's miserliness on the choice of *vin en carafe*; assuming, as one should, that this *tête à tête* takes place in Leopoldstadt or Grinzing, nobody in their right mind would dream of drinking anything but *heurig* white wine on draught). The tension has been on tenterhooks while the lackeys depart and Mariandel decides to sit down to table. For this moment we are on Ochs's side, not least because the music is marking time for a new waltz; it is Ex. 41⁴, perhaps (if we believe Roland Tenschert) a reminiscence of *The Blue Danube*. It is destined to furnish the great moment of the whole opera: but just now it is no more than one of several waltzes, to which Mariandel pretends that she cannot drink wine, that she should not remain there. She runs to the alcove and discovers the bed (Ex. 17 followed by Ex. 29). Who, she asks, will sleep there? Ex. 41⁴ answers, quite blandly, and Ex. 41⁵ follows it up as the Baron attempts to propound his philosophy whereby no man accompanied by his sweetheart should think of anyone else, fiancée or no. Cavalier is cavalier, sweetheart is sweetheart. Ex. 41⁶ arrives, and Mariandel sits back, inviting the first kiss.

But as Ochs responds Ex. 1 and Ex. 17 strike in; he suddenly finds his lust cooled by the fatal resemblance to Rofrano, and the waltz tempo is diverted. The man in the trapdoor raises his covering too soon. The Baron is horribly disconcerted. But Mariandel has seen nothing, and there is nothing, she protests, to see. Ochs is seriously upset, takes a good gulp of wine, and confesses he must be suffering from congestion of the brain (appropriate music). Fortunately at this moment the next waltz strikes up on the café orchestra and it is Ex. 35, very firm and consoling. Mariandel comments pleasurably upon it, tactfully since it is Ochs's own favourite song, as we know. It makes Mariandel cry by its beauty, which rather surprises him—he had always thought it pretty jolly; and, in a memorable phrase, Strauss manages to bring back, not well motivated, Ex. 22 (I suppose Valzacchi is never far away, and I also suppose that a good symphonist will always remember a good theme in a suitable structural moment). Ochs's bodyservant has been dispatched and gawps inside the room for a last look, intercepted by his father. The new waltz melody Ex. 41[8] now joins the waltz-sequence, and Mariandel appears to have fallen upon boozer's gloom (*Es ist ja eh als eins*), moaning that time blows everyone away. This is not at all to Ochs's liking, and he is sure that the cause of her melancholy is a tight corset; after all, the music has become excessively woeful and chromatic (almost like one of Salvador Dali's limp watches). Ochs gets up to ease her tightness, and feels the need to doff his wig. In this moment the various waltzes begin to merge curiously and he sees strange faces in the wall of the room. When he turns to this evidently willing seducee, she is impervious, ready to welcome advances, but her face puts him off—it is too like Rofrano's; and indeed Ex. 17 and Ex. 1 tell us why. There is no threat there, however, and he is calmed. But not for more than a moment. These ghosts or apparitions continually rise before him; they have even the rhythm of another authority, Ex. 6 (Faninal rather than the Field-Marshal). He cannot ignore them. They are everywhere. As he protests, the dummy window opens and Annina appears (Ex. 40), addressing Ochs as her deserter-husband, then disappears. Ochs does not know what to think; Mariandel crosses herself against witchcraft. Annina comes through the main door, followed by Valzacchi and the inn staff who pretend to restrain her and, in a Bohemian accent that makes one doubt her earlier Italian, claims Ochs as her lawful mate, promising the aid of the Empress Maria Theresa (a tremendous florid cadence), and vengeance on this Mariandel who is evidently trying to supplant her in his affections. Her claims are supported by four noisy children who storm into the room towards Ochs, saluting him as their Papa! Ochs has many sins to his discredit, but these are not among them, and he is justifiably aggrieved. Behind his back Octavian is making sure from Valzacchi that someone has gone to fetch Herr von Faninal. The Landlord and Valzacchi advise Ochs to beware of the Watch Committee who are unsympathetic towards bigamy; they even consider it a capital offence. Ochs regards the whole affair as a monstrous infamy, wrenches open the window and shouts for the police, to the distress and lamentation of the tavern's Landlord.

The Inspector of Police, with two constables, arrives on the spot without a moment's pause, and with a theme of his own, instantaneously authoritative (the police in those days were, even more than in 1911, a power to respect in Vienna).

42

In the long-held moment of the Inspector's arrival Valzacchi shows signs of panic, but is consoled by Octavian who is sure of his authority if it be necessary. The Inspector demands, in his firmest tone of voice, what is wrong. Ochs answers that, because of his arrival, all is obviously right; if the policemen will get rid of this vile rabble, supper can continue as planned.

Ochs expects too much, though. A wigless old man in his shirt-sleeves commands no more respect with a Viennese city policeman of 1745 than any other wigless shirt-sleeved man (Ochs looks in vain for his periwig). And the Inspector promptly declares as much. He is not the Landlord? Where is the Landlord? The host steps forward and is publicly trounced for allowing such an affray. Is this fat fellow a Baron? Can anybody vouch for him? Baron Ochs indicates Valzacchi, who will not by any means vouch for such a thing. This is something like a disaster for Ochs (crash goes a cymbal) but mercifully Leopold junior has a bright idea, and tears off (in the direction of the Feldmarschallin's palace, it later turns out). Mariandel seems to have panicked, ostentatiously, so that the Inspector's attention is drawn to her as she yells in terror and plunges for the exit which, carefully chosen, turns out to be (Ex. 17 inverted) the bedroom-alcove. The awkwardness of the situation, as far as concerns the Watch Committee, is now fully apparent. Ochs attempts to bluster his way out by pretending that he is having quiet supper with his fiancée (Ex. 21 gently and persuasively). The Inspector at once insists on knowing this fiancée's name, much as Ochs protests, and so very stupidly Ochs obliges with her complete names, Sophie Anna Barbara, legitimate daughter of the noble Herr von Faninal. 'Here I am,' answers that gentleman, much too promptly for Ochs's liking (a brilliant reshuffle of the Ex. 28 ideas) —for Faninal has been called here, overtly at Ochs's wish, though actually by Valzacchi. And at this point Ex. 34 makes an important and for some time active reappearance. There follows a comic scene in which Ochs tries to pretend that this old fellow is *not* his father-in-law, that he ought not to be here at all, and has nothing at all to do with the chambermaid under Ochs's betrothed protection. Faninal and the Inspector put the truth in perspective; Ochs tries to pretend that his congestion of the brain (apparition music) is to blame, but all in vain. When Faninal is asked to identify Mariandel as his daughter, he loses his temper altogether, and calls for Sophie to be brought from the carriage downstairs in the street (Ex. 42, imperiously). Ochs, foreseeing her arrival, renews his efforts to find his wig, and Strauss brings out a new theme, dealing with discomfiture and basically related, not to any Sophie theme, but to Octavian's Ex. 2².

43

The extensive activity of this theme from now on usually involves chromatic alteration of the fourth note, as shown, and only reminds us how flexibly Strauss treats his symphonic materials.

No wig is to be found, but the children choose this instant to yell 'Papa', as Sophie, announced pathetically by Ex. 30, reaches the scene of crime, while Faninal attempts to rouse her shame at this sight of her bridegroom (Ex. 29) and the family disgrace (Ex. 28). Sophie at first is merely delighted; here is the excuse of excuses. But Faninal's shame grows stronger and stronger as he sees the implications which the chorus have no hesitation in bringing home to all and sundry. He collapses and has to be supported next door, to be revived by cooling draughts and suitable medicaments.

Ochs has now miraculously recovered his wig, and with it much of his composure. He asserts his full weight and dignity and proposes to take Mariandel home—a brilliant and illuminating combination of Ex. 38, rhythmically revised (the Luck of the Lerchenaus) and Ex. 14, the theme of the fiancée who, Ochs still pretends, is Mariandel. The chambermaid is, of course, unwilling to do any such thing, and lets out a suitably protesting moan to Ex. 41⁴ and Ex 41⁸, which Ochs attempts to silence with promises of marriage and Baroness-ship. The Arm of the Law has no intention of allowing this to take place; he has dispatched everyone save (for further dramatic, but unrealistic, purposes) Annina and the four supposed children. Mariandel now breaks free and offers to tell the Inspector a secret in strictest confidence (Ex. 43 very prominent, but also, most comically, Ex. 41⁸). While the chambermaid disappears behind the alcove curtains, the Baron, very embarrassed, attempts to assure the remaining policemen that Annina is quite unknown to him. Suddenly he remarks the amusement of the Inspector as, one by one, Mariandel's clothes are thrown out of the alcove; and unseeing observers are also amused by the counterpointing, inestimably witty, of Ex. 43, Ex. 41⁸, Ex. 29, and Ex. 1, all on one another's heels, and protracted far beyond Ochs's patience, until Octavian's head pokes from out of the curtains.

It is too much for Baron Ochs. He almost breaks free of the constables who are holding him back, crying that he has to save this girl under his protection. But at this moment the Landlord opens the centre doors and announces Her Highness the Princess Feldmarschallin.

Marie Thérèse has been called by Ochs's natural son, so we gather from his glowing looks as he follows her in and runs to Ochs. We are suddenly aware that she has been off-stage ever since the end of Act 1, and that, as Hofmannsthal had realized, she was then already the most important person in the drama, and is still so. We are also aware that, without her, the nobility of the drama has dropped to nothing, and now is hoisted aloft again, as if with block and tackle. For, at any rate since the Presentation of the Rose, we have heard no music so splendid and dignified, and so heart-warming, as the stream of melody which now unfolds in expansive grandeur upon the orchestra. If anyone has the heart to reflect upon musical history and musical style at this supreme moment, we are not in the reign of Maria Theresa (though at any time in the last act and a half we might conceivably have felt ourselves there) but in the reign of Edward VII (I will not say of Kaiser Wilhelm because he disliked *Rosenkavalier* and it did not suit his *milieu* in any case).

The cellos play Ex. 1, the horns whoop aloft in some transformation of Ex. 43, and the violins pull out Ex. 3 longer than ever before, and more eloquently. One almost fears the degradation and condescension involved in so godlike a person actually talking to ordinary people; but of course the Feldmarschallin does so; she is not a puppet. She sees the fearful, apologetic head of Octavian, the fulsome gratitude of Ochs, and humble obedience of the Inspector. At once she recognizes the Inspector as her husband's ex-orderly, much to his pleasure.

Ochs too sees Mariandel's head between the curtains and orders the creature to stay out of sight, though he tries not to let the Marschallin notice. Noises at the side door distract him, and Octavian is able, unobserved by him, to leave the alcove, now in Rofrano clothes, and apologize to Marie Thérèse for her being brought to such a place. The side door is burst open by Sophie who, oblivious of anyone else in the room, advances with a message for Ochs. This is, as far as he is concerned, no moment at all for his fiancée to appear; but it gives Octavian a chance to slip a word to Marie Thérèse. And his dearest friend recognizes the position at once, approves the girl, and cuts off the past by addressing him frigidly as Rofrano—not even Octavian.

Sophie does not see the Marschallin, ignores Ochs's protests, and firmly delivers a mouthful to her ex-bridegroom. He must never show his face again within a hundred paces of Château Faninal—all this at top speed with spicy orchestral interjections, wherever possible, of Ex. 28. Ochs rounds on her, but she has disappeared, and while he protests he is tapped on the shoulder by his rescuer the Feldmarschallin, who tells him firmly to remove himself. Crash! The octave drop of Ex. 37 introduces a dignified, brief recapitulation of that section from Act 2. He can best preserve his dignity, she says, by departing with a good grace. Ochs is, for once, speechless as Ex. 1 on the flute and Ex. 14 on the violin expound a situation clear to the Marschallin, far beyond Ochs's comprehension.

Sophie stands in the doorway and hears the Marschallin dismiss the Inspector with the explanation that the whole thing was a harmless Viennese hoax; it was more than a hoax to Sophie. The police retire. The Marschallin and Sophie catch one another's eye, for the first time, and Strauss memorably underlines the moment by counterpointing Ex. 14 and Ex. 3—during the whole of this part of the third act one finds Strauss exerting all his dramatic virtuosity to pit the many characteristic themes together in different combinations; one can find other examples in modern opera (above all in *Wozzeck* and *Albert Herring*), but nowhere, I think, with more precisely compassionate and human effect.

Ochs is unwilling to do as the Marschallin says; he has no intention of letting a rich marriage, quite apart from his parental property, go. In answer to his objections the Marschallin raps out a word of command, and Rofrano, now in his own clothes (Ex. 2^2, all the more affecting in context), steps forward and greets Ochs. The Baron recognizes the identity of Octavian and Mariandel; he had almost suspected it (if the opera had been less extended, Hofmannsthal could usefully have made more of this). The Marschallin repeats, more firmly, her judgement about the Viennese hoax (poor Sophie again repeats her words), adding that she never intended her Mariandel to be seduced, and that she now nourishes a strong prejudice against all men—in general, that is.

Ochs's thick intelligence just begins to grasp the implications—who is Mariandel, how she got into the Marschallin's bedroom, *et cetera*. What is he to think? Firmly the Marschallin instructs him that he is not there to think at all, since he is, she assumes, a cavalier. And here she uses Ochs's get-out musical phrase Ex. 34 with utter finality. Ochs confesses himself enchanted by the Marschallin's gracious attitude to the whole affair, her willingness, like his, to forgive and forget. His Mahlerish transformation of Ex. 11 returns, and he asks leave to go and make peace with Faninal. The Marschallin's patience is not exhausted; but there is a finality in her voice as she orders Ochs to retire quietly—the octave drop, firmly and lethally, three times (as in Mahler's Sixth Symphony)—since the whole affair of his marriage (Ex. 21) is now over and done with, together with everything connected with it. Perhaps the Marschallin senses what this means for little Sophie standing by—it means the ineffable bliss of Ex. 32, recalled now by cellos, as Sophie repeats again the Marschallin's peremptory words. Ochs is for the first time quite flabbergasted; the effort has tired the Feldmarschallin who looks for a chair. Octavian provides it. The Baron is still not willing to admit defeat. The final blow is the menace threatened by the reprise of Ex. 17 plus the third-act introduction music, as all the conspirators and tavern staff begin to crowd upon him. He knows when the game is up. Loudly and decidedly he calls to his bodyservant: Leopold, we're off.

But they aren't. For all these people bar their path, while Annina, with ultimate irony, recalls his Luck of the Lerchenaus tune, Ex. 38, joined by individual calls from everybody in the inn who has contributed to the evening's entertainment including, last indignity of all, the bogus Papa-calling children.

Somehow, in the mêlée, Ochs fights his way out. Only Octavian, the Marschallin and Sophie are left in the room. The languid waltz of Ex. 41^6 is sounding as Sophie again repeats the Marschallin's words, 'only a farce'. Octavian is aware of his duties to both women. It is the Marschallin who sends him to comfort the little girl—Go, you are a real man, she says scornfully, but the music only offers Ex. 41^8, from his female impersonation days. Octavian's attempt at comfort is sharply repulsed; Sophie knows with whom she is competing (Ex. 3, to be exact). Octavian protests; Sophie protests in return. From her seat on the tavern chair, the Marschallin begins to repeat, like a hieratic utterance, her prophecy, which she knows is now coming true: Today or tomorrow, or the day after tomorrow (Ex. 27). It brings out voices in half-communing, half-musing motion, and it sets in motion the sensuous regretful thirds of Ex. 3^2. As the three voices become increasingly intense in their separate convictions, Ex. 4^2 crowns them all with its decision. And so, when Sophie returns Octavian to his old love, saying that she has to see her father, Octavian remains caught between the two of them, not knowing which way to turn, since he is torn between two fires.* His embarrassment is acutely portrayed in the short, hesitant musical phrases. Ex. 3 takes control. The Marschallin walks over to Sophie, looks searchingly at her, ignoring Octavian, and openly asks her if she has so quickly fallen in love. Sophie rattles out a quick-fire answer of evasion about shock, parental affection, etc. The Marschallin takes up the music, which first came in Act 1 at the poignant moment when she vowed that parting must come lightly, with light hands and a light heart; she said it then, perhaps only half in earnest, if we believe Strauss; but now she repeats the sentiment with practical, self-sacrificial intention, merely telling Sophie not to prattle so much, but to let the older woman see to Faninal while the younger one's pale cheeks are cured by the medicine of her young cousin. It is the sweetest, most gracious and most moving speech perhaps in all opera. It would stand on its own as spoken drama; with music it is almost unbearably poignant. The effect on Octavian is to turn Ex. 3 into a new, dominant-seventh climate, as he stumbles words of gratitude. Marie Thérèse pauses on the threshold of the door into the room where Faninal is resting. Octavian stands between her and Sophie. A solo trumpet recalls Ex. 32; Octavian tries to express to Marie Thérèse what he feels, but he gets no further than her name. The real intensity of what they feel, and we feel with them, comes from inside and can only be voiced to them-

* In retrospect this situation has its exact mirror-image in the closing scene of *Capriccio*.

selves. And this is a moment when these three persons, whom we have learned to love, unwrap all that is most secret in their hearts, beginning with the Marschallin who acknowledges an old promise to love Octavian so well that she would, when the time came, yield him to another girl, and love his love for that successor; joined by Sophie who feels as she does in church, wanting to kneel before this other woman, and yet to do her some injury since in giving she also withholds something of Octavian; and then Octavian, himself bewildered, aware of the change, questioning, afraid, but only certain of his love for Sophie. Their three voices blend in marvellous euphonious counterpoint, the top line passing, like the Norns' rope, from each to each, at a pace so expansive that we who listen feel time suspended. And if we know that the main theme of this trio is a reprise of the comic Ex. 41^4, we think none the less of it. It binds the act more closely, and creates stronger connexions between farce and serious emotional portrayal. You can think it an absurd idea to use such a theme for such a purpose; and you can think similarly of the Country Dance tune which Beethoven turned into the monumental finale of the *Eroica*.

The close of this trio is something which only Strauss could have written: the voices rise on an E major arpeggio, and then the G sharp is turned enharmonically into the dominant of the home key D flat major; with this switch we know that the Marschallin's decision has become fact, and that lovers have changed places. The final cadence is still moment-ously ringing out as the Marschallin calls God's blessing on this pair, and slips quietly through the door. Ex. 1 rises powerfully up the D flat chord and switches into G major, with a burst of sunlight. Ex. 14 shines out, and Ex. 32. The orchestra subsides into a humming serenity. Sophie and Octavian begin their final love duet which commentators have likened to Mozart and Schubert, but is still in concept unthinkable to any century before our own. As their first verse ends, Faninal walks, apparently quite well, out of the adjoining room with the Marschallin on his arm. Young people are like that, he comments. Oh yes, answers the Marschallin, with an infinity of understanding. Sophie and Octavian have not set eyes on them. They sing the second and final verse of their duet (with Silver Rose obbligato so to speak), ending with an ecstatic treatment of Ex. 32 rising in thirds to top B. As he kisses her, her handkerchief falls on to the floor, and they run out. After a moment Mohammed runs in (Ex. 7), looks around, spies Sophie's handkerchief and dances out with it, whereupon the curtain falls.

Does Octavian keep Sophie? Who will be the Marschallin's next lover, and when? Is Mohammed's last appearance as innocent as it looks? Like *Capriccio*, *Der Rosenkavalier* ends with several question marks.

6

In 1945, when the liberating troops walked up the drive of No. 2 Maximilianstrasse, Garmisch-Partenkirchen, they were met by an old man, tall but now stooping, with a white moustache and heavily lined face. He held out his hand and said in English, 'I am Richard Strauss, the composer of *Der Rosenkavalier*.' Strauss's prestige in Nazi Germany by this time stood rather below freezing-point; he had openly voiced his disapproval of the war, and of the Nazis' contribution to it, had been threatened with death, and only had his eightieth birthday acknowledged in a cold and (except in Vienna) most secretive fashion. He had little money and little food, but he and his wife had survived. Could any musician convey his identity to a foreign soldier? Strauss gambled on the popularity of one work, *Der Rosenkavalier*, in America where his loved and devoted Lotte Lehmann had spent the war, still singing the part of the Feldmarschallin. 'I am the composer of *Der Rosenkavalier*,' he said, and the soldiers knew what it meant; he might as credibly have said *Fidelio*, so much a part of inherited culture was the opera he had written. It had long become a classic, a piece of operatic history. Indeed from the very first it was never intended as a modern work. It was a stylistic regression from *Elektra*, designed by Hofmannsthal to throw the emphasis on vividness of characterization, convincing evocation of atmosphere, and chiefly on a theme eternally true, a European myth, a post-Renaissance fairy-story. It is not modern, and never was; but *Der Rosenkavalier* remains tremendously realistic, denying the changes of time which it discusses, a period-piece of modern times, but hall-marked with a special authenticity. Perhaps we should condemn it as a twentieth-century remake of Dresden china—like stockbroker's Tudor, or Van Meegeren's Vermeer forgeries. But it is neither a bogus vulgarization of a past style, nor a forgery. Astonishingly, *Der Rosenkavalier* makes its effect primarily as a post-Freudian document about human relationships and personalities; the Viennese charm, the Edwardian rococo, the sumptuous post-Romantic euphony, all seem subsidiary. From the librettist's point of view the opera was overloaded with music; it obscured or altered what he wanted to say. But it enabled Strauss to progress further than ever before with his exploration of symphonic technique in opera, and with the musical transference of the spoken drama into the sung drama. The public fell delightedly upon it for the waltzes, the comedy, and the moments of lyrical expansiveness. But the student, for whom opera is music-drama first and foremost, loves it and reveres it for the scenes in which Strauss discovers how to pass between different levels of articulate emotional expression, as in the Marschallin-Octavian scene at the end of Act 1, or in the third act from the entry of the Marschallin until the end of the trio.

The passionate admirer of Strauss will accord first place in his honours list probably to *Elektra* for its unsurpassed positivity of psychological observation through musically progressive vocabulary, or else to *Die Frau ohne Schatten* for its grandeur and diversity of musical imagination. But both these qualities are to be enjoyed in *Der Rosenkavalier*, which wears best on repeated hearing, if only because it is the Strauss opera that we hear most frequently, and that never (even in a poor performance) fails to renew our love.

Ariadne auf Naxos

OPUS 60

Opera in One Act with Prologue

LIBRETTO BY HUGO VON HOFMANNSTHAL

Characters in the Prologue:

The Major-domo	SPEAKING PART
Music Master	BARITONE
The Composer	SOPRANO
The Tenor (later Bacchus)	TENOR
An Officer	TENOR
The Dancing Master	TENOR
The Wig-maker	BASS
A Lackey	BASS
Zerbinetta	SOPRANO
Prima Donna (later Ariadne)	SOPRANO
Harlequin	BARITONE
Scaramuccio	TENOR
Truffaldino	BASS
Brighella	TENOR

Characters in the Opera:

Ariadne		SOPRANO
Bacchus		TENOR
Naiad		SOPRANO
Dryad	*Three Nymphs*	CONTRALTO
Echo		SOPRANO
Zerbinetta		SOPRANO
Harlequin		BARITONE
Scaramuccio		TENOR
Truffaldino		BASS
Brighella		TENOR

I

The ink was hardly dry on the score of *Der Rosenkavalier* before Strauss began to importune Hofmannsthal for their next opera. He assumed, at first, that it would be *Semiramis*, but Hofmannsthal had given it up in despair, and was now considering 'a fantastic play: a simple plot divided into three acts, sombre but not monotonous—for which music might very well be conceivable although originally I thought of the music only as accompaniment, subordinate.' This was provisionally entitled *Das steinerne Herz*, a Hofmannsthalian elaboration of the fairy-story by Wilhelm Hauff. Early in 1911, and probably while composer and librettist were in Dresden together for the première of *Der Rosenkavalier*, they decided to create together a little thanks-offering to Max Reinhardt for his work on the production; it would be a new German version of a Molière play, with incidental music by Strauss, designed for Reinhardt's company in Berlin. In March 1911 Hofmannsthal wrote to Strauss about two further plans: a thirty-minute chamber opera called *Ariadne auf Naxos*, in which *commedia dell'arte* comedians mingled with eighteenth-century opera characters; and a new magic fairy-tale about two couples, which in due course became *Die Frau ohne Schatten*, and which immediately put *Das steinerne Herz* out of Hofmannsthal's head.

Hofmannsthal thought of *Ariadne* as an intermezzo, in their joint work, between *Der Rosenkavalier* and *Die Frau ohne Schatten*; but one that might result in a 'new genre which apparently goes back to an older one —since all development takes place in spirals.' It was, he wrote, an intermezzo necessary to him in order to become better acquainted with music, and in particular with Strauss's music, so as to achieve a much more complete collaboration than in *Rosenkavalier* which satisfied him as a textual-musical entity very much—but not entirely. Strauss's symphonic texture and shaping evidently did not appeal to Hofmannsthal, mainly no doubt because it took the form out of the librettist's hands. He was anxious to develop the importance of separate musical numbers connected by *secco* recitative—precisely the concept of opera which Strauss, following Wagner, was developing away from. And indeed the history of *Ariadne auf Naxos*, absolutely crucial to Strauss's future development as an opera composer, is one of the composer's coolness and failure to appreciate how much it meant to his 'dear poet'. He regarded it, initially at least, as a rather boring chore, quite irrelevant to his path as a creative artist. *Die Frau ohne Schatten* interested him much more, and he was also negotiating at this time with Gabriele d'Annunzio for an opera libretto, with the special desire for 'an absolutely modern subject, very intimate and highly neurotic in psychology'. The Italian poet never became his collaborator and eventually Strauss himself had to write his neurotic and intimate modern drama *Intermezzo*.

It was two months later that Hofmannsthal realized how *Ariadne* could effectively be combined with his Molière adaptation for Reinhardt. He had thought only of the lesser-known Molière plays, but *Le Bourgeois Gentilhomme* ended with a Turkish Ceremony that could well be dropped in favour of the opera which Jourdain would be understood to present for the entertainment of Dorante and Dorimène. Molière's five acts could be cut down to two. Quickly he sent Strauss a draft sketch: Zerbinetta did not find her way into this, but Hofmannsthal had the idea of putting the chamber orchestra on the stage. (The Deutsche Theater in Berlin had no adequate orchestra pit.) Reinhardt was attracted by the idea. Strauss at once saw the weakness of the foreshortened Molière, and the impossibility of asking first-class instrumental soloists to cavort in costume on the stage —Reinhardt would have to raise and reconstruct his orchestra pit. But the sketch did at once show Strauss quite clearly the best musical shape of *Ariadne*, and the disposition of roles. Ariadne he saw as an alto, Bacchus a lyric tenor (eventually these became a fairly strong lyric soprano and a youthful dramatic tenor). Zerbinetta would be the star of the show (Selma Kurz, Frieda Hempel, and Luisa Tetrazzini were Strauss's choices) with a show-stopping solo rondo and variations; among the other set numbers immediately envisaged were Ariadne's recitative and aria, Harlequin's solo *Lieben, Hassen, Hoffen, Zagen*, and the hymnic march trio for the nymphs *Töne, töne, süsse Stimme*; there would be a final ensemble which did not quite eventuate. Strauss's first thoughts were of a twenty-piece orchestra with solo string quintet, and harpsichord (which became a pianoforte), as well as harp, celesta, and harmonium. He left no doubt at all that he found the piece cold and uninspiring, much in need of vivid poetry that would stimulate his music even if the plot was a bore.

The prominence thrust by Strauss upon Zerbinetta, who was Hofmannsthal's afterthought (borrowed, I have suggested earlier, from Molière's *Les Fourberies de Scapin*) rather surprised the poet, but he accepted the notion and even derived from it the main philosophical idea of the opera, though he never accustomed himself to the diabolically difficult and, for him, rather vulgarly exhibitionistic solo *Grossmächtige Prinzessin* which Strauss wrote for her. He made one vain attempt, two years after the second version was complete, to persuade Strauss to write new, less demanding music for this aria. And right from the start he assured Strauss that none of the three star singers named by the composer would be financially possible if their show was to enjoy a run and make some money. In fact, Kurz sang Zerbinetta in the Vienna première of the second version, and Hempel almost consented to take the part in the world première at Stuttgart.

Strauss began writing the music for *Le Bourgeois Gentilhomme* in May 1911, and proceeded to *Ariadne* before his poet had completed the libretto. He kept urging Hofmannsthal to saddle his Pegasus and make the dramatic climaxes more sunny and dionysiac—*Freude schöner Götterfunken* was Strauss's ideal. When in July Hofmannsthal sent the last pages of text, he expressed the 'hope that setting it to music will be a joy for you, and that I have not failed'.* He had done his utmost to sell the piece to Strauss by constant propaganda, but of course the situations and characters were much too formalized to strike sympathetic chords inside Strauss, and he much upset Hofmannsthal by his cool and rather tactlessly patronizing acknowledgement of the complete text. Hofmannsthal's reply was a letter explaining the inner meaning of *Ariadne*, and in due course we shall read it in the expanded form that the poet wrote for publication at the time of the première. Strauss, of course, climbed down and apologized, with the quiet protest that such important themes could not be hidden and left for people to pick up like clues in a treasure hunt; if the composer failed to get the gist, would not the audience and the critics be similarly at a loss? So vital an idea must be built into the action, not left to receptive imagination. Hofmannsthal was again on the defensive, explaining that the opera would be introduced by a new scene in which the actors preparing for the performance would be told that the comic and serious operas must be given simultaneously; this would give occasion to explain what *Ariadne* is about. Strauss observed how important this scene must be, and even suggested that the opera's composer might be shown having a love-affair with Zerbinetta 'so long as he is not too lifelike a portrait of me'. And this in time found its way into the so-called *Ariadne II*. I suspect that this was the moment when Hofmannsthal decided to let the composer interrupt Zerbinetta's recital of the *Ariadne* plot to her comedy troupe, and explain Ariadne's monoandrous nature and the theme of fidelity which, though Hofmannsthal maintained it constituted the special theme of the work, is at the root of every one of the half-dozen operas he wrote for Strauss.

It soon became clear that the Deutsches Theater in Berlin was incapable of mounting a production with an orchestra of thirty, and Strauss began to look elsewhere. Hofmannsthal heard of this, and put his foot down: only Reinhardt (for whom the work was written and to whom it is dedicated) could be allowed to present this *Bourgeois-cum-Ariadne* to the world. Strauss had been thinking of Dresden, but found the theatre impossibly large, and the smaller Dresden theatre unsuitable too. Munich in the Residenz Theater was conceivable, but everywhere there would be the difficulty of obtaining official goodwill for a company and producer from elsewhere. Hofmannsthal was near to tearing his hair over the

---

* English translation by Hanns Hammelmann; the German is not published at the time of writing.

difficulties when Strauss managed to persuade the Intendant of the Court Opera at Stuttgart to accept a world première in their small theatre, with Reinhardt and his Berlin company, with Strauss conducting a hand-picked orchestra of soloists, and with a cast led by Emmy Destinn as Ariadne, Karl Erb as Bacchus, Friede Hempel as Zerbinetta—something of a quality that had never been heard outside Bayreuth. This arrangement was agreed—though in the end none of these singers appeared in the world première, and half the Molière cast was from Stuttgart. The dinner scene in *Le Bourgeois Gentilhomme* with its musical accompaniment was, incidentally, Reinhardt's suggestion, in the course of a meal at which Strauss and Hofmannsthal were both present; Reinhardt maintained that for a composer with Strauss's descriptive gifts a menu for dinner would be a marvellous stimulus. Perhaps he was joking quietly, but Strauss obliged, with suitable musical quotations or descriptions for salmon, hock, mutton, and larks' tongues. Strauss's music was complete in score by 21 July 1912. There were many problems to be solved yet; the literary and musical ones were the least awkward. One of these was the prosaic affair of a public banquet to be held after the première; Hofmannsthal was almost in tears at the prospect of having to mix with Press reporters and Stuttgart Philistines who would all get drunk and call him *Du*, just when he needed to hang on to his precious memories of a beautiful evening. His scruples were respected and he shared a table with intimate friends. Not Strauss, nor Reinhardt: Hofmannsthal was pathologically selective about the company he kept. It is one of his least sympathetic traits.

The rehearsals were stormy. Guest artists were unwelcome in Stuttgart. Ernst Stern, the designer, has retailed in his autobiography the difficulties made by ignorant officials about his settings; when they objected to the pattern of a costume, he was able to embarrass them by proving that it had been carefully designed according to the specific instructions of the spoken play. Every form of intrigue and sabotage was put in the way of this première which, it does not seem to have struck people, would enhance rather than depreciate Stuttgart's artistic credit. When the dress rehearsal came, most of the technical staff had been ordered to officiate at a performance elsewhere in the town, and the resultant improvisation augured unhappily. Destinn was unavailable, but Strauss managed to engage a young soprano whom he had admired in Offenbach's *La Belle Hélène*—Maria Jeritza. Karl Erb could not leave Munich, but Hermann Jadlowker from Vienna was able to sing Bacchus. For the star-part of Zerbinetta none of the glittering coloratura prima donnas could oblige, and the part fell at short notice to Strauss's first Chrysothemis and Feldmarschallin, Margarethe Siems from Dresden—how many Marschallins have been able *afterwards* to perform such a feat? All went well on 25 October, however, and the Press reports were mostly favourable, though the opera fans were bored by the length of the Molière play, and the drama fans by the presence of an opera much longer than they, or Hofmannsthal, had bargained for. Richard Specht, critic of *Der Merker* and later a Strauss biographer, suggested that the Molière should be separated from *Ariadne*, and the latter provided with a sung explanatory Prologue—which had already occurred to Strauss and in due course happened.

It was not wholly public schism that precipitated the second version of *Ariadne*. There were in fact a large number of productions in other cultural centres during the next seven months, one of them in London under Beecham, with Somerset Maugham's translation of the play, Herbert Tree as Jourdain, Eva von der Osten (the first Octavian) as Ariadne, and Hermine Bosetti (Hofmannsthal's first choice) as Zerbinetta. But in most places the management found it appallingly expensive to have to engage a large acting troupe as well as singers for the piece. Few actors and fewer producers were capable of doing justice to this stylistically difficult piece—classical French comedy into the accepted German acting style didn't go. As early as two months after the première Strauss and Hofmannsthal were discussing a revised version of the opera without the play, but with a sung Prologue. By January 1913 Hofmannsthal had the new Prologue in his head: the Composer was now beginning to take a new and commanding place in this scene. By June he had the new Prologue completed; he intended it to be set entirely in *secco* recitative—imagine! Strauss was by now sated with disappointing performances of *Ariadne I*, unwilling to revise it at the moment, but equally sure that the first version was the best, the second a makeshift. Furthermore, he had a musician's deep-rooted antipathy to the idea of drama *about* a musician—an idea always treated falsely or superficially. Hofmannsthal did not press him, and Strauss finished the ballet *Josephslegende* and the opera *Die Frau ohne Schatten* before returning to the *Ariadne* Prologue in April 1916, when he discussed the idea with his colleague Leo Blech in Berlin. Blech put forward the suggestion that the Composer should be regarded as some young prodigy, like Mozart, in his early teens, and should be cast as a soprano part. Hofmannsthal now objected that the Composer must convey an aura of greatness and spirituality and authority—in fact, he meant the Composer as a self-portrait, a memory of 'Loris'. Strauss managed to persuade him that 'since tenors are so dreadful' and baritones wouldn't sing the part, their own Octavian must be the choice; this type of singer is always the most intelligent in any company, and they would have no difficulty in casting the part anywhere.

On May Day Strauss began composing the new Prologue—its text is for the most part identical with that of the equivalent scene in *Ariadne I*. Monsieur Jourdain and Paris have vanished, leaving 'the richest man in Vienna' to command this entertainment. In place of Jourdain's lackeys there is a glacial Major-domo. A short new episode, hardly a scene, finds Zerbinetta flirting with the Composer who, for a moment at least, becomes resigned to the deformation of his *opera seria*. In the opera itself some cuts were made (they will be mentioned in due course), and the ending was altered. Instead of the closing song and dance for Zerbinetta and her partners, after the apotheosis of Bacchus and Ariadne, and then Jourdain's final, wistful speech, the authors gave Zerbinetta a brief, mocking reprise of her rondo, and then a short, concluding boil-up of the love duet. Strauss would have liked the opera to end with a curtain speech by the Composer: this would have rounded off the 'play within a play' element emphasized in the Prologue (as we have it, *Ariadne II* starts by pricking the balloon and then blows it up to full size); on the other hand, it would have obliged the impersonator of the Composer to remain in the theatre for more than an hour after the interval—which star singers would little relish. The conclusion-trying of the collaborators shows how banal and unhelpful any alienation ending must have been, and how right it was to leave Zerbinetta as the representative of reality at the end.

The revised version was complete by 20 June 1916, less than seven weeks after Strauss had begun it. The première was fixed for Vienna where Franz Schalk, as musical director, had given the Court Opera a reputation for fine performances of Richard Strauss's operas. Here was Strauss's original Ariadne, Maria Jeritza, and here the Zerbinetta of his dreams, Selma Kurz. Here too was Marie Gutheil-Schoder, Strauss's favourite Octavian (and Electra!), destined for the part of the Composer. The Intendant of the Opera House, Hans Gregor, was a business man rather than a musician. When the cast-list for the new première was fixed, Gregor perhaps sensed that Gutheil-Schoder might not be pleased with so small a role; he also wanted to bring on a new soprano just arrived from Hamburg. His own explanation was simply that 'a double seam holds more firmly'. At all events he had young Lotte Lehmann coached as understudy to the great Gutheil-Schoder. And so, when the first rehearsal arrived, and Frau Gutheil-Schoder sent her apologies, Gregor suggested that the understudy, who was already in the house for a rehearsal of *Lohengrin*, should sing through the part. Schalk agreed with a bad grace, but Lehmann had hardly sung two phrases before Strauss began to express the greatest interest in her. Next day, Frau Gutheil-Schoder again absented herself; again Fräulein Lehmann sang the part, and by now Strauss was convinced that she was a perfect choice, and must be given the first performance—even in preference to the great star. Lehmann was terrified of arousing her senior colleague's jealousy, and Gregor very nobly bore the burden of her wrath (Gutheil-Schoder later became a fine Composer in the Mannheim première under Furtwängler, according to Strauss).* Lehmann became a Viennese star overnight after the *Ariadne II*

* This première is not included in the list in *ATV*, Vol. 1, p. 577

première on 4 October 1916, and went on to become one of Strauss's greatest interpreters in many roles. In the London première of *Ariadne II* she sang the title role, while that of the Composer fell to Elisabeth Schumann.

By this time Strauss and Hofmannsthal were taking the next logical step, and re-forming *Le Bourgeois Gentilhomme* as a three-act play with Strauss's incidental music, expressly for Reinhardt's Deutsches Theater in Berlin. This ended, of course, with the Turkish Ceremony, not the opera. Strauss composed ten further numbers of incidental music. The Berlin première of *Bourgeois Gentilhomme II* took place in the Deutsches Theater on 9 April 1918; Strauss himself conducted the Vienna production in the Redoutensaal in October 1924. And by this time he had made his concert orchestral suite which has done most to popularize the delightful *Bourgeois Gentilhomme* music. Strauss's Opus 60 consists, therefore, of four items: (*a*) the two-act Molière play followed by *Ariadne I*; (*b*) *Ariadne II* with sung Prologue; (*c*) *Bourgeois II*: the three-act Molière play with incidental music in seventeen numbers; (*d*) the orchestral suite of nine numbers. For the purposes of this operatic study *Ariadne II* is clearly the version to select for description, reference being allowed to musical discrepancies between it and *Ariadne I*.

2

The Prologue has an orchestral introduction that, with its potpourri working of themes, would count as an overture if it did not, at a certain point, audibly begin to move into the action which brings up the curtain and prevents a finite concert-close; this is a loss to concert programmes but a gain to music, since the great quality of this Prologue is its conveyed impression of being written down almost in one breath.

Busy C major, pompous thumps of tonic and dominant in the bass (which will be recalled when the major-domo enters for the second time), and a fiery, typically Straussian theme—referred to in the chapter on *Guntram*—which characterizes the young composer.

1

This is only its first phrase; Ex. 1 grows by repetition until it breaks simultaneously into Ex. 2¹, still connected with the Composer, and Ex. 2² on bassoon and horn which is concerned with Bacchus, and rather recalls the transfiguration theme in *Tod und Verklärung*.

2

The sound of this opening is typical of Strauss's chamber orchestra in *Ariadne*. He has three desks of violins, two each of violas and cellos, and one of basses. He writes individual parts for each desk most of the time, and asks for copious double-stopping, but he uses the whole string force together, in eight individual parts, only once in the whole Prologue. The purpose of this unusual departmentalization is to enable him to subtract rather than add notes and sounds, to thin not thicken the texture. And this helps to make every wind or brass entry tell with real significance. Ex. 1 carries an ambivalent hint of C minor and so the second subject quite logically takes the key of E flat major, and flows majestically forward in Ariadnesque triplets.

3

A hectic babble of semiquavers belongs to the Composer's Music Master, but in the opera to the comedians. There is no point in quoting these phrases because they alter shape all the time, retaining only the characteristic mood of nervous frenzy. They take the music into F major, where the bassoon drops a suggestion of the *commedia dell'arte* troupe and their song-and-dance act.

4

The last of the principal themes to appear is that of the closing love duet, sumptuous and sonorous in D flat major, Strauss's favourite key.

5

When the horn brings back Ex. 2¹ we seem to have started a development section, but this is in fact the point at which the screw turns and drama begins. There are hints at new *commedia dell'arte* themes and at

17 The Major-domo announces his Master's change of plan. *Ariadne auf Naxos* at Glyndebourne, 1953.
Cast from L. to R.: Fritz Ollendorff, Murray Dickie, Kurt Gester, Mattiwilda Dobbs, Richard Lewis,
Sena Jurinač, David Franklin, Sesto Bruscantini, Dorothy Dow, Marjorie Thomas, April Cantelo,
Edna Graham

19
Apparition of the Phantom Lover:
Die Frau ohne Schatten at Munich, 1939

Hermann Bahr, who collaborated with
Strauss for a time on *Intermezzo*

21 The Skat Party in *Intermezzo*, Dresden, 1934

the rhythm of Ex. 9 below, and as the pace grows hotter, up goes the
curtain. It discloses the backstage space of a large drawing-room which
has been fitted up *ad hoc* as a private theatre. There are dressing-room
doors to right and left for the stars of the performance and entrances from
either side. There is a table in the middle of the area—and often a spinet,
though this is a relic of *Ariadne I* in which it is used.

The orchestral activity is on the part of the Music Master, who has just
caught sight of the householder's Major-domo and rushes precipitously
and anxiously towards him so as to find out if rumour rightly says—
though he can hardly trust his ears, even with Ex. 4 on the strings to
encourage or discourage him as the case may be—that his pupil's wonderful *opera seria* is really and truly to be followed by a low farcical entertainment. The words tumble out of him in *secco* recitative, sometimes
accompanied by harmonium continuo (all too rarely audible). The
Major-domo, on the other hand, being Philistine and full of scorn towards
all manifestations of art, speaks his remarks in haughty unaccompanied
prose. He leaves no doubt that his master's wishes alone are worthy of
respect, those of a musical employee, who has moreover already been paid,
completely insignificant. The opera, says the major-domo, will be given,
after it the *opera buffa*, and punctually at nine o'clock both parts of the
spectacle will be finished in time for a grand display of fireworks outside.*
That is obviously that, and so the Major-domo goes on his way, while the
Music Master wonders how on earth he can break the news to (Ex. 1)
his pupil.

Small diversion. A lackey conducts an officer to Zerbinetta's dressing-
room, knocks on his behalf, and is kicked out of the officer's way for his
pains. The servant is pulling himself together when the young Composer
(Ex. 1) walks in, sees him, and asks for the orchestral strings to be
assembled for final rehearsal (noises of tuning-up). The servant answers
with sarcastic rudeness: from his mysterious innuendoes we gather that
the players are providing table-music for milord's dinner party (Ex. 4
with a countersubject). Slightly annoyed, the Composer decides to
rehearse with Ariadne (a hint at Ex. 9), but the servant indicates that he
is unlikely to have much luck, and departs chuckling. There is no response
to the Composer's knock—it is at Zerbinetta's door—and he vents his
indignation on the impudent lackey, only to find a new tune running
irresistibly in his head.

(It is a tune that Strauss had written for the first act of *Le Bourgeois
Gentilhomme*, where it also figures in the overture.)

* When *Ariadne* was given at Glyndebourne in 1962 the audience leaving the opera
house was regaled with just such a firework display—a particularly happy idea.

If only there were time to insert it in his opera, the Composer wishes; he improvises words to the phrases. But more important is to ensure the success of what he *has* written. Bacchus must be reminded that he is a young god, not a conceited tenor puppet. Woodwind and celesta introduce the Bacchus theme.

7

The Composer knocks at Bacchus's door, which is flung open, not for him, but to reject an incompetent wig-maker. The Composer starts to address the tenor, but the door slams noisily again. The Composer is still seeking paper to write down his new song. Out of her dressing-room, much to his surprise, comes Zerbinetta, scantily dressed and chatting with her Officer; and from the other side the Ariadne (harps in her home key of D flat major) taking leave of the Music Master. But the Composer may not enter her dressing-room; his teacher says she is with her *coiffeur*. Zerbinetta is now talking to her Dancing Master, who expresses scorn for the *opera seria*. The Composer asks his teacher who this charming girl may be, and this gives the old man a chance to break the news of the *opera buffa*. The boy is aghast: dances, trills, and provocative jokes to follow *Ariadne*? The dances are suggested by a theme from the overture:

8

and the *opera seria* by a hint at Ex. 11. The Composer is inconsolably infuriated, and berates his Maecenas for creating this bridge from the lofty world of *Ariadne* to the banal one of the audience. Exs. 1, 2^1, and 4, and the hint of Ex. 11, tumble over one another. How can one ever again know inspiration, if this is the result?—and just such an inspiration came to him only a minute or so ago: he sings the new song, Ex. 6, improvising words to it (exactly as in *Le Bourgeois Gentilhomme*), and busily begins to write it down.

The four clowns from Zerbinetta's troupe march drolly out of her dressing-room (curious—were they there when she received her admirer?), and Zerbinetta presents them. They remind the Composer of the undignified fate in store for his masterpiece, and he leaves the room angrily. The Prima Donna comes out of her dressing-room to confer with the Music Master; she too is disgusted to find herself in the company of a low comedy team, the more so since Zerbinetta and the Dancing Master are passing comments on the boredom of the opera, and the most favourable placing of the *buffo* entertainment, bearing in mind the effect of a good dinner on the audience (Strauss quotes here from the Dinner Music in

Le Bourgeois Gentilhomme). The Music Master assures his Prima Donna
that when the performance is finished no one will remember anything but
Ariadne; the orchestra quotes her Hermes theme:*

9

A lackey announces that the party is leaving the dinner table; the
performers must be ready to begin; Ex. 9 and Ex. 4, with quicker
rhythmic counterpoints, portray the hubbub as the actors assemble.
But in great pomp, and with a fanfare of drums, the Major-domo
reappears with an urgent instruction from his master: the two operas,
comic and serious, are to be performed simultaneously, complete with all
their music, so as to finish promptly for the fireworks at 9 p.m. It has
occurred to their employer that this minor adjustment will help to relieve
the depressing effect of an opera set on a desert island. But there is no
time to lose, for the party are even now about to take their seats on the
other side of the curtain.

The Composer regards the idea as not only vulgar but impossible; his
teacher's mention of the fee that will keep him for six months (clinking
coins are suggested by the triangle) does nothing to reconcile him. The
Dancing Master assures them that Zerbinetta, a mistress of improvisation, will have no difficulty in matching her part to the context of *Ariadne*,
if only the Composer will remove some of the more lengthy and dangerously tedious passages (Strauss and Hofmannsthal doubtless aimed this
episode at Schuch, whose cuts were famous). By way of example we hear
Ex. 9 turning very fluently into Ex. 4. The Dancing Master persuades
them to exercise the blue pencil on *Ariadne*; and we have the amusing
spectacle of both Bacchus and Ariadne imploring the Music Master to
abbreviate the other's part—references to Ex. 7, Ex. 9, part of what sounds
like Ex. 10[3] in *Elektra*, and two other themes from the *Ariadne* opera,
Ex. 20 and this one

10

The Dancing Master now explains the plot of *Ariadne* to Zerbinetta,
much to her amusement. His breezy résumé is interrupted by the Composer who tries to convey the higher meaning of Ariadne's longing for
death, her spiritual inability to give her love to more than one man. When
the young god Bacchus comes to claim her (I thought as much, comments
Zerbinetta, ever realistic), she gives herself to him because she believes

* Strauss lifted this bodily from an abandoned Watteau ballet, *L'Enlèvement de
Cythère*.

him to be the messenger of death, and in the act of yielding she dies and is reborn. Exs. 20, 2^2, and 5 are woven together in the Composer's explanation, towards the end of which the strings are given nine independent parts for the only time in the Prologue (and for one bar only!). Zerbinetta's practical common sense, viz. frivolity, is not at all touched by this lofty interpretation; try as the Composer may to show that Ariadne is that rare creature, the woman who never forgets, Zerbinetta can only see another girl waiting for the next boy-friend. And in these bald terms she passes on the action to her fellow-comedians. But the Composer has not yet finished: he takes up his interpretative exposition partly to himself, to a soft and solemn Ex. 9 on the trombone, and Ex. 2^1, new-born in pathos on the bassoon, emphasizing the transfiguration that Ariadne undergoes and through which Bacchus himself is changed from human to divine status. Ex. 5 boils to a grand climax as the Composer's tones grow more and more impassioned: through what other experience, he asks them, can one become a god? Even Zerbinetta is moved to admit that he is talking sense at last. What, in this sublime moment, can Zerbinetta possibly add to his music, he asks in despair.

Very gently she gazes into his eyes, and murmurs that a moment is as nothing to a gaze:* on the stage she plays a coquette, while in her heart she yearns only for the one man to whom she might be eternally faithful —all this in melody and harmony and orchestral texture of intoxicating voluptuousness, so that we, like the Composer, are enchanted by the magic spell of Zerbinetta's sexuality. She leaves him in a state of blissful adoration, lost to the scurry of actors in all directions, and the frantic efforts of the Music Master to convince the Prima Donna that her prestige will not suffer if she consents to appear on the same stage as Zerbinetta. When the old man comes to rouse the boy-genius, he finds him still in a state of exaltation, pouring out an inspired belief in the beauty of the world, and the power of music to raise brave souls of every sort to a loftier seat around the throne. This is, effectively, the climax of the Prologue, one of Strauss's finest inspirations—inspired, it may be added, by just such a rhetorical outburst as he had begged Hofmannsthal to grant him†—and it is worth noting how carefully it has been prepared, from the Composer's first interruptions of the Dancing Master's explanation, through his later solo and the glorious flirtation duet with Zerbinetta to this noble paean which itself induces a recapitulation of the overture. How much one wishes that the Prologue had ended here. Yet the author's purpose was to demonstrate that downs occur as well as the ups in the creative artist's life; and so his last note is interrupted by a shrill whistle from Zerbinetta as she comes running from her room with her fellow-comedians. All the

* There is an untranslatable play on words here: '*ein* Augenblick *ist wenig, ein* Blick *ist viel*'; ['a twinkling of an eye is nothing, but the twinkle is everything'].

† 'Perhaps you know my passion for Schilleresque hymns and Rückertian flourishes' (letter to Hofmannsthal, 27 May 1911).

sublimity has collapsed in the compromise which, as his teacher recalls, he himself permitted in a weak moment. And there is no time to savour his misery for the opera has to begin, and he presumably has to act as *maestro al cembalo*. Away he storms into the orchestra pit, and down comes the curtain.

3

Ariadne figures in Greek mythology as part of the extensive saga of Theseus. She was the daughter of King Minos of Crete, who exacted an annual tribute of youths and maidens from Athens; these boys and girls were sacrificed to the monster, half-man, half-bull, known as Minotaur. Prince Theseus of Athens determined to end this cruel custom and volunteered to go to Crete as one of the sacrificial victims. Ariadne fell in love with him, and in return for his promise to marry her, she helped him to slaughter the Minotaur, and escape with the other Athenians. On their way home to Athens, they stopped at the island of Naxos or Dia in the Aegean Sea, and here Theseus abandoned Ariadne, some say because Bacchus visited him in a dream and demanded Ariadne's hand, others say because he had fallen in love with another girl.* Such is, in essence, the myth on which Hofmannsthal based his drama.

The overture sets the scene for a grief-laden heroine. It is as ambivalently chromatic as the Composer's Ex. 1.

11

The horn very soon adds another theme, belonging to Theseus who abandoned Ariadne.

12

One phrase contributed by woodwind has further bearing on the Theseus–Ariadne relationship.

13

The music quickens and brings back Ex. 10.

The curtain rises to reveal the cave on the island of Naxos. Ariadne, inert, is surrounded by three Nymphs: Naiad, Dryad, and Echo. They

* Mary Renault, in *The King Must Die*, turns her into a craving-drunk Bacchante from whose sight Theseus recoils on the spot, but this is not an Ariadne that Hofmannsthal's readers would recognize.

ask one another if she is still sleeping after her bitter lamentation—a thematic chord-progression.

14

Soon they turn spontaneously into a smooth florid G major trio (reminiscent of Wagner's Rhinemaidens, full of melisma and flowing melody with descant).

15

Ariadne awakes and laments her broken heart and living death.

16

This is her in-turned theme of woe, alternated with another, more positive idea (connected, as will be seen, with Theseus).*

17

One of the Nymphs is Echo, and she repeats the sound of Ariadne's groans. Ex. 16 resumes as Harlequin and Zerbinetta muse disconsolately, but still passively on the lady's grief. Ex. 12 introduces the first of Ariadne's very skilfully linked solos, her recollection of Theseus, *Ein Schönes war*, derived from Ex. 13.

18

Ariadne muses on the Tristanesque dual integration of her love for Theseus (Ex. 17 returns, and Ex. 10). The comedians, in the wings,

---

* In *Ariadne I* Jourdain and Dorante exchanged remarks here. These characters have fallen away, but their remarks are still included in the score (like the Prima Donna's insistence in the Prologue on seeing the no-longer-existing Count Dorante).

conclude that she is mad (*toll*). Ariadne answers that she is *toll* but alive—
the pick-up of remarks here contradicts the idea that it is the opera which
is finite and the comedy improvisatory; we are not to take the premises
of the Prologue seriously! Harlequin, a sympathetic German baritone,
attempts to console her through a song which teaches that the heart can
bear everything, given the will to survive: *Lieben, Hassen, Hoffen, Zagen.*

19

But the comedians are forced to conclude that this serenade was
ineffective. Ariadne begins her principal *scena* with Ex. 9 (*Es gibt ein
Reich*); her mind, distracted, runs on the blessed land of the Dead, so
much purer than this world (the world of Theseus, and Ex. 12). She
awaits Hermes, messenger of Death, who will transform her into one of
his own.

Ariadne takes up and passionately expands Ex. 20 (which owes something, by the way, to Ex. 15), as she begs Hermes to relieve her of the
burden of life—the aria turns the corner to its close with a wonderful fall
from top B flat (surely inspired by Tosca's *Vissi d'arte*).

20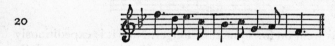

The comedians, as a group, now attempt to alleviate her grief with a
vocal quartet (*Die Dame gibt mit trübem Sinn*). This begins in melancholy
F minor, then brightens into the major with Ex. 4 (*Es gilt, ob Tanzen, ob
Singen tauge*) which is spread out into an extended cheerful fugato.
Zerbinetta also takes part in this, and there are references to Ex. 25
(happy outcome) and to a voluptuous phrase, otherwise insignificant,
from the big coloratura aria into which Zerbinetta now launches. *Grossmächtige Prinzessin* remains, as far as most of us know, the show-stopping
virtuoso coloratura star solo to end all show-stopping virtuoso coloratura
solos. In its original form it flew higher and involved even more hurdles:
for *Ariadne II* Strauss transposed the most fiendish portion, the rondo,
a tone down, and this is usually done even in *Ariadne I* performances; top
F sharps are not to be picked off trees like apples in September. The solo
remains a soprano's ultimate challenge, not least because she has to
appear frivolously gay throughout it. Almost every phrase has become
quotable, like *Hamlet*. But while we goggle aurally at the amazing
accuracy and spirit of the performer, it is also worth paying attention to
Hofmannsthal's words, which further hammer home the message of the
drama. Zerbinetta is aware of Ariadne's plight and is anxious to rationalize

it with examples from her own rich experience of masculine deceit. She
too has been 'translated' by sexual integration, has vowed faithfulness,
and has accepted every new lover as a god (dramatically speaking, from
the opera audience's point of view, she is jumping the gun here). Her
recitative is followed by a fluent cantabile (*Noch glaub' ich dem einen*),
then a florid arioso (*So war es mit Pagliazzo*) of which the two themes
need quoting:

Then having dispatched a spirited cadenza she settles down to a
flouncing rondo, *Als ein Gott kam jeder gegangen*, in Strauss's most
bourgeois, captivating vein.

In *Ariadne I* this went on for some time longer. Now it is expeditiously
halted by Harlequin, who uses Ex. 21² to seduce Zerbinetta as gracefully
and firmly as possible; Zerbinetta's vocal technique wriggles sensationally
with delight. They creep into a quiet corner while the stupider clowns,
in a comic trio, seek Zerbinetta everywhere, partly to independent
material, partly to Ex. 21² (and partly to a waltz very close indeed to the
Mariandel waltz version of Ex. 1 in *Rosenkavalier*). This ensemble was
substantially shortened in *Ariadne II*, but it still pads the structure too
vacuously to sustain complete concentration—it is one of three weak spots
in the piece, for all its liveliness.

A fanfare on the trumpet is heard. The Nymphs return in haste to
announce the approach by ship of a 'charming boy, a young god, Bacchus'
(Ex. 2²); their admiration is further depicted in a new theme, whose
subsequent transformations begin to sound curiously like Lehár.

Ex. 7 is also quoted, and, very prematurely, a part of Ex. 25. The
Nymphs tell us at length about Bacchus's parentage, birth, and upbringing; his credentials are unimpeachable. This is his first excursion into

romance, and the next new tune will be associated with Bacchus's new-found manhood.

24

He has just left the island of Circe (off Terracina below Rome), and is sailing towards Naxos, having survived, by sheer divinity, the evil effect of Circe's magic potion (Wagner's *Tristan* chord makes an appropriate appearance). The ensemble of Nymphs unfolds in thematic melody, very typical in formation. Ariadne comes from her cave, called by the Nymphs. Bacchus stands on the height of a neighbouring cliff, still calling (rather tactlessly) for Circe—to Ex. 7 and then Ex. 24. Ariadne recognizes him as the leader of her destiny, and the Nymphs fall serenely into a thalamic hymn, which we may or may not regard as a good invention.

25

Ariadne hails him with Ex. 20 and with Ex. 23; he is destined and desirable. Bacchus approaches. Strauss makes an enormous and audible cut of a long and sparkling solo for Zerbinetta, and Bacchus appears by Ariadne's cave. Ariadne mistakes him, first of all, for Theseus, but recognizes her error and acclaims him as the longed-for god of death. The Nymphs tactfully withdraw. Ariadne and Bacchus salute one another, solemnly and at cross-purposes—she thinks only of Hermes and Theseus, Exs. 9 and 20, he only of Circe. Gradually their surprise and shyness are reconciled through misunderstanding. Ariadne accepts him as a power for metamorphosis (at last Ex. 3 reappears), and their long voyage seems to begin, by submediant modulation, culminating in ecstatic outpourings of Ex. 5. A canopy descends upon them as the Nymphs, now with Ariadne, repeat their hymn. Zerbinetta comes out and mockingly repeats her philosophy that every god you meet stuns you into acceptance. From behind the canopy Bacchus and Ariadne are heard in rapturous duet. Bacchus and the welling Ex. 5 have the last word, and the opera closes momentously but very briefly in Ariadne's key of D flat major.*

4

It is fascinating to trace the growth of *Ariadne auf Naxos* from the half-hour Intermezzo, which would teach Hofmannsthal rather more about

* In *Ariadne I* Bacchus's last words were followed by an extended reprise of Zerbinetta's rondo, with a dance for her and her partners. In this at least the earlier version has the advantage.

collaborating with a composer, to the two-hour *Ariadne II* in which Strauss sailed off on a new tack and Hofmannsthal obviously felt he had justified his existence and his immortality. And then to sit back and consider just what *Ariadne* is for, and how far it justifies Hofmannsthal's confidence.

Hofmannsthal took his job as Strauss's librettist quite seriously; he thought continually about what makes a great opera libretto great, and among his required reading was Da Ponte. I would not be surprised if *Ariadne* was inspired by Hofmannsthal pondering on the balance of serious and comic, formal and uninhibited elements in *Don Giovanni* and perhaps *Figaro*, then on the two art-forms, *opera seria* and *opera buffa* that are married in heaven by these great works, and thence to the bland confrontation of both elements as a technical experiment. The Ariadne and Bacchus story allowed him to develop his favourite idea of constancy, and to explain how a one-man woman could submit to another man's embraces. But the collaboration of the *buffo* comedians helped him to present this theme with a diversity and formal compartmentalization that he regarded as suitable for music—and desirable for a composer who favoured the symphonic architecture that was always in danger of reshaping (and therefore spoiling) the librettist's careful plan. Hofmannsthal was often reminding Strauss that no other author of comparable distinction was so unselfish as to work actively with an opera composer; and of *Ariadne* he declared that the whole project was designed simply as a vehicle for Strauss's music, to give the composer pleasure. But already he had evidence that Strauss was bored with the whole idea; Strauss drew inspiration from real people and their human predicaments, especially of the mind, and these do not occur at all in *Ariadne* where the characters are dummies of the ventriloquist Hofmannsthal. The purpose of *Ariadne* was quite selfish: to project a literary idea which was taking hold of the poet's imagination, and to force the composer into a subservient role so that the beauties of the poetry would not be lost. When Strauss gave prime emphasis to Zerbinetta (because she would enliven the music of an otherwise dreary and artificial piece) Hofmannsthal may have realized that *Ariadne* could become a telling allegory of their artistic collaboration: Hugo von Ariadne living alone on his creative island, awaiting the transfiguration of an idea; Zerbinetta-Strauss deriving pleasure and satisfaction from such lowly stimuli as Savonarola and Rückert—and the two united only through mutual incomprehension. This, at least, is my interpretation; if it is true it explains why Hofmannsthal so continually and peevishly attacked Strauss for not appreciating *Ariadne* as a serious work of art.

The idea behind *Ariadne* is a very fine one. So is the theme of *Die Frau ohne Schatten*, but that is presented in a much more direct, human fashion (even allowing for symbolism and magic): the *Ariadne* idea, on the other hand, is wrapped up inside a polythene cover of rococo conceits and pretty *chi-chi*. These should not cloud the perceptibility of the meaning; and yet the meaning is clouded—for ordinary opera-goers, as for the composer when he first read the libretto—by the hot air which gets through the cracks in the polythene and renders the inside surface of the envelope opaque. Hofmannsthal had accordingly to explain himself to Strauss in his famous letter of July 1911, and at Strauss's request enlarged and rephrased this for publication at the time of the Stuttgart première. His article, published in the *Neues Tageblatt* on 12 October 1912, is of high importance to an understanding of *Ariadne*, and some of the more pertinent paragraphs are here given in an English translation:

'You ask me the meaning of the transformation which Ariadne under-goes in Bacchus's arms, because you feel that here is the vital moment, not only for Ariadne and Bacchus, but for the whole work. . . . Transformation is the life of life itself, the real mystery of Nature as creative force. Permanence is numbness and death. Whoever wants to live must surpass himself, must transform himself: he has to forget. And yet all human merit is linked with permanence, unforgetfulness, constancy. This is one of the deep fundamental paradoxes on which existence is constructed, like the temple at Delphi on its yawning crevasse. . . . So here we have Ariadne confronting Zerbinetta, as once Electra confronted Chrysothemis. Chrysothemis wanted to live, nothing more; and she knew that anyone who wants to live must forget. Electra cannot forget. How could the two sisters understand one another? Zerbinetta is in her element when she is careering from one man to another; but Ariadne could only be one man's wife, can only be one man's relict. She tears her garment; it is the gesture of those who want to escape from the world. This is the end of all things, she says, and it is as sad, though not as final, as much said by Electra, for whom Clytemnestra's bedchamber is the world, and the world is Clytemnestra's bedchamber. For Electra nothing remains but death; but here the subject is taken further. Ariadne too imagines she yields herself to Death; and "her boat sinks, only to float on new seas". This is transformation, miracle of miracles, the true secret of love. The unfathomable depths of our nature, the bond between us and something unidentifiable, everlasting, which from our childhood, and even from the time before birth, was close within us, may shut from within and leave us lastingly, detrimentally paralysed; shortly before Death, we anticipate, they will re-open: something of the kind, though it can hardly be put into words, is revealed in the minutes which precede the death of Electra. But in a being not so marked out by fate, a gentler force than death will also unlock these depths; love permeates that being; if love takes hold with its full power, then the utmost depths are released from paralysis: the world is restored to this person, yes he can conjure up a vision of the world even magically as here and hereafter simultaneously.

When Ariadne sees before her transfigured self that the cave of her sorrows has been changed into a temple of joy, when her mother's eyes gaze at her out of Bacchus's cloak and the island turns from a prison into a Paradise—what does she realize but that she is in love and alive?

'She was dead and is alive again, her soul is in truth transformed—and of course it is truth at a higher level, so how could it be truth to Zerbinetta and her like? These vulgar life-masks see in Ariadne's experience precisely what they are capable of seeing: the exchange of a new lover for an old. And so the two spiritual worlds are ironically connected in the end, by the only possible connexion: incomprehension. . . .

'Bacchus is a counterpart of the vulgar mask of Harlequin, as Ariadne is a counterpart of Zerbinetta. Harlequin is pure Nature, soulless and without destiny, though he is a man; Bacchus is a boy and full of destiny. Harlequin is anyone, Bacchus is unique, a god on the way to his divinity.'

There is much more, and it is beautifully expressed, though the transcendental terms wilt in translation, and may nowadays be thought unhelpful in any case. *Ariadne* is popular today because of its stylized presentation of a strongly committed idea: this is particularly so of *Ariadne II* where we have the added attraction of a dynamic, realistic Prologue to contrast with the static, formalized opera. We grasp the existence, if no more, of an ambivalence between Ariadne and Zerbinetta, Bacchus and Harlequin, perhaps even Bacchus and the Composer (young men on the way to a rich destiny). But if we survey Strauss's whole achievement we may incline to place the *Ariadne* opera, at least, lower than Hofmannsthal would have liked. The music of the three Nymphs plays gracefully on the surface of euphony, but it is not very strong, even for its dramatic context; the clown music is at its best in *Es gibt noch Tanzen* where the rondo-like thematic entries preserve their freshness right to the end, and in Harlequin's pretty solo *Lieben, Hassen*, and of course in Zerbinetta's show-stopper. The final duet of Bacchus and Ariadne is a lengthy failure: their mutual misunderstanding is effectively conveyed by bitonality (D flat and A major, for the most part, but more generally the contrast of a flat key and a sharp key), and the scene goes on its way to a primitive but decidedly intriguing scale-tune (Ex. 5); but there are signs that Strauss was working at less than full inspirational stretch here. He did not find much stimulus in the 'amphora' tenor of his day. For the transfiguration or metamorphosis music he fell back on the mysterious tinkling of the Rose Presentation in *Rosenkavalier*, and on a bombastic bulldozing texture that hopes to transport the listener by sheer force, though it usually sounds no more than a wilful uglification of the chamber-orchestral sound which is so imaginatively used elsewhere. If the serious part of *Ariadne* comes off, it is because Ariadne's solos—*Wo war ich?*; *Ein Schönes war*; *Es gibt ein Reich*—are all noble and ardently imagined in music. It is an opera of considerable charm, and makes a

significant contribution to the twentieth-century development of chamber
opera. But in the tale of Strauss's fifteen operas it makes a less progressive
step, and if I have called it the crucial work in Strauss's collaboration with
Hofmannsthal, this is because with the completion of the Prologue Strauss
declared himself won over to the cause, so inimical to his fruitful development, which Hofmannsthal had been urging upon him: 'Your cry of pain
against Wagnerian music manufacture has gone deep into my heart and
has pushed open the door to a quite new landscape in which, led by
Ariadne, especially the new Prologue, I hope to make my way along the
path of an entirely un-Wagnerian opera of action, mood, and humanity.
I now see the way clearly before me, and thank you for opening my
eyes . . . I promise you, that I have now cast off the whole musical
armour of Wagner for ever.'

Strauss had yielded supremacy to his reactionary co-author. He was
giving hostages to old age; he was fifty-two.

Die Frau ohne Schatten

OPUS 65

Opera in Three Acts

LIBRETTO BY HUGO VON HOFMANNSTHAL

The Emperor	TENOR
The Empress, his Wife	SOPRANO
The Nurse	MEZZO-SOPRANO
A Spirit Messenger	BARITONE
The Guardian of the Threshold	SOPRANO OR COUNTER TENOR
Apparition of a Youth	TENOR
The Voice of the Falcon	SOPRANO
The Voice from Above	CONTRALTO
Barak, the Dyer	BASS-BARITONE
His Wife	SOPRANO
The One-Eyed	BUFFO BASS
The One-Armed } *brothers of Barak*	BASS
The Hunchback	TENOR
Six Children's Voices	THREE SOPRANOS, THREE CONTRALTOS
Voices of the Nightwatchmen	THREE BASSES

I

Mention was made in the previous chapter of the more or less simultaneous conception by Hofmannsthal of *Ariadne auf Naxos* and *Die Frau ohne Schatten*, the former designed as an Intermezzo for his better understanding of words written for music. The first intimations of the new three-act opera are to be found in Hofmannsthal's notebook, dated 26 February 1911:

'The Woman without a shadow, a fantastic play. The Empress, a fairy's daughter, is childless. She obtains a stranger's child. In the end she gives it back to its real mother ("only by transcending").* The second couple (as against the Emperor and Empress) are Harlequin and Esmeraldina. She wants to remain beautiful. He clumsy and good. She gives up her child to a wicked fairy disguised as a fishwife; the shadow as a bonus.'

Hofmannsthal set this fairy-tale idea before Strauss to find out whether it should be an opera or a play with incidental music: 'it stands', he wrote, 'in general terms, to *Zauberflöte* as *Rosenkavalier* does to *Figaro*; that is to say that mimicry is intended in neither case, but only a certain analogy.' The whole thing would be highly colourful, 'palace and hovel, priests, ships, torches, rocky passes, choruses, children—it all hovers with real power before my eyes and even disturbs me at work and has quite pushed the other project, *Das stienerne Herz*, out of my mind because it is so much more bright and joyful.'

Strauss and Hofmannsthal accordingly met in Vienna on 31 March to discuss the plan. Hofmannsthal had at first intended Harlequin and Esmeralda (again the *commedia dell'arte* characters, so unappealing to Strauss's realism and humanity) to talk in broad Viennese dialect. During the conference they decided, according to Hofmannsthal's diary, 'that both couples would be treated in the same style, in poetic speech (*höhere Sprache*): instead of Harlequin and Esmeralda, or the Viennese tailor and his pretty discontented wife, appeared the Dyer and the Dyer's wife'.

It was not for another six years that these bright and fruitful ideas were transformed into *Die Frau ohne Schatten*.

The long period of gestation was partly due to Hofmannsthal's particular creative mind, which worked well only at certain times and seasons, and partly to the complexity of the subject. He stated elsewhere that for him artistic creation meant 'the scrupulous transference of one's whole personality into another world'; the world of *Die Frau ohne Schatten* is a vast and multifarious one, hard for us to comprehend in all its complexity, and how much more difficult for its creator to expound *ab initio* logically

---

* An allusion to the Goethe couplet quoted as motto for the opera (p. 174).

and lucidly. Hofmannsthal had again and again to beg Strauss for patience. During the summer of 1912 he worked out much of the dramatic detail on a walk in Gastein with his friend Rudolph von Bodenhausen. In September 1912 Hofmannsthal could at last claim that he now 'owned' the subject, 'joint for joint, scene for scene, every transition, every build-up (*Steigerung*), all as an entity and yet in detail to the point where I can really say, "this is safe".' But he was not yet ready to set the libretto on paper. During March and April, Strauss and Hofmannsthal spent several days together driving through Italy, discussing *Die Frau ohne Schatten* in greatest detail. In the following autumn (Hofmannsthal's most creative season) he wrote the first act, and also began the long short story which bears the same title. The libretto of the first two acts was complete and in Strauss's possession, and the last act had been fully sketched, before the declaration of the First World War retarded progress: 'Hail our brave troops; hail our great German Fatherland,' the poet wrote at the end of the sketch. Hofmannsthal was given a diplomatic post which obliged him to travel much, occupied the greater part of his energies, and left little time for literary creation. He was only able to resume work on the third act in January 1915 and completed it in the following April. The two collaborators were simultaneously preparing the revised version of *Ariadne auf Naxos*, and Strauss did not finish composing the third act until September 1916. In June of the following year the scoring was completed.

Hofmannsthal had made up his mind that so large and scenically demanding a work would be impossible to produce during wartime. They laid *Die Frau ohne Schatten* aside until peacetime, and Strauss began work with Hermann Bahr on *Intermezzo*, and with Hofmannsthal on *Bourgeois II*. Meanwhile the authors did consider where they might best turn for a première of *Die Frau ohne Schatten*. Munich seemed the best idea from the point of view of an enlightened and intelligent audience. But when in May 1918 it seemed possible that Strauss might be invited to become co-director of the Vienna Opera, together with Franz Schalk, and replacing Hans Gregor, the Austrian capital took first claim. Strauss signed the contract in September 1918, and the appointment was made public on May Day 1919. The Vienna Opera, now a State institution, had suffered badly from the material effects of the war, and had come down to once-weekly performances, matinées at that. Strauss entered on his appointment as artistic director, with Schalk as chief conductor, and began to draw up elaborate and ambitious plans. These involved a large and exciting repertory—it was particularly stipulated that Strauss should conduct not only his own works. The first major première was Pfitzner's *Palestrina* which had been given in Munich two years earlier. Emperor Franz Joseph's name day, 4 October, was customarily set aside for important novelties, and in 1919 it was automatically assigned to *Die Frau ohne Schatten*, but the première was eventually put back to 10 October, the first great evening of the post-war Vienna Opera. Franz Schalk conducted. The highly distinguished cast included Maria Jeritza as the Empress, Lotte Lehmann as the Dyer's wife, Aagard Oestvig as the Emperor, Richard Mayr as Barak, and Lucie Weidt as the Nurse. Alfred Roller, the scenic designer, fell surprisingly short in realizing the magical effects which abound in the piece; indeed, in post-war conditions, no German or Austrian opera house was yet able to do these justice. Roller had, however, made a careful prompt-book with Hofmannsthal and the producer Hans Breuer* whom Hofmannsthal declared 'mimically very gifted' (Breuer had been a celebrated Mime in The Ring, was a pun intended here?). The production was enthusiastically received; for the first time in Strauss's career the critics were all favourably impressed. But the productions elsewhere, which followed fairly quickly considering the difficulties involved, were poorly staged or poorly cast; the German première at Dresden under Fritz Reiner was particularly unhappy, due to political intrigue as well as unsatisfactory casting and designs—it almost ended the long association between Strauss and Dresden. Since that time, new productions have usually been historic events. The great operatic public has, as Hofmannsthal and Strauss foretold, taken a long time to accept an opera so thoughtful in content, though many musicians agree with the authors that this is the finest and most inventive of all their joint works.

2

Hofmannsthal and Strauss both realized that listeners to this opera must not come unprepared; it expounds an extremely delicate and searching philosophy of human life expressed through a complex system of symbols. We have seen the protracted thought that Hofmannsthal put into the libretto. Strauss's task was to support and clarify the text, never allowing music to obscure or confuse its motivation or progress. His musical presentation of this world of ideas is remarkably consistent. The action, it will soon become clear, moves on three planes: the spirit world of Keikobad and his slaves, of the Falcon and of the Unborn Children whose voices call to their parents; the human world of Barak, his wife and brothers; and a vaguer intervening plane of existence inhabited on different levels by the Emperor and his wife, who are linked with the upper and lower spheres through the malevolent machinations of the Nurse (Die Amme), and who must show themselves worthy of one world or another in the course of the drama. Strauss's thematic language distinguishes carefully between these worlds and their relationship; the more human a character is, the more his music emphasizes the interval of a

* Strauss wrongly remembered (BUE) the producer as Wilhelm von Wymetal, with whom Roller categorically refused to work.

third; thus the Dyer's brothers, entirely human, are first characterized by
a theme consisting purely of major thirds (Ex. 11). Magic, the unworldly
and the spirits are pointed by emphasis on the intervals of the fourth;
thus the motif which seems to refer to magic and metamorphosis consists
of rising fourths, perfect, augmented, and diminished (Ex. 5); Keikobad,
ruler of the spirits, is represented by a phrase (Ex. 1) which spans a
fourth, but which includes a third, presumably because Keikobad also
rules humanity; the motif in which perfect fourths are most strongly
presented is Ex. 4, which refers to the shadow (as the symbol of parent-
hood) or its absence, with special reference to the Empress whose quest
for a shadow is the subject of the opera—and this may be because it is
the absence of a shadow which holds the Empress to the spirit world,
while the ability to bear children raises humanity above the bounds of
materialism and the earthly span. By placing such emphasis on the
various planes of existence (Strauss furthered this by using a chamber
orchestra to accompany the spirits, full orchestra for mankind, and
soloists from the large orchestra for the Nurse who links the two worlds)
Strauss makes the world of *Die Frau ohne Schatten* more clearly perceptible, and he is assured of a sharp thematic perspective when he reaches
his own musical commentary in the purely orchestral sections. It should
be stressed again that in *Die Frau ohne Schatten* as elsewhere the themes
are not always definitely associated with set persons, but rather with states
of mind or action—this will be made more clear as the plot unfolds.

Hofmannsthal summed up the principle of the opera in a quotation
from Goethe:

> *Von dem Gesetz das alle Wesen bindet*
> *Befreit der Mensch sich der es überwindet.*

(Man frees himself from the law that binds all existence by transcending it.)

The Empress attains humanity, not by persuading a woman to part
with the shadow that she in her wilful discontent does not require, but
by realizing that human consideration for other people (i.e. the community) is more important than selfish happiness, and so being willing to
sacrifice herself and her husband for two other not apparently superior
persons. In doing so she frees them as well as herself and her husband.

Hofmannsthal sets the action in the South Eastern Islands. The region
is apparently one merely suitable to an exotic fairy-story, but the narration
involves various names, customs, and traditions peculiar to certain speci-
fiable Eastern cultures: thus Barak is Arabian, Keikobad and the identification of unborn children with flying fishes are Persian. Hofmannsthal
took his ideas from Goethe's *Hafiz* poems, Rückert's translation of *Saadi*,
from the *Arabian Nights*, and no doubt from dozens of other sources. By
mingling the traditions and mythology of different places Hofmannsthal

prevents later commentators from too definitely fixing a time or place for the action.

The preliminary argument is as follows: the Emperor of the South Eastern Islands devoted his time to falconry; one day, while hunting with his favourite falcon, he captured a gazelle which sank to the ground beneath the Falcon's claws, and was transformed into a woman. She was the daughter of Keikobad, Ruler of the Spirit World. Her mother had a penchant for humanity; her father had given her the power, by means of a Talisman, to change herself into whatever shape she chose. She won the Emperor's love and became his Empress, but his pride and noble upbringing caused him to keep her apart from the world in a palace where the roles of day and night were reversed. By night they lay in one another's arms, in a union that, being purely selfish and sensual, was not blessed with children and so did not band them with the rest of humanity. By day the Emperor pursued the chase while the Empress stayed in the palace, forbidden to be seen by anyone but her guardian or Nurse, a deliberately ambivalent character, partly daemonic, partly grotesque, who hated mankind and willed its ruin. When the Emperor won Keikobad's daughter her Talisman was seized by the Falcon, who disappeared and did not return. As a result the Empress lost her power of metamorphosis (the symbol of her place in the spirit world), but she remained a transparent being, a source of light who casts no shadow. Without the shadow she could not become a mother, which is to say a participant member of the human race. Mythological lore declares that the man who marries a peri must turn to stone if he does not within twelve moons turn his wife into a childbearing woman. The Nurse, who was naturally malevolent although not maleficently powerful, longed that her charge might preserve her spiritual transparency and return to the Kingdom of Spirits. Each month at the new moon a Messenger came from Keikobad asking the Nurse for news of the shadow. The action of the opera begins on the coming of the twelfth moon.

3

The overture, inasmuch as there is one, consists of a single sinister and heavy phrase enunciated three times by tenor and bass tubas against dark, low-pitched wind and brass chords. The theme belongs to Keikobad, Ruler of the Spirits.

1   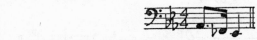

At once the curtain rises to disclose the Nurse crouching in the darkness on a flat roof in the Emperor's palace, outside the bedroom of the

Emperor and Empress. The Nurse is represented by a more angular and ambiguous theme.

2

The dark sound yields to light as the Nurse notices a glimmer on the water below, senses the presence of her master and bows before the apparition which materializes out of the darkness.

3

It is not Keikobad but his Messenger; the twelfth Messenger for the twelfth moon since the Emperor captured his fairy bride. His message is brief: does the Empress cast a shadow? (*Wirft sie einen Schatten?*)—the orchestra announces the Shadow theme. It is really a theme of Shadowlessness, and refers also to the Empress.

4

None, answers the Nurse; light passes through her body as if she were glass. The Messenger chides her for allowing the girl to be stolen away. But, answers the Nurse, how could she follow a bird or a gazelle?—if only Keikobad had not given his daughter the gift of metamorphosis. The Shadow theme takes on a distorted form, associated with magic and transformation.

5

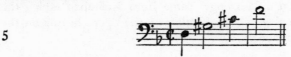

Keikobad's daughter, she tells the Messenger, is now indoors, lying, as every night, in the arms of the Emperor who is a huntsman and a lover and nothing further (we take it that he is not bothered by imperial duties of State). They refer to the Emperor always as Him. He is characterized by two themes: the first, introduced by solo viola, in duet form with Ex. 4 on solo violin, represents the Lover, and the unfruitful (therefore unhuman) love that he makes to her.

6

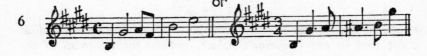

The Messenger announces that the Empress has three days in which to acquire a Shadow. Failing this she will be returned, with the Nurse (who is delighted at the prospect), to Keikobad's domain. As for the fate of the Emperor he will, according to an old folk-tradition, be turned to stone.

7
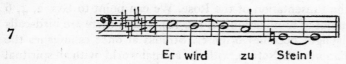

This grim edict is announced below a variant of Ex. 2 suggestive of the disaster for which the Nurse longs. The Messenger vanishes and almost at once the Emperor himself, young and handsome in his hunting uniform, steps on to the balcony as dawn begins to break. He is accompanied by fragments of Exs. 6 and 7, now in the forefront of the Nurse's mind. The Emperor is going out hunting in hope of finding his favourite falcon again. A weird chord and descriptive hoarse cry portray the bird.

.8

The Emperor describes how he captured the gazelle which turned into a woman, and the orchestra breaks passionately into a lyrical tune which has gradually been built up during his narration, a theme associated with the Emperor as huntsman and lover—for him both pursuits are the same.

9

Now he will hunt for three days while the Nurse must guard his wife and tell her that for him she is the prey above all prey; we hear on the horn the theme associated with prey and the other object of the chase.

10

Ex. 9 surges up as the Emperor departs. The Nurse and the Stone theme remain behind, as well as some of the Emperor's servants who are dispatched summarily. The Nurse hears the Empress stirring in the bedroom; the orchestra heralds her entrance with a miraculous orchestral passage, surpassing in transparent brilliance and delicacy all the miracles of *Salome* or the Presentation of the Rose. We can point to Exs. 2, 4, 6 (inverted, a symbol of humiliation, cf. Ex. 12), and 8; there are bird-calls too, and the daylight becomes brighter. Strauss at once establishes the Empress's affiliation with Nature, with the animal world, with all spiritual beings as opalescent as the high, crystalline tessitura of her initial vocal music. She longs to recover her gift of metamorphosis, to fly again with the birds; and she bewails her loss of the Talisman. Then in the sky she sees a falcon hovering; it is the lost red Falcon, still bleeding and still weeping. She calls to it, and can understand the Falcon's answer: How should I not weep? The woman casts no shadow and the Emperor must turn to stone! It is a curse, the Empress now remembers, which was written on her lost Talisman. The Falcon's voice recedes into the distance.

The Empress implores the Nurse to help her find the shadow. The Nurse explains the Emperor's guilt in presuming to change his peri-bride into a woman, and the meaning of shadowlessness which is infertility and for which he, not she, must pay: a shadow may possibly be found and bought, but only by searching for it in the foetid, lethal world of mankind. We hear the theme which will chiefly be used for Barak's brothers.

11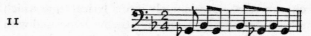

The two of them must descend to the world of mankind and live among men while the Emperor is away. We hear a new theme, connected with the necessity for the peri-Empress to demean herself—a mythological tradition in the East, but also a feature of Western fairy-stories.

12

The Emperor's Hunting theme breaks out again as the Empress declares herself undismayed. The Nurse takes up her words ('a new day dawns') and reveals her scorn for the race of men in a long solo. At the climax (*Der Tag ist da*) a new, drooping phrase enters—it has been much heralded in previous developments—and now mingles with the Nurse's Ex. 2 which is plainly concerned with malevolence against humanity. Its associations are with the dull, banal, unpleasant life of humanity in the Daytime of Mankind.

The Empress's voice joins that of the Nurse, and the two descend to earth below, while the orchestra describes their flight, developing Exs. 1, 13, 6, 9, 7, 12, 8, 6 in that order. Just after the main appearance of the Stone theme, Ex. 11 begins to toll out on two of the orchestra's five Chinese gongs, and this dinning becomes more insistent and rapid until the curtain is lifted again upon the world of men, humble impoverished men—the hut of Barak, the poor, good-hearted, industrious Dyer, a simple, squalid abode hung round with the implements and fruits of his toil—as indicated in Barak's Artisan theme.

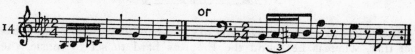

Barak lives with his three brothers as well as his wife. At curtain-rise the One-Eyed brother is sitting on the One-Armed brother, trying to throttle him. The third, Hunchbacked, brother tries to separate them. Barak's wife finds a bucket of water and throws it over them, whereupon they turn and abuse her as a discontented inhospitable shrew. The oboes portray these delightful characteristics with a vital new theme; it concerns not so much Mrs Barak as the discontent which devours her.

Barak appears in the doorway and sends the lads to work outside; he turns to stack up a pile of skins for dyeing, and his tribulations are hinted at in a fragment of tune on the oboe.

When the wife calls for the immediate removal of Barak's brothers, he reminds her (*Kinder waren sie einmal*) that they were once children, and we hear the theme later to be associated with the Unborn Children (it contains the Keikobad rhythm, and its corollary shows a 'contented' variant of the theme that portrays the wife's discontent).

The bracket equals Ex. 19 inverted.

Barak asks when his wife will replace the brothers with children of her own: Strauss brings back the love theme, Ex. 6, associated with the Emperor and his unfruitful loving. Barak is answered by Ex. 15, Ex. 6, and a shrewish outburst. (Hofmannsthal had, at the outset, suggested that Pauline Strauss should serve, strictly between themselves, as the model for the Dyer's wife.) In a duet he meets her nagging and self-justification with quiet resignation (Ex. 15 is combined very tellingly with the alternative part of Ex. 13, and Keikobad's Ex. 1 is mixed with the rhythmically similar Ex. 17—since children are sent to us by Keikobad). Barak's simple goodness shines out as he kneels down to work again in a radiant D major orchestral comment.

18

Strauss was presumably referring to this when he wrote to Hofmannsthal that, whereas he found the Empress hard to set to music, the character of Barak was succeeding well (*sehr gelungen*). Barak, as we shall see, has some of the most eloquent music in the whole opera—and it is interesting to compare this character with that earlier Good Man, Jokanaan in *Salome*, who gave Strauss so much trouble, and who now seems by contrast so much less lifelike and dramatically positive. His wife quietly and sullenly answers that in three and a half years of marriage she has steeled herself to avoid motherhood (Ex. 4, fragment marked x—an inversion of Ex. 17); now he must steel himself to abstain from wanting children (Ex. 16). His resigned, sad reply refers only to the blessing which must come out of her hard and arrogant words. A grand, lyrical and expansive melody associated with Barak's patience is set in one of Strauss's most human and favourite keys, D flat major, lengthened in a warm orchestral comment from Strauss, the family man.

19

Fragment y shows a built-in allusion to the inversion of Ex. 17, already remarked in Ex. 4. The fragment x will subsequently have to do with the Empress's anxieties for Barak's future happiness. The extension of Ex. 19 makes copious reference to Ex. 17 in its upright form. The wife makes a sour comment (Ex. 15), and Barak, wares on his back, trudges off to the market, singing a snatch of a folk-like song.

Immediately the music revives the magical flight motifs, and particularly that of the Empress's self-demeaning (Ex. 12); Nurse and Empress, in serving-maid's clothes, are suddenly and magically present in the dingy room. The Dyer's wife asks, with some surprise, the purpose of their visit and a new fortissimo unison theme on wind and strings answers: to make her sell her shadow.

20

The Nurse tries to pretend that she takes Mrs Barak for a princess, kisses her feet, and extols her beauty. On being assured that this is the Dyer's wife (Exs. 15 and 7 tell us that she is an ideal person to save the Emperor), the Nurse loads her with further flattery worthy of an Oriental trader, and the Empress longs to kiss the Shadow that she casts (as well as the Shadow part of Ex. 4, two horns softly and stonily intone Ex. 7). Must this exquisite beauty bear children (like those cripples associated with Ex. 11), asks the Nurse? The Dyer's wife takes all this for cruel sarcasm, and weeps while the Nurse whispers, rather louder than necessary, that alas their visit is fruitless; the woman knows the Secret —her vocal line here traces the bass of a theme to be associated with the Mystery, the ordeal which is the subject of the third act.

21

The Dyer's wife overhears, as intended, and asks to know more. She learns that she can sell her shadow, and bargain for unthinkable delights and riches and power. The theme of the Bargain, Ex. 22, is connected with the Shadow, of course (Ex. 4), and with the theme of Unfruitful Love (Ex. 6).

and

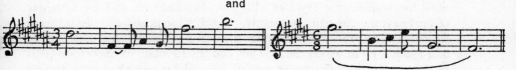

I quote two alternative forms of the theme; the second is heard almost at once, just after the Shadow theme has been put into two keys at once, thus showing that Mrs Barak's own is at present worthless to her. The Nurse assures her that such things fetch high prices, and she conjures visions of jewels and other luxuries, including servants, to tempt the Dyer's wife with sensuous bliss. The wife appears richly but scantily clothed, surrounded by slaves and a phantom lover. They vanish into thin air before long. The Dyer's wife, now returned to her rags, asks how she could attain this luxury, and how to sell her shadow; the Nurse asks if she regrets that she has brought no little Dyers into the world. The wife denies this with the Discontent theme, and the Nurse states the terms of the barter: *Abzutun Mutterschaft auf ewige Zeiten*—Renounce motherhood for ever (here is the full Renunciation theme, Ex. 20). The bargain will take three days to complete, during which time the two visitors will dwell as serving-maids (Ex. 12) in the hut here, after which the Shadow changes owners, and Mrs Barak enters upon a life of gracious leisure. She now hears Barak returning; he will need supper and his bed. The Nurse relieves her of these duties, conjuring with supernatural assistance (Ex. 1) five little fishes from the air into the frying-pan, and magically dividing Barak's bed into two separately disposed parts, before she and the Empress depart to the tune of Ex. 17, that of Unborn Children. These now raise their voices (with Ex. 16) from inside the frying-pan where, incarnated as fish, they are frying. They call on their mother to let them into the house; she is tormented by their voices and her own guilt (the two are of course identical, though the orchestra uses Ex. 15 to express the latter). The theme of the children, preying on the wife's mind, accompanies Barak as he returns from market. He is shown his supper and his bed, and his wife tells him of the two servants who are to join their household. Even at this news he does not complain (we hear the theme of his contentment), though in his suppressed anxiety he has lost his appetite. In the distance are heard the voices of the watchmen in the street singing a solemn and sonorous hymn in which they exhort couples to love one another and praise love's work. Barak sighs and lies down to lonely rest. The curtain falls.

4

The trials are in progress, says Hofmannsthal in his synopsis; for all four must be cleansed, the Dyer and his wife, the Emperor and the daughter of the fairy; the one pair too earthly, the other too proud and distant from the earth. The process is musically expressed as the development section of a symphony in which the first act had the function of exposition (first in the upper then the lower world). It will be remarked that a great profusion of thematic material has been presented in this act; the developmental nature of Acts 2 and 3 is confirmed by their thematic dependence on these now familiar phrases; only half a dozen new themes remain to be presented.

We are again in the house* of the discontented wife, so the orchestra

---

* Hofmannsthal's original intention was to place this scene in the same setting as the previous one; Clemens Krauss was responsible for the tradition of setting it outside Barak's house.

reminds us, the house of unfruitful love where the wife dreams only of her phantom lover.

23

Barak is making ready for the market, helped by the Empress, now in the garb of a servant; the Nurse kneeling before him tells him to return soon. On his departure she begins to tempt the wife, whose hair is now adorned with pearls, offering to summon her phantom lover; but the wife wants no lover, though the Nurse insists he is in her thoughts. To themes of Keikobad, herself, and the lover, the Nurse seizes a broom and kettle, and conjures from the shape of the one and the voice of the other this Phantom Lover (see Plate 19: *Er und der Gleiche*—The very one, says Barak's discontented wife, and yet not he). The Nurse and an invisible chorus coax the wife to be unfaithful to her husband; the Empress, aware that she is doing wrong, is anxious lest Barak return and meet Keikobad's spectral slave, so much his opposite. Her pangs of conscience are expressed in a touching melodious phrase.

24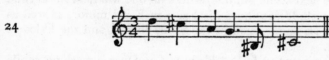

Barak does return, to Ex. 14, but not before the Nurse has spirited everything away. Barak has done well at market and is surrounded by a horde of begging children as well as his three brothers who are looking forward to a large meal; their ensemble is based on a cheerful variant of Ex. 16. His wife chides him tearfully, but he tells the company to take no notice, though we know that his heart is increasingly heavy, and he senses that someone is appealing to him for help. He gives the Empress some of the food that the others are gobbling up, and offers some to his wife, but she turns on him again, declaring that she prefers to nourish the bitterness in her mouth, not to sweeten it with the sweetmeats he offers. Strauss gives a new theme to Bitterness.

25

All express their various feelings in an ensemble which ends the scene; Barak's Exs. 14 and 16 and his wife's Ex. 25 being prominent. The ensuing Intermezzo takes up the Barak themes, then sinks on to a D major cadence which is broken by the harsh cry of the unhappy Emperor's Falcon. We have returned to the fourth and most doom-laden of the candidates destined for Keikobad's ordeal.

Outside the Emperor's hunting-lodge, the Falcon hovers: we hear also a minor mode version of Ex. 6 and the hunting-call Ex. 10. A long and touching cello solo, based on Ex. 6 and Ex. 9, looks strangely forward to the string writing in *Metamorphosen* which the dejected and disenchanted Strauss was to write thirty years later. The Emperor rides on, dismounts, and hides behind a tree, watching the house. Why has the new-found Falcon led him here; must he still hunt the Empress? His monologue is imbued with haunting melancholy, not least through the Falcon's motifs. He soon finds that the house in which she had said she would spend these three days is empty; and with his mounting suspicion (Ex. 12) the music strains upward in tonality (to the Shadow theme which explains why the Empress is not at home). He hears the sound of someone approaching. The Empress and her Nurse come noiselessly through the trees and slip into the hunting-lodge. The Emperor is aghast with sadness, for he senses that they have been among mankind; his wife has lied to him and must therefore die as his prey (Ex. 10). He prepares to kill her, but rejects every available weapon. The Stone theme (Ex. 7) declares that his heart is already turning to stone. He calls the Falcon to lead him away to some rocky cave (cf. the next scene but one) where no one will hear his crying. The orchestral interlude continues his Ex. 9 in E flat minor, as well as a terrifying full brass enunciation of the Stone theme, and the Falcon's vanishing screech.

The third scene returns us to Barak's hut. The Dyer is working, while his bitter wife (Ex. 25) nags sullenly, and the Nurse waits impatiently to resume her temptations. Barak is thirsty; his wife refuses to demean herself (Ex. 12) by serving him, and the Nurse prepares a drugged drink for him. While his wife continues to taunt him he lies down, promises to go to market later, and sleeps. The wife is angry with the Nurse and, when promised many beautiful hours of Ex. 6, declares that she wants to get away (the music suggests to her lover Ex. 23) from the clutches of this inquisitive and all too knowing old serpent. The Nurse again suggests that she should conjure the Phantom Lover. The wife resents any favour from the hand of this sinister procuress, yet she cannot avoid thinking of the Young Man, so the Nurse is at once able to summon him; we hear his unearthly voice (which should come from the prompter's box, not from the actor). The Dyer's wife, the Nurse, and the Young Man join in a concerted trio in the course of which the Nurse, by blowing at the fire, causes the Phantom to fall as if unconscious. The wife, appalled, tries to awake Barak with the help of the Empress who throws water over him, while the Nurse crossly has to dematerialize the erotic vision. Barak sits up, and the wife complains that he is not looking after her. Barak asks how his tools come to be on the floor; he senses that mysterious powers are interfering in his life, and is worried chiefly about their effect on his work and his ability to earn food for all his dependants. His wife coldly remarks, in a scherzando solo which begins with the Renunciation theme, Ex. 20, that he should be ashamed of his dull intelligence. As for food, he need not worry about her; one day when she goes out of the house she will not return. With this, she and the Nurse depart, leaving behind the Empress who collects Barak's handiwork together. He hears a noise and asks, Who is there? I my Lord, your servant, she answers, and the wide-ranging melody of Ex. 19 in D flat major tells us that his goodness has begun to make a profound impression upon her and her conscience (Ex. 24). She is already becoming aware of human sympathy—and so is half-way to deserving her Shadow. The ensuing Intermezzo reshapes Ex. 19, as if it were a dominant minor ninth, into a superficially indepen-dent motif of Anxiety, though its provenance shows who is inspiring the Empress's anxiety. The Intermezzo enlarges on her qualms which have to do with the behaviour of her supposedly loyal Nurse, with the Emperor as lover and huntsman, and with the stony fate that she knows to be decreed by her own father, Keikobad.

All this, we realize when the curtain rises again, is passing through the Empress's mind as she lies in uneasy slumbers in the hunting-lodge, her Nurse asleep at the foot of the bed. A further procession of relevant themes haunts her nightmares, chiefly the Anxiety motif. She mutters in her sleep and then a new fanfare-like phrase suggests that she foresees a stern judgement for her traffic in the wife's Shadow. The Judgement theme, not yet set in its detailed outline, is finally as follows:

26

The Empress sits up with a shout: Barak, I have sinned against you! and the motif of Anxiety takes up her cry, though she now seems to have fallen firmly asleep. She dreams of an enormous rocky cave with a door in its side (Keikobad, Ex. 1, rules here); the Falcon's cry is heard, and the Emperor appears and pauses before the door. Ex. 21 tells us that he is taking his place for the great ordeal. There is a sound of rushing water and distant voices call: To the water of life, and: To the brink of death. The Falcon repeats the warning on the Talisman. The Emperor knocks at the door; it opens, and he passes inside. The Empress wakes up, and realizes that the closing of the door behind her husband heralded his trial (Ex. 26) and sentence (Ex. 7). She knows that she is guilty, and longs to take her husband's punishment upon herself. This scene, like the one in front of the hunting-lodge, is crucial to an understanding of the dramatic development: they are scenes of interpretation as much as action; they also contain some of the most glorious music in the opera. The Inter-mezzo which grows out of this nightmare scene continues its themes and is finally dominated by the motif of Keikobad, which persists after the curtain has returned us to Barak's hut.

The three days are almost up, and the hut grows darker and darker although it is noon. The Spirit of Keikobad broods over the lower regions of the orchestra, and the Anxiety theme (Ex. 19, variant) is also to be heard; the Nurse senses that superior powers are at work, and her own plans are in danger. Barak's brothers howl with ignorant terror; Barak himself feels hemmed in, and his wife is even more querulous than usual. The Empress's anxiety and pricking of conscience are tempered by gratitude at finding a really good and exemplary human being in Barak. These conflicting emotions are deployed in a grand ensemble dominated by Barak's Ex. 14 and the brothers' Ex. 11. The wife has been working her way to an hysterical outburst. Behind her trifling complaints she is oppressed, the orchestra hints, with thoughts of her approaching renunciation of motherhood (Ex. 20, variant), the magical metamorphosis that will be her reward (Ex. 5), and an anxiety (Ex. 19, variant) for that outcome. She turns to Barak and blurts out through the sounds of storm and lightning that she has been receiving a lover (Ex. 23), and now intends to forswear motherhood (Ex. 20) and in token has bartered (Ex. 22) her shadow (Ex. 4) for a rich reward.* Barak, in the utmost consternation, calls to his brothers to light a fire and discover if this nonsense is true. The fire, when kindled (with contrariwise appropriateness, to Ex. 4), reveals her shadowless. In the following ensemble the brothers shout and curse (plenty of Ex. 11's human thirds) and the Nurse is jubilant, but the Empress cries aloud that she will not accept a shadow stained with blood, for Barak now threatens to slay his wife. A new, strongly rhythmical theme portrays Retribution.

27

As the voices stop, a sword springs by magic into Barak's outstretched hand. The brothers exert all their force to restrain him. But the miracle resulting from her irresponsible confession has wrought a change in the Dyer's wife now as she turns to her husband and, in a wonderful lyrical solo, admits that she has not yet done what she admitted to, but that she is willing to die for having thought of it. Barak lifts the sword, but it is spirited out of his hand. Ex. 1, Ex. 5 and Ex. 21 explain that punishment is not for Barak to execute. The earth opens and swallows up the Dyer and his wife; the brothers fly yelling out of the door; through the cracked walls (down the street, if the scene is set outside the hut) a river

---

* A bald description with thematic references must seem to support all the scornful strictures of anti-Wagnerites. But in effect Strauss's symphonic genius elevates this Uncle Tom Cobley recital of nameplates to an eloquent and challenging musical argument, and this enumeration is only a reminder of what he is arguing about.

flows. The Nurse calls the forces of darkness to her aid; a boat appears by magic, and setting the Empress in it she and her mistress float away. Distant fanfares announce the coming judgement.

5

The solemn brass chords which open the last act sum up Hofmannsthal's opening words of explanation: 'The Spirit world is opened up, and surrounds those who are being tried; but the last and most exalted ordeal is still to come.' Out of the darkness a solo bassoon dwells on Discontent, Anxiety, and Nightmares. Then the voices of the Unborn Children begin to wail on flutes, clarinets and celesta, and the curtain rises. We see an underground cavern divided into two parts by a thick wall. On the right, Barak sits brooding; on the left, his wife cries to the voices to stop calling —she did not renounce them. Neither the Dyer nor his wife is aware of the other's proximity. She calls to him, full of repentance and humility and love. Barak sings, to the finest melody in the whole score, of his duty to protect his wife.

Her voice joins with his in a duet on Ex. 28. Barak longs to see his wife once more, to comfort her and bid her not to be afraid—here again the theme of his radiant goodness, Ex. 18, from the first act, is heard. A magic voice tells him to mount the enormous staircase which is suddenly visible (see Plate 20). His wife calls even more passionately for him (to reminders of Ex. 27), and then she too is told to climb higher. The clouds conceal the scene while the orchestra dwells on Ex. 28 and Ex. 19 (the evidence for their joint acquittal), as well as on Ex. 16 and the Anxiety theme; later we hear the fanfares of judgement.

After a tiny pause the music becomes more uneasy (Ex. 4 and the

Anxiety Ex. 19); through the clouds there becomes visible the rocky face which the Empress had seen in her dream; amid a virtually seamless texture of symphonic counterpoint we are made aware of the spiritual link between the conscience-ridden Ex. 24 and the fateful Ex. 7. The door of the cave is open now, and on the steps waits Keikobad's Messenger. The boat appears, carrying the Nurse and the sleeping Empress, and moors by magic at the foot of the steps on which the Messenger hides. The Emperor is here (with Exs. 6 and 7), and so is Keikobad: the orchestra tells us so. The Empress hastens to disembark as soon as she wakes; the Nurse urges her to escape at once, and is dismayed to find that the boat will not move. Recognizing the door, the Empress mounts the steps; trumpets sound from within the cave. She knows what is inside, and that Keikobad, her father, is the Judge; but she is determined to share her husband's trial because, unlike the Nurse, she knows the meaning of duty—not by rote but by experience. She recognizes this moment as part of a superior ordeal (Ex. 21), that her humiliation and life among men (Ex. 12) are evidence on her behalf, that her conscience (Ex. 24) will speak for her as well; she senses, the music further declares, the presence of Keikobad's Messenger (Ex. 3), and the integrity of her marriage to the Emperor (Exs. 4 and 6 together). Remembering how often Hofmannsthal complained about Strauss's dull-witted incomprehension of the issue at stake in *Ariadne*, it is of the highest interest to remark how, in *Die Frau ohne Schatten*, he at every turn makes the inner meaning of the drama come alive—simply because the real humanity, quite lacking there, is so prominent here. Strauss's 'incomprehension' of *Ariadne* was a condemnation of the theme (even though Hofmannsthal's explanation may incline us to accept a certain relevance in his special pleading). Here, however, we cannot help recognizing with Strauss the outstanding importance of the message.

The Nurse insinuates that all will be well if only they can escape; she clings to the validity of the Bargain, the hope that even with a Shadow all will remain as it was; to cross this threshold is worse than death. The Nurse is obviously counselling a reactionary policy which has no substance, worse still, no justification in the human logic or morals to which the Empress is now committed (the duplicity is confirmed in the suggestion that the Empress shall have a Shadow, yet remain transparent). The Nurse's remarks prove to the Empress that she is being cheated by her guardian. She resolves to go her own way, whether to life or death. The Nurse promises her a terrible punishment for straying among humans, but the Empress hears the call to Judgement (Ex. 26) and she is adamant; her conscience, Ex. 24, has sustained her integrity: I belong to them—you are no use to me, she tells the Nurse, and the Emperor's Hunting theme is heard as she goes inside.

Barak and his wife are heard calling to one another and they approach, first one, then the other; the Nurse sends them off in opposite directions, with a curse, and calls on Keikobad for help; the echo of his name sounds sixfold (a stunning moment) round the rocks. Her loyalty to Keikobad's daughter definitively reveals her nature; she would give her security for Keikobad's presence, but its spirit and meaning she cannot understand. The Messenger now emerges from the door through which she tries to pass: he spurns her loyalty to a personal, spiritually unjustified ideal (the voices of Barak and his wife emphasize in an ensemble the Messenger's meaning) and orders her to depart in the little boat, and to wander wretchedly for ever among the humans that she hates. We may very easily ignore the point of this condemnation, which is central to the whole drama. The Nurse is rejected for the selfsame reason that the Empress is received. It is ideals, as well as people, that matter—or, rather, people matter because of the ideals they represent. Thunder and lightning erupt and the orchestra further develops familiar themes in an Intermezzo; far away Barak and his wife are still calling in desperation for one another, while spirit-voices exhort them to reverence (Ex. 21).

The music slows down, and now we are within a temple in the rock; there is a veiled niche at the back. Barak and his wife can still be heard as the Empress, encouraged by hidden voices, is led in by slaves who vanish. She approaches the niche, to a violin solo (based on Ex. 4), and implores Keikobad in a solo of high sublimity. She has learned the meaning of the human shadow and now desires to know her place among mankind. A spring of golden water rises in front of her (it seems to promise only unfruitful love). A spirit, the Guardian of the Threshold (male alto voice), bids her drink, and the woman's shadow will be hers; her husband will be free, and she will be safe. But she hears the wailing of Barak and his wife: Blood is in this water, she declares, I will not drink it— and the fountain subsides. The Empress affirms her place in the human world: here I have sinned and here I belong. She has been addressing the figure behind the niche, assuming it to be Keikobad. But the Chinese gongs toll Ex. 11 and show that her addressee is human. The veil becomes transparent and reveals the Emperor on a throne; he is entirely petrified but for his pleading eyes. This is, for the Empress, the greatest moment of ordeal and, exceptionally, her terror is expressed in unaccompanied speech. She cannot save him by condemning two human people. Unearthly voices repeat the message of the Talisman, and the Emperor disappears as the fountain rises again. The Guardian of the Threshold tells the Empress to say: I will, and she will have both shadow and Emperor; but she hears Barak and his wife, and knows that they will be the price of her submission. The water rushes, tensely dinning. From the innermost being of the Empress comes an anguished cry: I will not.

There is a long pause. Then Ex. 4 returns; light shoots down from above and throws a sharp shadow behind the Empress and across the temple. The Emperor rises from his throne and pronounces the Empress's reward: When the crystalline heart smashes with a cry, the Unborn Children hasten like starshine, the wife beholds her husband, and she casts an earthly shadow. The voices of the parents and their Unborn Children join together, and the Emperor's cantabile theme (Ex. 9) announces that his prey is now truly his wife. The Cherubim which the Empress thinks to hear are her unborn children, unborn but now promised. They combine in an ensemble of joy. Ex. 9 caps the triumphant ecstasy of this, and Ex. 26 pronounces the delivery of justice; similarly, Ex. 20 resounds in affirmation of a selfish act prevented by the Empress's selfless will. As Emperor and Empress embrace, the scene changes to a beautiful hilly landscape centred on a golden waterfall. Barak and his wife hurry from either side to its brink and, from above, the Empress's shadow falls across it and turns into a bridge on which the earthly couple are reunited. They and the Imperial, but now fully human, couple join in a jubilant quartet, and the voices of the Unborn Children—six little Dyers and a whole choir of boys for the Emperor and Empress—make their rejoicing complete. Justice has been done, and the trombone fanfares bring *Die Frau ohne Schatten* to an end.

6

'We,' wrote Hofmannsthal (meaning 'you', one suspects), 'have missed lightness of touch in *Die Frau ohne Schatten*.' The general opinion is that it was Hofmannsthal who ruined its chances of success by overloading the piece with symbolism. Many listeners, having come unprepared to *Die Frau ohne Schatten*, have been mystified; they expected either a realistic drama or a fairy-story, and found neither. I have tried to show how simple and natural, and yet full of meaning, the libretto is, even if it involves more characters than necessary. It is the most pretentious of these Strauss–Hofmannsthal operas; it is perhaps the most 'pretentious' opera in operatic history. And yet it is possibly the most moving and beautiful of all. Its world, Hofmannsthal hoped, might be that of *Die Zauberflöte*. It is nearer to the inner, thoughtfully spiritual world of *Tristan*, more closely perhaps of *Parsifal*, since it discusses the union of man and woman not only with one another, but with God (whether or not we call him Keikobad), and with the whole of human creation. Some have said that Strauss failed to rise to the sublimity of Hofmannsthal's text. These commentators, I think, prejudge the case, simply out of a feeling that Strauss could not possibly comprehend a drama so deep and far reaching in implication. Yet the opera as a whole, once one has comprehended its real human significance, owes its impact to Strauss's music, which heightens and clarifies the issues to an extraordinary degree. I am even of the opinion that the music, in the most vital scenes, realizes Hofmannsthal more meaningfully than the text by itself enables one to understand. The grandeur and subtlety of the orchestral colours, the masterly control of symphonic technique (unequalled even in *Don Quixote* or *Der Rosen-kavalier*), and the vocal characterization summon an admiration that one may, given full understanding, be tempted to express about no other Strauss opera. (*Elektra* compels a different sort of admiration.) Strauss, in *Die Frau ohne Schatten*, found the inspiration for his masterpiece. It would be vain to wish that he had applied himself earlier to the idea; at that time he would not have done it justice. (One might as well wish that Hofmannsthal had given him the stimulus of the excitable romantic themes which he suggested and which represented his primitive needs.) In *Die Frau ohne Schatten* he deployed all his gifts to their utmost. This is the last Wagnerian opera of inner psychology and it is also the last pantomime opera. Stravinsky has declared that, when he decides to compose, he hopes to 'leap a little in spirit'. In *Die Frau ohne Schatten* Richard Strauss leaped by an extent that he had not—nobody could have —suspected earlier. The characters of themselves are an *élite*, their music elect among all his other works. There are fine things in *Helena*, in *Arabella*, but they are at an almost ridiculously lower level. Even the characters of *Der Rosenkavalier*, much more familiar through frequent performance, do not cut so deeply at the level where they invite us to become different people, to exercise the repentance of Greek μετανοία which means a change of mind as well as an apology. *Die Frau ohne Schatten* is possibly Hofmannsthal's greatest claim to immortality, but it was Strauss who justified the claim.

Intermezzo

OPUS 72

A Bourgeois Comedy with Symphonic Interludes, in Two Acts

LIBRETTO BY RICHARD STRAUSS

Christine Storch	SOPRANO
Little Franz (*Bubi*), *her eight-year-old Son*	SPEAKING PART
Hofkapellmeister Robert Storch, her Husband	BARITONE
Anna, the Chambermaid	SOPRANO
Baron Lummer	TENOR
The Notary	BARITONE
His Wife	SOPRANO
Kapellmeister Stroh	TENOR
The Business Man	BARITONE
The Lawyer	BARITONE
The Opera Singer	BASS
Resi, a Young Girl	SPEAKING PART
Fanny, the Cook	SPEAKING PART

I

By the time Strauss approached the end of *Die Frau ohne Schatten* it was clear to him that he had to go on writing operas—they were his *métier*—and that the next one must be quite different. Ever since *Guntram* he had been wanting a realistic subject: he had collected an assortment of more or less humanly inspiring librettos about more or less inspiring characters, but his work on *Elektra* (Greek myth), *Der Rosenkavalier* (Viennese baroque), *Ariadne* (myth plus baroque *commedia dell'arte*) and *Die Frau ohne Schatten* (German *Arabian Nights*) inclined him to something as cheerful as *Rosenkavalier* and more up to date than anything he had yet attempted—something to suit his own special gifts, dare one say, rather than those of any librettist. Hofmannsthal was not interested in this sort of development: he had mooted the first ideas of *Arabella*, which were to be exactly what Strauss eventually needed, but for the moment the poet's mind ran on the timeless themes of antiquity: 'let us make mythological operas: they are the truest of all kinds.' For Hofmannsthal perhaps, but at this moment Strauss needed a modern theme and atmosphere of a kind that Hofmannsthal found, as he had repeatedly observed, in poor taste. When Strauss proposed something of the nature to him, Hofmannsthal sent him to the Viennese critic and dramatist Hermann Bahr.

This talented writer and amiable man (1863–1934) is now best known as the author of a stage comedy, *Das Konzert*, still popular in German-speaking countries, and as the husband of the great soprano Anna Bahr-Mildenburg (a famous Clytemnestra). Bahr had also been responsible for a long and highly distinguished (but not very critical) notice of Strauss's *Elektra*. He would, one begins to fancy, have been an ideal collaborator for the Strauss who longed to write twentieth-century operetta, to be the legitimate successor of Franz Lehár, producing stage-works of strong popular melodious and dramatic appeal with that extra element of serious psychological investigation that no operetta had yet attempted. Bahr could have supplied him with this as Hofmannsthal could not; and similarly for the serious, exploratory operas, Wolzogen or some other author of like creative inclination might well have drawn out the greatest of Strauss's pioneering creative possibilities. But that is another hypothetical story. Hofmannsthal made the recommendation in August 1916, and a month later the two men met in Salzburg, Bahr's home town. It was here that they elaborated the rough outlines of *Das eheliche Glück* (*Wedded Bliss*) which was to become *Intermezzo*.

Bahr made a draft sketch during October, but the composer, while appreciating its splendid features, took exception to a certain element of rough, hobbledehoy or 'yobbish' (*burschikos*) character in it. Strauss's proposed subject was autobiographical, dealing with a composer-conductor and his capricious domineering wife. Everybody knew how sharp-tongued Pauline Strauss had always been; but Strauss, who suggested the story, knew that he loved and respected his wife for other qualities which Bahr had found difficult in his libretto to incorporate, given the fairly unsympathetic facts of the original scenario and the authentic incident on which it is based. He had further difficulty in creating a vivid but tactful character out of the third principal actor in this little domestic drama, the wife's party companion Baron Lummer. Both collaborators, in fact, were dissatisfied. But at New Year 1917 Bahr was agreeing to try again.

Strauss's chief concern at this point was that the libretto should float lightly across the surface of the music, leaving all the main comment and elucidation to the composer. Bahr, a modest but sensitive musician, understood this well, and when Strauss resumed his inquiries in June 1917 (the score of *Die Frau ohne Schatten* was now completed), Bahr answered that it would be most useful if the composer were to note down suitable scenes. Strauss's efforts won Bahr's whole-hearted approval; they were exactly what was required and he promptly advised Strauss to go ahead on his own—only Strauss could properly characterize the story, and Strauss could equally well find the simple, everyday words for a conversational drama of a deliberately undemanding nature. Bahr explained all this in a generous and appreciative letter of July 1917. The composer accordingly set out his ideas quite quickly during a week's stay in Dr Krecke's Sanatorium in Munich. By the second week of August he was able to send a draft libretto for Hofmannsthal to look at (the poet doubted if he would be a good judge of it). Strauss does not, on the other hand, seem to have communicated any further with Bahr on the subject. In the following year he returned Bahr's sketches, and a subsequent letter, very friendly in tone, does not mention *Intermezzo*. His suggestion that Bahr should write him another quite original libretto on the subject of marriage, and specifically Strauss's marriage seen from another angle, bore no fruit—predictably.*

Work on *Intermezzo* proceeded quietly, and slowly too, for between 1919 and 1924 Strauss's time was further taken up by his post at the Vienna State Opera. In 1920 he toured South America, in 1921 the United States (with Elisabeth Schumann), and in 1923 South America again. He also managed to complete the little-known ballet *Schlagobers* ('Whipped Cream'), and to devise, with Hofmannsthal, a new version of

---

* Strauss planned a cycle of five domestic conversation pieces with small orchestra, first because he wanted to establish a new genre, second because 'one could make ten pieces out of my wife'. If he came no further, he did at any rate complete three operas about marriage: *Die Frau ohne Schatten*, *Intermezzo* and *Die Ägyptische Helena*—and they are three in a row. It might be argued that *Die schweigsame Frau*, *Friedenstag* and *Die Liebe der Danae* are also about married couples.

Beethoven's *Ruins of Athens*. He completed *Intermezzo* in Buenos Aires on 21 August 1923, during his tour with the Vienna Opera.

2

The obvious location for the première must have seemed to be Vienna. But Strauss's position in Vienna had now become rickety, partly through difficulties with his co-director Schalk, partly through the intrigues and counter-intrigues which are part of the good Viennese citizen's possessive passion for *unsere Oper*. Strauss's resignation was inevitable; he was only waiting to make certain that the job did not go to the dreaded Weingartner. At all events he decided that the première of *Intermezzo* should once again be given to Dresden: Fritz Busch was now in command as music director, and Strauss was promised that standards had risen to their former heights, and that such a débâcle as the Dresden *Frau ohne Schatten* première was no longer possible. Intimacy was the essence of *Intermezzo* with its conversational style, its subject matter, and its small orchestra—double woodwind, brass, three horns, modest percussion, piano, harp, harmonium, and small string forces (eleven first violins, nine second violins, five violas, five cellos, and three double-basses); the production was therefore given not in the large house but in the smaller theatre, where the première took place on 4 November 1924, as part of the celebrations for Strauss's sixtieth birthday. Lotte Lehmann was engaged to portray Christine Storch* (alias Pauline Strauss), Joseph Correck impersonated the composer—wearing a mask to emphasize the composer's real-life identity. The stage designer, Adolf Mahnke, who had visited Garmisch to sign the contract for the première, modelled the sets for Storch's house on Strauss's Garmisch home (though the Storch home in *Intermezzo* is supposedly on the Grundlsee near Salzburg). The composer was kept in ignorance of this until the last rehearsals, when he expressed surprise not unmixed with apprehension.

Fritz Busch has left an interesting account in his autobiography† of Strauss at this time, and his reactions to Strauss's work which were admiring but ambivalent (Busch had been such a Strauss-worshipper as a boy that he and his brother began composing a symphonic poem on *Max and Moritz*, out of sincerest flattery, and then abandoned it, being sure that so brilliant a subject must already figure among the composer's

---

* Strauss gave the première to Dresden on condition he might have the choice of singer for this vital role, and so it was that Dresden's rule of home casts for premières was broken for a guest singer from Vienna. After the first performance Grete Nikisch, a Dresden company member, took over the part. It may also be recalled that Schumann–Heink had taken Clytemnestra in the première of *Elektra*.

† *Aus dem Leben eines Musikers* (Zürich, 1949), translated as *Pages from a Musician's Life* (Hogarth Press, 1953).

work in progress). Busch was especially puzzled by the discovery that Strauss, 'in spite of his marvellous talents, is not really penetrated and possessed by them like other great artists but, in fact, simply wears them like a suit of clothes which can be taken off at will. . . . His favourite game of Skat, at which he was very seldom beaten, often seemed to be nearer to his heart than his music.' On the subject of music, however, Busch found that he and Strauss spoke much the same language; Strauss reciprocated this by giving the première of his next opera to Busch as conductor, dedicating *Arabella* to him, and offering to make a reduced orchestral score of *Der Rosenkavalier* if Busch would conduct it at Glynde-bourne (but alas this project was never realized in the lifetime of the two musicians).

Intermezzo was quite quickly taken up by other opera companies. Erfurt gave the piece two days after Dresden; Hamburg and Karlsruhe followed in December, Berlin under Georg Szell in March 1925. The Swiss première in June was given by the Dresden company and in the following November Karl Alwin (Elisabeth Schumann's second husband) conducted the Spanish première at Barcelona (in Italian). It reached Munich in 1926 under Knappertsbusch, and Vienna the following January under Strauss himself. It was in Vienna that Hofmannsthal heard it for the first time and was surprised to discover how serious the work had turned out to be.

Premières are one thing, repeated revivals another; and despite a fairly long stay in the Dresden repertory, *Intermezzo* did not hold the stage, though it is still given from time to time in Munich and Vienna. Hofmanns-thal later maintained that *Intermezzo* had been denied wide popularity because it offered no dramatic tension, but only a character portrait: Baron Lummer is such a 'shadow-figure' that one feels no concern either for the husband or his ebullient wife. Strauss accepted all this, but added that he found 'so pretty and logically elaborated a character portrait more interesting than any so-called plot'. He hoped that one day a generation with a more highly developed theatrical sense would come to esteem *Intermezzo*. Hofmannsthal's reservations about the libretto were not shared by Max Reinhardt, who told Strauss that he would like to produce *Intermezzo* as a spoken play without touching a line. Strauss dedicated the work to his son Franz, an accomplished Skat player himself, as well as the Bubi of the opera to be described in a moment.

3

The origin of *Intermezzo* was as follows: in 1903 an Italian opera company was giving a season at the Kroll Opera in Berlin under the conductors

Josef Stransky and Arturo Vigna. One evening Stransky went for a drink in the Hotel Bristol with the company's leading tenor Emilio de Marchi (who had been Puccini's first Cavaradossi in *Tosca*) and the impresario Edgar Strakosch. While they were conversing in Italian, Marchi and Strakosch were approached by a none too shy young lady who had heard them talk, put two and two together, and promptly asked for a free ticket for the opera. Marchi told her to apply to the Kapellmeister Stransky, whose name he consistently mispronounced 'Strausky'. Josef Stransky conveniently forgot about the incident, and so the bright young lady looked up Strausky in the telephone book, found Hofkapellmeister Strauss and at once sent him the following note: 'Dear Sweetheart, do bring me the ticket. Your faithful Mitzi. My address: Mitzi Mücke, Lüneburger Strasse 5.' (She used the intimate second person singular, which implies that she had at least spent a little time with Stransky.) The letter arrived at Strauss's address while the Master was on holiday in the Isle of Wight, after a concert tour which had brought him to England. His wife opened it, didn't even question the circumstances, immediately assumed the worst and visited a solicitor with a view to divorce. Strauss was completely baffled when faced with his wife's accusations of adultery, couched as these were in the emphatic, impassioned tones natural to an ex-Wagnerian soprano. Not even his suggestion of some confusion with his colleague at the Hofoper, Edmund von Strauss, weakened Frau Pauline's conviction. Strauss confided in his friend Friedrich Rösch who contrived to elucidate the truth. *Intermezzo* was perhaps Strauss's way of laying this old ghost by laughing at it.

Baron Lummer also had his origin in life: he was, the composer told Bahr, 'a shy, taciturn youth whose confidence-trickery only emerged when, half-ashamed, he tried to extort money from my wife, having awoken her sympathy by his modesty and need for help till she saw qualities in him that only existed in her lively imagination'. Two other real people, the business man (*Kommerzienrat*) Willy Levin, and the singer Paul Knüpfer (a famous Ochs) also figure briefly in the Skat scene which opens Act 2. For the rest it may be added that Frau Strauss was notoriously house-proud, had continuous trouble with her domestic staff (though the faithful Anna survived her mistress's tantrums for thirty-four years) and that she talked incessantly about her husband.

4

Strauss had asked Hermann Bahr to leave a good deal to music, and in his own score to his own libretto there are more than fifty identifiable themes; one can reduce their number, even for a fairly detailed synopsis, because a good many do not persist from scene to scene. The curtain rises almost at once on early morning in the dressing-room of Herr Storch who is packing his bags for a trip to Vienna. The precipitous opening theme leaves no doubt of the disputatious relationship that exists between Robert and Christine Storch, and the enormous gap that seems to divide them on practically every subject.

It will be seen that this contains three ideas: (a) being about the two of them, (b) the running semiquavers about the talkative wife, and (c) about the harassed husband. Christine calls for their maid Anna.

An-na, An-na!

Robert begs her not to upset the servant who will leave as so many have already done, giving her the bother of hunting for another. Christine's chatterbox Ex. 1b is now given a more durable form.

The couple are plunged at once into an animated discussion which extends to her insistence that he has a proper breakfast, and her pleasure at being rid of him for a while. She yells again for Anna to remember the trunk keys—there was that time in Campiglio when they had to wait a week before they could open their baggage. And when he protests that it was her fault she changes the conversation to his job, which keeps him at home while other husbands are at work (married musicians and journalists are familiar with this complaint), and gives her more responsibilities. She details them; but he does not account them serious work—and the new oboe tune suggests that serious work is the intellectual sort which he does.

This idea is more firmly implanted a moment later when it is taken up and extended in sumptuous D flat major by full orchestra. Christine plays into Robert's hands by mentioning that necessity of thinking ahead which is every housewife's headache. This gives him the leading point that thoughtful work (such as his, a beautiful version of Ex. 3 implies) is the creative artist's business; and it is also, or should be, a pleasure. No work is a pleasure, answers Christine. His efforts to persuade her that less strenuous work would help the smooth running of the household, only lead her to deride his less distinguished ancestry (Pauline was a general's daughter). Finally the husband stamps off to breakfast with two full D major chords that conclude this particular instalment of the argument.

At once the chambermaid Anna rushes into the room, packing suit-cases in all directions under a cross-fire of reminders from her mistress, first about food for the journey, then medicines to preserve her husband's health. Again Christine remarks how glad she will be to get him out of the house; this time to a theme pointedly associated with loneliness.

5

And indeed the maid persuades her to admit that she will find life lonely in this enormous house alone with the child; the oboe suggests another theme of loneliness to be prominent later, in a slightly different form.

6

p espressivo

Anna suggests that Madam might relieve the tedium by going tobog-ganing (appropriate glissando on piano and strings). Madam is bored by the idea. Robert, having breakfasted, returns to collect his luggage. He does not speak, and when asked why, answers that it is in order to avoid arguments. The strings storm up an arpeggio in the theme of Frau Storch's tantrums.

7

f

And so of course they fall to abusing one another. Christine is parti-cularly eloquent on the indecorous publicity of the musician's life; he is always having to parade his feelings before the bloated stall-holders (Strauss here quotes the love duet from Gounod's *Faust, Laisse-moi, laisse-moi*, on the trumpet). The maid announces the arrival of the sledge (cheerful jingling in the pit) to take him to the station, and Christine refuses to kiss him good-bye until he reminds her that he might have an accident—which transforms her at once into solicitude personified. She begs him to keep warm, sit in a central compartment, go to bed early, and embraces him passionately—but when he asks her to write, her good temper vanishes at once, and he leaves in a rage, she merely commanding him not to miss the train. An animated and warm-hearted orchestral passage clarifies the shape (outward-moving wide intervals) of an earlier, unquoted idea, now a symbol of the bonhomous conciliatory husband.

8

Frau Christine's chatterbox theme, Ex. 3, is involved as well. She sits down at her dressing-table and Anna does Madam's coiffure (falling scales and harp arpeggios), though Madam jumps up almost at once to see if her husband is waving goodbye from the street (Ex. 8 and Ex. 4 in double harness), and to wonder, with all his urge for travelling, if he has not some Jewish blood in him (Strauss makes a comic quotation from Schumann's *Spring Symphony**). Anna counters that, after all, the Master has a lovely profession, which sets Christine's objections in motion again to Ex. 4 and Ex. 7. Why, the publicity is so unpleasant that her husband had to forbid mention of her in his biographies [though he writes an opera about her]. Anna offers a pert comment and is curtly shut up; she continues combing. The little son runs in for advice about boots in the snow; then the housemaid announces the arrival of the tax-collector, who is told to send the bill through the post; then Frau Storch remembers she must telephone to the fruiterer for rose hips to make her husband's favourite jam; finally the cook wants to know about the menu. What a busy morning; obviously she cannot accompany her husband on his travels. Anna offers a polite word about the Master's kindness to his wife, and again her temper and Ex. 7 come to the boil; it is his passive conciliatory nature that enrages her most, and his scorn of the whole sex, his sly reserve, all make her the unhappiest woman in the world (Ex. 5). Very helpfully the telephone now rings. Frau Storch is surprised and much cheered by the invitation from a female friend to go tobogganing. At once her energies are roused, and as the scene ends she is wondering what to wear and, once again, yelling for Anna. Darkness descends, and the orchestra takes up the animated themes of Frau Christine's Ex. 3 and Ex. 7, the music of her telephone conversation, Ex. 2 ('Anna, Anna!'), and finally Ex. 8 which turns into the tobogganing glissandi, since the

---

* Schumann was not Jewish, and I suspect that Strauss was confusing the theme with one by Mendelssohn.

scene now discloses the local sledge run, where parties are descending one after the next. A young man enters on skis, and the strings play us his rather empty-headed, non-committal theme.

The man is called Baron Lummer; characteristically Strauss made him a tenor, and gave him these shadowy harmless themes (indeed Ex. 9^2 is quite close to the Shadow theme in *Die Frau ohne Schatten* which is perhaps why Hofmannsthal found him a 'shadowy' figure). The chatter-box Ex. 3 joins the texture. From up the hill Christine yells the equivalent of 'Olly, olly' (*Bahn frei*), and descending much too soon after the previous toboggan collides with Baron Lummer who is floundering across the track (their collision occurs in her D major and his F minor). They curse one another briefly, then introduce themselves; Frau Christine knows Lummer's family from Linz, or rather her parents did. They arrange to see one another again. The curtain falls and the orchestra resumes Ex. 9, Ex. 3 and the composer's private protest, Ex. 1. By degrees the orchestra reaches waltz time and the piano inaugurates the famous waltz scene. Significantly enough, a good deal of the writing is in Baron Lummer's characteristic fourths (as in Ex. 9) harmonically, and later melodically. The curtain rises on a dance in the inn at Grundlsee; Christine, exhausted after her dancing, enters with the Baron. She promises to keep him strictly to his cure (he claims to be suffering from migraine), chatters about her husband, and is soon persuaded to go on dancing. The orches-tra resumes a waltz theme inaugurated just before their entry; it is a theme with associations of the absent husband.

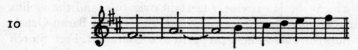

Strauss gaily extends the waltz-chain; is he trying a little too hard to revive the glories of *Rosenkavalier*, and is his inspiration now at less than its freshest? The waltz fades away on violas and basses, the piano plays three fat C major chords, and the new scene reveals a furnished spare room in the house of the local Notary. Frau Storch enters with the Notary's wife; she proposes to rent it at her own (or rather her husband's) expense for Baron Lummer whom she has taken under her wing. She chatters ceaselessly about this protégé (Ex. 9), his migraines (B flat minor triad on brass), his talents as a botanist, his heritage of illness, his need for extra furniture, extra cleaning, extra nourishment, and of course about her husband. Finally she accepts the room, and the curtain falls for an orchestral Intermezzo which toys lyrically with Ex. 3 and Ex. 9 (the rising octave theme begins to recall Sancho Panza!) among less enduring material.

The next scene shows the wife in her dining-room, reading over a letter she has just written to her husband about the charming Baron Lummer, with Ex. 3 for her open-hearted narrative, Ex. 1 for her attachment, and Ex. 7 for her determination to wear the trousers, even over a protégé— whom after all she needs when she is left alone. She meditates quietly about the Baron (Ex. 9) in waltz-time, and about her subordinate role as a celebrity's wife (Ex. 4). She even reminds herself of the critic (Hanslick) who called her the composer's 'better half'—we hear the first 'Adversaries' theme from *Ein Heldenleben*. Fanny the cook comes in to do accounts, and is told to reckon on the Baron at dinner. Here he is, already; he is put to arithmetical sums for the household bills, and then they chat politely. No, he cannot stay to dinner. No, she does not know the friends in question. No, he has not done much today. At each topic the music promises to develop into something, only to tail away into the embarrassed broken octaves of his second theme, Ex. 9^2. Finally Frau Storch is reduced to reading the newspaper with him; she is much excited by the news that Frau von Hupp is divorcing her husband who has been flirting with an actress—scandalous! Attempts to draw out the young man on his studies are unfruitful: it seems that his family will only support him if he reads law, and this he finds quite uncongenial (Strauss's musical comment is a whispered, free, but elaborate canon, most descriptive of legal argument). However, the subject encourages him to approach Frau Storch on another matter, though only after she has instructed the Nanny to give Bubi his bath, rejected the idea of writing letters, and settled down again with the paper. The Baron puts out feelers as to her kind interest in his career as a naturalist (Ex. 10 as a soft horn solo), and the extent to which—he is extremely hesitant over this, and the violins match his stammering with a descending scale that recalls Baron Ochs's Ex. 17 in *Der Rosenkavalier*—she is prepared to encourage it. Frau Storch is not giving her full attention to this request for help; she is still catching up with the latest news of old cronies. When at last she senses in which direction the wind is blowing (Ex. 10 now on the violins with suitably off-putting counterpoints in duple time), she assures Baron Lummer that her husband will help him to acquire some scholarship or grant—her husband with his noble breeding and excellent connexions (we recall her comments on these in the opening scene) is unusually practical in such matters, for an artist. She launches, with the aid of Ex. 1c, Ex. 1a, Ex. 8 as well as Ex. 10, into a panegyric of Robert Storch, his success, his modesty, his industry. For his wife's sake, her husband will take an interest in the Baron; she admits that they quarrel now and then, but never seriously, for he fulfils her every wish (Ex. 7, very determined on the violins, shows why). The Baron begins to press his need for assistance even before Herr Storch's return, but she turns his hints neatly aside, with the hope that the Baron can remain at Grundlsee until her husband's return (Ex. 1 inverted), promises to maintain their friendship and adroitly packs him off, since it is time for her evening meal; she hopes he will be in better spirits (Ex. 9 inverted) when they next meet.

This has been a long conversational scene, fairly full of incident, and full also of fleeting musical themes that do not subsequently reappear; it is the scene in which designedly the most admirable and likeable characteristics of Frau Storch are brought forward. In her phrases of goodbye to the Baron, with their pedal point on C, there is almost a suggestion of the Feldmarschallin taking leave of Baron Ochs, but with the difference that this time the great lady is rather fond of the quasi-villain. Christine and a richly divided string orchestra now subside into a serene and dreamy monologue in A flat (*Ein hübscher Mensch*) in which Ex. 9 and Ex. 10 merge together, as Christine merges the figures of her husband and her gallant, and bestows on this dual beloved a warmth of affection that comes easily when one is lonely.

This ought to be a solo highlight from *Intermezzo* to be sung at concerts or on records, and if it has not achieved this distinction, the reason is simply that the soprano has only twenty bars to sing before the curtain falls and the orchestra continues her reverie at length, coming to a firm close in A flat before the next scene begins. The snapshot construction of *Intermezzo* does not find time for vocal highlight-numbers; this, perhaps, is another reason why it has not won wider favour.

Scene 6 finds the Baron lying on a sofa in his digs, smoking a cigarette, while woodwind serenade him with Ex. 9 and a fragment from the orchestral waltz scene, which had now better be quoted.

He jumps up suddenly and calls down the corridor to his landlady to send up his trunk, in case he has to leave. Chords (piano and strings) built in fourths, i.e. Ex. 9, chatter away as he privately curses his pretty but dull protectress who believes in his migraines but would probably not respond to a declaration of love (Ex. 1a). His true light-of-love (or as true as he can manage), a young girl in skiing clothes called Resi, looks into the room, much to his horror—what if the landlady should see her and tell Frau Storch? He sends Resi away, and sits down to write Frau

Storch a letter (Ex. 10, in a hesitant version, a canon, with Ex. 9 as countersubject on clarinets) telling his full heart . . . a very cheerful orchestral interlude takes up his piled-fourth chords and lets us know that his letter is not inspired by tragedy.

What the letter contains we learn as soon as Scene 7 reveals the Storch dining-room. Christine holds his letter, expostulating over fourth chords: he asks her for one thousand marks—ridiculous, the end of a promising affair (Ex. 10 on bass clarinet). At this moment Baron Lummer bursts into the room, snow all over him from his walk here; Frau Storch brusquely sends him to clean himself; when he returns she reads him a strict lecture on his impoliteness in sending such a letter. A further lecture (Ex. 7 portends the wagging finger) is interrupted by the arrival of a servant with a letter. Frau Storch sees that it is addressed to her husband, but thinking she recognizes the handwriting she opens and reads it. Horror and fury overtake her (a variant of Ex. 1c, shortly followed by the inversion of Ex. 1a). She reads the letter aloud: 'Dear Sweetheart, send me two more tickets for the opera tomorrow. Afterwards in the bar as usual. Your Mieze Meier.' Trumpets and lower strings pronounce the tragedy in Christine's heart.

13

Baron Lummer offers help and Ex. 9, but she can only repeat phrases from this appalling document, and eventually asks him to go home, which he is relieved to do. In high tragic form Ex. 13 thunders forth; she writes her husband a telegram: 'You know Mieze Meier, your faithlessness proven, this is good-bye for ever', and calls Anna to dispatch it and then pack all the trunks at once as they are leaving for good. She sinks exhausted into a chair as the curtain falls and the orchestra takes up an animated, passionate commentary on her feelings, Ex. 1a, Ex. 13, Ex. 6, the hesitant Ex. 10, Ex. 9, and Ex. 7, a grand emotional parade of themes in Strauss's most ardent vein, fully but not thickly scored.

When the curtain rises again Ex. 6 now wails in F minor on the cor anglais against a tiptoe rising scale figure for violins. Frau Storch has crept into Bubi's night-nursery, very unwisely, to release her self-pity before the sleeping child; the boy wakes up, hotly defends his father, and tearfully refuses to go away with Mother who is so nasty to Daddy. Ex. 6 is now quite close to the theme of the Unborn Children in *Die Frau ohne Schatten*, as Christine kneels weeping by the bed of her apparently alienated child. This is both vocally and expressively a beautiful scene, and would claim separate performance if only an audience could, out of context, feel any sympathy at all for the wife. We are almost asked to regard her self-dramatized wailing as a joke, and this is perhaps why

Strauss, in the last years of his life, was begged by Clemens Krauss and
Rudolf Hartmann to re-cast *Intermezzo* in three shorter acts removing this
scene, which makes a beautiful but slightly ludicrous end to the first half
of the opera.

5

The second act begins with one of the Skat parties that were Strauss's
great delight, and at which he was more uninhibitedly himself than at any
other time. *Jetzt wird's gemütlich* (Now it's going to be pleasant) he would
say as he sat down with his friends, Ernst von Schuch or his son, Leonhard Fanto the artist, Tino Pattiera the singer, Willy Levin the famous
art-collector, Paul Knüpfer the basso. The introduction for strings
exudes *Gemütlichkeit* and is based on this very pleasant, relaxed phrase.

14

After a little while the piano joins in, imitating the shuffle of cards with
nice accuracy (though Strauss had already used a similar effect for the
Baron alone in his lodgings, and the presence of piled-up fourth chords in
both passages may seem a little confusing).

15

The curtain rises as this motif returns after more of Ex. 14. The
lawyer (perhaps Mautner-Markhof?), Singer (Knüpfer), the Conductor
Stroh, and the Business Man (Levin) are sitting at Skat in the house of
the last-named—we are supposed to be in Vienna, but Levin lived in
Berlin, and the room should be hung with fine modern paintings for
which Levin was noted. Storch is expected, and before his arrival the
four friends are discussing his wife; Levin pronounces her *Ein Ekel,
einfach ferchterlich* ('A loathsome thing, simply dreadful')—woodwind
remind us of Ex. 1a. They begin their hand* and Stroh calls 'Aces high
on the table', a difficult call, much circumscribed by rules.† Nevertheless

---

* Skat is a card-game which can be played by four or five persons.
† Schuch junior once asked Strauss if he really meant this call; the composer replied:
'Stroh is a tenor, so he gets it wrong.' And indeed Stroh loses the hand.

they continue to gossip during play (significantly card-play is discussed in spoken dialogue, gossip set to music). Stroh sticks up for Frau Christine as a much maligned person who looks after her husband well. While they are scoring Robert Storch enters (Ex. 1a *inversus et rectus*) apologizing for delay at a rehearsal—evidently of *Figaro*, for the muted cellos interpolate the opening of the overture to that opera (the quotation is so soft as to be easily missed); and the bass-singer quotes Othello's (but not Verdi's) 'Hast thou prayed tonight, Desdemona' when Storch sits down to play. Storch praises *Skatchen* as the only relaxation after music (wood-wind underline the remark with The phrase from the *Tristan* Prelude), and the Business Man adds the rider '. . . especially when the wife is far away', so of course Storch has to counter that he loves his wife dearly, even if he prefers male company for Skat. The Business Man's further teasing is broken off for a new hand but conversation soon returns to Frau Storch, (Ex. 7), and the letter which Robert has just received from her about her young companion (first part of Ex. 9). The Singer raises metaphorical eyebrows but Storch knows better, he claims (Ex. 1c and Ex. 7), better too than Levin whom she once unjustifiably abused; she has trained him (by her Ex. 3) into self-discipline. They continue their badinage, Storch with quiet, rather serious assurance and a long melody in F sharp major; he maintains that the rougher type of woman is the best type (Ex. 1c inverted). For a minute he has to stop play to read a telegram which has arrived. But what he reads puts cards and joking quite out of his mind. It is his wife's telegram which Stroh reads out for him (Ex. 13). The telegram is unsigned, as usual with Frau Storch. Cellos and basses introduce a new phrase.

16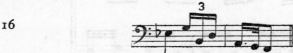

It carries the implication that this fracas too will be happily mended. Stroh is surprised that his colleague also knows Mieze Meier, whom he describes as a 'so-so, la-la'. Bassoons characterize her from Stroh's point of view (the alternative sixth note later becomes usual for this theme).

17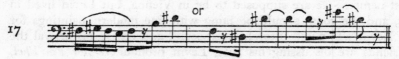

Stroh is inclined to treat the message cynically but Storch is genuinely upset, and feels obliged to ask his card-partners to excuse him. He leaves in haste, while Ex. 1a follows him in vehement imitation with elements of Ex. 13 and also a chordal theme, indicative of his anxiety and bewilderment.

18

The four friends are left ruminating in surprise on this sudden disaster; as the singer quotes from *Parsifal*: *Schwach auch er, schwach alle*—'If he is weak, everyone is weak', and again, from the Hermit in *Der Frei-schütz*—'Does one mistake deserve such a sentence?' With promises to attend later to Storch's affair, they return to their Skat, and strings with flute again portray their agreeable pastime in an interlude which refers to Ex. 1a and Ex. 16, and does not lose Ex. 14 until after the curtain has gone up on the next scene with a new fourths theme, derived from Ex. 9 on wind and brass to show that this is the house where Frau Storch has installed the Baron. It is into the office of the Notary, who owns the house, that Christine steps; she has not come to see the Baron but to employ the Notary as her representative in an action for a divorce—though he aggravates her (Ex. 7) by assuming that the Baron is somehow involved. She is aggrieved by the Notary's unwillingness to break up the marriage of a musician whom he respects, and by his conviction that her evidence is decidedly flimsy. When he refuses to proceed further without first consulting her husband she stumps out of his office (Ex. 6 and Ex. 1 in harness). Most odd, comments the Notary, to Ex. 18.

There is another stormy interlude involving Ex. 16, again Ex. 18 and Ex. 1, Ex. 4, Ex. 13 and also Ex. 9 inverted. The tempest is still raging in the orchestra when Scene 3 discloses the Prater in Vienna, where Robert is pacing back and forth in despair and bewilderment, trying to solve the riddle and cursing his wife's impetuosity. Kapellmeister Stroh comes running through the rain, to Ex. 17; in great embarrassment he confesses that he, not Storch, is the friend to whom Mieze Meier wrote that note. He has visited the lady and established the truth. Towering with rage on a top G Storch expresses his gratitude before bursting out at top speed with a harsh rebuke to the colleague who has allowed him to be impli-cated in his petty amours, upset Storch's wife, and deprived him of three nights' sleep. Stroh is responsible and Stroh must make amends by going personally to Grundlsee to attest his guilt and Storch's innocence in such manner as to convince Frau Christine of the truth. Both hurry off through the rain, and as the curtain falls the orchestra blazes into C major, with Ex. 7, Ex. 4, Ex. 17, and a pounding pattern on the timpani that recalls the shouts of 'Rofrano' in Act 2 of *Der Rosenkavalier*. They all exhale relief in the composer's mind.

The Interlude ends more peacefully with Ex. 1c and Ex. 4; then with Scene 4 Strauss plunges once more into a Presto of close contrapuntal imitation and furious confusion, equalled only by the sight of Frau Storch's bedroom. The curtain rises on a disarray of clothes, trunks and other chattels, through which Frau Storch picks her distracted way as Anna attempts to pack. It seems she has sent Baron Lummer to see Mieze Meier in Vienna, but forgot to give him a photograph of her husband for purposes of identification. She returns to the packing, alternately searching for what she has already packed, and scolding the servants for mistakes that she herself has made. When Anna protests, she is at once dismissed and abused—and a moment later treated as if nothing had happened. At the moment when Frau Storch begins to weaken towards her husband, a new telegram arrives and Anna persuades her mistress, who has left all communications from her husband unopened, very reluctantly to read this one which announces the forthcoming arrival of Herr Stroh to explain the confusion. Almost at once he is announced; Christine refuses to listen to what she is convinced will be a patchwork of concocted lies. But again Anna persuades her to interview the Conductor. The curtain falls and the orchestra bursts into a jubilant Interlude based on a 6/8 version of Ex. 4, and scored quite amply. Evidently it depicts the joy with which Frau Storch is convinced of her husband's complete innocence, for when the curtain rises on the last scene, in the dining-room laid for breakfast, she is voicing her delight at Robert's imminent return. He is announced (to Ex. 1a and Ex. 1c) and she is on the point of running to meet him when she pulls herself up and decides (Ex. 13) to receive him coldly and unapproachably. And so it is that when he enters greeting her warmly she refuses his embrace, gives him only her hand, and adopts a stand-offish attitude so unjust and hypocritical that we blush for a composer who could portray such a wife on the stage, and for the wife who connived at the exhibition.

Robert innocently and amiably asks: Why this fuss? It is, she replies, because he has not sufficiently taken account of the pain he has caused her; like Donna Anna at the end of Mozart's opera she demands some time to recover from the shock and disillusionment. His sweetly reasonable protests only harden Christine's resolve, and eventually he completely loses his temper with her, and storms out of the room. Her only comment is that she knew it would end like this one day.

At this moment Baron Lummer hurries in with the news that he has seen Fräulein Meier who knows Kapellmeister Storch very well. Christine now turns the tables altogether, informs the Baron of the real explanation, of her husband's return and presence in the house, and of her own unshaken confidence in his innocence from first to last. She invites the Baron to return later and make the acquaintance of her husband, then bids him goodbye. Robert returns to the room as the Baron leaves the house, and on learning the identity of the guest, admits that the Baron was his reason for returning home—the Notary had written to him. He believes wholly in his wife's innocence, but believes also that it is bad for a wife to be too much alone. There are always gossips—much as

Christine may reckon herself above suspicion. And he suggests that they make their peace, now and forever. He questions her discreetly and amiably about the Baron, and wheedles from her the ultimate outrage—the request for one thousand marks, which makes him laugh enormously. The music turns quietly and with an access of gorgeous string polyphony into A major. Exs. 10 and 11 come into their own. Robert offers gently to help the boy. Christine admits herself no longer interested: he is too shy to be worth arguing with, and she needs to argue in order to sustain her pride and self-respect. Now, however, she is determined never to quarrel with Robert again. She has discovered how dreadful it would have been to lose him, even if he had been the guilty party. She admits that it was his rage a moment ago which convinced her. A major has given way to F sharp minor, and now F sharp major as she speaks her love for him, words he would have suffered much more fear and misery to hear. Isn't that, she asks, what one calls a truly happy marriage? And in this sunset glow of euphony the opera ends.

6

Intermezzo, 'this harmless little slice of life', as Strauss called it in his reminiscences, is not to be considered very seriously as a spiritual experience or even an emotionally convincing one. Mention has already been made of the questionable taste exhibited by a composer who sets up his own wife as an Aunt Sally for the public's amusement, part shrew, part clown, often apparently hypocritical (e.g. the final scene), never very likeable; and pencils next to her a gentle, rather flattering self-portrait. It may be that a generation less close in life to the Strausses will be able to laugh uninhibitedly at the comedy—shrews are a legitimate comic subject, and there are certainly many amusing features in the treatment of Christine Storch, many opportunities for a talented singing actress with a strong personality.

The further away a production moves from the sources of the plot, and the more independently of history the principal roles are characterized, the easier it is to enjoy a performance of *Intermezzo*. In a more remote posterity it may happen that *Intermezzo* will be valued as an historical document, the last of Strauss's autobiographical compositions, a more intense operatic equivalent of the *Symphonia Domestica* which itself has autobiographical connexions with *Tod und Verklärung*, *Ein Heldenleben*, and *Eine Alpensinfonie*, and more tenuously the *Parergon* for left-handed pianist and orchestra which Strauss wrote a year after *Intermezzo*. One can also admire *Intermezzo* for the remarkably youthful quality of the music which Strauss could write about himself at the age of sixty; this too may well seem significant to future students of musical history and the psychology of the creative artist. These students may also see the piece as a therapeutic exercise, not only a cure for Frau Pauline's suspicions, but for Strauss's feelings of guilt about his own more or less harmless lapses from marital faithfulness. Primarily though, *Intermezzo* remains interesting and stimulating as a technical exercise of a definitely creative order; and it was the technically progressive aspect of the composition which Strauss emphasized in the two prefaces which he wrote for the score. (The earlier version was not published until after his death and much, but not all of it, is more comprehensively included in the published second draft.)

These prefaces remind us of Strauss's lifelong preoccupation with the marriage of words and music (this symbol of man and woman remains implicit below the surface of the quarrels between chatterbox Pauline and musician Richard, but in the end it was brought into the open and formalized in *Capriccio*), the audibility of both in performance, and particularly the ideal timing of the various speeds at which speech-music should most naturally occur in the theatre.

In the course of writing his first four operas Strauss mastered the problem of audibility by perfecting a technique of dynamic variety in his scoring so that noisier instruments and heavier masses of sonority were marked down in varying degrees, quieter instruments and prominent strands of texture kept at an appropriately audible level. Strauss acknowledged a debt of experience to the orchestral discipline obtained by Ernst von Schuch at Dresden, and as a first-rate conductor himself he discovered that it was possible to conduct a performance of *Elektra* in which every word could be understood by the audience without loss of musical audibility. *Der Rosenkavalier*, and particularly its first act, taught him that the tempo of musical speech was a problem by no means yet solved in the works of the great opera composers, nor easily to be solved. Mozart must have sensed the interconnexion of spoken dialogue with *secco* recitative, and this with orchestral recitative, and so to arioso and eventually aria; but although he achieved some marvellous transitions in *Così fan tutte* (and, though Strauss does not mention it, a superb example in the *Don Giovanni* scene which ends with *Or sai chi l'onore*), he did not take the opportunity in *Die Zauberflöte* to make the next transition between spoken dialogue and sung dialogue. Strauss, in the prefaces to *Intermezzo*, traces the history of this speech-music development through Beethoven and Weber to *Rienzi* and *Rheingold*. This last opera, together with Verdi's *Falstaff*, Mussorgsky's *The Marriage*, and the Prelude to *Ariadne II* (as well as the later operas of Janáček which Strauss is unlikely to have known) are the sources of the *Intermezzo* style. Strauss was anxious to create a traditional composing practice for musical conversation and its links in operatic word-setting, so that his younger contemporaries and successors would know automatically how to pass fluently and naturally from one to the others. He wanted these effortless changes of level to come off in less than perfect performances. To this end he warned performers of *Intermezzo* to pay special attention to the dynamics of the orchestration, to the contrapuntal texture which Satan inflicted on all German composers so that they would never shine in opera, the importance of the verbal consonant as the singer's means of riding orchestral sound, the danger to verbal clarity of the naturally guttural German voice, and the inclination of these voices to force in order to be heard, whereas Strauss had noticed that clearly articulated consonants at *mezza voce* were most effective of all in making themselves understood. All these practical considerations were in Strauss's mind when he wrote *Intermezzo*, as they had been in the *Ariadne II* Prologue and less successfully (Strauss decided) in the Nurse's music of *Die Frau ohne Schatten*— but this was surely because the Nurse's speech is at a loftier, more concentrated level than conversation. The vocal style of *Intermezzo* remains at the light level of the *Ariadne* Prologue, but is worked out in a much greater variety of moods, often rapidly alternating in Christine's part—so that the music often sounds like a chamber orchestra *Rosenkavalier*. Strauss was further developing the mercurial, integrated and flowing, but thematically very flexible style of the *Ariadne* Prologue over a much longer time-span. The above-given analytical synopsis charts the appearances of the most important themes; there are many others, though doubtless deliberately less striking in character, and recapitulated seldom but with extreme discretion, so that one hesitates to quote them all. It is a much less powerful symphonic technique than that of *Die Frau ohne Schatten*; the serious opera student must feel that many of the themes are too impersonal, too easily forgettable between one scene and another. Towards the end of the first scene of *Intermezzo* for example, Frau Storch's telephone call with a friend is accompanied in the bass by a tiny phrase, a dropping octave with an inverted mordent at the bottom; this is taken up in the first interlude. It does not reappear until Act 1, Scene 5, and then in inverted form, as it were, a new idea and still a subsidiary one. Nondescript themes are a serious drawback to the captivating power of *Intermezzo*. And yet, as a masterpiece of operatic craftsmanship, it must command the highest admiration; some of the tunes may not be memorable, but they are superbly contrived. And there is a *joie de vivre* and self-assurance about the piece which draws the Straussophile to any production or revival of it. There is something to be said for the Krauss–Hartmann plan to remove the scene at the child's cot and play the opera in three acts. Accordingly Act 1 would end after Scene 5, the orchestral postlude of which reaches a full-stop in A flat major, and the second act at the end of the second scene, with the Lawyer's last words and the tonally indecisive C–E flat on flute and clarinet—but this is not ideal, and Strauss

hotly defended his own structure, reminding Clemens Krauss that
though Puccini would doubtless have done this, he was not Puccini. In
the last analysis one is driven back to the autobiographical nature of
Intermezzo, and to Fritz Busch's perceptive observation that Strauss wore
his marvellous talents 'like a suit of clothes which can be taken off at
will'. Was Strauss aware of this chasm between the man and the artist?
Did he return to daily domestic life as a musical theme in the hope of
finding an integration of his musicianship with the most vivid source of
musical inspiration, as a recharging of his creative batteries, so to speak?
Perhaps not entirely for this reason; certainly he wanted to broaden his
scope as an operatic composer beyond the sublime *chi-chi* of Hofmannsthal's librettos; and certainly he wanted to acquire mastery over the small
pit orchestra, which he had grasped almost, but not quite fully, in the
Ariadne Prologue. And yet Busch's remark may explain *Intermezzo* more
completely than anything else. He needed to make an opera out of life,
not out of a charade. And at sixty the simple, ordinary aspects of life
become more treasurable and inspiring than ever before.

Die Ägyptische Helena

OPUS 75

Opera in Two Acts

LIBRETTO BY HUGO VON HOFMANNSTHAL

Helen, Wife of Menelaus	SOPRANO
Menelaus	TENOR
Hermione, their Child	SOPRANO
Aithra, the Daughter of an Egyptian King; a Sorceress	SOPRANO
Altair, a Nomad Chieftain	BARITONE
Da-ud, his Son	TENOR
Two Servants of Aithra	SOPRANO, MEZZO-SOPRANO
Three Elves	TWO SOPRANOS, CONTRALTO
The Omniscient Sea-Shell	CONTRALTO

I

It is well known that Helen was the most beautiful woman in all antiquity. She was the daughter of Zeus, who ravished her mother Leda in the disguise of a swan. Helen was accordingly, but unscientifically, hatched from an egg; her sister was Clytemnestra, her brothers the Dioscuri, Castor and Pollux. According to one legend Helen was abducted while still a child and put in the safe keeping of Theseus's mother Aithra—a name we shall re-encounter in Hofmannsthal's opera. If this was so, she found her way back to Sparta in time to be given away in marriage by her foster-father, King Tyndareus, to the richest of all the Achaean princes who came to woo her. Her chosen husband was Menelaus, who eventually joined her on the throne of Sparta after the death of Tyndareus and the Dioscuri. Helen bore Menelaus a daughter Hermione.

Far away in Troy, King Priam's wife Hecuba gave birth to a son (her second) who was exposed at the instruction of the royal soothsayers. The boy survived, and was carried home by a shepherd in his knapsack. For this reason he was named 'Knapsack', the Greek word for which is *Paris*. While tending his flocks on Mount Ida, south of Troy, the handsome foundling Paris was appointed by Zeus to judge the famous beauty competition between Hera, Athene, and Aphrodite, the prize being a golden apple which Eris, goddess of Discord, had inscribed 'For the Fairest' and carelessly tossed into the assembly of the gods. Each of the three ladies bribed Paris to award her the prize, but Aphrodite succeeded by promising the love of the most beautiful and passionate of all mortal women, Helen of Sparta.*

Aphrodite won the prize, and she was as good as her word. Paris was restored to his native position at Priam's court; Menelaus visited Troy, and took Paris back with him to Sparta, so that Paris could make a sacrifice supposedly required of him. He wooed Helen shamelessly and successfully, and as soon as Menelaus went off to Crete to attend a funeral, Paris sailed away with Helen who took Aithra with her, but not Hermione who was only nine years old at the time. In due course Menelaus and his fellow-princes from Greece followed them across the Aegean Sea and for ten years the Trojan War was waged.

In the fourth book of the *Odyssey* Homer brings Telemachus to the court of Sparta, ten years after the end of the war, where he finds Helen and Menelaus ruling in blissful domesticity. How does this connect with the Sack of Troy, when Menelaus dragged Helen away to his ship,

* Robert Graves, in *Greek Myths*, rouses the interest of the Straussian operatic student by linking Helen and Ariadne as fertility goddesses both worshipped in the images of dolls swinging from trees—a custom by which children's swings were invented.

vowing to murder her either on the high seas or as soon as they reached home?

This was a problem which puzzled Hugo von Hofmannsthal in his reading of the classics; and it had puzzled the classic authors of antiquity as well. A Sicilian poet named Stesichorus is credited with the solution upon which Hofmannsthal's libretto is based; having written a powerful poetic denunciation of the adulteress who brought thousands of bold and noble soldiers to untimely death, Stesichorus was struck blind, and was eventually informed that this was the vengeance of Helen herself, now an immortal spending eternity on the island of Lemnos in the Black Sea where, with her posthumous husband Achilles, she gave a non-stop recital of Homeric poetry to all the heroes who had taken part. (Lemnos is now a Rumanian penal settlement; and no wonder!)

Stesichorus promptly and tactfully produced a new poem which explained that not Helen but a phantom of air went off to Troy with Paris; the real Helen remained unsullied until she was reclaimed by Menelaus after the Sack of Troy. And in due course the details, often confusing, of this tale became established. Stesichorus recited his poem in public, and at once recovered his sight.

Modern readers are best acquainted with this whitewashing episode of the saga through Euripides's *Helen*, a work based, scholars have convincingly argued, on earlier and extremely familiar, but now lost, dramas on the story. From references to these we understand that when Athene set the Trojan War in motion, Hera (acting as patroness of marriage) took care of Menelaus's interests by bringing up a strong breeze which diverted Paris's ship to the salt pans in the Canopic mouth of the Nile. Hermes thereupon spirited the real Helen to Memphis into the protection of King Proteus (he with the original Protean gift of quick-change), while a phantom was put in her shape on Paris's ship. King Proteus had a daughter named Idothea or Theonome, who was an infallible prophetess, and Hofmannsthal has identified this sorceress with Aithra, or rather with two Aithras: for as well as the mother of Theseus and Helen's nanny, there was also an Aithra who was the daughter of Oceanus, the wife of Atlas, and the mother of the Hyades (seven daughters who figure in 'Green grow the rushes-o' as the 'seven stars in the sky', and also, with their brother Hyas, as 'eight for the April Rainers'—Hyades means Rainers). Oceanus was antiquity's name for the Atlantic Ocean, so called because Mount Atlas supposedly dominated one of its shores.

It is on Mount Atlas that Hofmannsthal places the fortress ruled by Aithra's father, presumably Oceanus, to which Helen was wafted en route for Troy, by Hermes. Euripides uses a version of the tales whereby Menelaus, returning with Helen from Troy, is blown into Egypt, finds the real Helen, accepts her explanation—which is confirmed by sudden dematerialization of the phantom Helen—and, after playing a trick on

22 Hermann Prey and Hanni Steffek as Robert and Christine Storch in the Munich production of *Intermezzo*, 1964

23 The arrival of Menelaus (Karl Ostertag) and Helen (Viorica Ursuleac) at Aithra's palace: the All-Knowing Sea Shell can be seen between them: Munich production, 1940

24 Altair (Hans Hotter) pays homage to Helen (Viorica Ursuleac): Munich, 1940

25 Mandryka (Hans Hotter, R.) asks Count Waldner (Georg Hann, L.) for Arabella's hand: Munich. 1939

26 Arabella (Lisa Della Casa) brings the glass of water to Mandryka (Hermann Uhde) in the closing scene of the Munich production, 1953

27
Richard Strauss and Fritz Busch
outside the Dresden Opera House

28
Stefan Zweig, librettist of *Die
Schweigsame Frau*

the suitor who wanted to wed her, sails back to Sparta. Homer, too, made Menelaus wander for eight years after the Sack of Troy, before landing in Egypt* where he discovered, from Proteus, the cause of his troubles (he had not sacrificed to Zeus) and so put himself in a position to sail safely home.

Hofmannsthal, we have seen, regarded myth as the truest of all dramatic subjects. And he was particularly fascinated by myths of metamorphosis and human faithfulness. He was not content, however, to retail the myth of two Helens as it has come down to us; he needed to explain it and make the symbols real for a modern audience. Between 1920 and 1923 he worked out his own recension of the drama whereby Menelaus lost his hatred for his adulterous wife and accepted her back in a spirit of unclouded love before leaving Egypt for Sparta. The 'phantom' Helen is too unconvincing an image for a modern writer. And so Hofmannsthal gave us simply one Helen, who pacifies her husband by a conjuring trick,† and then insists, for the sake of her integrity, on undoing the spell so that he may accept her for what she really is. 'Helen,' he says, 'must have complete possession of the man to whom she belongs.' The crux has been even better summarized by Oscar von Pander: 'By far the majority of men in love substitute the *likeness* of the inamorata for her real person; they erect a statue on a pedestal, so to speak, which is able to conceal the terrible truth under a veil of iridescent allure.'‡ The figure of the husband, Menelaus, was influenced, Hofmannsthal admitted, by his experience of war victims; and so it is that Menelaus can be tranquillized by drugs and by illusory persuasion, but will only be returned to normal life when he is made aware of everything in the past and what it means. In the first act he fights a phantom Trojan War over again, and he returns to a virtually phantom bride—or so he regards Euripides's 'real' Helen. She is not as real to him as the much beloved for whom he fought ten years, the guilty adulteress whom he believed slaughtered in his nightmare. He therefore has to kill a 'real' Paris, the innocent Da-ud, in order to recognize his own guilt, and divorce Helen's past actions from her worth as an individual.

Perhaps it is a pity to have given away the story so early in the chapter but *Die Ägyptische Helena* has persistently been denigrated as feeble, trivial, factitious and naïve. And if it is not the strongest of the Strauss–Hofmannsthal operas, it is not as weak as some critics have maintained.

---

* History explains these visits to Egypt, far out of the route between Sparta and Troy, by Dardanian and Achaean invasions of North Africa.

† Aithra's potion of *oblivion soave* (as Monteverdi's very realistic Arnalta calls it) occurs in the fourth book of the *Odyssey*, where Helen is said to have acquired it from one Polydamna in Egypt. The authors of *Die Ägyptische Helena*, particularly Strauss, were anxious that listeners should realize that potions of this kind are an accepted part of antique myth, in all civilizations, adopted in order to abbreviate the exposition of drastic action. In an age of quick-acting tranquillizers we may find Aithra's little bottles less stupid than audiences of 1928 did.

‡ O. von Pander, *Clemens Krauss in München* (Munich, 1955).

Strauss, who did not think it worthwhile to redeem an old flop when he could spend his energy in creating a new success, was persuaded to reshape and improve *Helena* five years after its première, and without his librettist's guidance. And he had a special reason for doing so; for the theme of marital trust and affectionate illusion, so nobly treated in *Helena*, was one which he had developed at an everyday level in *Intermezzo*, and which was always in his mind.

2

When, in 1916, Hofmannsthal invited Strauss to collaborate in some more mythological operas, 'the truest kind that exists', Strauss was not impressed; he needed something more actual and directly self-identifying, and so he wrote *Intermezzo*. But having tackled this ever-present inspiration, he was ready to treat similar emotions and conflicts at the formalized level of myth, when, in 1923, Hofmannsthal proposed *Die Ägyptische Helena*. As with *Ariadne*, he did not for some time appreciate the real point of Hofmannsthal's dramatic idea: what he did look forward to, I believe, was an opera about Greece and Egypt, countries which he knew and had been inspired by, and to an opera about *La Belle Hélène*. Most of all he looked forward to what promised to be a light opera, almost operetta, with spoken dialogue, melodrama, and all the various kinds of recitative culminating in true arioso lyricism. *Die Ägyptische Helena* would, he was sure, allow him to take the speech-music techniques of *Intermezzo* a decisive step further in another more formal, but not more cold, direction. For some time he intended a good part of Hofmannsthal's libretto to be spoken by the characters—though in the end everything was set down for singing, and the whole is far heavier and more exalted than any operetta.

In June 1919 Strauss asked Hofmannsthal for a political satire set in late Grecian times, and with Jeritza as a hetaira out of Lucian. Here is perhaps a beginning of *Die Ägyptische Helena* which was always conceived by the authors in terms of Jeritza (Strauss had first seen and fallen for her in a performance of Offenbach's *La Belle Hélène*). Hofmannsthal's immediate response, however, was the rough scenario of *Danae oder die Vernunftsheirat* (much later worked into a libretto by Josef Gregor) which he sent to Strauss on 23 April 1920. Some time before April 1923 Hofmannsthal talked to Strauss about the idea of an opera on the return of Helen and Menelaus from Troy—this much we know from an essay on the piece written by Hofmannsthal shortly before the première. Strauss, who was touring America, greatly looked forward to the new Hofmannsthal libretto, and hoped it would contain opportunities for ballet in each act—his way of expressing a need for something light and attractive. (In retrospect we must admit that he had never, since *Elektra*, wanted or needed a serious subject, though all his operas, even his own *Intermezzo*, had turned out more serious than he expected.) In September 1923 Hofmannsthal named the cast for which he was writing *Helena*: the title role, now and always, belonged to Jeritza; Oestvig or Tauber should be Menelaus, Lotte Schöne was Aithra (at one stage called Sistre, but not for long), Hans Duhan (the Music Master in *Ariadne II*), would be Altair, and Jerger should be Da-ud (but Strauss never considered a baritone for this role). Hofmannsthal was at constant pains to stress that the Elves in Act 1 must sound malign and frightening—Strauss never quite met him on this issue—and that the Omniscient Sea-Shell should appear comical and mysterious, which it has never done (it usually looks like a rococo television set). Strauss, who had by now fallen in with Hofmannsthal's operatic ideals (after all, he could not easily find a better librettist, and he was beginning to feel too old for pioneering, unlike Schoenberg), confessed himself delighted with the libretto as parts of the first act reached him; he found that it inspired music perfectly naturally, even though he suggested different ordination of the scenes—this was adopted. Hofmannsthal in turn proposed manifold cuts, but Strauss observed few of these. All this happened in 1923. Strauss and Hofmannsthal were able to meet often in 1924 thanks to the composer's Vienna post which did not terminate until the end of the year, and their letters are not of particular interest on the subject of *Helena*, apart from one in which Hofmannsthal strongly recommends that the Elves should be sung by male voices (Strauss's ensemble of girls seems a dreadful mistake, visually and audibly). During this year Strauss drafted the composition of Act 1. But he found difficulty in settling down to Act 2, and one can sympathize, since the emotional inspiration is no longer present; the second act is devoted to an intellectual problem whose solution involves repetition of the earlier action at a different level—not recapitulation so much as the re-presentation of events already just presented. This is a formal, but not fundamentally realistic idea.

Strauss managed Helen's first solo in Act 2—a marvellous lyrical invention whose excessive length can be put out of mind by a radiant and convincing soprano—and the ensuing duet. But the advent of the nomad cohort halted his creative machinery, and though his hesitancy was alleviated by a visit to Hofmannsthal at Rodaun so that he was able to move forward, Hofmannsthal was persuaded that the libretto needed some more cuts, and by the end of the year he had tightened the second act considerably. Strauss's anxiety to include plentiful passages of speech, alone or with accompanying music, seems to have been squashed after a letter from Hofmannsthal on 12 February 1925; the poet sensibly suggested that Verdi's technique in *Falstaff* might prove fruitfully influential, though Act 2 still contains some sections of dry recitative close to the style of *Das Rheingold*. In March 1926 Strauss was ready to play Act 1 to the poet, and for this purpose he persuaded Elisabeth Schumann to learn Helen's first scene in only a few hours; she sang the three Helen solos so beautifully (though her voice was too small for the part in the theatre) that Strauss inscribed the autograph voice part from which she had learned her songs, 'to the first Helen: Elisabeth in memory of 27 March 1926'.

There was a small diversion in September 1926 when Dr Paul Eger, a well-known theatrical manager, pressed Hofmannsthal to observe the symmetries by ending the opera with the apparition of Poseidon as Aithra's lover (she begins the opera with a song of yearning for him); fortunately this came to nothing, though the episode would have been possible if Strauss had preserved his diminuendo end of the second act. Since Poseidon never materialized, and the opera simply ended with a fade into the distance, Fritz Busch, the chosen conductor of the première, objected, and three days later Strauss produced a revised conclusion, fortissimo.

But before this, Hofmannsthal had made a protest of his own (6 May 1927) against Strauss's proposal to cast Da-ud as a travesty role (the poet, it will be remembered, had thought of the virile baritone Alfred Jerger), and Strauss compromised by giving the part to a tenor, with optional suitability to a mezzo-soprano—it was so done at the Metropolitan première in New York.* The remaining letters were concerned with some lapses—Strauss had again set a stage direction to music, Helen's *Schon im halben Schlaf hinein* which remains in the score because it fits well enough; and he had made Menelaus sing words intended solely for Helen (new words had to be written) and with problems of casting. Both authors had conceived Helen as a role for Jeritza, and they had agreed to another Dresden première. But Jeritza's fees were now too extortionate for Dresden and so Strauss suggested Elisabeth Rethberg. Hofmannsthal was not at all pleased by this idea—he thought the lady too dumpy and bourgeois, and was unswayed by promises of Rethberg's gorgeous singing which had so impressed Strauss in *Die Frau ohne Schatten*.† Eventually the partners agreed to a Dresden première under Busch with Rethberg on 6 June, followed on 11 June (Strauss's birthday) by a Viennese première under Strauss with Jeritza. Strauss was very anxious that Hofmannsthal should help critics and public by publishing an elucidatory foreword, and by writing a synopsis of the action for the programme. (This seems to have been a new feature of opera programme books, which Strauss

---

* Da-ud's part lies more naturally for a mezzo-soprano; the first Italian tenor who took the role at Dresden, Guglielmo Fazzini, found it uncomfortably low, and Strauss cheerfully revised it to suit Fazzini's voice.

† From the number of necessary references in this chapter to Helen's beauty it will be seen that the part can only be given to an extraordinarily glamorous soprano with so voluptuous a voice that it will reduce strong men to abject surrender.

regarded as a poor substitute for reading the libretto.) Hofmannsthal produced not only a synopsis printed in the libretto, but an article couched in the form of an imaginary interview between him and the composer. And Strauss made a radio broadcast about *Helena* with the critic, Dr Ludwig Karpath, as interlocutor. Strauss completed the score on 8 October 1927.

The première, on 6 June 1928, opened a week's celebration of the Dresden Opera House's jubilee. Fritz Busch, who conducted, had been ill during rehearsals and a good deal went wrong when he took over direction. The producer was Otto Erhardt whom the authors had agreed was good, but no genius, and therefore they took pains to acquire Marie Gutheil-Schoder as assistant producer.* Elisabeth Rethberg sang the title role (she had given up an American tour in order to do so, being a native of Dresden), Curt Taucher was Menelaus (soon replaced by the young Max Lorenz). Maria Rajdl sang Aithra, Friedrich Plaschke was Altair. Leonhard Fanto designed the rather too baroque décors (Hofmannsthal had asked for female costumes like Paris fashions)—later designers created more solid, more Hellenic designs. Even if one discounts the reactionary critics, this seems to have been a less than potent première. Five days later followed the opera's baptism in Vienna under Strauss, with Jeritza, Gunnar Graarud (a famous Tristan) as Menelaus, and Margrit Schenker-Angerer as Aithra. Five years later Clemens Krauss conducted *Helena* at the Salzburg Festival and collaborated with the producer Lothar Wallerstein in a new version which somewhat rearranged the second act, even to including two sections newly composed most unwillingly by Strauss. At Berlin in 1935, and Munich in 1940, Rudolf Hartmann placed the first part of the first act out of doors, so that the tempest, the arrival of the ships and the fight with the Elves, were all made visible to the spectator (see Plate 23). I shall try to show the reader where the two versions differ, while basing the synopsis on this accepted second version.

Die Ägyptische Helena made its way to the major German opera houses, to New York (where Jeritza, not Rethberg, as some accounts state, sang the title role, where Da-ud was assigned to a woman, and where the role of Hermione was dropped after the first night), to Zürich, Antwerp and Budapest. In 1933 Krauss and Wallerstein persuaded Strauss to drop Hermione's short sung utterance, since it was dramatically off-putting and invariably badly sung by the terrified young chorister. Since the war the sung part has been reinstated at Munich where *Helena* remains in the repertory. It has never been given in Britain.

* Leo Wurmser has written highly interesting recollections of the initial rehearsals (*Music and Letters*, January 1964).

3

It has been intimated above (p. 219) that, as far as Hofmannsthal's Menelaus is concerned, the War of Troy is by no means over; it has to be fought again before he can be cured of his war-madness. The opening orchestral bars re-invoke that war, the cause of Menelaus's suffering. The opera begins with flutes and clarinets squealing out the meaning for both sides, of the 'face that launched a thousand ships'.

This is Helen, the cause of the Trojan war, and in the figure marked x, the world's most dazzling beauty. Sometimes Ex. 1 seems to refer to Troy itself (though motif x is always Helen, very often in augmentation), but the 'topless towers of Ilium' have a striking succession of brass chords.

This Trojan theme is subsequently to be recognized by the initial tritone progression (marked a) which has a special thematic importance; but the melodic contour of the whole theme is sometimes used independently. During the first statement of these big chords, the strings interject a florid counterpoint, parts of which have thematic significance and are quoted. Ex. 2b usually refers to Paris, 2c always to Menelaus, 2d more generally to Troy. The curtain now rises, and two harps strike up a fortissimo D minor arpeggio which is connected with the sea-god Poseidon.

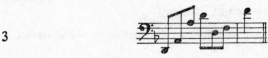

The scene shows (if we follow Rudolf Hartmann's version, which had Strauss's blessing) a terrace outside the palace of Aithra (pronounced

'Ah-ee-tra') on the shores of a Mediterranean island not far from Egypt. Aithra sits on a high-backed throne, a servant plays the harp on a stool at her feet. There is a table laid for two (Aithra lives in constant hope that Poseidon, her lover, will come to dinner), and a giant Sea-Shell stands on the terrace. It is evening and the sea is dark. Clemens Krauss thought it a mistake on Hofmannsthal's part to begin an opera about Helen by showing a beautiful woman sitting on a throne who eventually turns out not to be Helen at all. But this need perplex nobody if Aithra's costume is made recognizably Egyptian and recognizably that of a sorceress.

Above the thrumming of the harps an oboe plays an exotic dance-melody (it could almost have come from *Salome*), and when it is over Aithra stands up and at once begins an extended invocation to Poseidon who, she says, has too long left her to pine for him in loneliness. A hollow contralto voice comes from the Sea-Shell, which is Aithra's companion and a magical source of information. Poseidon sends her greetings and messages of love and faithfulness; he is detained in Ethiopia. Aithra is upset by the news, and her servant offers to fetch a tranquillizing potion of lotus juice which will relieve her chagrin. The potion is portrayed by two ideas, one scampering, the other sinuously chromatic (not unlike Wagner's Tarnhelm motif in *The Ring*).

Aithra indignantly refuses the tranquillizer; she needs companionship not drugs. At this moment the Sea-Shell begins to sing about a man who stands up, on board a ship where all others are asleep. The Shell's voice is supposed to be curiously distorted, and the serving-maid crouches beside it to interpret; Ex. 2c tells us that the man is Menelaus. He is descending to a cabin where sleeps his wife, the most beautiful woman in the world. Besides Ex. 2 melodically on cellos and basses and Ex. 1ˣ severally, the clarinet announces this sinuous phrase.

The man kisses her. Then, to the consternation of the Sea-Shell, he prepares to slay the woman with a cutlass. Ex. 2 remains prominent when the Sea-Shell reveals the identities of the couple, to a noble and beautiful B major triad derivative of Ex. 1ˣ, softly breathed out by woodwind and violins as a special Helen theme.

6

The Sea-Shell implores Aithra to avert this murder by invoking her magic arts. Aithra commands a storm to beat upon the ship and tear it apart. Ex. 3 on the trombones hears and obliges, and the strings seethe and surge vividly while organ chords off-stage depict the wreck of the ship. The Sea-Shell reports that Menelaus is swimming ashore carrying Helen in his arms; Aithra subdues the storm at once, and calls for a torch to light their way to shore. She is agog to meet and talk with Helen, here in her palace; a brief reference to her opening soliloquy and to the Troy chords of Ex. 2, and then, at the words 'Helen of Troy', a soft and solemn new phrase.

7

Sometimes, meditates Aithra while the first three notes of Ex. 1 are spread out and reshaped, dreams do come true. And as she hides herself in an adjoining room, there are echoes of the oboe melody at the start of the scene. Echoes of Ex. 3 as well. Then silence and an empty terrace.

The serving-maid runs up from the beach with the torch, conducting a handsome man in light armour, carrying a cutlass in his teeth, and dragging behind him the paragon of all loveliness. They are left alone. Helen finds a looking-glass, and tidies her hair. Menelaus (who, according to Homer, is distinguished by his red hair) lays down his cutlass. Ex. 7 on the bass-clarinet breaks the silence. Menelaus wonders whose house this is. Helen, at once mistress of the situation, remarks (derivative of Ex. 5) on the fire, the table for two, and the implicit invitation to sit down and eat. A king and queen are clearly expected here in this splendid place (Ex. 6, immensely impressive and Valhalla-like on the brass). They are now embarked on a lyrical duet in which Helen has decidedly the prima donna's share—this was the first section which Elisabeth Schumann sang to Hofmannsthal. Thematically it centres on Ex. 5 and Ex. 2. She is attempting to restore his confidence, cheerfulness and love; he is morose and unforthcoming (because, of course, he is still determined to slay Helen as the cause of ten years' battle and carnage, and an adulteress into the bargain). Aithra, watching from behind a curtain, finds him unimpressive. Helen now fetches a goblet of wine from the dinner table, and offers it to Menelaus in a dignified solo based on Ex. 7 (*Bei jener Nacht*), one of the highlights of the work.*

* It bears a distinct resemblance to the Goethe setting *Durch allen Schall* which Strauss wrote in 1926 for Romain Rolland's birthday.

At the conclusion of her song she touches the rim of the goblet with her lips, and offers it to him. But he refuses it with a bitter sneer about Paris and his brothers. Brightly Helen turns this to wooing account, and now offers him a fig from which she has bitten a morsel. Again he refuses. But she shows no surprise or disappointment, even when he reveals his murderous intentions. Does she, he asks, recognize the crooked weapon? Low woodwind and double-basses intone a phrase associated with the cutlass.

8

Certainly she knows it; the music plunges turbulently into 7/4 metre and fragments of Ex. 2 as she identifies the weapon with which Menelaus slew Paris—so that, she concludes, she might be restored to her husband's arms. I must bring up my daughter,* he rather smugly announces, to respect the principle that a woman belongs to one man only; she counters that Hermione is her daughter too, and she, Helen, belongs only to Menelaus. He calls on the gods above to help him in his undertaking, she on the powers below to shield her from his violence. They burst into the coda of their duet, she invoking the protection of Mother Earth and Night (*Erde und Nacht*), he abjuring them. Their phrases are made of the Menelaus theme preceded by another, a new one, which I quote together with three later derivatives.

9

The orchestral commentary to this strenuous duet further involves Ex. 6. Helen and Menelaus end on a top C. He is obviously about to slaughter her at this instant. But Helen's appeal to subterranean powers has been heard—by Aithra who casts a spell on Menelaus† while she calls up her Elves, green-eyed, sinister spirits of mischief, to distract the

* Hofmannsthal blandly ignores the historical facts: Hermione was nine when Helen went to Troy; the Trojan War lasted ten years; it took Helen and Menelaus eight years to reach Egypt. Therefore Hermione would by this time be twenty-seven, and her mother in the mid-forties. But Aithra, later in the act, implies that it is only nine or ten years since Helen was abducted.

† This stage direction was added by Wallerstein and Krauss for the Salzburg version as the only possible means of making the following scene clear to an audience.

attention of this hot-headed ruffian. Since they are spirits the Elves have no theme of their own; their music is scherzando, lightly scored, and based on transformations of the Helen theme Ex. 1^x, and the Menelaus Ex. 2^3. Aithra's invocation is vocally agile and florid, as she instructs the Elves to delude Menelaus with a second Trojan war. Helen waits in an ecstasy of death-wish for the stroke of her husband's cutlass; Menelaus's hand is stayed by her beauty each time that he raises the weapon. Near at hand but partly invisible, a three-part chorus of Elves, with four soloists, simulates the clash of arms and calls out: Paris is here. Menelaus is distracted. Do the dead want to die again? He storms off in the direction of the phantom warriors whose laughter can be heard.

Aithra steps out and comes to Helen, explaining that this is Poseidon's house, that she is Aithra's guest, and Aithra will save her. The Sea-Shell retails Menelaus's rampaging through a mist in search of the phantoms Paris and Helen. Meanwhile Aithra exerts her arts to dry Helen's clothes, renew her radiant beauty (Ex. 5) and remove all tension and anxiety with a draught of lotus juice—the slave-girl repeats her testimonial to its effectiveness (television commercials and tranquillizers have taken much of the magic from this bit!). In duet Helen and Aithra agree, to Ex. 5, that two mutually trusting women are stronger than any warrior, richer than any king. Helen drinks again (Ex. 4^1), grows drowsy, and is supported by two slave-girls as she croons her love for Menelaus, half-asleep—this is where Strauss set the stage direction. Ex. 2c becomes the opening of a languorous lullaby at the end of which she falls completely asleep. The Elves are audibly closer now and Helen is carried by the slaves into Aithra's bedroom, dressed in Aithra's most exquisite dress, and laid on her bed just before Menelaus bursts back on to the terrace, bits of Ex. 2 at his heels, sword in hand. With a cry, twice echoed by Elves (a marvellous polytonal effect), Aithra hides behind a curtain. Menelaus is remembering how he slew, not a moment ago, Helen and Paris together; his sword seems drenched in blood, and he hides it quickly (it is in fact clean and bright). Aithra steps before him saluting him as her guest, bids him be seated, and calls for the lotus draught (Ex. 4^1 mixed with Ex. 2). Menelaus is greatly surprised when Aithra asks him to talk quietly, so as not to disturb the slumbers of his wife. In a fervent solo he calls passionately on the gods to restore his happiness. Aithra's answer is to explain to him (Ex. 2d) that since the day when he went hunting, nine years ago,* he has not seen his wife; when Paris laid hands on her (Exs. 2 and 1), the gods laboured for Menelaus and gave Paris a phantom Helen, a creature of air (specifically Ex. 1); the Elves echo Aithra's phrases. Menelaus's dangerous hot temper (red hair, no doubt) is assuaged with more lotus juice, as Aithra tells of her father's

---

* Hofmannsthal wrote: 'thrice three years and a year' but Strauss omitted to set the extra year to music.

castle on Mount Atlas (*Am Hang des Atlas steht eine Burg*), where she grew
up with her two sisters Salome* and Morgana. One day Helen was
brought to the castle where throughout the years of war she lay in a
magic sleep, dreaming that she was in the arms of Menelaus, while the
phantom Helen made free of all Troy. Again the invisible Elves echo
Aithra's words (there is a short cut here marked in the full score of the
revised version, but it looks unauthoritative and serves little purpose).
Menelaus is greatly astonished by this intelligence, and suspects, when
told he will see his true bride, that Aithra is a zombie-raiser; his outburst
is characterized by a hard, lucid, strong orchestral texture that is typical
of Strauss's Greek operas (we find it in *Daphne* and *Danae*, and supremely
in *Elektra*, but not in the baroque *Ariadne*). In the ensuing duet with
Aithra the colours grow increasingly rich and warm, until a long pedal-
point on B at the end of a splendid orchestral Intermezzo is resolved on a
soft E major chord, for strings and backstage organ.

The scene has changed to Aithra's bedroom where Helen lies asleep.
A solo horn exhales Ex. 9^2; strings gently depict the rise and fall of
Helen's breast. Slowly she opens her eyes: 'An Angel' cry two invisible
Elves; but their fellow-spirits add mocking laughter. Cellos introduce a
scale melody that hints at Happy Ends.

10

While Aithra whispers hush to her Elves, Helen, refreshed and radiant
from sleep, sits up on the bed, and Menelaus hardly dares to contemplate
this vision, as beautiful as when he first saw her. Ex. 5 has acquired a new
voluptuousness and distant affiliations with Brangäne's Dawn Song in
Tristan und Isolde. As Helen gets off the bed Aithra quickly brings her up
to date with a résumé of *Am Hang des Atlas*, sung at Menelaus as if to
remind him. Helen, all modesty and shyness, asks him if she is still his
only love, and Aithra in triumph asks him if this could ever be the proud
harlot of Troy (Ex. 1). Now it is Menelaus who hesitates, uncertain if he
is worthy of this unsurpassed creature. The shy couple, the triumphant
Aithra (who soars to top D), and the mocking Elves unite in a lively
ensemble. Helen is the first to take action, telling Aithra that her husband
loves another; she herself has never left him, he was with her while she
slept. They are now clasped in one another's arms, man and wife, and
Aithra prepares to send them aboard ship to sail home. But Helen, a
little afraid of Sparta, asks for a brief stay alone with her husband somewhere where the names of Troy and Helen are unknown. Aithra suggests
an oasis at the foot of Atlas, and promises magical transport for them.

* This Salome is accented on the second syllable, as distinct from the daughter of
Herodias.

They fall in with the plan, and each in turn extols this access of complete happiness—though Menelaus's ecstatic solo pointedly incorporates Ex. 1, the Other Helen. Aithra, meanwhile, is whispering to Helen that she will send a chest of necessary luggage, notably a flask of lotus juice which Menelaus may require in order to put away wicked thoughts. Their trio is resumed, and the melody flies from one voice to another, as in the *Rosenkavalier* trio. Menelaus and Helen are left alone in the bedroom which now grows dark as Ex. 6 (or rather the version sung by Helen in her first aria) thunders forth, followed by the Trojan Ex. 2, and the ecstatic Ex. 10. The Elves' mockery can still be discerned. Aithra crossly orders them to be silent, and very quietly Strauss combines Ex. 1^x, Ex. 2c, Ex. 1 and Ex. 2. Peace descends and with a last augmentation of Ex. 10 on the horn, the act closes in serenest E major.

4

The second act opens passionately with Ex. 7, which subsides into an undercurrent of Ex. 1^x as the curtain rises to reveal a sizeable tent in a palm grove below Mount Atlas. Menelaus is asleep, Helen is twining pearls in her hair while regarding herself in a golden looking-glass and soliloquizing, in expansive vocal phrases that look forward to Strauss's *Four Last Songs*, on the bliss of this second honeymoon (*Zweite Brautnacht!*). This marvellous solo, rich in thematic reminiscence, appears in performance to have been written in one breathless sentence, a single act of inspiration. A superb soprano with first-class breath-control brings down the house with *Zweite Brautnacht!*; but such sopranos are rare.

Menelaus awakes (the lullaby transformation of Ex. 2c) still bemused by the events of the previous evening and astonished by the soothing yet invigorating effect of the magic potion he drank. Helen promises him more of the same drink, and their questions and answers, expressed in quatrains that soon begin to sound rather stiff and prim, fall easily into a dialogue duet chiefly concerned with a voluptuous transformation of the Protean Ex. 5. This version, which first appeared near the beginning of *Zweite Brautnacht!* should perhaps be cited separately.

11

When Helen searches in the chest for the lotus drink, she accidentally lets Menelaus's cutlass clatter out on the floor. Menelaus runs to pick it up (Ex. 8 and now Ex. 9^3 on the trombone), and sadly recalls the woman he struck down with it. In the light of day he recognizes the proximity of

the fit which led him once to destroy a phantom Helen, and might again
send him in murderous pursuit of the real and radiant, but still apparently
phantom, creature who stands before him.

This wild and frightening outburst convinces Helen that the fit is a
deep-seated psychological disorder that can be suppressed temporarily by
drugs but will have to be thoroughly cured by more drastic, physical
means if she and he are to live happily ever after. She throws the lotus
juice into the chest and vows to face the problem and solve it somehow.*

The solution now presents itself, did she but know it. Sounds of horses'
hooves are heard, the stamp of a cavalcade. Strauss lets us know that they
are relevant, for the stamping figure is compounded of the three notes
that make up Ex. 2c, as was the Elves' theme in Act 1. The point is that
Menelaus can only rid himself of suspicion and insecurity by fighting
the Trojan War again for its own sake and not for revenge on Helen. The
phantom war with the Elves was no real cure because it was effected by a
trick. The true cure on which Helen is determined (though she does not
yet divine its nature) has to be carried out in daylight on a patient fully
conscious, so to speak. The cohorts now approaching will enable it to be
achieved successfully, as we shall discover. In some peculiar but sensible
fashion they represent the Trojan host.

Helen cries for Menelaus to protect his own (Ex. 2b on horn and
violins, the Paris theme), just as a detachment of desert warriors in chain-
mail takes up position in the grove beyond the tent; runners enter and
prostrate themselves before Helen, and are followed by the chieftain of
the district, Altair, a majestic figure who kneels before Helen, touches the
earth and then his forehead in homage, and rises. Altair has his own
sombre theme for bass-clarinet and double-bassoon, suggestive of his
dignity, stature and ruthlessness.

12

The initial tritone also suggests a psychological link with Troy and
Ex. 2. Black slaves bring in a rich carpet as a gift for Helen who now sits
on the chest, as on a throne; Menelaus, with drawn sword (Ex. 9³),
standing behind her. She signals Altair to step on to the carpet, and to
speak. He tells her that the princesses Aithra, Salome and Morgana have
commanded him to lay their land at the feet of this unknown stranger.
All this time he has not once raised his eyes; now he does so and is almost
blinded by her godlike beauty, and moved to an even greater reverence.
More gifts are brought in; three veiled maidens run forward and fall at

* Two separate cuts in this final part of their duet are much to be frowned on, as
obscuring the force of this decision, and its cause, and as falsifying the symmetry of the
musical structure.

her feet, and now a company of young boys takes their place, among them
Altair's son Da-ud. The chieftain, who cannot remove his eyes from
Helen and has clearly fallen a victim to her beauty, depreciates these
unworthy tokens of homage and offers the deaths of these boys for her
sake, for one single glance from her golden eyelashes.* Altair offers this
alarming and drastic present in the name of Da-ud, as a repetitive and
passionate motif eventually makes clear. As so often with Strauss the
first appearance of Da-ud's theme is not the definitive one, and accordingly I quote the later form in D flat.

13

Menelaus is immensely impressed by this spectacle, which recalls
Troy's homage to the Helen now lost to him, particularly when Altair
and the young men raise their swords to the heavens and offer to pour
out their blood in the sand for a sigh from Helen's lips (here we have
Ex. 13 as quoted). And Da-ud, stepping forward, proclaims that it is
right to die for such unequalled beauty. His tiny aria in D flat roused
Fritz Busch to rebuke Strauss for including anything so cheap and
mawkish. The composer answered that without such lapses no opera
would appeal to the public—where would *Tannhäuser* be without 'O Star
of Eve'? But it may have been subsequently that he marked Da-ud's solo
to be sung 'quietly and yearning, but without any trace of espressivo'.
Da-ud withdraws, but Menelaus cries out suddenly that this is Paris
come again, a shameless suitor to his wife; and Ex. 13 is combined with
Ex. 1^x. In highest excitement he reaches for his sword (Ex. 9^3). Helen
attempts, none too successfully, to soothe her husband; Menelaus
suggests that he is out of place here; and Altair mutters a sour comment
on the boorish behaviour of the goddess's favourite. However, he is
prepared to offer gifts to Menelaus too, if that will please Helen. A brass
ensemble backstage summons the warriors to a hunt, slaves bring in a
small armoury from which Menelaus is invited to choose a gift for himself, and woodwind introduce a new Altair theme, ultimately derived
from Ex. 12.

14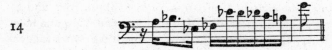

Menelaus, his temper now mastered, proudly recalls the glorious
weapons that he wielded on the fields of battle and in the blazing streets of
Troy (Exs. 2c and 2b, Exs. 1 and 9^3 tell us what they were and why). Altair

* The horns at this point make a quite unexpected but appropriate reference to the
Empress's theme in *Die Frau ohne Schatten*.

promises him equally good sport in the hunting field; he has planned a
hunt in Menelaus's honour, and for companion he will give him Da-ud.
Altair adds that he hopes the prey will be worthy of the hunters; Ex. 6,
Ex. 1ˣ and Ex. 5 tell us the prey that he is already stalking. With a signal
to Da-ud to remain with Menelaus, Altair leaves the tent. Menelaus too
has ideas of his own about the prey he intends to hunt; he repeats
Altair's words to Ex. 13, as Da-ud steps forward and greets him solemnly.
The whole episode and its characters seem strange and dreamlike to
Menelaus (Ex. 4², the lotus potion, and Ex. 5, the dream Helen). The
hunting calls are still sounding, and slaves accompany him into the tent
where he arrays himself for the chase. Da-ud is left alone with Helen, and
he too is a victim of her beauty. For a moment he cannot bring himself
to look at her face, then he suddenly declares his infatuation to an
aspiring new idea.

15

Helen warns him to beware of the fire which will melt him like wax,
but Da-ud confirms that she is born to be queen of the sun, and he to be
her slave until death (Ex. 13 again). He prostrates himself and leaves the
tent, while Helen smiles after him with some amusement. Menelaus is
now dressed for hunting (Ex. 2) and Helen steps towards him, with his
helmet. Menelaus reminds her, in a little aria, that he was once sent out
hunting by just such a lovely nymph, and when he returned she had gone
away, and now is dead. He asks this nymph her name and Helen protests
lightly that he should know the name of his own soul's soul. With courtly
but obviously distraught phrases of admiration he excuses himself; the
hunting horns call him. She recommends him to take a more suitable
hunting weapon than his cutlass, but he clasps it to him as the object
now, in a time of wandering among strangers, closer to him than any
other. Look me in the eyes at least, she asks, and recognize me. While
lower strings play Ex. 5, and the harp Ex. 1ˣ, high violins and flute
insinuate a new theme associated with full remembrance. I append four
later versions of the same idea.

16

16

Menelaus replies that looks of this kind can prove costly; when he returns from hunting another woman may be there in her place (Ex. 2). He storms away to the huntsmen as Ex. 12 sounds in the distance.

Helen wonders distractedly how she can release Menelaus from his fit of madness. And at this point in the opera Krauss and Wallerstein persuaded Strauss to accept the first of their numerous changes. This first alteration affects only the content and meaning of Helen's self-questioning soliloquy; in the original version Hofmannsthal's words obscured in poetry Helen's realization that her young, pretty Helen-image is not the one Menelaus loves, and that tranquillizers do not remove the urge to hate, mistrust and destroy. Krauss and Wallerstein therefore removed Hofmannsthal's seven lines, and substituted four much more simple and direct ones (completely innocuous in style). Strauss refitted the beginning of the first line to the old music, and rewrote twenty-five old bars as eighteen new ones, at first keeping approximately to the old pattern (a thematic figure not quoted here, and Ex. 5), then removing the reference to Ex. 4[1], and simplifying the version of Ex. 7 which refers to the rejected magic potion. The new music is quite neatly dovetailed, but I wonder if any substantial gain was achieved. Helen has expressed these sentiments already.

Ex. 4[1] returns presto. The three veiled slaves sent by Altair to tend Helen are visible again. Two are searching in the chest, the third unveils and reveals herself to Helen as Aithra who has flown quickly to undo her slave's mistake. A second bottle of medicine was packed in error, and Aithra feared that Menelaus might have taken the wrong one, the draught of Remembrance (Ex. 16[2]), the lethal potion avoided by all the blessed ones. Much to Aithra's surprise, Helen declares that this is precisely the medicine required to cure Menelaus; the other drink had merely caused him to regard Helen as a phantom substitute for the dead Helen of Troy. You always win, my dear, remarks Aithra complacently. If that is so, answers the other, I shall win today or never, and through this drink (Ex. 16[2]).

We come now to a more complicated series of alterations in the Vienna version, and it may be as well to detail the alternatives in parallel.

Dresden Version 1928

A Aithra protests, but Helen and the two servants mix the draught of Remembrance (Ex. 16^2 and 4^1).

B Altair enters and pays court to Helen as the fairest bird a hunter could catch (Ex. 9^4, Ex. 1, Ex. 12). Quasi-oriental music is heard from the palm-grove (and a florid bass-clarinet obbligato from the orchestra pit), and Altair invites Helen to a banquet of unparalleled splendour which he will give in her honour (Ex. 16^1 sonorously on six horns). Savage and cruel his people may be, but he knows how to pay tribute to beauty. Better than Menelaus, he hints.

C Aithra's two serving-maids watch the progress of the hunt through the tent-flaps. A falcon (quote from *Die Frau ohne Schatten*) is catching a gazelle; Menelaus and Da-ud are galloping together after it.

D Altair presses his courtship. Let the young men kill themselves (Ex. 13) for her sake; he woos by other means. Helen warns him not to go too far (Ex. 16^1) lest the gods take vengeance; Aithra from the inner tent joins her in duet. Altair threatens to possess Helen by force if need be, however many other lives it may require; young men's voices are heard, as if dying for hopeless love of her.

Vienna Version 1933

A This episode removed to section G, and partly re-composed.

B This section follows directly on Helen's remark about winning now or never, and is unchanged, but for the removal of Altair's last remark about Menelaus.

C This section omitted. The girls' commentary is set to music in section E.

D This complete section links on to B, without musical change.

E The serving-maids resume their delighted commentary on the excellent hunt (Ex. 2, melodic outline in the bass), which suddenly turns into a fight between Menelaus (Ex. 8 and 2c) and Da-ud (Ex. 2b=Paris).

E This now begins with the commentary about the falcon (the quotation remains) and the gazelle, re-composed more transparently. From the beginning of the fight the old music is retained, though the texture is thinned out and some words are reset.

F Aithra joins her servants in time to report with sorrow the murder of Da-ud. The hunt is called off with renewed fanfares of Ex. 12.

F This section is retained without change, apart from a couple of orchestral erasures at the very beginning.

Altair, in his infatuation, wildly dismisses Da-ud's death as unimportant, and speaks only of the feast that evening which Helen and Altair and no other shall enjoy (Ex. 13 and Ex. 12, and the oriental band, and Ex. 16³).

To a solemn funeral march on Ex. 13 and Ex. 15, Da-ud's body is carried on a carpet into the centre of the tent where Aithra and her maids busy themselves with the corpse. Helen stands alone; Altair has retreated into the back of the tent. Trumpets proclaim Ex. 2a, and wind and brass alone continue the frigid march with the Ex. 2 outline and Ex. 8, as Menelaus walks slowly and fixedly into the tent, drawn cutlass in hand. He stands as if moonstruck before the body (Ex. 13, passionately, on strings and horns, Ex. 2 chords on wind and brass fortissimo).

Helen calls gently (Ex. 16¹) to Menelaus, who recognizes her for the first time (Ex. 16²). She removes his sword and rebukes him tenderly (Ex. 6), as a mother rebukes a baby, for having killed his companion. Altair mutters that they will fight to the death. Menelaus has forgotten the deed, and she reminds him that he mistook Da-ud for Paris who had to die so that Menelaus might return to—whom? To her, he replies, who is dead, and all those others who died unthanked around him. But she is alive, Helen answers (Ex. 16^1) and she is your wife, not I (Ex. 1^x flares up). Menelaus gives her a look of horror, turns to Da-ud's body and promises his dead friend that he too will go the same way.

G Helen promises Menelaus a sacred draught (Ex. 16^2) even though Aithra gives warning that, with Altair's retinue at hand for the imminent banquet (offstage band), this is not the time for the potion. Altair's troops are dangerous. Helen, who has now finished preparing the drink, tells Aithra to be quiet. Here and now begins Helen's own banquet.

G Helen's first remark has identical music, notated in half values (6/8 instead of 6/4). From here on, there are new words and new music. Menelaus answers that one drink alone is holy to him (viz. poison), that which restores him to her who is dead. She promises him this drink. Aithra's earlier remark about danger is reset without stage-band. Then follows the potion-mixing from A, the final section of it unchanged. Aithra prays for Poseidon's aid, to music based on her opening solo from Act 1. A duet for Menelaus, who is prepared for death, and Helen, preparing for Remembrance (even though it too brings death), turns into a trio with Aithra, and leads immediately into—

H Altair's troops now become visible, marching in solemn procession (Ex. 16¹, with the off-stage oriental band's tune, and the tramp of horse-hooves, eventually Ex. 12, all very fast and tense). Eunuchs, kneeling outside the tent, invite Helen to the feast. Aithra senses danger and again warns Helen. The eunuchs describe themselves as sacrificial victims for Helen.

H This is retained with the addition of a lengthier warning for Aithra, to words from the Dresden G.

I Distant thunder is heard. Aithra and her maidens listen and implore Poseidon's aid. Helen sends Altair's slaves outside and orders the tent-flaps to be closed. She shows Menelaus his cutlass, held aloft by a serving-maid, and the goblet containing the Remembrance potion.

I Helen's orders are set afresh to the music of Aithra's first phrase, and this enables a cut from here to the end of the section with the composition of one new bar.

J Altair's slaves outside mourn for Da-ud. Aithra urges the defiant Helen to give Menelaus the lotus juice.

J The lament, in its last bars, now includes Aithra's warning and Helen's defiance. Helen adds her last sentence from the Dresden G to two new bars, still on Ex. 16². From here until the end the two versions coincide.

Before we continue, it must be said that Strauss's musical revisions constitute a magisterial example of how to revise completely without having to work too hard. The resettings and dovetailings, and orchestral retouching, and even some of the new composition on existing material, are the work of a consummate craftsman, who knew dramatically, as well as tonally, precisely what was required, and knew also that to re-compose entirely afresh was (even for lateish Strauss) to endanger the unity of musical style.

To a version of Ex. 5, oddly like Wagner's Treaty theme in *The Ring*, Menelaus pushes Aithra and her servants aside and takes his grateful leave of Helen, as the phantom (Ex. 16⁴ and Ex. 1) who came to comfort him for one night on the death of his real wife, and who now purifies him (Ex. 6) with this lethal drink. As Helen raises the goblet to her own lips, he protests that the drink is for him. She answers with a reprise (almost painfully close to light opera in effect) of her Act I aria *Bei jener Nacht*, with some elaboration of scoring and a duet part for Menelaus. Since it is a fluent lyrical solo, we are glad to hear it again.

Menelaus drinks (Ex. 16^2), and gazes up at Helen (Ex. 9^3) who cries to Aithra for help: Remembrance, Helen always knew, spells Death for her, but now she fears it. Aithra promptly answers that Helen's child is approaching—another, more helpful aspect of memory. Ex. 2 blazes out. It may or may not be the reminder of Hermione that restores to Menelaus the full meaning of his love for Helen. But, in all events, he drops his sword, looks her full in the face and recognizes the identity of the living phantom and the dead Helen who was so much more alive for him (Ex. 1^x becomes the beginning of Ex. 2). At last the various, till now mutually exclusive, Helen themes (Ex. 7, Ex. 5, Ex. 6, Ex. 16^1, Ex. 11, Ex. 16^2, Ex. 1^x and Ex. 1 itself and Ex. 16^4), are integrated for him in the person of the heroine-wife who stands before him, and whom he apostrophizes in the grandest, most rewarding music that Strauss ever wrote for a 'frightful' tenor—but of course he was thinking of Richard Tauber. Aithra reminds him that he would not now love her so much if there had not been two Helens, and all three of them join in a splendid, forward-flowing D flat major trio.

Ex. 12 brings this celestial transport back to reality. Altair takes command of the situation: he orders Helen to be appropriated for himself, Menelaus to be taken and bound. But, as his orders are being carried out, Aithra hears the sound of an approaching throng, recognizes her own troops, draws back the curtain (Ex. 16^2, presented as the B–A–C–H motif which Strauss had appropriated before) and reveals a huge crowd of Poseidon's armed troops; at their centre sits Hermione, clad in gold, on a white horse. Poseidon's Ex. 3 blares out on trombones, the Egyptians cower, and Aithra reveals herself to the complete humiliation of Altair. Aithra directs Helen's attention to her daughter who now dismounts, walks into the tent and asks Menelaus for her beautiful mother. Ex. 11 wells up as Menelaus gazes at his wife. See, child, he answers, what a mother I bring you (and perhaps it is appropriate to recall that these were his very words at the end of the first act).

Hermione is remounted, horses are led forward for Helen and Menelaus and they sing a last joyous duet of reunion in octaves before riding away. Ex. 10 speeds them on a triumphant way as the curtain falls.

5

When *Die Ägyptische Helena* had its American première at the Metropolitan Opera, the highly respected critic W. J. Henderson declared that 'The Metropolitan has known some sorry opera librettos, but none more puerile, more futile, or less interesting than this. . . . The orchestration is extraordinarily good. . . . But there is nothing new. One hears the voice of an elderly man babbling his reminiscences.'

For the Straussophile it would be encouraging to reply that one hears the voice of an elderly man, and a much less estimable one, regurgitating his prejudices. But Henderson's is the sort of comment that any confirmed opera-goer might voice on *Die Ägyptische Helena*. I have tried to indicate something of the veiled deeper meaning of Hofmannsthal's libretto which, when one has torn aside the modesty-veil of poetic imagery, makes the piece seem not only interesting but true, valid and modern—in some respects *Helena* is as finely imagined and perceived as any of Hofmannsthal's opera librettos. And yet the half-tutored opera-goer is liable to miss the vividness and conviction which encourage him, on first encountering *Die Frau ohne Schatten*, to probe further into its significance. And this is perhaps because, Helen and Aithra apart, the characters do not really live. Menelaus is as much a phantom as his hallucinations of his wife. The Egyptian chieftain and his son are puppets. The twofold repeated intrigue does not live up to its well-meaning, psychological intention.

Strauss's music, on the other hand, is particularly rich in vocal lyricism, a complete reversion from the conversation-style of *Intermezzo*, and an almost primitive, but oh so ingratiating, transition to the fluent conversational lyricism of the next opera, *Arabella*. *Helena* is, in this context, surprisingly formal in structure, though the cohesive symphonic technique is even more thoroughgoing than my analysis has suggested. There are many other themes, and all are used more industriously than this account, directed towards the thematic interpretation of the dramatic action, may imply (once the reader has grasped the meaning of the Sword theme, he does not need to be directed to those passages when it accompanies the word *Schwert*). The score is distinguished also, for much of the time, by a toughness and muscularity of harmony and scoring which may make a greater impact on the student of Strauss than on the less analytical opera-goer. To a sympathetic ear the musical invention is attractive rather than strong; it is particularly unequal in the Altair episode—and this, I am sure, was the unwitting stimulus for the Viennese version—but at other points one is retrospectively reminded that Strauss must have intended spoken dialogue, and then simply half-cooked the musical insertions instead of composing them.

If one erects an identification parade of Strauss's Hellenic operas (always excepting the quite un-Hellenic *Ariadne*) *Elektra, Helena, Daphne, Danae,* the place of this opera is seen to fall some way below *Elektra,* and far above the Gregor operas in sheer dramatic and musical style. But among the Hofmannsthal–Strauss operas after *Der Rosenkavalier,* it must seem, from every point of view, the least inspired and the most factitious, the opera most likely to be dismissed as a trivial charade. To do so is to judge the superfice without attending to the content underneath. The characters of *Helena,* like those of *Ariadne,* do posture, and do not on the whole turn from puppets into credible people. But as with *Ariadne,* so *Helena* has a theme worth listening to and thinking about—even if one comes to the conclusion that the theme ought to have been more cogently treated by both authors. Their last opera, maddeningly enough, was to be much more novelettish and pretty-pretty, but also much more successful.

Arabella

OPUS 79

Lyrical Comedy in Three Acts

LIBRETTO BY HUGO VON HOFMANNSTHAL

Count Waldner, Retired Cavalry Officer	BASS
Adelaide, his Wife	MEZZO-SOPRANO
Arabella ⎱ their Daughters	SOPRANO
Zdenka ⎰	SOPRANO
Mandryka	BARITONE
Matteo, an Officer	TENOR
Count Elemer ⎫	TENOR
Count Dominik ⎬ Suitors of Arabella	BARITONE
Count Lamoral ⎭	BASS
Fiakermilli	SOPRANO
A Fortune-Teller	SOPRANO
Welko, Mandryka's Bodyguard	SPEAKING PART
Djura ⎱ Servants of Mandryka	SPEAKING PARTS
Jankel ⎰	
Hotel Porter	SPEAKING PART
Arabella's Chaperone ⎫	
Three Card Players ⎬ SILENT	
A Doctor ⎪	
A Man-in-Waiting ⎭	

I

The origins of Arabella go back to 1910 when Hofmannsthal wrote a short novel: *Lucidor—Characters for an Unwritten Comedy*. This is about Frau von Murska, a well-born but impoverished widow of Russo-Polish origins, who has two daughters, Arabella and Lucile. Arabella, idolized by her mother, was in reality the image of her dead father: 'A proud, discontented and impatient, very handsome creature, quick to disparage, but concealing disparagement in a perfect formality, respected or envied by men, and loved by many women, of a dry temperament. Little Lucidor on the other hand was nothing but heart.' For, out of caprice, the eccentric mother had chosen to parade her younger daughter Lucile as a boy, calling her Lucidor. One of Arabella's admirers, Wladimir, is greatly fancied as a son-in-law by Frau von Murska but Arabella cares nothing for him; Lucile on the other hand adores him and, seeing Arabella's unconcern, writes love letters to him, forging Arabella's hand (which she had long learned to copy, as her own handwriting was ill-formed); later she welcomes him at night to her bed, under cover of pitch darkness, and by her whispers persuades him that she is her sister. Wladimir is forbidden ever to show the 'daytime Arabella' any sign of the favours he has received. When at last, on the eve of the family's departure from Vienna, he breaks his promise, Lucidor resolves the tangled skein by appearing as the girl she always was.

Much of this plot was carried over into Hofmannsthal's libretto for *Arabella*. The figure of Mandryka is suggested in the character of Herr von Imfanger, 'a nice and thoroughly elegant Tyrolean, half peasant, half gentleman', but not seriously considered as a husband. The figure of Frau von Murska is more vividly characterized in the novel, Arabella less so, but also less sympathetically than in the final version of the later opera. The real value of *Lucidor* is that it explains the travesty of the younger sister in a plausible manner; and since the secondary (or is it primary?) plot of Zdenka and Matteo has always been a stumbling block, a situation widely regarded as absurdly artificial if not actually tasteless, it will be as well to quote some appropriate sentences from *Lucidor* on the subject.

'The idea of letting the younger daughter appear *en travesti* for the duration of the stay in Vienna occurred like lightning, as did all Frau von Murska's inspirations, and yet had the most complicated background and concatenations of thought. The chief motive in play was to engage in a truly remarkable game of chess against an old, mysterious, but fortunately actually existing, uncle who lived in Vienna and for whose sake (all these hopes and tyings-up were extremely vague) she had perhaps fundamentally chosen this town for their stay. [It is later explained that the uncle was a misogynist.] At the same time, though, the disguise also had other, quite real, quite prominent, causes. It was easier to live with a single daughter than with two of not quite the same age; for the girls were actually separated by four years; in this way one survived with fairly small expenditure. Then there was a still better, still more correct, position for Arabella if she was the only daughter rather than the elder one; and the truly pretty small brother, as a sort of man-in-waiting [the German word is *Groom*], set the beautiful creature somewhat in relief.

'One or two chance circumstances came into question: Frau von Murska's inspirations never stemmed entirely from unreality, it was only that they connected in a peculiar way what was real, the data, with what seemed possible or attainable to her imagination. Five years previously Lucile (she was a child of eleven and had been having typhus at the time) had to have her lovely hair cut short. Moreover it was Lucile's preference to ride astride. . . . Lucile accepted the disguise as she had accepted much else. She was patient in temperament; and even the absurdest things quite easily become habit. Moreover, as she was painfully shy, she was delighted by the thought that she need never have to appear in the drawing-room and play the growing girl. . . . It is not usually given to mankind to see what is there. Also Lucile had really boyish, small hips, and nothing else that might too obviously betray the girl. In fact the matter remained undisclosed, even unsuspected, and when the turning point came, and made of the little Lucidor a bride, or even something more feminine, the whole world was astonished.'

During 1910, when *Lucidor* was written, Hofmannsthal attempted without much success to turn it into a scenario; he returned to the task in 1921 and 1922, seeing in it perhaps the answer to Strauss's request of 1916 (and on many another occasion) for 'a realistic comedy with true and interesting human beings . . . either predominantly lyrical in content, like *Der Rosenkavalier* with its magnificent Marschallin, or burlesque and full of parody like Offenbach.' In September 1923, after completing *Intermezzo*, Strauss again called for 'a second *Rosenkavalier* without its mistakes and *longueurs*. This you must write for me, I have not yet had my last say in this vein.' Hofmannsthal was preparing *Die Ägyptische Helena* for Strauss at this time, but he took up the composer's point: 'I believe I feel exactly what you mean by a second *Rosenkavalier*. The action would have to be set in Vienna, around 1840 or so, rather unpretentious, good-humoured, and also cheerful. . . . I have an idea of the plot. It takes place among young people, and ends with a multiple wedding. But I must let it develop inside me. . . .' Hofmannsthal was considering it again in November 1924, and in 1925 he tried to turn *Lucidor* into a vaudeville with a modern setting; Arabella's suitors would have to be a psychoanalyst, a chiromancer, an astrologer and a physical training instructor; and the scenes would take place in a *café-dansant*, a beauty salon, and at a spiritualist tea-party. Fortunately this idea did not long detain Hofmannsthal. By the time Strauss had finished *Helena* in October 1927, indeed a few weeks earlier, he was clamouring for a new subject: 'oil to prevent my imagination from going rusty'. Hofmannsthal was now toying with a parallel theme to that of the *Arabella* one.

'Two years ago I made notes and a scenario for a comedy, and then laid them aside. The title was *Fiaker als Graf* (*Coachman as Count*). The subject was a real one in my youth, but today the action would have to be set back—I thought to 1880, but perhaps even to 1860. Yesterday evening it occurred to me that this comedy might perhaps be suited to music, with a light text, mainly in telegraphic style ... and that the whole thing has a real breath of *Rosenkavalier* in it.' He proposed to make a light operatic scenario of these sketches, 'in the style of *Rosenkavalier*, but still lighter, more French, if I may say so, still farther from Wagner'.

A month later he had again rejected *Fiaker als Graf* as too tenuous (the very title may lead us to agree with him), but salvaged certain ideas and motifs from it for a three-act comedy, 'almost operetta', 'with five or six very vivid roles'. The two principal girls, sisters, were contrasted 'like Carmen and Micaëla, one very sparkling, one tender and humble'. By this time the character of Mandryka, the suitor from Croatia, had materialized—Hofmannsthal mentioned several possible exponents, including Chaliapin, but carefully specified Richard Mayr as impossible, so as not to further the link with Ochs; besides, Mandryka is the opposite of Ochs, half peasant, but exquisite in his manners.

Hofmannsthal met Strauss in Vienna on 16 December 1927 and told him the story of *Arabella*. Strauss seems to have taken it for granted that Mandryka, not a female character, would hold the centre of the stage; and for Strauss, the champion of the operatic soprano, this was a disappointment. Hofmannsthal quickly undeceived him (22 December 1927) and enlarged on the nature and relationship of the characters, in a manner particularly revealing to us of posterity who are trying to probe further than the facts of the ultimate *Arabella* libretto. He suggested that Viennese waltzes should play a lively part in the music, and rather later admitted that the action stemmed in part from *Lucidor*, and that Max Reinhardt had been responsible for suggesting it as the basis of a musical comedy rather than a spoken one.

The scenario seemed by now to be clear, and Hofmannsthal spent the first half of 1928 in writing the libretto, the first act of which he sent to Strauss on 2 May. Strauss was thoroughly enthusiastic and grateful, but knew at once (it usually took him some time) that the structure was wrong and the character of Arabella too vague. The following year Hofmannsthal revised the first act entirely; his original version, with its cuts and intermediary rewriting, was published in 1954* and from it we can see that, although Strauss was quite right, the revision did remove important aspects of Arabella's character, her cynicism, fatalism, and dislike of all sentimentality such as nourished her mother's being. All these traits are made clear in the original act; but there was not yet the Fortune-Telling scene, or the entry of Arabella, or the *Aber der Richtige* duet, or the *Mein Elemer* monologue—moments that none of us would willingly forgo.

It may be interesting to compare the first and the final forms of this act.

1928	1929
A Zdenka importuned by creditors, including hotel porters.	A The same, enhanced by Adelaide's conversation with the Fortune-Teller.
B Zdenka and Matteo.	B Similar.
C Arabella and Matteo. She cold, he begs for a letter from her. She agrees.	C Arabella and Zdenka. Some words addressed by Arabella to Dominik in F of the original are here expanded into the (very uncynical) *Richtige* duet.
D Zdenka and Adelaide. The daughter begs to be allowed to put away boy's clothes.	D Elemer (alone) calls on Arabella (cf. F of the original).
E Waldner and Adelaide discuss financial troubles and possible suitors for Arabella.	E Absorbed into G; and postponed entirely until then.
F Dominik, Elemer, and Lamoral call on Arabella, gossip with her and Adelaide. Meanwhile Zdenka gives further reassurances to Matteo. Waldner sits writing.	F Zdenka and Arabella. Arabella sees a handsome mysterious stranger (Mandryka) in the street.
G Resumption of E. Arabella overhears and shocks parents by her cynical attitude to her 'mating'.	G Waldner and Adelaide as in original E and G.

* *Die Neue Rundschau*, Vols. 3 and 4.

1928

H Waldner alone, then with Mandryka. Waldner's delight at having money.

I Waldner tells Adelaide, who tells Arabella, of Mandryka's proposal. Arabella cynically fixes an appointment to meet him, and tells her father that Zdenka should live a girl's life.

J Arabella decides to marry a rich building contractor (abhorred by her snobbish mother) and have Zdenka to live with them. Zdenka, desperate that Arabella will not take Matteo, imagines finding his suicide corpse.

K Matteo is promised a letter by Zdenka. She conceives the plot for that evening in a short solo which ends the act.

1929

H As in original version Waldner eventually leaves the apartment to go gambling.

I Zdenka's second scene with Matteo from K of the original.

J Arabella sends Zdenka to change.

K Arabella's monologue about Elemer and marriage.

The number of scenes is almost the same, but the contents differ considerably, and the structure is a good deal more compact in the 1929 version, even if we regret that the 1929 libretto omits the big septet in Scene F, and the quartet that Hofmannsthal inserted into I on first revision at Strauss's request. But the final Act 1 might very well have been changed yet again if Hofmannsthal had lived longer. The version that Strauss set was devised after Acts 2 and 3 had been considerably reshaped to suit Strauss. Throughout the preparation of the libretto Strauss came forward with suggestions, sometimes ludicrous, sometimes acutely perceptive. Where his musical share was concerned, he was immediately sensitive to what was and was not appropriate in musical drama, as opposed to theatre. Hofmannsthal, for all the sensitive self-esteem that went with his elegant and inventive mind, was able to bear with Strauss's forthright objections. He protested, almost excessively from first to last, that *Arabella* was his finest work. But when Strauss found a hole to pick, he accommodated the composer with exceptional promptness and goodwill. Their collaboration had never been more amiable, the tone of their letters more friendly, than during *Arabella*. And the result is curiously that *Arabella* is not only Strauss at his most effortless, but also Hofmannsthal at his most authoritative. The composer cannot have made life easier for his poet with his suggestions for a monster Croatian ballet, plenty of traditional songs that Mandryka could sing to national folk-airs (Hofmannsthal begged Strauss to steer clear of a hero who keeps popping out of the action, *à la Lilac Time*, to remind us of his own songs), and a tragic conclusion in which Mandryka shoots himself and is then handed the famous glass of water. Yet Strauss supplied Hofmannsthal with apt, as well as ludicrous, schemes from which the poet could judiciously select. Poor Hofmannsthal had been lavishly praised by his friends for this draft; now he saw that it would have to be drastically revised. Even then Strauss was not content; he condemned the insipidity and unsympathy of Arabella, the tedious behaviour of Mandryka, and the lack of characterization in the trio of 'noble nonentities'. In desperation he suggested that Mandryka should overhear the appointment for Matteo's assignation with the supposed Arabella, that he should flirt with the coachmen's mascot, Fiakermilli, and that Arabella's mother should dally with one of her daughter's lovers—all of which was duly incorporated in the second act—so that then, and only then, could Arabella, the most apparently compromised person, emerge finally as the one guiltless party, alone fit to hand the glass of water to her betrothed.

Hofmannsthal counselled Strauss to patience until the whole libretto was ready. That date was Christmas Eve 1928, and a few days later he read the three acts to Strauss, who seemed happy—though not for long. Further revision was retarded in the following spring by Hofmannsthal's ill-health, and a relapse occurred in the summer. By 2 July, however, he could claim that only one scene was still missing from the entirely new first act; that the tempi of the several scenes were now more effectively geared for music; and that Arabella had become stronger and more dominant. On 6 July Strauss asked for a monologue with which Arabella could end the first act. This would lend variety yet coherence to the three finales, would make a suitable point of repose for the audience after an act chiefly consisting of conversation, and make a successful solo for the principal soprano. All this fired Hofmannsthal's imagination; four days later the beautiful solo finale, *Mein Elemer*, together with the rest of Act 1, was sent to Strauss. It was his last letter to his collaborator. The composer's telegram of thanks and congratulation arrived on the day that Hofmannsthal's son Franz, who had taken his own life, was buried; an hour or so after the funeral his father died of a sudden stroke. The date was 15 July 1929.

2

Some rude remarks have been made during the course of this book about Hofmannsthal's misuse and misguiding of Strauss as a great twentieth-century composer, in order to further his own ambitions as the first great opera librettist since Da Ponte, and the most thoughtful, poetic of all operatic poets. That Hofmannsthal was a poet there can be no doubt at all; his sensibility was extremely fine, though he understood the place of music in sung drama hardly at all compared with Strauss; and as several of their joint operas show, his judgement of dramatic structure was decidedly fallible. His feelings for subject-matter, character, diction, were altogether beyond Strauss's field of vision; we can remark this not only in his comments on Strauss's suggestions for plots and action but also in those passages, scenes, whole acts, where Strauss could not truly comprehend the beautiful ideas which his poet had struggled to convey. In *Ariadne auf Naxos* Hofmannsthal always felt that the material was too far above Strauss's head, but Strauss was probably right in countering that the great ideas had been opaquely and therefore clumsily realized. In *Die Frau ohne Schatten* the symbols clash and jangle so obtrusively that ordinary opera-goers have never bothered to discover whether so lengthy and obscure an opera really means anything that might one day be worth understanding. *Die Zauberflöte* is also an opera with many hidden meanings; but the symbols are few and clear, the language that of a simple, yet thoughtful person. *Die Ägyptische Helena* contains ideas as fascinating and as modern as any that Hofmannsthal gave to Strauss—once we have grasped them, they belong to contemporary people like us in the audience, and in performance we almost forget that the drama took place before the return of Orestes in *Elektra*. The earlier opera belongs to an expressionist climate; the latter, to a psychoanalytical one. The scenery is virtually irrelevant. And the same is true of *Arabella*. But as later productions attempted to correct, *Arabella* is an opera completed in a textually imperfect state. It is good, it is convincing, it is glorious because Hofmannsthal's figures for an unwritten comedy that was at last written are good, convincing and glorious.

Hofmannsthal—and one says this with due regard for his exceptional sensibility as well as his immense prestige in twentieth-century literature —had more imagination than dramatic technique or operatic sympathy. His influence on Strauss was so strong that he aged his collaborator aesthetically and idiomatically before his time. And yet Strauss's later collaborators were pygmies beside Hofmannsthal, particularly as regards the propulsion of Strauss's operatic development. Each of the Strauss–Hofmannsthal operas inhabits a quite different musical-dynamic climate. Can we say the same of the Strauss–Gregor operas? I think not.

3

Life after sixty, a sexagenarian musician once said, is one non-stop funeral service. Even so, Strauss was gravely shaken by the untimely death of his poet, ten years his junior, in the middle of a supremely promising operatic collaboration. It was necessity as much as piety that spurred him to set the *Arabella* libretto as it stood on the day of the librettist's departure from the world. He set to work promptly. By 13 September 1930 he told Frau Hofmannsthal that the first act was almost completely sketched. Strauss hit a bad patch of inspiration in the middle of Act 2 (as we can hear), and it was not until the autumn of 1931 that he could write to Fritz Busch of Dresden that the whole opera was now in finished initial sketch; but age was beginning to tell, and he remarked several times that he would be in his seventies before it would be ready for performance. He was wrong. The score was completed on 12 October 1932. He dedicated it jointly to Alfred Reucker and Fritz Busch, respectively the Intendant-Producer and Musical Director of the Dresden Opera, intending them to take charge of the première. And then in March 1933 came the Nazis. The two dedicatees were relieved of their posts and became refugees. Strauss, greatly shocked, withdrew the score. But the Dresden Opera insisted that the contract must be fulfilled. Strauss only consented on condition that he should personally approve all the participants. Topography, the setting in Vienna, was as much responsible for this insistence as musical scruple or (which never meant much to Strauss) politics. Eventually he gave his consent to a première at Dresden on 1 July 1933. The Viennese Clemens Krauss conducted, and Viorica Ursuleac, subsequently his second wife, made her name in the title role. Also from Vienna came the Mandryka, Alfred Jerger, and the rest of the cast included the Hungarian Margit Bokor as Zdenka, Friedrich Plaschke (whose wife Eva von der Osten, the original Octavian, was artistic adviser on the production) and Kurt Böhme. Josef Gielen produced and the designer was another Austrian, Leonhard Fanto.

The Dresden première was fairly successful, that in Vienna with Lotte Lehmann as Arabella much more so. But people seem to have made up their minds, almost without bothering to think, that *Arabella* could not be much good. Those in Germany denied the validity of an opera whose librettist had died four years before the first performance; those abroad clung complacently to their conviction that *Der Rosenkavalier* had been the end of Strauss, and therefore the end of their need for cerebral activity connected with his subsequent works. There were, however, premières (among others) at Berlin (under Furtwängler), Berne and Stockholm, before the end of the year; in 1934 at Monte Carlo in French, London (a production by Otto Erhardt, largely based on the Dresden cast), Buenos Aires (conducted by Busch), Amsterdam (under Strauss), Antwerp and Budapest. In 1939 Munich celebrated the composer's seventy-fifth birthday with a new production by Rudolf Hartmann who, by means of the revolving stage, split the second act into three scenes and, omitting the final waltz and chorus, linked the second and third acts without pause. In 1942 Clemens Krauss asked Strauss to rewrite the second act for a Salzburg production so as to omit Fiakermilli, a character for whom he found no musical justification, 'a painful Auntie Trill', he called her.* Strauss agreed that she was an unsatisfactory character, but decided that it was too late to overhaul the part fundamentally. *Arabella* did not have its American première until 1956 when it was given at the Metropolitan Opera. Two other productions are worth recording, a Berlin one in 1953 where the producer was Richard Strauss junior (Bubi of *Intermezzo*), and one at Santa Barbara, California, in 1960, produced by Lotte Lehmann, Vienna's first Arabella.

4

Hofmannsthal specified several conflicting dates for the incidence of *Arabella*; the final one is 1860, and the action takes place entirely on the morning and evening of Carnival Day, Shrove Tuesday, of that year. Count Waldner, a retired cavalry officer, lives with his wife and children in a smart hotel in central Vienna. (Viennese Straussophiles have identified it as the Hotel Munsch in the Neuer Markt, or the Hotel Erzherzog Karl, both popular with aristocratic refugees—such as the parents in *Lucidor* were.) He has evidently exhausted his army pension at the card-table, and the family letterbox is groaning with unpaid bills. His wife Adelaide has grown more superficial, less cultured and less cranky since we first met her as the Widow von Murska in *Lucidor*. Her decision to dress the younger daughter Zdenka as a boy springs from no tortuous whim but from the severely practical consideration that the parents are too poor to bring out two daughters in Viennese society. Of Arabella's suitors, Matteo (*olim* Wladimir) is no longer her mother's favourite; Adelaide now prefers Count Elemer, one of three rich army playboys who are courting Arabella *en trio*.

Silly Countess Waldner is hard at it, when the curtain rises, in consultation with a Fortune-Teller; Strauss, the master of tone-painting, gives a *trompe l'oreille* description of the shuffling and laying out of cards (different from the one in *Intermezzo*; Skat is not the same thing at all as fortune-telling). Below the playing-card theme is heard the motif associated with the penniless Waldner family.

* The German *Trillertante* is an untranslatable pun on *Dilettante*.

Zdenka is in the room as well, putting papers in order, perhaps bills, perhaps a new letter that she has written in Arabella's hand to Matteo, assuring him of eternal devotion. Each time the doorbell rings she goes to ward off the creditors.

The Zdenko–Zdenka complex, an odd one at best, makes more sense when one knows the original in *Lucidor*. It might have been made for Strauss to set to music. Strauss had created Octavian and horrified Hofmannsthal by making trouser-roles of the Composer in *Ariadne II* and Da-ud in *Die Ägyptische Helena* (which he did because he disliked tenors). Now, as if to tease him, Hofmannsthal produced a realistically justified trouser-role.

Adelaide calls to Zdenka to leave the bills on the table; and violas introduce Countess Waldner's own theme.

The cards have nothing encouraging to tell her of the legacy that the Waldners expect so anxiously, but they can vividly describe Count Waldner and his ill luck at gambling. Adelaide sets all her hopes on a rich marriage for Arabella, and upper wind match Ex. 3 with a rising scale that represents the salvation of the family.

Violas launch the career of the gay and charming Arabella theme.

The Fortune-Teller has something more helpful to offer on this subject. The Officer whom she sees so clearly, and whom Zdenka identifies as her adored Matteo—

—is not the successful suitor. The bridegroom-to-be is a foreigner, summoned by letter. That he is the Right Man (*Der Richtige*) we know from the Slavonic folk-song quoted briefly by horns.*

7

The trumpet identifies him as Mandryka.

8

Adelaide wrongly assumes that he must be Count Elemer, one of Arabella's playboy suitors.

9

She also learns that delay to the successful conclusion of the marriage will come through another girl, Arabella's sister, and Countess Waldner is obliged to explain to the Fortune-Teller about Zdenka.

10

Ex. 10^1 represents Zdenka's real nature, Ex. 10^2 her outward appearance as a boy. The Fortune-Teller insists that the danger is there; and Adelaide, much embarrassed by the presence of Zdenka, whisks the good lady into her boudoir for a more private session.

Zdenka, left alone, puts the audience further in the picture; Matteo had been forbidden the house by Countess Waldner for fear of compromising other suitors. Zdenka is convinced that Arabella must love him as much as she herself does. The creditors are probably all the more attentive

* Strauss wrote down the original folk-tune as a footnote in his short score. Since it does not seem to have found its way into either published score, I cannot do better than follow his example.

because they must have heard that the Waldners intend to leave Vienna (this is no doubt a hangover from *Lucidor*; the only other mention of departure is a wild suggestion from Adelaide that they should all go and keep house for Aunt Jadwiga, but it is typically unpractical). Zdenka utters a prayer for Matteo and Arabella and money. At the climax of this soliloquy, two new themes are introduced.

11

This is associated with Zdenka's loving nature. Ex. 12 is concerned with Matteo's transports of passionate longing.

12

The little solo ends with a charming slow waltz based on Ex. 10[1].

Matteo slips quietly into the room (Ex. 6) for a report on Arabella's activities, and a complaint of her coldness towards him—so opposed to the warmth of her letters. The reason for this is given in a theme played by flute and a moment later by clarinet: this is the opposite of Ex. 7; it means the Wrong Man. Arabella is not, in reality, remotely interested in Matteo.

13

Matteo insists that Arabella must write again this very day, and hurries out with wild threats of foreign service and suicide. Poor Zdenka is at her wits' end when she is fortunately interrupted by Arabella's return from her morning constitutional with a chaperone. Arabella is accompanied, not by any of her own themes, but by that of the Carnival Ball at which she is to be Queen.

14

Today being Carnival Day she has received presents from all her admirers. Her eyes light first on some roses (a half-conscious allusion to the Silver Rose motif) and she asks (Ex. 4 and Ex. 8) if a Hussar by any chance brought them for her. In fact they are from Matteo, who is Ex. 13; the entire male sex is divided, for Arabella, into those who are Wrong, and one who will be Right. Arabella puts down the roses hastily, too hastily for Zdenka, who is pained that her adored Matteo should be so scorned by her adored Arabella: the clarinet shows us Arabella through Zdenka's eyes.

15

Arabella turns to the presents from her three noble admirers, whom she finds excellent company but equally Wrong Men for serious romance (Ex. 13 again). Zdenka finds them worthless compared with Matteo, and now Ex. 15 on violas and bassoon is mated with a surging arpeggio on the cellos—this is Matteo's third, physically compelling theme.

16
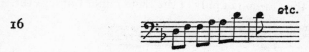

Zdenka pleads Matteo's cause so passionately that Arabella warns her it is time she became a girl at last. I don't want to be a woman like you, cold and a flirt, answers her sister. Arabella is in earnest this time. Strauss slips the gear-lever one notch in the direction of aria as the cor anglais sadly echoes Ex. 13, and strings unfold the long melody of Arabella's serious mood.

17

She expounds her continual surprise to find how quickly her heart can warm to a man, and equally quickly turn away from him. And yet she knows that when the Right Man appears (Ex. 7), she will recognize him at once and never swerve from her love again. This is the famous, and sensuously most beautiful duet *Aber der Richtige* with its richly divided string texture, its allusions to Ex. 8 at the return to the main tune, and its swaying, soaring thirds for the sisters at the conclusion.

The duet is applauded, so to speak, by the jingle of sleighbells in the street. Elemer has won the privilege, over Dominik and Lamoral, of taking Bella for a drive. Because it is Carnival (Ex. 14) she will go with him, and also because she must make her choice tonight before her coming-out Carnival ends. Zdenka imagines Matteo's suicide if another is chosen (Ex. 6)—she will find his body, kiss his icy lips. Arabella explains what brought the Hussar into her mind; she saw one, a foreigner, gazing at her in the street this morning, and prayed that he would send her flowers. Mandryka's foreignness is expressed in the following theme, which is related to Ex. 17 (since he and Arabella were made for one another), but independently used.

18   Mandryka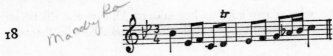

Meanwhile here is Elemer, introduced by a Polonaise on Ex. 9, and radiant with the triumph of having Arabella to himself, a triumph slightly soured by the necessity of taking her young brother along too. Their conversation (all that is left of the vocal octet in the first version) is gay and immensely spirited—there is only one pull-up when Arabella talks of having to choose a husband before the night is out. The three Noble Nincompoops, as Strauss neatly described them, exist purely for light and romantic relief. But Elemer is a romantic figure, ardent as well as dashing; the second of his themes makes this clear when the horn softly plays it as he calls her the Queen not only of the Ball tonight but for ever.

19

His speech is full of such *fleurettes*, and many of them are answered in the orchestra by Ex. 13 or Ex. 7; there is even a classic example of thought-less label-tying when Strauss brings out the Right Man theme for Arabella's mocking comment that Elemer and his friends are 'a right bunch' (*Ihr seid schon die Rechten*). At one of these gallantries however, about the power of a girl's look, the first violins breathe a theme of long-ing henceforth much linked with Arabella.

20
espress.   (♭) (♮)

As Elemer leaves to console the horses while Arabella is changing for her ride, she points gaily at the sleigh then exclaims to Zdenka: her foreigner (Ex. 18) is outside in the street again. But she dare not hope too much, for the stranger passes by (Ex. 8 rather sadly, and Ex. 4 inverted for unsalvation).

Count Waldner comes in, and is met by his wife who dismisses the children—your father has worries, she explains, and Ex. 1 tells us why. He scans the letters eagerly; alas they are all bills. He had hoped for a letter from one Mandryka, an old army comrade, rich as Crœsus, a noted womanizer to whom Waldner had sent a portrait of Arabella in the faint hope that the longed-for rich suitor might be he, old man or no. Deaf to Adelaide's proposal that they should all leave Vienna, depressed by the mountain of Final Notices and the absence of even fifty gulden for his luck in the gaming house, Waldner rings for a brandy, only to be told that service in Room 8 must be on a strict cash basis. Ex. 8, as well as Ex. 1, is in his thoughts, but automatically he dismisses a caller announced by the waiter, then sees the visiting card, and reads the name with joy: Mandryka! The caller has fortunately insisted on seeing Waldner, and is received.

Mandryka is tall, powerfully built and elegant, about thirty-five years of age, his manner is direct and comradely, his appearance fairly suggestive of rusticity (this probably only means that he has a ruddy and cheerful complexion), his behaviour utterly dignified, as his entrance theme (Ex. 18 solemnly on horn quartet) and the sombre, rich-toned scoring of the whole scene, full of divided strings and of rests for high-lying instruments all suggests. Waldner goes to meet him with open arms, then recoils in surprise, for this is not his old army comrade. Mandryka explains; he had received a letter from Waldner (it is now bloody, since on the same day he was attacked by a she-bear), passed on to him as the only surviving Mandryka (and therefore Ex. 7)—Waldner's friend, his uncle, being now deceased. He proposes to come at once to the point; Strauss gets there even more quickly with a literally wooing theme, that of Mandryka as suitor, which I quote in a later, more typical form.

21

Is the subject of the enclosed portrait, Waldner's daughter, still un-betrothed? Waldner assents. Was the intention that old Mandryka should fall in love with Fräulein Waldner and ask her hand in marriage? Waldner tries to parry this masterpiece of thought-reading. Mandryka, part unfamiliar with Viennese talk, part afraid that some sophisticated urban hint might pass over his head, hangs on Waldner's every embarrassed syllable —and then takes the initiative, using his uncle as an imaginary suitor for Arabella's hand (a glorious development of Ex. 21). Now that the uncle is dead, he continues, it is the nephew who is the heir to the Mandryka wealth and who himself asks (need one add, not unsuccessfully?) for Arabella to wife; the whole process is carried out with that immensely tactful, longest-way-round-is-the-shortest-way-home verbosity that is indigenous to the countryman. It happens to suit the context by allowing Mandryka a long solo with a rapid *cabaletta* in which he relates the tale of his illness after meeting the bear, the anxiety of his servant, the sale of a forest to get the money to come to Vienna and court Arabella. . . . Quite without boasting Mandryka reveals how enormously rich he is, and gradually the idea of his wealth creeps into the musical texture; Strauss told Leo Wurmser that it was one of the Slavonic folk-tunes he had borrowed.

22

And at this point he draws out his wallet to show the proceeds of sale. Waldner stares goggle-eyed at what is no less than an oasis to the thirsty traveller. His enchantment does not pass unnoticed. Mandryka begs to lend him a thousand gulden—as a favour to his prospective son-in-law, he adds tactfully. 'Do help yourself, please,' he offers.

23

Teschek, bedien dich!

Waldner is pressed without embarrassment into accepting two such notes. Mandryka adds that he would wish too to meet Arabella and her mother; not now—one must prepare for such a holy occasion—but at some suitable moment—he will be staying in the hotel. And so saying he departs taking with him Ex. 17 which is so close to his own Ex. 18.

Waldner is almost hysterical with joy at the sudden access of wealth. Again and again he repeats Mandryka's words *Teschek, bedien' dich!* ('Please help yourself'), to the bewilderment of the waiter and Zdenka, and then he leaves in triumph—for the gaming table of course. Zdenka (thinking always of Matteo's Ex. 12) is convinced that trouble has softened her father's brain. Matteo makes another brief appearance and is promised a letter at the Ball that night. He escapes as Arabella returns, urging Zdenka to dress for their sleigh ride. For the sleigh ride and, Zdenka adds almost in despair, your Elemer. Zdenka sings the words to the dropping seventh in Ex. 20. At once a solo viola rejects the name with Wrong Man (Ex. 13), and lower wind and strings admit this is only Zdenka's idea of Arabella's future (Ex. 15). It would be sad, says the oboe, if he were the Right Man (Ex. 7 in C sharp minor); but the salvation, remarks the viola *en passant*, of the family (Ex. 4). This is a typically articulate Strauss orchestral passage. Arabella repeats Zdenka's taunt: 'My Elemer'; it sounds strange. She knows that she longs with over-whelming anxiety for—what? We know the answer to be *Der Richtige*. He is not (Ex. 12) Matteo. Ex. 7 turns into a quick waltz, but it is still in the minor mode until she thinks again of her handsome unknown suitor, and then the music comes marvellously to the boil, an inward, restrained boiling-point with strings heavily subdivided as in *Ariadne*. The thought of marriage with Elemer brings out Ex. 17 on two soft trombones, as if she were stepping on somebody's grave—is it the foreigner's grave? Ex. 7 turns cheerful and she decides to forget him (he is doubtless already married) and look forward to the Ball. As the sisters leave the hotel suite it is of Zdenka and Elemer that the music tells us. Both these are optimistic for their hearts' desire; both will be dis-appointed—though for Zdenka and for Arabella there is in store a brighter fulfilment than either ever allowed herself to imagine.

5

For Strauss, one may feel, there was indefinable optimism in the flat keys; some of us may share with him the feeling that, while they adorn the stave, comfort is in store for the soul. The second act opens in such rosy hopes, in B flat, with the first enunciation of the Staircase music which stands as the symbol of a happy end.

24

We are in the anteroom of the main hall in the Hotel Sperl at Leopold-stadt, a district of Vienna, during the Coachmen's Ball on the same evening. Waldner and Mandryka are waiting (Ex. 23) as Arabella and her mother descend the stairs from the ballroom, surrounded by admirers and themes of gaiety (Ex. 14) and loveliness (Ex. 5). Mandryka presses Waldner's hand with such excitement that the prospective father-in-law fears for his card-playing arm (Exs. 1 and 2). Arabella is so awed by the sight of her Right Man that she has to wait alone for a moment before coming down to be presented to Mandryka. The parents tactfully disappear—the admirers have already gone to find new partners. The suitor and his intended are left alone. Both are shy, both know their own minds but seem fearful lest their desires are not the same. They stammer formalities and invitations and confidences while the three 'noble nonentities' in turn come forward to beg the next dance, only to be invited to apply later. Meanwhile Mandryka reveals himself a widower (*Ich habe eine Frau gehabt*), and with a painful deliberation unlocks his feelings for Arabella. For an anxious moment the Wrong Man theme floats by—it is Mandryka's not Arabella's anxiety. He gathers courage so much that Arabella is almost afraid of his ardour. But she regains her composure (helped by the respite of an invitation to dance with the third of her gay cavaliers) and helps Mandryka by revealing her knowledge that he wishes to marry her. He declares it himself, and she reverts to the *Aber der Richtige* music, admitting that her love at first sight was not mistaken. Love flows like a river through her words. Mandryka takes up the image, and recalls a custom of betrothed girls in his village—the idea of bride-winning brings out another theme, for oboes, horns and lower strings, the Slavonic folk-tune of Ex. 26. These girls go down to the river Danube at bedtime, draw a cup of clear water and present it to their intended as a symbol of chastity and eternal allegiance. Mandryka's account, punctuated by horn calls of Ex. 7, turns the strings to a betrothal theme distinct from the later song.

25

Arabella takes up this melody to express the love that she reciprocates herself. The inner joy which her avowal provokes in Mandryka is outwardly expressed in the wide vocal leaps of Ex. 21. Arabella and Mandryka pledge their troth in a solemn duet, whose words (*Und du wirst mein Gebieter sein*) look back to the Book of Ruth and her vow to Naomi: 'Whither thou goest, I will go . . . where thou diest, will I die, and there will I be buried.'

26

There is a quality of naturalness and humanity about this scene that is deeply moving on paper, overwhelmingly so in the theatre. Strauss's orchestral commentary flows as easily and grandly as the Danube through Vienna, and his vocal lines ride it with the expert abandon of well-tried swimmers—though here the metaphor breaks down, since Strauss, who loved dearly the duetting of lyric soprano and high baritone, designed the setting for these voices and made sure that the current would never be too strong for the swimmer's technique. Chiefly, though, the scene derives its special quality from Hofmannsthal, who here struck a vein of poetic dialogue more happily judged, because more realistic, than anywhere in his operas with Strauss. In the most successful passages of the earlier Strauss–Hofmannsthal operas one senses by comparison the weakness of other dialogues where the librettist was aiming too consciously at art; and in this Mandryka–Arabella scene the acute nervous sensibility is the more sharply felt by us at the receiving end because Hofmannsthal has so skilfully judged the dialogue in terms of two fundamentally simple people. Simplicity is Mandryka's natural voice; and Arabella, after cultivating the mask of sophistication as a defence against the outside world, suddenly falls in with her suitor's vocabulary. She expresses herself in the plain language of a girl who knows that sophisticated conceits will simply frighten away the suitor on whom she has set her heart—and who, in finding the direct language of plain words, discovers that she can best express what is in her heart. This quality of highly poetic simplicity is to be felt at the topmost level in her reprise of *Aber der Richtige*, and in the biblical reminiscence of *Und du wirst mein Gebieter sein*. Something of the same direct eloquence pierces through the period language of *Der Rosenkavalier* in the Octavian–Marschallin scenes, especially that with Sophie preceding the final trio. We miss the quality, where we might expect it, in the Barak scenes of *Die Frau ohne Schatten* because Hofmannsthal's sights seem fixed on lofty sentiments which he fears to cheapen by directness. One begins to feel that his poetic potency grew weaker the more he aspired after high art (which impelled him towards the nebulous decorative preciosity called 'high camp'), and stronger the more closely he geared his art to nature and humanity. Helen and Menelaus are much more interesting characters than Arabella and Mandryka, but they are infinitely less real and compelling.

When the orchestra has played lovingly with the Betrothal music, Arabella suggests that her intended should return to the hotel while she dances farewell to her girlhood. After a moment's disappointment, expressed only through Ex. 13, he gladly grants her freedom for the evening, but insists on remaining where she is. And now the whole party streams into the anteroom, led by Dominik who introduces their spokeswoman, Fiakermilli the coachmen's mascot. She claims Arabella as Queen of the Ball, the brightest star in Vienna, a town with a flair for star-spotting; her solo *Die Wiener Herrn* is a lively florid number, tearing up to top Ds at the drop of a coachman's *Zylinder*, and making appropriate references to Arabella's Ex. 5. Strauss seems to have seized gladly on such a helpful compendium of Zerbinetta, and Adèle in *Die Fledermaus*, at a moment of shrewdest brilliance and gaiety, and to have given no forethought to the drab vulgarity which the song suggests unless the singer has a trim, jewelled vocal technique and the artistry to convey plebeian fun without musical tastelessness. This must have been the cause of Clemens Krauss's plea to the composer, quoted earlier. Milli's solo melts into a waltz for dancing. Mandryka and Adelaide exchange a few blissful civilities; simultaneously Zdenka comforts the wretched Matteo as best she can. Adelaide fetches her husband who embraces the saviour of the family fortunes, and they prepare for supper. Mandryka decides to push out the boat with fleets of champagne bottles (delightfully giggling trills for flutes) and acres of flowers (a strong suggestion of the waltz from Strauss's song *Schlechtes Wetter*). Waldner has already disappeared to the card-table in the hope of maintaining a run of luck; Mandryka and Adelaide depart to the ballroom.

Here comes Arabella on the arm of Dominik, bidding farewell to the first man who courted her. Elemer succeeds him, full of impetuous optimism; but he too is thanked and sent away, not without protest. Thirdly Lamoral to whom Arabella grants the warmest of the dialogues, musically considered, and crowns it with a loving kiss (Ex. 7 in augmentation on the horns almost makes him think he has been chosen) before taking him off for a last waltz. It is the tenderness with which Arabella carries off this process of mass leave-taking that endears to her audience a character not basically as lovable by half as Zdenka. Arabella's personality retains little of the hardness associated with her in *Lucidor*; in the opera libretto she has acquired reserves of affection and

gentleness the extent of which it is the story's business to draw out. The
two dance away and the orchestra follows them in glamorous waltz
tempo with Ex. 5 and Ex. 14 as suitable counterpoints to elegant waltz
tunes. Matteo lurks in the anteroom, and now what seemed a very
subsidiary, rather quaint sub-plot takes the limelight, casting formidable
shadows over the main intrigue (and this of course was vital from a
dramatic point of view, since the Arabella–Mandryka story would otherwise be feeble material for an opera). Zdenka returns to assure Matteo
(who orchestrally stammers with apprehension) of Arabella's love. As she
speaks Mandryka approaches to supervise the arrangements for supper;
he overhears the confidences, during which Zdenka gives Matteo a letter
purporting to come from Arabella. Matteo (for reasons explained in
Hofmannsthal's original libretto to Act 1) fears the worst of this. Zdenka
persuades him to feel it, and what he feels is the key to Arabella's bedroom—an onomatopoeic theme.

27
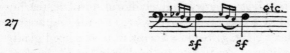

Stupid Matteo comments aloud on it, and leaves only just before
Mandryka, who has overheard, decides to take action, calling his body-
guard Welko to stop Matteo—without success. But Zdenka's deception
(it is the key to her own room) is made plain in a strong unison theme for
strings.

28

The supper party has begun to assemble; Arabella's hour of leave-
taking is not over yet, so that Mandryka is tempted to feel ridiculous in
his suspicions, although nagging fears, chiefly concerned with Ex. 27,
interrupt his attempts at consolation through alcohol (sociable Ex. 23).
He sends his servants to search for Arabella throughout the ballroom.
One of them returns with a letter from Arabella excusing herself for the
rest of the evening. Further inflamed (he asks if the envelope contains a
key), Mandryka flings himself into an attempt to get everyone, chiefly
himself, thoroughly drunk; and he begins to flirt with Fiakermilli, singing
her a savage song, full of sarcastic musical references to Ex. 26 and Ex. 27,
about an incautious lover who loses his girl. Fiakermilli echoes his phrases
with nice irony. But Adelaide begins at last to feel concern for Arabella;
she is answered roughly by Mandryka, as is her husband, though he puts
a practical face on what seems an awkward turn of events and suggests
that they and Mandryka and Waldner's own card-party should return to
the hotel to look for Arabella. Mandryka adds (Ex. 23) that meanwhile

those in the ballroom may consider themselves to be his guests. Hurrah! they shout in a coda that is sarcastically jubilant, but customarily omitted, since the Munich version plunges without pause into the Prelude to the third act.

6

The third act opens with an extended Prelude depicting the appointed rendezvous and passage of love between Matteo and Zdenka-would-be-Arabella (what hidden motives here!) with an ardour and realism that yield nothing to the *Rosenkavalier* overture dealing with the same subject. The persistence of Arabella's Ex. 5 is obviously in Matteo's mind, but the Prelude is mainly concerned with the six themes of the two parties physically involved. When the curtain rises above the slow, simmering ecstasy of Zdenka's first theme, Ex. 10^1, a slow waltz involving Matteo's Ex. 12 pushes home the similarity of the two themes because (as with Arabella's Ex. 17 and Mandryka's Ex. 18) their owners were destined for one another.

We see the main hall of the Waldners' hotel, with two flights of stairs ascending to the floor above. Up there Matteo is seen closing the door of what he still believes to be Arabella's room; he is not yet properly dressed, and when the house bell rings he vanishes.

Arabella enters the hall, themes of Carnival and her Right Man ringing in her head. She sits for a moment in a rocking chair, singing a simple, folk-like ditty (*Über seine Felder*) before preparing to go upstairs to bed. This delectable moment of calm between the storms makes happy references to Ex. 22, Ex. 26, Ex. 18, Ex. 4 and two Arabella themes, all without a trace of effort. Matteo peeps over the banisters, and is astonished to see Arabella; he can hardly believe (with reason) that she has so quickly and unobservedly come downstairs again; she, on the other hand, is displeased to see him at all. They converse at cross purposes (a good deal of the deceptive Ex. 28) about each other's present and immediately past whereabouts, Matteo proving quite exceptionally inane, even by his own standards. He tries to thank her for what she has granted him; she, of course, is at a loss to explain his gratitude and when pressed with times and places denies that she was upstairs a quarter of an hour previously. Matteo is almost more beside himself than usual when the hotel bell rings and the deputation of family and others enters at rapid tempo. Adelaide complains of the noise in the foyer; Mandryka sees Arabella with that cursed key-man Matteo and orders his servants to pack for the homeward journey. Arabella alone remains calm and firm, upheld by the certainty of Ex. 24. The parents try to dispel the unrest and discontent; Mandryka asks to beg his excuses of Arabella, with financial recompense (Ex. 23) if necessary. He has lost interest in the marriage since finding her with the object of his firmest suspicions. Arabella pierces through the heavily ambivalent innuendo and asks if Matteo has had any claim on her as strong as that of her fiancé Mandryka. Matteo hesitates and Mandryka's suspicions seem tragically confirmed. His politeness to all and sundry could be cut with a knife. Waldner proposes a duel between himself and Mandryka, but realizes just in time that his pistols are pawned. A crowd of hotel residents collects and a little hushed ensemble ensues. Arabella, urged by Mandryka to admit her complicity, denies with all her strength that Matteo is her lover, and swears that she is telling the truth. Mandryka confronts her with the rendezvous made by her brother on her behalf—she almost divines the explanation—but not quite. The music stops. She refuses to speak further with Mandryka. He is now prepared for a duel with Matteo, and lights a cigarette.

At this moment a voice from the first landing cries for Papa and Mama. Down the stairs comes Zdenka, in a nightdress, her boy's hair suddenly revealed at girl's length (we are never told how this was able to happen, but perhaps we had better not ask). Zdenka intends to say farewell to one and all before jumping into the Danube, there to drown her shame. Adelaide, suddenly recognizing the scandal of transvestism, orders her to hold her tongue till death. Waldner gives his wife similar orders, with the reminder that this repays her for her masquerade-making. Zdenka, *in extremis*, tells Arabella what has happened, and reveals her sex to Matteo who has not, even now, guessed the truth; he was destined for a glorious career in the army. Mandryka, on the other hand, could sink through the floor for shame. Arabella calms her sister's fears and, by her personal radiance, the fears all round. With a lift of her hand she has Mandryka almost prostrate before her. He rises and asks Waldner to accept Matteo as a son-in-law (*Brautwerbung kommt*). All is well, as the Staircase theme confirms. Waldner can go back to his cards. Adelaide can lead Zdenka back to bed. Matteo, having succeeded beyond his deserts, can disappear, as befits his behaviour. The crowd can return to bed or whatever.

Arabella is left with Mandryka; she asks for no more discussion until next morning, but requests that his servant bring her a glass of water to her room, to cool her mind and thirst. The lamps are lowered. Mandryka stands wretched and solitary with his remorse in the hall, a million reproaches and at least half a dozen themes chasing one another round his head.

But the light on the landing suddenly falls on Arabella. The Staircase music begins for the last time, at full stretch, including Ex. 7 and other allusions, as she descends holding the glass of water, grace and dedication in her features, Welko quietly following her. It is one of the great moments in all opera, Hofmannsthal's last and perhaps most moving theatrical *trouvaille*, not to be remembered or witnessed without a transport of emotion. Mandryka perceives the exquisite appropriateness

29 Karl Böhm, who conducted the premières of
Die Schweigsame Frau and *Daphne*

30 The Mock Wedding ceremony in Act 2 of *Die Schweigsame Frau*: Kassel, 1954. Note maritime details in décor

31 Joseph Gregor with Richard Strauss

and significance of what she is doing (for this is the bridal custom that he taught Arabella in Act 2), and he shrinks from her greatness of soul. As she reaches the bottom step of the staircase, during the descent of which her mouthpiece, Richard Strauss, has confided the thoughts that she and her beloved share, she begins the finale of the opera, *Das war sehr gut, Mandryka*. She had thought, she says, to drink the water alone, for purely selfish refreshment, until an ocean of love swept over her as she saw him there in the darkness, and she knew she must leave the drink untouched, and bequeath it to her loved one on this evening when her girlhood finds its end. Mandryka drinks with deep reverence, then smashes the glass on the stone of the staircase. Their betrothal is complete. 'Will you stay as you are?' he begs her. 'I cannot be otherwise,' she answers. 'Take me as I am!' She falls into his loving arms, kisses him goodnight and for the last time runs up the stairs to her solitary room.

When one first gets to know the opera, one wonders if such a flower of the social world could ever live happily ever after on a farming estate. But a careful study of Arabella's character and of the way she expresses herself in her two duet scenes with Mandryka leaves no real doubt that here she has found her ideal level. She knew that flirtation and adulation and gay rides in the Prater must end as soon as she grew up, and she had decided with a firmness that some girls, and particularly eldest daughters, take upon themselves as their badge of independence that growing-up and taking her own responsibility was her next step in life. Arabella is really quite a simple girl and her pride comes from simple integrity, not from self-preservation (like Christine Storch) nor sophisticated ambition (like the Dyer's wife). She will make Mandryka a perfect farmer's wife, an ornament to any society, and she will live a life of pure happiness in doing so.

7

At the time of Strauss's death it was widely assumed that none of his operas after, at the latest, *Ariadne I* was much good. A few knowledgeable musicians believed, rather from a spirit of optimism, in *Die Frau ohne Schatten*; but there were not many who felt disposed to quarrel with Boris Goldovsky's pronouncement that 'the genius turned into a routine and even commonplace composer for the last thirty-five years of his life'.

Yet since that time *Arabella* has risen sharply in general esteem and popularity. Productions are widespread and well-attended, it has been recorded complete for the gramophone; it may even be considered the most popular Strauss opera after *Der Rosenkavalier* in chronological terms (though *Ariadne I* and *Capriccio* are strong contenders). *Arabella* has great popular appeal: glittering, lilting and sensuous or sentimental music, coloured with masterly skill; a gaiety touched with real feeling, and for a moment or two with suspense and anxiety, but completely free of the German heaviness which for better or worse took hold of Strauss whenever he had previously attempted a light touch; a piquant set of situations set in a very glamorous city during a romantic period; and an extraordinary collection of characters, led by a young, beautiful heroine waiting for Mr Right to arrive.

It all begins to sound like a cinema film, and if one did not know that Hofmannsthal had put an enormous quantity of work into the subject over some twenty years one might imagine that he had wanted to caricature a certain sort of romantic film story. What peculiar people they are! The prim, rather condescending heroine, dedicated to setting her life in order; her transvestite sister, ripe for a nervous breakdown; the superstitious, wildly fanciful and extravagantly sentimental mother; the posturing, complaining, corny-gesturing officer with the high-pitched strangulated voice (but Matteo should always be given to a decently proportioned, fairly handsome tenor—he is not a laughing-stock; in fact Arabella was once, briefly, in love with him); the puffy, unpractical, distrait father, who will clearly never win a card-game in his life—he is nearly related to Baron Mirko Zeta in Lehár's *Merry Widow*; and the proud, ardent, florid, gesticulating foreign landowner who throws his money right, left and centre, and is clearly several feet larger than lifesize. The three puppet Counts, the Fortune-Teller, the yodelling Fiakermilli—not to mention the gypsy fiddler, the Jew and the building contractor, whom Hofmannsthal intended to include—what a bunch!

Hofmannsthal must have been aiming at operetta and its extravagant world, or rather at a world in which Lehár characters would, by the librettist's superior powers, come magically to convincing life. He was able to convince himself that the exercise was spiritually worthwhile because the subject of *Arabella* is his favourite subject of Lovers' first meeting—that moment which he described in discussing *Der Rosenkavalier* and which he turned to poetry in Arabella's *Aber der Richtige*:

Aber der Richtige—	But the right man—
Wenn's einen gibt für mich auf dieser Welt—	if there is one for me in this world—
der wird einmal da stehn,	he will stand there one day,
da vor mir	there in front of me,
und wird mich anschaun und ich ihn,	and will look at me and I at him,
und keine Zweifel werden sein	and there will be no doubts
und keine Fragen,	and no questions,
und selig werd ich sein	and I shall be happy
und gehorsam wie ein Kind.	and obedient as a child.

It is perfectly possible to find weaknesses or shortcomings in *Arabella*, and still to find it an enchanting and inspiring opera, deserving its popularity. There is, for example, a shortage of concerted ensembles in it, and it must be accounted a pity that Hofmannsthal removed the family quartet from Act 1 (Section 1, second version) and did not allow for a quartet of the lovers in the final act. But larger set pieces do exist in the opera, and there are several fine duets. The dramatic tension is not too skilfully controlled in the second and third acts, and leaves little doubt that Strauss would have further badgered his poet about these scenes. Yet sufficient fine material remains, and has given Strauss real inspiration enough to justify the claim that in *Arabella* the two collaborators were working for the first time on completely equal terms. The uncluttered straightforwardness of the poetic diction, the perfectly judged weight and tunefulness of the music were exactly what they both wanted. *Arabella* is a happy end to the most important chapter in Strauss's operatic career.

In 1935 Strauss wrote his own summing-up of what Hofmannsthal had meant to him:

'Hofmannsthal was the one and only poet who, besides his strength as a poet and his gifts for the stage, had the sympathetic ability to present a composer with dramatic material in a form suitable for setting to music —in short the ability to write a libretto that was simultaneously stage-worthy, satisfying at a high literary standard, and composable. I have ogled and negotiated with the leading German poets, even with D'Annunzio, repeatedly with Gerhart Hauptmann—and in fifty years (as Paul Heyse once remarked in writing) my only find was wonderful Hofmannsthal. He not only had the inventive gift of discovering musical subjects, he had—although he himself was scarcely musical (like Goethe he had a clairvoyant intuition for music)—a simply astounding flair for the sort of material which, in given circumstances, corresponded to my needs.'

Die Schweigsame Frau

OPUS 80

Comic Opera in Three Acts

freely adapted from Ben Jonson's comedy *Epicoene*

LIBRETTO BY STEFAN ZWEIG

Sir Morosus		BASS
Widow Zimmerlein, his Housekeeper		CONTRALTO
Schneidebart, the Barber		BARITONE
Henry Morosus		TENOR
Aminta, his Wife		COLORATURA SOPRANO
Isotta		COLORATURA SOPRANO
Carlotta	members of an opera company	MEZZO-SOPRANO
Morbio		BARITONE
Vanuzzi		BASS
Farfallo		BASS

I

Strauss's distress at the death of Hofmannsthal has been described together with his generous summing-up of the poet's influence on his life. It occurs in a posthumously published note on the history of *Die schweigsame Frau* which Strauss wrote down in 1935. At the time of Hofmannsthal's death Strauss had a whole opera libretto, that of *Arabella*, to serve as the best medicine in his loss. As his composition progressed he became convinced that his work as an opera composer was finished, that he would never again find another decent librettist. On 27 October 1931, at about the time when the sketch for Act 3 of *Arabella* was completed, Strauss had a visit from his friend Anton Kippenberg (1874–1950), an amateur music lover and the managing director of the Insel book-publishing firm, who was on his way to visit the celebrated Austrian author Stefan Zweig at his home in Salzburg. Strauss seems to have lent Kippenberg the libretto of *Arabella* to read, and he casually asked the publisher to inquire whether Zweig had any suitable material for an opera.

Zweig, who had been a close friend of Hofmannsthal and a long-standing admirer of Strauss's music (though until now they were not acquainted), wrote back two days later to Strauss, sending him a present of a facsimile Mozart letter from Zweig's own vast and famous collection of manuscripts, and proposing an unspecified musical plan which they might, at Strauss's convenience, discuss together. Strauss answered that he longed to complete his gallery of female portraits with a swindler or a spy. Hofmannsthal had always pooh-poohed suggestions of this kind, but Zweig was much less egoistic in his approach to opera, particularly with Strauss whom he so much admired. Hofmannsthal had always regarded himself as a necessary restraining influence on Strauss's all too fallible artistic taste. Zweig insisted, from the start, that he accepted the invitation to collaborate in an opera 'only for the pleasure of stimulating a great man'; and he harped continually on the theme of humility, embarrassment in the presence of those whom he admired, absolute readiness to pass on his work to some other writer if Strauss did not approve. Zweig's letters to Strauss are often painfully, sometimes comically, self-depreciatory and, in the Dickensian sense, 'umble. Zweig had two possible ideas in his head; they were not of the highly stylized, abundantly symbolic kind that Hofmannsthal had cultivated, Zweig suggested, perhaps to excess; for Zweig an opera libretto must be intelligible without reference to a printed book of words, just as a good novel must be appreciable to a cinema audience.

The two men met in Munich on 20 November 1931. Zweig outlined a

ballet scenario, which Strauss found much too strenuous; and a version
of Ben Jonson's *Epicoene*, based on Thieck's translation. This second had
been used by Mark Lothar for an opera *Lord Spleen* in 1930 (and earlier
by Salieri in 1800 for *Angiolina, ossia Il Matrimonio per Susurro*); but
Strauss at once recognized it as an ideal subject for himself. Zweig was
deeply impressed by Strauss's 'abstract and infallibly objective' power of
self-analysis, his recognition of his own limitations and immediate
perception of the sort of situation he could best use. He told Zweig that,
on the verge of the seventies, he could no longer command the musical
inspiration of the young man who composed *Don Juan* and *Till Eulenspiegel*. He needed words, and a certain degree of dramatic complexity to
spur his inspiration. He added, according to Zweig: 'I am not blessed
with long melodies as Mozart was, I only get as far as short themes.*
But what I do know is how to turn a theme, paraphrase it, extract everything that is in it, and I believe nobody today can do this as well as I can.'

2

Strauss left Zweig to think *Sir Morosus* out by himself. He had the
scoring of *Arabella* to complete,† and in April 1932 when he inquired
incidentally after the Jonson libretto he was on tour in Italy. In May or
June he visited Zweig in Salzburg and they made more detailed plans,
resulting in a sketch scenario in June. Strauss was conducting *Fidelio* at
Salzburg in August and further consultation must have taken place then,
since Strauss was making musical sketches for *Die schweigsame Frau* by
1 October, a fortnight before he hailed the arrival of the Act 1 libretto
with *Bravi, bravi, ganz ausgezeichnet* ('Bravo, bravo, absolutely excellent')
—a quotation in German from his favourite Mozart opera *Così fan tutte*.
The second act libretto arrived on 16 December and this time Strauss
quoted *Die Meistersinger*: *Auch der zweite Bar gelang* ('The second verse
was good as well') though he voiced doubts on the length of the Aminta-
Morosus dialogue before and after the wedding scene; Zweig readily
agreed to reduce this. Already the composer was thinking, as with earlier
operas, in terms of spoken dialogue instead of linking recitative, and this
time he carried out his intention more thoroughly than in any of his
operas except *Intermezzo*.

* The reader may have noticed the preponderance of very short musical examples in
this book.
† Friedrich von Schuch tells us that Strauss in his enthusiasm was minded to postpone
the completion of *Arabella* in order to proceed with *Die schweigsame Frau*, but that he
was persuaded against this plan by the urgent entreaty of the Dresden Intendant Alfred
Reucker (one of the dedicatees of *Arabella*). The tale seems curious, and it is conceivable
that Schuch junior is thinking of 1933, after *Arabella* was finished, when Strauss withdrew the score because he wanted Reucker to produce and Busch to conduct the first
performance.

Zweig completed the libretto of Act 3 on 17 January 1933 and wrote at the end, *Plaudite, amici, comoedia finita est*—the last words of Beethoven. Strauss, not to be outdone, expressed his thanks with two lines of words and music from his song *Ich trage meine Minne*, Opus 32 No. 1.

The chief interest of this quotation is that Strauss remembered it so inaccurately; notes and note-values are quite different in the original. But this is quite characteristic of the composer who freely altered his own music to suit the special qualifications of special singers, and who, when the music for a recital was lost, improvised brand-new accompaniments for his songs.

Strauss wrote promptly to Professor Kippenberg, thanking him for his part in the creation of 'the best libretto for an *opéra comique* since *Figaro*'. Strauss began work on the short score of *Die schweigsame Frau* on 23 February.

On 7 March the Reichstag elections took place and, as many had foreseen, Hitler's National Socialist party came to power. It was in the same month that a boycott of all Jews was ordered; Josef Goebbels himself published an attack on Stefan Zweig, supported by quotations taken incautiously from the works of Arnold Zweig, an expressionist author whose literary adventures in sensual realism had recently taken the form of a novel examining the psychological meaning of homosexuality (*De Vriendt kehrt heim*, 1933), and who consistently inveighed against militarism, bureaucracy and intolerance.

Stefan Zweig was able to refute the attack without difficulty, but he took it for granted that Strauss would feel obliged to abandon work on *Die schweigsame Frau*, if only because his son Franz had married a Jewess, and the composer's earlier, most famous operas, were written in collaboration with Hofmannsthal, who was half-Jewish. 'In the National Socialist sense', Zweig explains in his autobiography,* 'he was very much in the red.' Nevertheless as Strauss had set his heart on the successful conclusion of this opera and on writing further operas with Zweig, he took the trouble to write to the newspapers confirming Zweig's refutation. We shall find in due course that Zweig was closely connected with

* *The World of Yesterday*, London, 1943.

several of the later Strauss operas, and find also that Strauss acted towards the Nazi authorities with more courage and defiance than has sometimes been credited to him. His defence of Zweig was nevertheless primarily selfish, secondarily artistic, and political not at all. Strauss was prepared to tolerate any régime that facilitated the production of his music. The Nazis, far from victimizing Strauss for his Jewish connexions, were anxious for his support as the greatest living German composer, not least because their unsavoury tactics had won the open hostility of most reputable artists. Strauss did his moral prestige no good by accepting an engagement at the Bayreuth Festival that summer, after similar invitations had already been refused by Toscanini and Fritz Busch on political grounds; and also by accepting the Presidency of the State Music Council (which was voted to him without his prior consent).* But for the official acceptance of his collaboration with Zweig he worked hard and determinedly.

3

Strauss completed the scoring of Act 1 on 21 January 1934, a hundred and forty pages of score in two and a half months as he proudly told Zweig. By May he had finished the whole opera in short score,† and begun the full score of Act 2; he also paid a visit to Goebbels, following an inquiry whether it was true that Strauss was writing an opera with Arnold Zweig, and obtained an assurance that no obstacle would be placed in the way of a première at Dresden for *Die schweigsame Frau*— Strauss could guarantee this for July 1935. Strauss had also asked Goebbels if the anti-Jewish propaganda might not be toned down and was told that so long as foreign Press reports continued to vilify Hitler's régime this would remain impossible. Strauss reported all this to Zweig, who was in London collecting material for a book on Mary Queen of Scots, and who attended the London première of *Arabella*.

The scoring of the opera was completed on 20 October, and in January 1935 Strauss added the potpourri overture to it. Before this, however, he had celebrated his seventieth birthday in June 1934, with plaudits from Nazi officialdom, and only a month afterwards found that Dr Goebbels had changed his mind. Strauss was at Bayreuth in July to conduct *Parsifal*, when Goebbels walked into Wahnfried, the Wagner family residence where Strauss was staying, and announced that *Die schweigsame Frau* was likely after all to prove an embarrassment to the Government.

---

* When sent a form to fill in for this *Reichsmusikkammer*, Strauss found the instruction, 'Give two well-known composers who will vouch for your work as composer'. Strauss named as his referees Mozart and Richard Wagner.

† As on two previous occasions he had set a stage-direction, *Mit Reverenz*, to music.

Strauss regarded the whole affair as grossly insulting, but replied that he had no wish to embarrass Hitler or Goebbels, and was ready to withdraw *Die schweigsame Frau* (which had already become known all over the world) from performances inside or outside Germany. Goebbels and all his minions had spent hours poring over Zweig's libretto in search of possible indelicacies or other undesirable matter and had been unable to find anything here or in Zweig's other work that might be construed as anti-German or politically unfavourable. Zweig, on the other hand, regarded himself proudly as a Jew first and an Austrian second, and he admitted to a secret joy in all the political harum-scarum his harmless comic opera had aroused. Any of us, for that matter, must raise a smile to think of the pompous face-saving that was set in motion by an innocent comedy devised solely for humour and euphony, qualities that meant nothing to Hitler and his thugs. Goebbels was obliged to note the force of Strauss's remarks, and could only reply that, even if he muzzled the Press, he would be unable to prevent stink-bombs from being let off at the première. But he would leave a final decision to the Chancellor. So Hitler too had to read this Jew's comedy and had also to admit that he could not object to it: it is not even about Germany. It makes fun of an English sea-dog, and therefore implicitly of Imperialism, British characteristics, and so on, all to the predictable amusement of a Nazi audience —were it not that the author was an outspoken and exceptionally gifted anti-Nazi Jew. By the end of September Strauss could inform Zweig that Hitler had given his blessing to the première.* And by this time too Strauss and Zweig were seriously discussing the opera which became *Friedenstag*, of which more in the next chapter.

4

A week before Strauss completed the overture to *Die schweigsame Frau* another tragedy befell him. Ever since he first wielded influence at the Vienna Opera he had striven to ensure the musical directorship of a sympathetic and broadminded man—and striven to keep out Felix Weingartner whom he regarded as a disastrous influence on the *Oper am Ring* (not least because Weingartner disliked Strauss's music). Now Clemens Krauss decided to take a post in Berlin and Weingartner was appointed at Vienna in his stead. Strauss wrote to a new friend, Joseph Gregor, that it was 'the collapse of the sacred, dear Vienna Opera', and the appointment certainly put paid to any Vienna production of *Die*

---

* Zweig in his autobiography claimed that Strauss had to talk personally with Hitler before permission was granted; but no other evidence for this famous rendezvous is forthcoming.

schweigsame Frau, or of any Strauss operas that could conceivably be withheld from the Vienna repertory.

Nevertheless there was the prospect of the Dresden première, and of other productions to follow in Berlin, Hamburg, Frankfurt, Munich, etc. During rehearsals at Dresden Strauss reported enthusiasm for Karl Böhm's conducting* and Josef Gielen's production, as well as Maria Cebotari's impersonation of the title role; 'it is a sure-fire hit, even if only for the twenty-first century', he wrote prophetically. The whole production was to go to London, aided by a Nazi subsidy, in November: 'the wicked Third Reich has, you see, its good sides'. There were even rumours that Hitler might attend the première.

How was all this possible, when the opera in question was written by a militantly Jewish author? The Nazi compromise was as simple as it was dishonest. Secretly it had been arranged that the Dresden première would take place without official cognizance of the librettist's name: the opera would be billed as 'freely adapted from Ben Jonson's comedy'. Two days before the première, on an afternoon when Strauss was in his hotel playing Skat with his friends Fanto, Pattiera and Schuch junior, he suddenly declared a wish to see a proof of the theatre handbill—plainly some friend of Zweig's had warned him of the method by which Hitler hoped to excuse his presence, and pay tribute to the official Nazi composer. Strauss had chosen a moment of relaxation when officials of the Dresden Opera would be in his private company. Schuch junior, then business manager of the Opera, waited until after dinner to place a proof-sheet in front of Strauss who turned the colour of a boiled lobster (his blushes were celebrated) and exclaimed, 'Unless Zweig's name is printed in type as large as Hofmannsthal's for *Der Rosenkavalier*, I go away tomorrow morning and the première can take place without me.' And in his own hand he corrected the attribution on the proof. A panic conference took place and it was agreed that Strauss's wishes must be respected. As soon as the decision was communicated to Berlin, Hitler determined not to attend the performance and Goebbels and his wife announced that their plane to Dresden had been unable to leave Hamburg.

Next morning the Nazi postal censors discovered a letter from Strauss to Stefan Zweig. It was stated to have contained defamatory remarks about the Dresden management, but there are none. Evidently it answers a letter from Zweig who must have voiced his Semitic grievances in a particularly vehement and querulous tone. The Gestapo seem to have been so stupid that instead of withdrawing Strauss's letter they made photo-copies, and then forwarded the original to Zweig. On reading the letter, Zweig must have known that he could have struck a

---

* Böhm had been brought in to replace the Nazi mediocrity who supplanted Fritz Busch as musical director at Dresden; this was one tiny triumph of German musicality over Nazi Philistinism.

blow against Nazism and earned some money by placing the document in the hands of *The Times*. It has been wondered why he did not do so. There are two reasons: Zweig knew that publication of this letter would put an end to Strauss's life or his career; furthermore it was the editorial policy of *The Times* during these years to print nothing which might sharpen Hitler's temper.

This was the letter which Zweig received:

Dear Herr Zweig,

Your letter of the 15th makes me despair! This Jewish egoism! I mustn't turn anti-Semitic. This racial pride, this feeling of solidarity— it makes even me feel different! Do you think I have ever let myself be guided, in any sort of action, by the thought that I am German (perhaps, who knows?). Do you think that Mozart deliberately composed in an Aryan manner? For me there are only two categories of human beings; the talented, and the untalented. And for me the populace only exists from the moment when it becomes an audience. It's all the same to me whether they are Chinese, Upper Bavarians, New Zealanders, or Berliners, so long as they've paid the full price at the box office. Now please stop plaguing me with dear Gregor. The comedy I have received is charming,* and I know perfectly well that it is entirely your idea. I won't accept it under an assumed name, any more than *1648* [the first title of *Friedenstag*]. So please let me beg you urgently to work out these two one-acters as soon as possible, and tell me what the expenses are. Let it be my worry what I do with them if you keep the matter a secret. Who has told you that I have involved myself so deeply in politics? Is it because I conducted a concert in place of Bruno Walter? I did it as a favour to the orchestra. Or because I stepped in for that other non-Aryan Toscanini? That I did as a favour to Bayreuth. It has nothing to do with politics. How the gutter press presents it is none of my affair, nor should you worry about it. That I hold office as President of the State Music Council? I do it to bring about good and prevent greater misfortune. Simply because I know my artistic duty. I would have taken on this tiresome honorary job for any government, but neither Kaiser Wilhelm nor Herr Rathenau asked me to. So be good, forget Herr Moses and the other apostles for a couple of weeks, and just work at your two one-acters. . . . The performance here is going to be splendid. Everyone is tremendously worked up! Should I therefore stop working with you? Never, on any account!

The première on 24 June was immensely successful, uproariously applauded, and very favourably noticed by music critics; even those for Nazi papers wrote enthusiastically about the libretto as well as the music and the performance. The second, non-subscription performance was

---

* The original source of *Capriccio*, which Zweig and Gregor had concocted between them on a walking tour of the Zürich district.

well attended and two further performances took place (though one Martin Mutscher reported to Hitler that only two had been given, the second almost empty). After this the opera was banned officially in Nazi Germany. Karl Rankl conducted the Austrian première at Graz on 1 February 1936,* and two months later it was given at La Scala, Milan, in Italian (Mussolini did not, at this time, subscribe to anti-Semitic policies). Zürich and Prague (where Georg Szell conducted) followed, and Rome followed Milan's example. Thereafter there was silence until the end of the war. An attempt, encouraged by pleas from Zweig and Strauss, to have the opera given at Salzburg in 1936, was cut off at the official source. Sir Thomas Beecham, having failed to obtain the promised Nazi-financed Dresden visit for Covent Garden, planned to produce the work in 1938 with Cebotari as Aminta, Charles Kullman as Henry, Alexander Sved as the Barber, and Josef Manowarda as Morosus. But this project also came to nothing. Too many German musicians were involved.

5

Strauss was not content to remain silent under this public, yet underhand, insult to his work. On 10 July 1935 he prepared a memorandum to his accusers, a direct result of the visit paid to him at Garmisch, four days earlier, by an emissary of the State Secretary Walter Funkl, who demanded Strauss's resignation from his official presidential post on what would be described as grounds of 'ill health'. Strauss gave his consent to the emissary, Otto von Keudell. Having summarized this interview Strauss particularized:

'Herr von Keudell produced a copy, often underlined in red, of a private letter to my friend and sometime collaborator Stefan Zweig. This had apparently been opened by the Saxon police, and so it is alleged (though according to Dr Frank illegally), denounced in several Berlin Government offices—even though the letter was signed externally with the full name of the sender. I was not aware that I, as President until now of the State Music Council, stood under the direct control of the State Police, nor that, after a lifetime's achievement of eighty major works "recognized throughout the world", I am not considered a "good German" above all criticism. Nevertheless the unprecedented event has occurred that Minister Goebbels had dismissed me, without vouchsafing any explanation at all of his confiscation of my letter which must remain completely incomprehensible to readers unacquainted in detail with the

---

* A semi-private concert performance had been given on 17 December 1935 by the Strauss Society in Vienna.

events leading up to it, and its connexion with a lengthy correspondence over purely artistic matters.

'The letter in question is a somewhat testy reply to Zweig's unwillingness for further collaboration with me in case this might damage my political position as President of the State Music Council (which I was pushed into) and might put further difficulties in my way. He did not want to hasten accusations by agitators that, as my collaborator, he was agitating for special indulgence. The beginning of the letter, about Zweig's Jewish egoism and his (admittedly understandable) solidarity with his persecuted racial fellows, demanded the obvious answer that no German ever thought whether he was composing German or Aryan music. Ever since Bach we have composed just as our talents permitted, and have been Aryan and German without thinking further about it. This can hardly be reckoned betrayal of our country but only faithful service to the fatherland, even when non-Aryans have written the libretto, as with Mozart and myself. The third and most heavily underlined passage—and here perhaps I am in conflict with Dr Goebbels who, as a statesman, regards the populace differently—says (and I point out that this is an entirely personal view, expressed in a private letter): "The populace, over and above two million, begins to count for me only at the moment when, as cultivated listeners, it becomes an audience and has paid the full price at the box office." This is not to say the fifteen to thirty Pfennig *Meistersinger* and *Tristan* audience through which (all theatrical administrators are agreed) our stages suffer the greatest material damage, and which need ever greater State subsidies if they are to fulfil their loftier cultural tasks. It is in fact a purely artistic matter, nothing to do with my purse as seems maliciously to have been claimed.' We may note in this connexion that Dresden Opera employees had had their salaries reduced by the Nazis.

'Let us,' Strauss continues, 'enumerate the sacrifices I have made in order not to set myself apart from the whole National Socialist movement from the very start. They began when I took over Bruno Walter's last subscription concert after Walter had been evicted. I did this as a favour to the Philharmonic Orchestra and at the ardent request of Julius Kopsch and Hugo Rach. I gave my fee of fifteen hundred marks to the orchestra. This started a storm directed against me in foreign, but particularly in Viennese Jewish newspapers, and caused me more alienation and damage in the eyes of all decent folk than the German government could ever make good to me. I was condemned as a servile, self-seeking anti-Semite; whereas, on the contrary, I have stated as often as possible to ordinary people here (and again often to my disadvantage) that I regard the Streicher–Goebbels Judaism panic as a disaster to German honour, a sign of weakness, the lowest possible weapon of untalented and lazy mediocrity against superior intelligence and superior

talent. I openly acknowledge here that I have received so much encouragement from Jews, so much selfless friendship, magnanimous help
and spiritual stimulus, that it would be a crime if I did not recognize it in
all thankfulness.

'To be sure, I have had opponents in the Jewish Press; on the other
hand I would call it, compared with that displayed towards my highly
disparate opposite, Gustav Mahler, almost friendly. My worst and most
evil enemies and opponents were Aryans—I name only Perfall, Oscar
Merz (of the *Münchner Neueste Nachrichten*), Theodor Göring, Felix
Mottl, Franz Schalk, Weingartner, and the whole of the recent Party
Press, the *Völkischer Beobachter et cetera.*'

I make no apology for giving these documents at length in English,
since they are unknown to English readers (and to many Germans, for
that matter), and they correct the impression that Strauss toadied wholesale to the Nazis. It is clear, furthermore, that as time went on his
attitude to the Nazi régime became more and more truculent, until in
1944 Hitler was only with difficulty persuaded to remove a veto on
the official celebration of Strauss's eightieth birthday, since the composer had openly declared that 'if I had had my way, there would never
have been glorious war heroes to be billeted on me, because there would
never have been a war'.

6

Strauss called his overture a potpourri, and composed it after the rest
was completed. It is gay, feather-light, brilliantly scored and contrived,
and fixes a quantity of themes firmly in our heads before we know their
precise connotations. Thus the first horn leads off with Ex. 14 (the conspiracy) as an ostinato above which violins add Ex. 17 (the unwedding of
Morosus) and, at the top of the scale, Ex. 16 (the termagant Timida).
Ex. 7 (Morosus's craving for quietness) and Ex. 2 (the housework which
prevents him from attaining quietness) furnish the transition section; and
a little later Ex. 13 (Morosus's tantrums, and in particular his decision
to disinherit Henry). The love theme, Ex. 8, looms in the bass, and
after a percussive, Rossini-crescendo, independent second subject,
another version of Ex. 17, more expansive, breaks in. During the
development Ex. 5 is suggested through Ex. 7. There is an even livelier
coda.

Jonson's *Epicoene* appeared around 1609, but Zweig treated it very
freely and, among other things, set the scene forward to about 1780.
When the overture ends and the curtain rises, we therefore see an
eighteenth-century living-room in a London house on a fine morning.
Models of ships, stuffed fish, ship's tackle, flags, and weapons of war

32 The arrival of the Holsteiner and his troops in the besieged fortress: Viorica Ursuleac, Hans Hotter and Ludwig Weber in the Munich premiere of *Friedenstag*, 1938

33 The deputation of townsfolk to the Commandant: Munich revival of *Friedenstag*, 1961

34
Der Baum allein, der singt . . .
the close of the Munich revival
of *Daphne*, 1964

35
Peneios (Georg Hann) prophesies the
arrival of Apollo: Munich, 1941

should all indicate that an ex-naval man lives here, and that Sir Morosus*
is exceptionally sensitive to noise of all sorts—for the doors are all sound-
proofed with blankets and sacking.

Just at the moment his housekeeper, Widow Zimmerlein, has the room
to herself, and she is dusting the furniture industriously. Her technique is
described in Strauss's music, and (Ex. 2²) her frustrated passion for the
sound of her own voice.

Hearing a presumably muffled knock, she opens the door and admits
Herr Schneidebart (or, in Jonson, Cutbeard), the Figaro of London
town, who has come to attend Morosus as soon as he wakes up. Schneidebart is fitly characterized in a stealthy, tricky, Eulenspiegelish phrase.

He is asked to wait since the master is still, and for once in a while,
God be thanked, adds this loquacious lady, asleep. Repose and sleep are
precious acquisitions and rare for Morosus; both have their own musical
images. This is sleep.

Here, for Widow Zimmerlein, are the time and the place and the listener
all together for a pleasant gossip (Ex. 2²). The barber only wishes to get on
with the job, but Widow Zimmerlein is not to be denied this heaven-sent
opportunity to voice her opinion that Morosus's phonophobia is due
to loneliness: what he needs is a good wife, experienced and industrious—

—and of course very taciturn:

schweig – sa- me Frau

* In *Epicoene* the old man is called Morose, according to the classical practice whereby
characters have one all-purpose name. Zweig simply named him Sir Morosus, but never
indicated whether he was Sir Morosus Smith or (as Arthur Jacobs's English translation
made him) Sir John Morosus.

(the 'silent wife' theme is quoted with the words later attached to it). It will be seen that Exs. 5 and 6 are virtually retrogrades of each other. The housekeeper's idea is that Herr Schneidebart should suggest to Morosus the ideal suitability of Widow Zimmerlein as a prospective wife. Schneidebart knows otherwise; he has heard her talk. A fearsome quarrel ensues (inversion of Ex. 6) and this wakes the master of the house, who storms out of the adjoining bedroom in his dressing-gown, waving his pipe at the housekeeper and ordering her to be off, which she promptly is. His cries for peace and quiet are sharply defined, but the eventual form of this important theme involves an extra note (the first one), and so it is quoted in its later final shape. The connexion with Exs. 5 and 6 will be noted, and Ex. 12 is not far away.

7

The Barber begins to shave Morosus, who continues to complain of the terrible noise in the vicinity—Strauss obliges with anachronistic quotations from Gounod's *Faust* waltz, Papageno's *Der Vogelfänger bin ich ja* and Wagner's *Meistersinger* Overture (drums only), as well as appropriate sounds of bell-ringing. The Barber talks in speech, Morosus in music very delicately scored. The old man grumbles that he cannot enjoy peace in his own house for the chatter and bustle of his housekeeper (Ex. 2). Schneidebart suggests that Morosus should get rid of the baggage and replace her with a young quiet wife.

8

Did Strauss consciously intend to echo the German traditional song *Freut euch des Lebens?*

Morosus protests that this is a contradiction in terms, except in cemeteries, but the Barber conjures up beatific scenes of domestic bliss and companionship in strong contrast to cold lonely evenings by an unlit hearth. The versatile uses to which Strauss puts Ex. 8 in the course of three acts might almost have been intended as a demonstration of his boast to Zweig that 'no one can extract all the contents from a phrase as well as I can'. He does not waste time indeed, for Morosus expresses his approval (*Ja, das wär schön*) to one variation of Ex. 8, and expatiates (*Irgendwen zu wissen*) with a second. There will be many later demonstrations of this all-purpose theme. One cannot call it a love-theme since its associations are also with domestic bliss and uxorial suitability, as well as, perhaps instead of, Romance.

Morosus is bound to conclude that much as he might fancy such a paragon, she would never take an old crosspatch like himself. To which the Barber replies with a canzona contrasting wise and foolish virgins. The silly girls only long for handsome young men who soon grow old, the wise ones go for character. The Barber's song begins with this phrase, one portion of which, Ex. 9^x, is generally connected with vacuous chatter, and has already made one discreet appearance in this role.

The canzona turns now and then into a duet as Morosus depreciates his chances, since his principal need is for tranquillity.

Promptly a din is heard at the door outside. Morosus jumps up and shouts for his stick, not to walk with but to belabour this disturber of the peace. The Barber drops his curling tongs in terror, and trombones with lower strings introduce a new theme.

A heated altercation between the noisy visitor and the housekeeper ends when the former bursts into the room (shades of *Der Rosenkavalier*!). Morosus fortunately recognizes him at once as his long-lost nephew and heir, Henry. The old man's menacing shillelagh stops in mid-air, and he calls the young man's name, while violins and violas produce an appropriate phrase.

It is not so much Henry's theme, though, as that of the company he has brought with him (this is a feature of Strauss's thematic technique to which almost every chapter of this book has had to draw attention). Henry, it seems, left his studies at Pavia University, being bored to extinction with legal studies (though violas and cellos deviously suggest Ex. 8 as the real explanation). Uncle Morosus is delighted by this attitude, so like his own days of yore when he ran off to sea. The associate phrase, for strings (*So sind wir nicht zu halten*), is closely linked with one in *Elektra* during the dialogue of Clytemnestra and her revolutionary daughter (Ex. 10^3 in *Elektra*)—a fascinating psychological connexion.

Now Henry has come home (Ex. 10) and Morosus joyfully sets aside plans for marriage (Ex. 6), and instructs the Barber to tend Henry in all his wants (Ex. 3). Henry, a trifle embarrassed, has to confess that he is not alone; downstairs he is awaited by the companions he has brought with him—his *troupe*. Morosus understands 'troops', and this makes his day: he will hear of his nephew's bold deeds in battle from Henry's own comrades in arms.

But the jerky, comical march to which the 'troops' enter (strings *col legno*) is far from heroic, like the company (Ex. 11). They are solemn, none too well dressed, certainly not in military uniforms. There are three men, also three women, and a mixed chorus behind them. Morosus is dumbfounded at the spectacle, even more when Henry introduces the Manager Cesare Vanuzzi, Carlo Morbio the famous Orfeo, and Giuseppe Farfallo, darling of Bologna; the leading ladies, Aminta, Isotta and Carlotta, and the rest unnamed. The penny drops. Morosus senses song. But not Henry as well? Not in public? Not for money? Vanuzzi boasts of Henry's prowess. But why in England? Morosus learns that it is for an opera season at the Haymarket Theatre, in response to public demand. Strauss supplies shamelessly anachronistic references to *Bella figlia dell'amore* and *La Donna è mobile* from *Rigoletto*, and his own *Mir anvertraut* from *Die Frau ohne Schatten*.

Morosus at last regains his outraged dignity. Let these ear-splitters bawl where they like, he will have nothing to do with them, and he hopes Henry will not insult him by consorting with them in town. Morosus's determination is expressed in a short phrase that traces a triad in second inversion, but is variously harmonized, most often in this form.

13

Henry has to admit that he is down to sing Orlando, and is looking forward to it. Furthermore his fortunes are allied with the company since Aminta is his wife. This is too much for Morosus, and he disinherits Henry (plenty of Ex. 13). The opera-singers, including Henry but excluding Aminta, protest in a lively and noisy ensemble. Morosus calls for hush, tells the Barber to find him a wife, a Parson, and a Notary, and storms into his bedroom.

Aminta was too much upset by this unwelcoming reception to join the ensemble, and she now shows her sweet and gentle nature in an apology to Henry for being the cause of his misfortune. The other actors resume expressions of outrage, to the music of their entrance march; their comments, inaudible in performance, are very amusing—Vanuzzi proposes to serenade the old man with brass bands until he revokes his decision, Isotta suggests they set fire to his house, Carlotta is chiefly annoyed at being called a whore ('Even for three hundred ducats and a diamond watch I refused to sleep with the Prince of Guastalla'). The Barber asks them not to be too hard on Morosus. They bring their ensemble to a full close (Strauss lays much emphasis on 'closed' numbers in this opera) and the Barber explains in spoken recitative what a dear old boy Henry's uncle is. His ears, alas, are super-sensitive because he once lost his ear-drums when the powder magazine of his ship exploded (appropriate orchestral description, and equally appropriate noises of sympathy from Aminta). Furthermore Henry is advised to return to his uncle's favour, since Morosus is extremely rich: there are some sixty or seventy thousand pounds' worth of gold in the cellar. Here a short arioso for the Barber (*Da unten im Keller*) provokes a little ensemble as the actors repeat, astonished, the figures cited (*Sechzig, siebzig tausend Pfund*). When the ensemble ends Aminta begins a canzonetta of her own (*Nicht an mich, Geliebter, denke*) offering to give up Henry for his own good. This turns into a duettino (charmingly reminiscent of Mozart's *Ah, perdona il primo affetto* in *La Clemenza di Tito*) tenderly and lightly scored, as Henry steadfastly refuses her offer, a gesture that the other opera-singers hand-somely applaud in another ensemble; Aminta here makes the first of many excursions high among the leger-lines.

The Barber can only regard this light-mindedness as fatal folly; where can any of them lay hands on so much wealth, and would we not all be happier having part of such a fortune? His main problem now is to find a wife for Morosus. He tries to interest Isotta and Carlotta. But Isotta is a happy soul and vows she would banish Morosus's dumps by laughing and joking; Carlotta, a born singer, would hope to cure him with fluent roulades day and night. Aminta follows these two solo verses with some phrases of regret and self-reproach, and Strauss then combines all three solos in one of his melted-honey female-voice trios. Neither of these two eligible candidates will do, the Barber decides. But suddenly he has an idea, worthy of Figaro's London counterpart, and when silence has been called in ten-part harmony Schneidebart expounds his plan above the following conspiratorial ostinato.

14

wie wär- es, wenn man Herrn Mo-ro-sus

The Barber's suggestion is a mock marriage, with three suggested candidates for Morosus's hand, with Parson, Registrars and all enacted by the opera singers. They can thus make sure that the old man will repent as quickly as possible, wish himself unwed and, when the hoax is revealed, be heartily thankful and welcome Henry back again. After a moment's bewilderment the company approves this plan and Henry launches the finale of the act, an extended ensemble for the eight soloists and chorus. They agree on their roles—Aminta, already disheartened by the cruelty involved, is overruled by the determination of the others 'to cure this uncle'.

Die-sen O-heim zu ku-rie-ren

The brilliant lightness of this stretta is enhanced, after the Barber's warning to plan in complete secrecy and silence, by a reprise of Ex. 15 at a quicker tempo. They all gather round Schneidebart as Ex. 13, repeated again and again, rings down the curtain.

7

Act 2 begins with another of Strauss's elegant eighteenth-century minuets; Morosus is putting himself to enormous trouble in order to look like a dashing suitor, and concatenations of baroque triplet figures (like Ochs's reverences) give a hint of the absurdity involved, just as softly pounding drums tell us how madly his heart is beating at the prospect of this new venture—Ex. 13 recalls repeatedly what sparked it off.

On the afternoon of the following day we find Widow Zimmerlein putting the finishing touches to Morosus's bridal attire, and doing her best to warn him against taking this disastrous step. He quite deliberately takes no notice; he knows, as Ex. 2^1 explains, what motivates her advice— she would like him for herself. He is indeed looking forward to being shot of her prattle (Ex. 2^2 again and Ex. 2^1 inverted=conquered). She has, though, an idea of what was plotted while she listened at the keyhole (Ex. 15 on violins), but her duplicity only inflames his irascibility, and when she comments that his costume is in better order than his head, he shoos her off to answer the door.

Here is the Barber with not one, but three girls (Am I a Turk? asks Morosus). As well as Ex. 6 we have Ex. 14 to remind us of the hoax— and the officials for a wedding to follow are on their way. But, the Barber urges in a short canzona (*Nur das eine lasst Euch bitten*), Morosus must hold on to his best behaviour in front of these shy and inexperienced young things (Ex. 12 and Ex. 6) or they will never accept him.

His canzonet over, Schneidebart introduces the three candidates, to a stiff little march. Carlotta is a farm-girl, rough and hoydenish; Isotta an affected bluestocking; Aminta a simple, down-at-heel young lady of the town. Schneidebart, emphasizing the solemnity of the occasion, introduces

Morosus (while Ex. 14 mocks the old man) who welcomes the young ladies: first Carlotta, who answers in heavy rustic accents and coarse spoken phrases, and is quickly turned down; the polymath Isotta whose accomplishments are rattled off by the Barber, and her own evident loquacity paraded against rapid scale-figures—she, obviously, will kill Morosus with her intellectual prattle before they reach the altar, so she too is refused. Aminta, now disguised as Timida, steps forward to Ex. 8, with a new suffix that later becomes thematically independent.

16

She very sweetly explains her lack of pretensions in a gentle quasi-parlando arietta. Strauss plainly responded with warmth to the situation, and obliged with a particularly ingratiating web of vaguely thematic diatonic material. All Aminta's replies are to Morosus's taste, and he acclaims her victorious in this curious Judgement of Paris—though Timida can barely believe the decision (Ex. 16) even when Schneidebart explains to her in detail (there is a quite gratuitous quotation from Tchaikovsky's *Italian Caprice* here). Morosus has to ask her, sincerely and gently, if she accepts him, and of course she does—to the pretended fury of the other two girls. Morosus sends the Barber for the Parson and Lawyers, and meanwhile takes the opportunity to calm Timida's anxiety and win her affection—so eloquently that her conscience nags her even more strongly than before. This fourth scene of the act, a duet for Aminta and Morosus alone on stage, is as touching and heartfelt as anything in the whole opera. We are reminded in retrospect that Strauss loved *Die schweigsame Frau* particularly because he could identify himself with Morosus, not as buffoon but as a dear old man winning the affection of a young girl by his gentleness and courtesy. Morosus is musically very much the hero of the opera; all the best music goes to him, in the duologue with Schneidebart (*Ja, das wär schön*, etc.), now in this duet, and later in the closing scene of the opera.

The duet with Aminta shares a fairly perceptible musical family likeness with that for Mandryka and Arabella in the second act of the previous opera, notwithstanding the difference in vocal timbres, the simpler themes (but two or three are close to *Arabella*), and the light, open texture. Ex. 8 makes humorous appearances, as do Ex. 12, Ex. 6 and Ex. 9^{x}. Ex. 8 ends the duet as Morosus kisses Timida tenderly on the forehead. And now the Barber returns with the officials for the wedding ceremony, who enter to a straightforward orchestral transcription of an anonymous *Almain*, No. XIV from the *Fitzwilliam Virginal Book*. Vanuzzi, disguised as a Parson, performs the equivalent of a Bidding, and Morbio, in the role of Notary, contributes a legal exordium (to an *Almain* by Martin

Peerson, *Fitzwilliam Book*, No. xc, transposed a tone lower). The marriage contract is signed, and its completion proclaimed by Vanuzzi to the anonymous piece; Timida has to be pushed into giving her signature. Morosus invites those present to remain for a snack; the ensuing ensemble is dominated by Aminta's unwillingness to play the sadistic part assigned to her. The company toasts the couple; Morosus is moved by the sacredness of the event. Into it bursts a gang of sailors (supposedly from Morosus's ship, but actually from the opera troupe, led by Farfallo) noisily insistent on celebrating the marriage. Morosus does not recognize their faces and is by no means glad to see them (Ex. 13). Farfallo opens a window and invites all the neighbours indoors, and much to Morosus's fury they appear in force, to Ex. 16, led by Henry who insists on the participation of the throng (Ex. 8). Bells and bagpipes (not notated in the score) add to the jubilation, which is highly painful to Morosus. It is amusing to find that their congratulations include a German song, *Hoch soll er leben*! (just before figure 119). Schneidebart takes the liberty of asking them to accept beer in the pub round the corner, to drink the newly married couple's health. Widow Zimmerlein's Ex. 2^2 remains behind when they are gone (though the stage directions indicate that she has already disappeared). The actors in their various roles depart as well, offering encouragement to Aminta in the part she has to play.

Morosus resumes, very tactfully, his wooing when they are all gone (to Ex. 8 in a new version) and remarks unhappily that Aminta seems upset (Ex. 8). She insists that she is content, so long as quietness remains the order of the day. But Morosus insists on discovering why she is not more obviously cheerful.

I want peace, she screams on a top C to her husband's terrified astonishment, and I must have my own way! Oboes and horns throw out a new theme (new, that is, since the overture) associated with the un-wedding of Morosus. At present only the first four notes are heard; the continuation given is only the most memorable of several variants.

17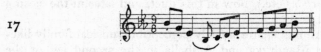

Aminta informs her putative husband that old conventions no longer apply to newly married couples. The house needs complete redecoration and manifold improvements before she can feel at home. She pulls down the existing decorations, and invites her husband to install better ones. Husband and wife fall into a quarrelsome duet. Nothing in the house will please Aminta; Morosus is too surprised to protest very much at the extraordinary change which has come over the shy young lady, though he does stick up for his pipe which also comes in for her disapproval.

At the worst moment Henry arrives and without exerting a finger turns

Ex. 17 into a bland triad figure without further implication (a metamorphosis of telling dramatic effect). Morosus greets him as a human
lifebelt for a drowning man; Ex. 17 has become too much for him.
Aminta answers Henry's basic questions with convincing rudeness, but a
half-Nelson or two (if this form of torture is not anachronistic in 1780)
calls her to obedience (Ex. 2^2, curiously but not unintelligibly), and she
wails her way into the spare room.

This, explains Henry, is the way to deal with silent women (Ex. 17 is
followed sarcastically by Ex. 6). Morosus thanks his saviour-nephew and
defends himself in a passionate solo. Henry promises to organize a
divorce in the morning, and Morosus leaves no doubt of his gratitude to
his nephew and his acceptance of Henry as his true heir, especially since
Henry promises to remain watchdog all night long in the living-room, in
order that his uncle shall get some much-needed rest (Ex. 7 in sundry
forms). The orchestral passage (chiefly for dark-coloured horns and
trombones), to which Morosus goes to bed and locks himself in, sounds
like a new theme, but it is still Ex. 17; the Barber's plot is succeeding.

As soon as Uncle Morosus is asleep Henry calls Aminta, who leaves her
room and comes to embrace him. Ex. 17 has turned from a conspiratorial
phrase into its dramatic result, a love theme, and the two married lovers
join in a duet expressing Henry's thanks and Aminta's feelings of
affection for the old man and distaste for her appointed role.

As they sing, Ex. 17 returns and with unexpected trenchancy we hear
the voice of Morosus from his bedroom calling to Henry as watchdog (it
is almost like a parody of Alberich and Hagen in Act 2 of *Götterdäm-
merung*). Henry assures his uncle that he has Timida firmly under
physical control—she cannot move from his arrest—which is true since
he is clasping her tightly. The music grows warmer, more richly polyphonic and no less melodious. Morosus, eased in mind, voices his thanks
on low D flat and Aminta echoes them in her resumed duet with Henry.
Her voice rises to her top D flat, and from near by Morosus utters the
same word *Dank* on the D flat four octaves below—a striking musical
invention. The curtain falls.

8

The third act opens vivaciously and in business-like fashion with an
energetic figure that represents the revolutionary goings-on *chez* Morosus.
Here is the beginning of the bland diatonic andamento fugue subject.

The commotion involved in this disastrous marriage finds a voice in the Ex. 18ˣ, which is often inverted during the act. When the curtain rises we see Aminta surrounded by her operatic colleagues, now disguised as workmen who are completely redecorating Morosus's living-room, knocking in nails to the first four notes of Ex. 18, importing a quantity of new furniture including a talking parrot that yells nonsense tonelessly but against screeching discords for wind and brass—it is to stand outside Morosus's bedroom. As Aminta is ordering the bogus workmen about, Widow Zimmerlein pleads for less noise. Aminta pays less than no attention; indeed she brightens at the entry of a harpsichord and her Singing Master (Henry in disguise) and is delighted when he asks her to sing an aria from Monteverdi's *L'Incoronazione di Poppea*. The workmen are sent away and Farfallo as accompanist strikes up. The 'aria' is *Sento un certo*, and it is very much adapted by Strauss from the delightful Intermezzo for Damigella and Valetto in Monteverdi's opera. The words are the same; the first four notes of the tune are the same— but they are on a different degree of the scale, in another mode and sung by the lady instead of the man; thereafter the rest is pure pastiche by Strauss. Ex. 19 shows Strauss's version,* and Monteverdi's original in C minor below it.

Sen·to un cer·to non so che—₃che mi pizzi·cae di - let-ta.

19

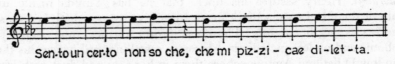

Sen·to un cer·to non so che, che mi piz·zi - cae di-let -ta.

Strauss's version becomes more and more florid and elaborate, and eventually turns into a duet with Henry. Top E, sustained by Aminta, brings Morosus out of his bedroom (Ex. 10) to plead in person for less noise; Aminta and Henry promptly embark on a new duet, this time supposedly from Legrenzi's *Eteocle e Polinice*; Strauss's virtuoso stratospheric vocal parts are soon set off by two more conversational ones for Morosus and the housekeeper, making a quartet (it is a pity that this should sometimes be cut). Henry and Farfallo noisily applaud their partners at the end of this operatic selection—Ex. 16 returns to remind us how much the shy young girl has altered—and she suggests an encore. But mercifully for Morosus's ears this has to be postponed, because Schneidebart (Ex. 14) now bursts into the room announcing the imminent arrival of the Lord Chief Justice and two Notaries. The divorce

* In later years Strauss decided that A major was uncomfortably high for this piece and at Zürich in 1942 he transposed it down into G major.

action must take precedence over everything. Timida has not officially been approached on the subject, of course, and the Barber is now asked to undertake this task (plenty of Ex. 17). Timida, however, declares herself well content with the marriage and has no wish to be divorced.

Quarrels? Only everyday arguments, common to every marriage and soon settled. Incompatibility? She is a meek wife and wears her troubles without complaint. The Barber reports failure to his employer (Ex. 18[x] represents Aminta's sharp tongue, we now assume) who offers alimony to any amount if only she will consent to a divorce. Schneidebart returns to the assault and now finds Aminta more accommodating, until a thousand pounds is mentioned. This figure, like the higher offers which follow, rouses her only to laughter. Parodying the manner of the broadsheet ballad, she announces her intention of always remaining true to her man. Another dispute is brewing, but now the Housekeeper announces the arrival of two carriages. These must be the Justices; Morosus is sent to put on his finest clothes, assisted by Widow Zimmerlein.

Enter Vanuzzi, Farfallo and Morbio in full legal attire, to the strains of an *In Nomine* by Bull (*Fitzwilliam Book*, XXXVII), transposed and set for bassoons, horns and trombones.*

20   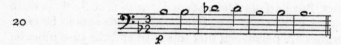

Vanuzzi makes a pompous opening announcement, and is deflated by Aminta who points out that Morosus is not yet here. The Barber regales the actors with tales of Aminta's shrewish deeds. Much relieved, the bogus Justices caper round the room and throw off a cheerful quintet, resuming their official manner in about nought seconds flat just as Morosus, splendidly dressed, re-enters. Vanuzzi now makes a shorter opening speech with Ex. 13 as well as Ex. 20, and reads the petition. Lady Morosus objects that she, at least, is not seeking a divorce, and the Lord Chief Justice decides that evidence must be brought by Morosus. Farfallo now launches into a full-scale list in Latin of the twelve impediments which justify matrimonial annulment, simultaneous translation being supplied by Morbio. Morosus seizes on the fact that he thought to have wed a taciturn wife and now finds her a volcano, but this is not enough. Further legal niceties have to be explained. Of these the Barber selects chastity (two horns in thirds); he can bring witness that Lady Morosus has had intercourse with another man—Aminta truthfully protests that she has had intercourse only with her lawful husband. The witnesses are brought in (Ex. 14) and prove to be Carlotta and Isotta in their second-act disguises. Timida protests that these are bribed false

---

* I have the strongest feeling after tracing these quotations that Strauss (or Zweig) simply looked at the first volume of the *Fitzwilliam Virginal Book* and picked out the pieces at random, just where the page opened on a suitable piece.

witnesses, much to the physical discomfort of Morosus; a lively quarrel ensues, and culminates in a grand passionate prayer by Aminta for the support of the Judges. The Barber, who has evidently appointed himself Counsel for the Prosecution (like Jonson's Cutbeard, he is a dab hand at the pertinent Latin phrase), agrees that she may have been faithful to her husband in the twelve hours since her marriage, but what before the marriage? He can call a further witness (Ex. 20 again). This is Henry in yet another disguise, fully bearded, and with a new transformation of Ex. 17. He freely admits to carnal knowledge of Lady Morosus. She hesitates to admit acquaintance with the bearded stranger, and Henry urges her, in a full-scale aria, to acknowledge their love.

21

Willst — du wirk-lich mich nicht ken- nen?

Lady Morosus explodes with passionate rage at the witness's protestations; but when pressed by Vanuzzi to say whether he is known to her, she cannot deny it, and Morosus appears to have won the case. 'Vivat Morosus' they all exclaim. Morosus thanks them all and Schneidebart calls for the verdict. But Farfallo does not concur with false findings since the contract of marriage nowhere stipulated that Timida should be *virgo intacta*; his colleagues are persuaded that this is so and the case must be dismissed.

Morosus is at the end of his tether. Remain tied to this she-devil? Never! (Ex. 17, Ex. 10, and Ex. 13). He will kill himself first. The others attempt to console him with suggestions of an appeal; and a big, fully scored ensemble is elaborated; in the middle of it Morosus makes for a bed and covers his head with the pillows to stop his ears. The Barber raises his hand, the singing stops at once, and the orchestra grows softer, slower, down to nothing. Aminta and Henry remove their disguises, go to the bed and kneel by Morosus. Ex. 15 on a bassoon provides an allusive bass to a hesitant clarinet solo, and Henry in an arietta invites his uncle to forget a bad dream, now vanished for ever, to look up and see that he is surrounded only by friends. Morosus takes his advice and gazes bewildered about him, then with horror sees what he takes for Timida.* Henry assures him that Timida has gone; only Aminta, kind and loving, remains. He asks Morosus's pardon, and promises a lifetime of filial devotion if his uncle will now accept her as Henry's wife.

Gradually light dawns in Morosus's fuddled brain; he recognizes that a trick—in fact Ex. 14—has been played on him, and he prepares to be wildly and violently angry, picks up his stick to belabour the conspirators (Ex. 13, over and over again)—and then suddenly sees the joke.

* Timida is her authentic name, but on various occasions she is jocularly or ignorantly addressed as Timidia.

Wind and trumpets trill absurdly on a dominant seventh, horns guffaw, and trombones and drums intone Ex. 13 in the manner of a *Ranz des vaches*. Morosus begins to laugh, helplessly, monstrously, hysterically but with a boundless and fathomless joy. He congratulates these versatile virtuoso actors whose art he so misjudged. He pronounces himself cured for ever of the marriage sickness, and calls for wine—even for music if the others wish it. Anyone who has endured a silent wife can endure all the noise in the world, he concludes. He sits down to table between Aminta and Henry, while the actors improvise a dance based on Ex. 5. Then Vanuzzi leads off a formal Vaudeville in praise of music, followed in turn by Morbio, Isotta and Carlotta in duet, then in quartet with the Barber and Farfallo, ending with a concerted chorus (without Morosus of course) to Ex. 17. Morosus, touched to the heart, waves his thanks. Vanuzzi signals his fellow actors to depart, and as they go each of them, including the Housekeeper and the Barber, offers a line by way of appendix to the Vaudeville. Henry, Aminta and Morosus are left alone in a silence broken only by a fragment or so of theme, notably Ex. 7 (*Ruhe* at last!).

The old man, wreathed in smiles of contentment, leans back in his chair as the strings play a gentle contemplative version of Ex. 8: How beautiful is music, especially when it is finished; and how wonderful a young, silent wife, especially when she is married to someone else. He takes a sip of wine, lights his pipe and, remarking how indescribably well he feels, clasps the hands of his adopted son and daughter-in-law. A fat, contented chord of E flat major brings down the curtain as the three of them sit silently and companionably together.

9

Ben Jonson's comedy *Epicoene*, produced in 1609, gave a new word to our language. It was Jonson's intention to ridicule those less-than-gallants who claimed to have slept with women they had plainly never touched; and to this purpose he had Sir Amorous La Foole and Sir Jack Daw, two pompous buffoons, swear in a court of law to the carnal knowledge of old Morose's wife Epicoene—and she is finally unmasked as a boy, much to their discomfiture. Jonson's play is crammed with bawdry, but he suggests nowhere that Epicoene has played the catamite to anybody in the cast; the word epicene has since, however, acquired hermaphroditic connotations.

Zweig could have provided Strauss quite easily with yet another trouser-role, and with an ensemble of female soloists in Jonson's polyandrous Collegiate of married women, that should have spurred the composer's vocal invention (one thinks of Jupiter's four concubines in *Die Liebe der Danae*). But Jonson's *Epicoene* had to be adapted fairly drastically, if only to remove obscure passages which are numerous, and to concentrate the proliferating, rambling action. Zweig retained the character of Morose, 'a gentleman that loves no noise', blended him with the Sea Captain Otter, explained his phonophobia, and made him a sympathetic figure. He retained the idea of a silent bride who, as soon as the wedding is done, becomes gregarious and talkative (Zweig borrowed liberally from *Don Pasquale* as well); he retained and expanded the barber Cutbeard, giving him much of Truewit's function in the original; and he borrowed much of the legal Latin jargon in the divorce action argued by Otter and Cutbeard disguised as shysters in Jonson, even to the *duodecim impedimenta* and the *carnaliter* (Jonson's macaronic sallies are much longer and are hilariously funny). He retained the nephew heir, called Sir Dauphine Eugenie in Jonson but merely Henry Morosus in Zweig. The rest, including the opera singers and the happy end, was Zweig's invention. One could wish that Zweig had adopted Jonson's happy quirk whereby Morose's servants have to answer him by 'showing a leg'; but Zweig could hardly have managed the superb stage direction, *Re-enter La Foole, like a sewer.**

Devotees of Jonson may accuse Zweig of removing the pith and vitality from the original, yet he did provide Strauss with a genuinely comic and lively libretto, roundly characterized in the main roles, perhaps even more attractively human than Hofmannsthal's comedies, though without their depth of feeling and significance, and catering in particular for Strauss's preoccupation with the various degrees of musical speech from plain spoken dialogue to the heightened poetry of aria. *Die schweigsame Frau* gave Strauss the only true comic opera libretto he ever had (as he acknowledged to Kippenberg—it was no insult to Hofmannsthal's memory), since it followed faithfully Jonson's dictum, expressed in the second prologue to *Epicoene*, that:

> 'The ends of all, who for the scene do write,
> Are, or should be, to profit and delight.'

Strauss loved *Die schweigsame Frau* with a special, fierce and abiding love. Naturally, of course, since alone of his operas it was clapped into concentration camp, as he phrased it. Naturally, too, because it was about a dear old man with a noisy, quarrelsome wife. And, even more naturally, because it gave free rein to his theories of musical speech, of pure, transparent musical comedy, of vocal writing (how neatly each character falls into one of his favourite vocal pigeonholes!), of light scoring *à la Intermezzo*—the orchestra required is larger but based on only six double-basses. And, although it is innocent of symbols or psychological

---

* It is not as cloacal as it sounds, though: a sewer is a waiter.

complexities, it is not without a moral: mutton may not dress as lamb, nor advantage be gained without corresponding disadvantage; prejudice, as well as pride, goeth before a fall.

All these qualities suffice to make of *Die schweigsame Frau* a welcome offering for the opera-goer who loves Strauss's music. But it is not the best Strauss by a long chalk; indeed for much of the time Strauss is playing the part of a magician who attempts feats of prestidigitation without benefit of props. The foregoing account of the opera has included quotations of the most memorable and personable themes in the opera, but some of these, and several others too flimsy to quote, are the merest nondescript diatonic tags, background material thrust uncooked into the foreground. And, as one studies the score, one finds again and again a promising, characteristic idea with dramatic significance behind it that Strauss subsequently forgets about. What he does with *Freut euch des Lebens* in Ex. 8 is miraculous; would that he had done more with Ex. 10 and Ex. 11 and Ex. 16. The student-analyst begins to wonder if the old master's concentration was failing him. Perhaps, after all, he needed ideas as well as situations, and perhaps he encouraged Zweig to set his sights too low. If Hofmannsthal lacked the directness to write a true, fully developed comedy as such (*Der Rosenkavalier* is, at least in part, a cynical tragedy), Hofmannsthal stimulated a quality of high-protein musical content that Strauss never quite recaptured in his later operas, and only arguably in the orchestral *Metamorphosen* and the *Four Last Songs*. It is all the more regrettable that Zweig was prevented from taking full literary responsibility for the later, more substantial librettos that he initially elaborated, out of his exceptional creative talent, for Strauss.

Friedenstag

OPUS 81

Opera in One Act
LIBRETTO BY JOSEPH GREGOR

The Commandant of the Besieged Town   BARITONE

Maria, his Wife   SOPRANO

A Sergeant-Major   BASS

A Corporal   BARITONE

A Private Soldier   TENOR

A Musketeer   BASS

A Bugler   BASS

An Officer   BARITONE

A Front-line Officer   BARITONE

A Piedmontese   TENOR

The Holsteiner, commanding the Besieging Army   BASS

The Burgomaster ⎱   TENOR

The Pastor   ⎰ from the Besieged Town   BARITONE

A Woman   SOPRANO

I

Stefan Zweig's complete libretto of *Die schweigsame Frau* was hardly in Strauss's possession before he began to look forward to the next Strauss–Zweig opera. He was aware that destiny had generously favoured him with a second chance to go on writing operas after his one-and-only librettist had been snatched from him. His relationship with Zweig was of the happiest; they esteemed as well as liked each other, and so Strauss thought happily of the productive years ahead together. Zweig's first suggestion (23 February 1933) was for another comedy, based on *The Pied Piper of Hamelin*; no more was heard of this, and there were other things to think about, not least Sir Morosus. Eleven months later, while working on the full score of *Die schweigsame Frau*, Strauss had another idea, *Calandria* by Bernardo Dovizi da Bibbiena (1470–1520); he was taken by the description in the recently published monumental *History of the Theatre* by Joseph Gregor which he had been reading (and about which he wrote an enormous letter to the author). Zweig now suggested Kleist's *Amphitryon*, which was not at all to Strauss's liking (though later he recommended Gregor to study Kleist's dramatic technique) or else one of the librettos which the Abbé de Casti wrote for Pergolesi*— Zweig was going to London and could look them up in the British Museum. It was from this research that *Capriccio* eventually grew. A particularly significant suggestion came from Strauss (2 February 1934) that something might be done with Henry III of Saxony and the Treaty of Constance in 1043. During the intervening months Strauss rejected this rather too Wagnerian mediaeval setting; but Velasquez's painting of the *Surrender at Breda* renewed his interest, and a little historical reflection pushed his thoughts towards the Thirty Years War and so it was another Treaty, that of Westphalia in 1648, which in the following July Zweig and Strauss discussed (as well as Casti's *Prima la musica e poi le parole*) when they met in Salzburg at festival time. They fixed on *24 October 1648*, the end of the cruel Thirty Years War, as the subject and provisional title of their next opera. The title was changed into *Friedenstag* ('Peace Day'), and Zweig in the end got no credit for it, but it was basically the same opera.

Zweig sent Strauss a quite detailed synopsis, on 21 August 1934, of the 'solemn festal one-acter'—tragic, humanistic, some might even say pacifist, but to Zweig it seemed heroic. He would remove all topical, overtly historical references so as to make the action anonymous and

---

* Zweig seems to have been wrong about this; none of Pergolesi's operas has a libretto by Casti.

timeless (and therefore, though he was careful not to say so, the more timely for a militant Germany). Zweig's synopsis outlines the action almost as it came out in the end; the chief development subsequently was the crucial active role given to Maria, the Commandant's wife, in the final scene—this was due to Strauss, who saw in this female role another prize exhibit for his much-treasured gallery of heroines. Zweig, the least selfish and vainglorious of men, was now, since the revelation in newspapers everywhere of official Nazi opposition to *Die schweigsame Frau*, more than ever ready to pass over his scenario to some other librettist who would be politically inoffensive. He suggested Rudolph Binding; later he was to propose Robert Faesi, a professor at Zürich University, and Alexander Lernet-Holenia, a Viennese, rather sensational poet and dramatist, and finally Joseph Gregor. Strauss rejected them all though; they could send him their own librettos if they liked, and he would consider them fairly. *1648*, like *Prima la musica* (which became *Capriccio*) was Zweig's idea, and only Zweig could realize it to Strauss's satisfaction. On 2 April Strauss reported that Nazi officials would not permit the production of a second Strauss–Zweig opera. Zweig's idea that the libretto of *Friedensvertrag* (Peace Treaty) or *Der westfälische Friede* (The Westphalian Peace)—*Friedenstag* passed through several titles—should be written with somebody else and Zweig's name finally omitted, struck the composer as distasteful. Nor did they proceed far with the synonym-pseudonym of Ast *vice* Zweig (both are German for the branch of a tree).

Strauss was on the other hand quite ready to work in secret with Zweig as Zweig, and to keep the completed operas in his drawer until such time as political conditions were favourable. But Zweig found this a subterfuge unworthy of a great composer; it would, with such a famous public figure, be impossible to keep the collaboration secret. On 26 April 1935 Zweig suggested Gregor as, to all intents, a puppet collaborator; Gregor was one of Zweig's closest friends—each read in draft everything that the other was writing—and he was, as Strauss knew, an outstanding connoisseur and scholar of literature, the theatre, and music, an ideal go-between. Zweig could no longer meet Strauss in Germany, and so spend time at Garmisch working out their operas in detail; but Gregor could. Strauss's loyalty to Zweig set him the more firmly against work with 'this learned philologist', particularly after reading Gregor's draft of *Semiramis*. This old relic of Hofmannsthal days had recaptured Strauss's imagination, and together with Zweig's proposal to adapt *La Celestina* by Cota and Roja, almost put *1648* out of the running. As late as 28 June 1935 Strauss was 'strictly refusing' to accept collaboration with Gregor. But already he had begun to weaken over Lernet-Holenia (until he read the plays of that 'noble poet', as Zweig described him, and declared them 'empty, tasteless and humourless'), and political pressure was increasing, since the personal disgrace of the *Schweigsame Frau* affair. On 7 July he met Gregor, by appointment, at a hotel in Berchtesgaden to discuss possibilities. Gregor had made his own scenario for *1648*, and as examples of his own work had also brought draft synopses of two Greek mythological operas, one on Daphne and her metamorphosis into the laurel tree, the other on Danae and the shower of gold (coincidentally a theme that Gregor's friend Hofmannsthal had, many years earlier, proposed to Strauss). Strauss read these three synopses very quickly, sometimes more than one at a time, and expressed interest. 'In a quarter of an hour,' relates Gregor, 'four years' work was decided.' Would Strauss have spent so short a time on these all-important plans if he had been really interested? We ask the question again, having read the fractious, discontented and unusually dull letters which Strauss sent to Gregor during their years of collaboration. Their relationship on paper seems an uneasy, one-sided one, almost like that of a managing director and his adoring but inefficient secretary. When Strauss became deeply interested in *Parole-Musica*, as he called *Capriccio* (the last of the Zweig operas, and the fourth to be elaborated with Gregor), he eventually cast his loyal librettist aside and wrote the libretto himself with Clemens Krauss. He maintained friendly relations, until his death, with Joseph Gregor, regularly beginning his letter *Lieber Freund Gregor*, or *Lieber Freund*, even before their collaboration began; whereas Gregor always addressed him more reverentially as *Verehrter Meister* or *Sehr verehrter, lieber Herr Doktor*. There is no doubt that he admired Gregor's scholarship and enjoyed sharing literary observations with this exceptionally knowledgeable man, but we cannot escape the conclusion that Strauss regarded their artistic collaboration as an unsatisfactory *faute de mieux*, and that he treated Gregor more roughly than any other of his collaborators. In the case of *Friedenstag* they achieved something worthwhile together in a comparatively short time. But during the elaboration of the *Friedenstag* libretto Zweig was at Gregor's elbow, and it was he who hammered out the tough suggestible ideas, and at least to some extent the actual lines which drew from Strauss an opera like no other that he wrote.

2

Gregor had already given something of his own to *1648* in the song of the Piedmontese Messenger early in the opera, one of the most purely captivating moments in the score—Gregor had heard it during the First World War when he was a soldier in the south Tyrol, and Strauss approved of this happy incursion of light on to a dark canvas, and asked Gregor to expand it. At the end of July Gregor accepted an invitation to stay in Strauss's villa at Garmisch and there work out *1648* and *Daphne* together, at length. When Gregor returned to Vienna in mid-August, he made a second version of the *1648* libretto, which Strauss found a decided improvement. But the end of the opera (now definitely entitled *Friedenstag*) was still not as Strauss had fixed with Zweig, and in November this perforce shadowy third party rewrote the closing scene for them, including bells, transformation, and final chorus of joy. Final agreements were settled between Strauss and Gregor at a meeting in Munich during December, and by 24 January 1936 Strauss had completed a fair copy of the short score. He played it to Gregor on the piano at Garmisch in mid-February, and by 16 June the whole full score was completed, even though March and April had taken Strauss away from home on a tour of Italy, France and Belgium.

Gregor had planned *Daphne* as a foil to *Friedenstag*, and Strauss's intention was to perform them together at a joint première in Dresden. When *Daphne* proved less easy to finish he entrusted the première of *Friedenstag* to Clemens Krauss at Munich where, preceded by Beethoven's *Creations of Prometheus* as a ballet, it opened the summer festival on 24 July 1938 with a dazzling cast including Viorica Ursuleac as Maria, Hans Hotter as the Commandant, Ludwig Weber as the Holsteiner, Georg Hann as the Sergeant-Major, Julius Patzak as the Private, Peter Anders as the Piedmontese, and numerous other now well-known singers; Rudolf Hartmann was the producer. The double bill followed on 15 October 1938 at Dresden under Karl Böhm (with Mathieu Ahlersmayer, Kurt Böhme, Marta Fuchs, Christel Goltz). Rudolf Moralt conducted the Austrian première (with Eva Hadrabova) at Graz on 25 October. Clemens Krauss conducted the Berlin and Vienna premières of both works in 1939. As the months passed and Nazi bellicosity rose, *Friedenstag* was cautiously dropped from the German repertory (though only after ninety-eight performances). Gregor saw and enjoyed the Venice première in 1940 under Gui, with Margherita Grandi as Maria.

Strauss decided that *Friedenstag* and *Daphne* were best given separately. Since 1945 *Friedenstag* has seldom figured in German opera houses, and more than seldom elsewhere. In 1964 it still awaits its British première.

3

The letter which Strauss wrote to Stefan Zweig immediately after they had discussed *1648* (otherwise *Friedenstag*) suggests that Bamberg must have been the intended scene of the opera. At one of the first Graz performances Gregor made a speech declaring that the events of *Friedenstag* had taken place there, not, admittedly, during the Thirty Years War but in 1809, when Major Franz-Xaver Hacker zu Hart was in command.

But Strauss and Zweig had been careful to remove all references to times and places. There were many cities, at the end of the Thirty Years War, being beleaguered by Lutheran troops from Holstein. *Friedenstag* might have taken place in any of them, and even this is unimportant. We are to keep company, for some eighty minutes, with a soldier who lives for war and who cannot imagine, let alone desire, peace. We are to sense the dullness, deprivation, spiritual poverty of wartime (Strauss had lived through and detested the First World War), and the purposeless servitude which it means to those who are forced into waging war when they are not dedicated soldiers. *Friedenstag* puts the whole validity of professional soldiery in question. No wonder that the opera was slipped into dust-covers after Hitler marched into Poland. It is a plea for tolerance and friendship between people who hold different opinions about creed, race, government and all the other beliefs on which Adolf Hitler was most narrow-minded. How infuriated he would have been to know that *Friedenstag* was the work of the Jewish poet whom he had taken pains to remove from greater Germany and influence over Germany's greatest composer. *Friedenstag* was perhaps Stefan Zweig's outstanding triumph.

For a composer in his seventies the music is exceptionally tough in tone of voice, comparatively as hard-shelled as *Elektra*, granted Strauss's interim reaction to diatonicism. It is also, in theme, harmonic format, and texture, much more Wagnerian than any of his operas since *Ariadne*, perhaps even since *Feuersnot*. To say this is not to forget the idiosyncratic neo-Wagnerism of *Die Frau ohne Schatten* with which *Friedenstag* is linked particularly closely in language—and I believe that these are the two Strauss operas after *Elektra* which have most to tell an audience in terms of moral persuasion as above mere entertainment. *Friedenstag* is a less great opera than *Die Frau ohne Schatten* not least because it is concerned with one dramatic event only, and that one poorly expressed in words—the point of the opera comes across almost wholly without a word being understood; the text hardly repays understanding (after completing *Friedenstag* Strauss said: 'I never want to read the word *Geliebter* [Beloved] again!') but it is still a great and inspiring one. Like *Die Frau ohne Schatten* it recalls Handel's remark to the Lord-Lieutenant of Ireland after the first performance of *Messiah*: 'I did not wish to entertain them, I wished to make them better.' Compared with these two operas, *Arabella* is a charming waste of time.

4

The scene shows the upper part of a fortress, stoutly walled and fortified (in parts patched hurriedly) with battlements above, and steps to the lower stories of the fortress, and so to the streets of a town that is being heavily besieged, after thirty years of tireless and bitter warfare, by an army from Lutheran Holstein. The war has been going on for so long that nobody any longer knows what it is about, nobody can remember what peacetime was like. Everybody is tired, hungry, apathetic—except the Commandant of the citadel whom we shall meet later.

The opera opens with a powerfully formulated theme representing the cruelty and *ennui* of war. The outline of Ex. 1, given by woodwind, traces a pattern of falling tritones (hard and unpleasing) separated by rising tones, so as to span a descending octave.

1

The odd-numbered chords are harmonized in triads, the even ones in whole-tone chords; all the harmony is touched in below the angular melody. When this cunning martial pattern has been traced, the basses set up a march rhythm, with a prominent fourth later associated with famine,* and a Mahlerian march tune, both quoted as Ex. 2.

2

The Sergeant-Major is inspecting the guard. He halts by a Private on look-out who reports dawn (Ex. 1). The Private talks of an offensive operation during the night against some poor farmer; it gained nothing, not even anything to eat. Nagging deprivation is suggested in the clashes and hopelessness of a new idea.

3

The Sergeant-Major speaks of the Commandant who, in full armour, pores all night over his plans, thinking always of victory and duty.

4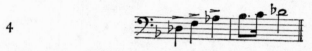

* Obviously it recalls *Parsifal*, Beethoven's Fourth Symphony, and Mahler's First. The whole march is quite close to the music of Kurt Weill. Archetypes are at work—as the Nurse in *Die Frau ohne Schatten* said, *Übermächte sind im Spiel!*

The soldiers are beginning to awake. Among them is a civilian from Piedmont who has brought a message through the enemy ranks and spent the night in the fortress. As he awakes the Italian sings an enchanting song full of happiness, soaring easily aloft, untroubled, a complete contrast to all life in the besieged fortress. A gentle string accompaniment supports his liquid, melancholy, but untroubled song about the rose which flowers and fades like youth. The last phrase of his verse lingers in the soldiers' minds.

5

The tune persists as the soldiers comment on the song. None of them has known life as this peaceable Italian knows it. He goes on singing, deaf and uncomprehending. The march figure Ex. 2 resumes; the other soldiers awake, and their lethargy finds expression in a rising figure that underlies their conversation.

6

They speak of operations (Ex. 1), of the enemy (quotation of Luther's *Ein feste Burg*), and of the contrast between Bible and gun. The tritone of Ex. 1 now turned into a perfect fourth on trombones, a motif of the hunger which is driving the civilian population to revolt. In fact they can be heard in the distance calling 'Hunger' on these two notes; a deputation is approaching the citadel, a place banned to civilians. One soldier tries to halt them; the accompanying motif on the trumpet refers not so much to soldiery as to the dedicated Commandant.

7

Nevertheless the crowd breaks down the main city door and begins the ascent to the ramparts, as the soldiers stand by for action (Ex. 1). The solemn March which brings this crowd on stage is called a funeral march, and again it involves Ex. 1. As soon as the deputation is complete, the Commandant of the citadel appears on the ramparts, and addresses the populace in a hostile tone of voice. He is, the authors tell us, a handsome man of about fifty, dressed in black, and he is clasping a letter to his bosom. This, he tells the crowd, is the Emperor's territory. A firm theme in thirds, bitonally harmonized, implies that he regards the incursion as inimical, for the first phrase is connected with the enemy.

8

The Commandant asks what is the meaning of their visit; the chorus answers: Surrender—to which he gives the Emperor's answer: Obedience or death, and flings a soldier's musket in front of the crowd as a symbol. His loyalty, musically portrayed throughout the opera by the tiny phrase of Ex. 7, is to this fortress, and since he is married to a strong heroic woman, Ex. 7 will be involved in her music as well.

The Burgomaster, Hans Stoss, puts the civic case to him (Ex. 3) that the enemy is no different from themselves, suffering, hoping, praying, but chiefly suffering. The Commandant remains unimpressed. The Parson talks of humiliation in the cause of victory. For the Commandant victory is an unattainable God, a credo meaningless to the crowd's calls of Hunger, Bread and Misery. At this moment an Officer from the front line enters hurriedly and announces that all the remaining ammunition is soaked through; he begs for the gunpowder that is kept under the fortress. The Commandant, however, is under Emperor's orders to hold the fortress at whatever cost. A woman breaks out of the crowd and sarcastically denounces the omnipotence of the Emperor whose decree murdered her children. Her outburst is supported by dull, hopeless appeals from the crowd. Now cry for victory, she taunts the Commandant.

The sun has risen, the Commandant's resolution is shaken. He tells the deputation to return to work and wait for a sign at midday.

9

This fatalistic, and in Ex. 1's sense, warlike theme suggests his plan. The sign will tell the populace when to open the gates and seek freedom. As he mentions the sign, lower-pitched instruments introduce a freedom theme that is at once taken up chorally; I give it in the soprano's version.

10

Ihr gebt uns Le - ben.

The populace at last feels relieved of doubt. The Commandant's promise means salvation. But even as they repeat their cries of: Life, life, he is privately voicing his scorn, for he has another idea, signified by Ex. 9.

The crowd disperses and the Commandant faces his Watch (Ex. 2 and Ex. 7), and addresses them. The jubilation (Ex. 10) does not mean surrender. They are to spread out the gunpowder below the fortress and bring him the fuse to blow it and the citadel to blazes. That will be the sign (Ex. 9). At first his announcement is received with horror. He now turns to the Sergeant-Major and, in a quasi-ballad (*Zu Magdeburg in der Reiterschlacht*), reminds him how as an orderly he once saved the Officer's life; now the Sergeant-Major must have his reward in escape. Solemnly the Sergeant-Major declares his intention to remain and die with his Commandant. He reminds the Corporal of a moment when the General gave him a sword to replace the one he had lost. Now let the sword be given back and the Corporal return to peace. The Corporal too refuses the offer. The Commandant approaches the Private who admits to hatred of war, unwillingness to slaughter, and distaste for heroism, but he too decides to remain with his Commandant. The Musketeer, Bugler and others are more sensible, and accept the offer to leave the citadel. The Commandant thanks them all, and particularly the Piedmontese equerry whom he dispatches home (what a pity that this attractive part is so short). He dismisses the Guards to their duties and retires to the battlements. The stage is left empty.

Ex. 2 is still sounding as a more expressive and warm version of Ex. 10 introduces Maria, the wife of the Commandant, who climbs the stairs to this part of the bastion, timidly but anxiously (dark-coloured instrumentation), especially when she finds nobody here at this vital defence-point. The music suggests two themes particular to her, but she is at one in her husband's wishes and also those of the citizens, and so, as wise interceder, her themes are those of Ex. 10 and Ex. 7 transformed. She is surprised to find the bastion empty, particularly since she has heard noise up here, as well as below in the powder-cellar, and she suspects what is in preparation (Ex. 9). Nevertheless she is optimistic; she is the positive, salubrious force in the drama (the stronger female equivalent of the Piedmontese), and she has sensed a thankfulness in the eyes of the populace that she has seen, a smile. Only there has been, is, and will be, no smile on her husband's lips. He is dedicated to the grimness of war. Her heart, full of love, is unlocked in a radiant E major aria (this is her key, as sombre D flat belongs to her husband) in which she recalls her husband's smile at marriage, a smile never repeated. The melodious section is interrupted by a strong passage, but gives way to her vision of the sun, optimism, joy, all that her husband has put away from himself.

11

This vision gives her hope but is dispelled by the appearance of her husband, the Commandant, on the battlements above; he is thinking of the Emperor's decree, as a theme for heavy brass implies.

12

The Commandant sees his wife out of bounds up here on the battlements. He tries to send her away with diplomatic explanations; but she
urges him to tell the truth. The truth, he answers, is bitter. It brings
death (Ex. 9). He reminds her of the terrible fate she will suffer at the
hands of the invaders. He begs her to descend into the town, for the arm
which embraces her now will draw her (Ex. 9) to the grave. In a duet,
based on her joyful Ex. 11, she vows to remain with him until death—
this transition of emotions is surely too quickly realized; it does not carry
conviction, even though musically a duet of this kind is welcome in
context. It ends with a quick section, very like that of Helen and Menelaus
in *Die Ägyptische Helena* (*Erde und Nacht*), in which she curses and he
praises the ideal of war. This is the passage at which Strauss objected to
the 'absurd' notion of a soldier after thirty years war still praising it as a
'splendid idea'. But the Commandant, who knows no other Credo, does
believe in this idea. That is why he is in the end proved wrong.

Their duet ends monumentally with Maria soaring to a top D flat and
Ex. 4 thundering forth on all the lower instruments of the orchestra while
Maria's radiant Ex. 11 pierces through the upper ranges of the score.
During a passionate, fully scored orchestral Intermezzo, the Commandant and his wife remain in a sublimely loving embrace, broken only,
as the soldiers ascend from below, when the Commandant orders the
Sergeant-Major to descend with the fuse. The euphonious ardent E flat
major pales into blank, practical D minor (Ex. 1) as marital trust
acknowledges the grimness and fatality of the situation. The music is
reduced to a drum tap on D, the tonic of the opera so far.

A cannon shot is heard, far away, then another. Ex. 8 suggests that the
enemy is inaugurating an attack. For the suicide squad it is a moment of joy;
they now have the chance to die in action. Hastily the Commandant seizes
the fuse from the Sergeant-Major who has returned, and extinguishes it.

But there is no sign of military action yet. The sign comes from a
distant bell, a new remote sound, putting a G on to tonic D. The lower
strings build up a new key, G major, and cellos begin a phrase that leaps
as high as hope.

13

For Maria the bell is like sunrise, on which all her hopes have been
fixed. She knows, before any of them, what it means. Another bell and
others afterwards, begin to peal; the inhabitants recognize them from

their location, but have never heard them before. The Commandant sees only an offensive here (Ex. 8, the enemy), but the Private on duty reports a gathering of the Holsteiners, not for battle, though approaching the citadel. The Commandant does not believe such a thing is possible, and orders preparation for fire. One of the officers reports ceremonial dress and a white flag, and though the Commandant automatically senses a trick, he is too late. The enemy troops have been let through the gate and are embraced by the people of the town. Now the Burgomaster with his retinue, all of them radiantly happy, appear, welcoming the promised sign (not at all the one intended by the Commandant). Their Commandant refuses to recognize the implications. They go against his long-nourished monomania for war, and the Emperor's edict (Ex. 12). But society, as the Mayor says, has already proved stronger than militarism. The enemy are being received as friends, and rejoicing is general in the town.

A solemn quick march, with *Ein feste Burg* in the bass, begins to unfold as the Holstein troops enter with the utmost dignity and ceremony. Their leader (bass) calls for the heroic man who opposed them. The Commandant of the fortress answers rudely, but his opponent doffs his hat and gives news of the armistice council at Münster which is agreeing peace. At this Maria and the crowd proclaim their joy. But the Commandant still suspects a subterfuge. The two argue in duet, at cross-purposes and with wonderfully contrasted effect. Their dispute is narrowed down to religious belief, and the Commandant draws his sword. But at this Maria intercedes with Ex. 10 as an answer to Ex. 7, and in a passionate solo urges her husband to drop his prejudices and believe in peace, a glorious concept that he has never experienced.

Her meaning is brought home by the metamorphosis of suspicious C minor Ex. 7 into confident E flat major, a wonderful and exhilarating sound, emphasized by the union of redeeming Ex. 10 and loyal Ex. 4. The two opposing Commandants look suspiciously at one another. Suddenly the Commandant of the fortress throws away his sword, steps forward and solemnly embraces the fellow-man who was his foe. The bastion is filled with people. They proclaim peace in a grand choral finale.

14

Sei uns ge - grüsst.

And if we are still thinking of structure, Ex. 14 can be linked with all the other themes that involve the interval of a fourth, whether open or militantly chromatic. Ex. 10 and Ex. 7 and even Ex. 1 are involved in this superb double chorus with soloists. The two Commandants are reconciled in a duet, Maria joins them exultantly, the chorus resumes, and finally they hymn the concept of peace in a strong C major block chorus.

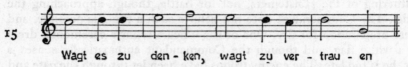

15

Wagt es zu den - ken, wagt zu ver - trau - en

It is a grand, overwhelming confirmation of the inspiring emotion towards which this drama has been steadily moving. There is an enormous quantity of diatonic C major at the end, but it is there to mark a point which audiences, long after Strauss's death, may well find fresh and inspiring. As Schoenberg said: 'There are plenty of good pieces waiting to be written in C major.'

Daphne

OPUS 82

Bucolic Tragedy in One Act
LIBRETTO BY JOSEPH GREGOR

Peneios, a Fisherman	BASS
Gaia, his Wife	CONTRALTO
Daphne, their Daughter	SOPRANO
Leukippos, a Shepherd	TENOR
Apollo	TENOR
Four Shepherds	TENOR, BARITONE, TWO BASSES
Two Maids	SOPRANOS

I

The beginnings of Joseph Gregor's collaboration with Strauss have been retailed in the previous chapter. At their first interview in Berchtesgaden it was decided that Gregor should proceed at once with Zweig's *1648* (*Friedenstag*) and with his own *Daphne*. Gregor had originally sketched his *Daphne* scenario under the momentary inspiration of an engraving by Théodore Chasseriau, a poor picture in which he was much struck by the chaste cold figure of Daphne as she begins to take root at her moment of 'transition into another world'—a Hofmannsthalian concept. Strauss connected the myth not only with the many operatic settings, from Peri to Schütz and Fux, but with Bernini's statue in the Villa Borghese at Rome which he used to visit whenever he was in the Eternal City—a likeness of the statue is reproduced as a medallion on the cover of the opera's vocal score and libretto.

Gregor records that he wrote his original scenario in a train on 21 June 1935—the longest day of the year, he noted, and therefore the one when Apollo journeys farthest through the heavens. He did not consciously lean on any particular version of the story, though as a self-taught student of the classics he was probably familiar with the accounts of Hyginus, Pausanias and Parthenius, since his version accepts, or at least acknowledges, features referred to by these authors.

The Daphne of mythology was the daughter of the Thessalian river-god Peneios, and was a priestess of Mother Earth, Gaia (Gregor makes Gaia her mother). Daphne was loved by Leucippus,* son of Oenomaus (whom we met in discussing *Elektra*), and also by Apollo. Leucippus disguised himself as a girl so as to enjoy Daphne's company; Apollo took revenge by advising Daphne and her friends to bathe naked. Leucippus's sex was discovered and the young ladies tore him limb from limb. Apollo then chased Daphne, but as he was about to catch her she called on Gaia for protection and was spirited away to Crete where she became Pasiphaë, mother of Ariadne and the Minotaur; in her place Gaia left a laurel tree from which Apollo twined a wreath in memory of Daphne, and declared the laurel sacred to himself.

Gregor saw this as a tale of man's reconciliation with nature, a mythological equivalent of man's reconciliation with man in *Friedenstag*, and also as a study of man's relationship with the gods. His first scenario reads as follows:

* Gregor uses Greek names throughout the libretto, not German ones, e.g. Leukippos not Leukipp; and in relating the contents of the opera I have retained his usage.

'Wonderful Greek landscape. Mankind identified with Nature and with the gods. Old Peneios is at once the river and the singing fisherman living by the river. Gaia is his wife and also the beautiful green earth by Peneios. Their daughter Daphne profoundly inaccessible. Games among the waters of Peneios; chorus of nymphs. Two suitors; the cowherd Apollo, wise, baritone, surrounded by his priestess-maids, and the young tenor Leukippos. Daphne remains enigmatic even when the cowherd shows her thunder. Leukippos, jealously pursued by Apollo, has the idea of disguising himself as a girl. This altogether alters Daphne's ideas and she now favours him as a girl-friend. By this mistake he achieves the goal of his desire. Daphne is now seriously disturbed and tells all to the cowherd. Apollo reacts as a god and as a man, and kills Leukippos with a thunderbolt. During choruses of mourning for Leukippos Peneios entreats Zeus to transform mankind back into their original shapes. Zeus grants this prayer, and amid the play of water-nymphs and in front of the flames cremating Leukippos the Daphne tree springs up.'

There are several interesting points here. Gregor later (6 January 1936) said that Gaia was a new invention, and from his letters to and from Strauss we understand that the original scenario involved subterfuge as a main theme rather than the identity of man and nature. We also gather that the first libretto of *Daphne* involved two gods in human disguise, the cowherd Apollo and the swineherd who turns out to be Zeus; a third god, Hermes, is brought in to reveal Leukippos's deception. Gregor rather regretted the abandonment of Zeus, 'an attractive character'; but Strauss rejected him as an 'infelicitous Wotan' and Gregor was content to treat him as the Jupiter of *Die Liebe der Danae*. It is interesting too that Gregor imagined Apollo as a baritone, whereas Strauss (who detested tenors) deliberately made this one of two tenor roles.

Gregor sent this first libretto of *Daphne* to Strauss on 3 September 1935; it had been read, improved and approved by Stefan Zweig. Strauss found it loose in construction and diction, ill-connected, lacking in contrast; it was 'written, not envisaged'—literature instead of theatre. Gregor, who had written it in a spirit of 'real and genuine enthusiasm', was much hurt by these strictures, particularly since several friends had praised the libretto (he later found out that all Strauss's librettists had been favoured with castigation of this kind, usually rather later in the day). Strauss poured a suitable quantity of oil in Gregor's direction, and several sharp words into Zweig's ear. The result was a second version by Gregor, made early in 1936. Strauss discussed this with Lothar Wallerstein, the eminent and highly skilled producer, and put him in contact with Gregor. He also thrashed out *Daphne II* with the librettist when they met at Garmisch in February for a play-through of *Friedenstag*. In April 1936 Gregor sent his third version of *Daphne* to Strauss, and the final recension was elaborated by the two together, during a stay on the Adriatic coast, and at Garmisch. Karl Böhm (to whom *Daphne* is dedicated) recalls a visit to Garmisch at this time, when Gregor upstairs was delivering the finished script, page by page, to Strauss downstairs who at once set it to music—and this is perfectly credible when one knows how much consultation had gone on beforehand, and how rapid and precise were Strauss's musical reactions to the written word.*

Gregor paid several visits to Garmisch during the composition of *Daphne*, but an important decision was taken in his absence. In May 1937 Clemens Krauss, who had liked the first version better than Strauss, was consulted by the composer about the choral finale—as the tree grew up round Daphne, the shepherds were to return and sing a hymn of wonderment and thanksgiving. Strauss was worried about this, and his colleague suggested that the transformation should be portrayed orchestrally, while Daphne's contribution should be wordless melisma. Strauss, and subsequently Gregor, approved this idea, and the result is one of the most magical passages in all Strauss's music—indeed a significant contribution to the history of musical theatre.† The two authors had a final consultation at Bologna in November, and Strauss completed the full score in Taormina on Christmas Eve 1937.

The première was given in Dresden on 15 October 1938 as a curtain-raiser to *Friedenstag* (though *Daphne* is some forty minutes longer). It was Dresden's ninth and last Strauss première, and with careful preparation, a superb cast led by Margarete Teschemacher and Torsten Ralf, Leonhard Fanto's cunning solution of the formidable scenic demands, and Böhm's inspired conducting, not to mention the melodious bucolic euphony of the score, it was adjudged more impressive than its partner in this double bill. Strauss had sufficient faith in Dresden and his trusty 'Böhmerl' to postpone his arrival until the last rehearsal, however; Böhm, in his enthusiasm, took such an ardent, homophonic view of the opera that Strauss, who desired clarity and polyphonic transparency above all for his scores, was obliged to call an extra rehearsal. And though he praised Teschemacher's performance in the highest terms, writing to Gregor who was unable to attend the première, he insisted that the Berlin *Daphne* should have the lighter-voiced Maria Cebotari in the title-role. Strauss made some interesting observations about the visual aspect of the

---

* Böhm also told me the delightful story of *Traum durch die Dämmerung*. Strauss found Bierbaum's poem one day, read it through, conceived the idea for a setting, and was then informed by his wife that she proposed to go for a walk and that he must accompany her. When he answered that he was working, she told him he had twenty minutes to complete what he was doing. By the time that she returned, ready to remonstrate, he had finished one of his most beautiful and polished songs. The story is historically just possible; the song was composed in the year that they were married.

† Strauss set the text of the choral finale as a nine-part *a cappella* piece, *An den Baum Daphne*, in 1943, and dedicated it to the chorus of the Vienna State Opera. The setting, for boys' choir and double chorus, is based on themes from the opera. Felix Prohaska conducted the première on 5 January 1947.

opera. At first he rejected the adoption of classical Greek costumes, especially for the women—they do not suit German singers, he said (one knows what he meant), and he advised Botticelli's *Primavera* as the model for Daphne's costume, Rubens for the rest. But after the première he reverted to a preference for antique Hellenic style, as shown on Greek vases of the sixth century. Singers like Cebotari evidently gave him an inkling that the fat old German soprano was going to become a thing of the past. The style of the music gives us some idea of his dilemma. *Daphne* is not a neo-classic opera but a post-romantic homage to Hellenic classicism. Its language is pure and transparent, relieved of all fatty tissue; the heaviest moments (Apollo–Daphne duet, Daphne's metamorphosis) are intense, but not romantically weighty. The Rubens idea is perhaps justified by the ritual marriage-dance at the feast, but Strauss's Daphne is not a Botticelli figure, and once one accepts the suitability of classical Greek costumes for the main characters, it is possible also to see the dance in a hard, primitive, unsophisticated light. After the première, too, Strauss decided that *Daphne* and *Friedenstag* were better given separately, and his ideal was that *Daphne* should be preceded by his *Couperin Suite* as a ballet.

The Dresden première was followed by the Austrian one at Graz, under Rudolf Moralt, on 25 October. Robert Heger conducted it at Cassel in November, Leopold Ludwig at Oldenburg in December. Krauss was in charge of the Berlin première in March 1939,* and the Vienna première in June. Karlsruhe timed its first performance under Joseph Keilberth for Strauss's seventy-fifth birthday on 11 June. Among later productions an open-air one at Budapest under Janos Ferencsik in June 1940 (in Hungarian) may be mentioned. When Strauss visited London in 1947 Sir Thomas Beecham planned a concert performance of *Daphne*, but a suitable cast could not be collected. Thomas Sherman conducted the U.S. première in New York, in concert form, on 10 October 1960; the American first performance had already taken place in Buenos Aires under Erich Kleiber in 1948 (with Rose Bampton and Set Svanholm). *Daphne* is quite frequently to be seen in German and Austrian opera houses, which take some pride in devising ever more ingenious and striking realizations of the final metamorphosis—though if we are all honest, the opera is fundamentally a very static piece of music drama, and would go quite well in concert form. It is only when one imagines an *Oedipus Rex* abstraction of *Daphne* that one recognizes the importance to the total effect of a landscape background and a scenic mood of relaxed, devoted eclogue; the style is expansive, not concentrated, and the drama has to fulfil itself at some leisure. This is surely why Strauss

---

* At rehearsals for this, the whole of the first scene was omitted, so that after the Prelude the opera began with the shepherds' chorus. Gregor managed to restore the missing scene.

called that extra rehearsal in Dresden. The music is all diaphanous clarity; it is the beginning of Strauss's last manner, the manner of the oboe concerto, *Metamorphosen*, and the *Vier letzte Lieder*.

2

Daphne is an opera about Nature, mankind amid Nature, man's relation to Nature and to the natural forces which antique civilizations worshipped as gods. In Thessaly, when the world was young, man and Nature were closely connected. The shepherds and cowherds lived in harmony with their fellow-men, their animals, and the changing seasons, more serenely and naturally than do the simplest peasants of our day. In such a community in Thessaly the one-time river-god Peneios could live as a fisherman, married to Gaia, Mother Earth herself. But their daughter Daphne was exceptional even in this society; she felt closer to the trees and flowers than to her fellow-humans. The blood in Daphne's veins is close to the sap in the tree, the water in the river, the grain and stone in the soil. She is pure, uncorrupted, unsavage Nature incarnate. Music's symbol for this first state of man is the tonic triad and beyond it the pentatonic scale (black notes on the piano). Strauss's *Daphne* is full of pentatonic melodies, and the Prelude to the opera serenely and warmly puts us into their frame of mind.

The stream of woodwind melody, as gentle and fertile as the river Peneios that sired Daphne, portrays this integral untroubled life. Later in the opera we may be tempted to believe that Ex. 1a refers to Daphne, Ex. 1b to her lover the sun-god Apollo; but the two phrases are part of one another (the triplet figure shows this) as she and he could never, in human form, be. These are both positive, animate Nature themes, not man and woman but sun and laurel. Equally general, cosmic as it were, is the second theme which ripples out of the first sentence.

The overture comes to rest on a rather civilized half-close in the dominant, and off-stage a mountain-horn is heard. Peneios is calling the

shepherds to the sacred festival of the blossoming grape, the feast of
Dionysos who will bless the union of all things with living fruits after
their kind, cattle, plants, people. This is Peneios's summons.

3

The scene reveals an olive grove by the river Peneios at dusk. The
fisherman's hut is supposed to be visible, and further away Mount
Olympus, home of the gods, can be glimpsed. There is a haze in the air;
to the eye it is a heat-mist, for the senses it is a presage of the divine
intoxication which overcomes celebrants of Dionysos's rites. Short
isolated phrases, like shepherds' or animals' cries, pierce the haze.

4

Sounds of cattle being driven home can be heard near at hand (in the
Kleiber Buenos Aires record the cowbells are noisier than the orchestra!).
The swirling mists take the pattern of a harmonic progression, human
in the triad, one might say, divine in the second chord with its construction by fourths (as Apollo's theme will bear out).

5

An elderly shepherd, Adrastes, comes to meet the young Cleontes who
climbs up from the river where he has been watering his flock. The boy
does not know of this feast for Dionysos; he learns that it is fixed by the
flow of the stream (i.e. Peneios).

6

The old man tells Cleontes to collect his sheep who must also, in their
fold, partake of the sacred celebration.

7

Two more shepherds pass by on their way to this feast, one called Clitos, one anonymous. Ex. 4 and Ex. 5 heighten the atmosphere of the forthcoming assembly. As they walk towards their byres the shepherds call their farewell to departing day. And while the sun smiles, Daphne, a girl, almost a child to look at, enters from the other direction, hears the shepherds' song, and contrariwise implores the bright day to remain and not depart. She feels her true self only at daytime, among the trees who are her brothers, the flowers who are her sisters, and the stream which reflects her image. The freely flowing, almost improvisatory meditation on Ex. 1 mirrors her thoughts, and should emphasize her close affinity with springing Nature (she is not a botany mistress, but a tree which has become flesh by mistake, and the purpose of the drama is to restore her to her rightful shape).

In her ecstasy she embraces one of the trees, and from behind it springs a young shepherd, Leukippos, a childhood playmate who has grown up into her determined but unwelcome suitor.

8

Daphne is not at all pleased to be discovered at such a moment, nor he to find that she prefers a tree to himself. He reminds her of the days when she loved to be pursued by the sound of his flute.

9

The tune reappears later in the opera, always associated with the flute and Leukippos's love for Daphne; the three notes bracketed as Ex. 9a are often detached and treated separately.

Daphne tries to explain that she still loves his flute-playing, since what she loves is not the player but the wind, her brother, who blows through the wooden pipe. What drew her to Leukippos was nothing masculine, but the blossom-red of his cheeks, the rivulet of sound from his flute, the sisterly gaze from his girlish eyes. Their conversation bursts into a fiery duet dominated by Ex. 1b, and by a surging arpeggio which may aptly be likened to Matteo's Ex. 16 in *Arabella*—they both suggest virile sexuality. At the climax of this duet Leukippos feels the power of the god Dionysos (Ex. 7): I am fortified, he cries, and Strauss responds by counterpointing Ex. 8 simultaneously in augmentation and double augmentation! Leukippos snaps his flute in two, and embraces Daphne ardently. She breaks free—the Dionysiac feast does not hold any enchantment for her—and goes towards her parents' house, while Leukippos runs dejectedly away in the opposite direction.

Daphne is met by her mother Gaia who has come to call her into the hut to make ready for the feast, and who has seen her tiff with Leukippos. She reminds Daphne that the feast is for the fertility of all nature, plants as well as men and animals. When the god is ready Daphne will blossom forth gladly, and in anticipation of this moment she should now dress herself in the festal robes which two girls are bringing to her. But Daphne can only bear to attend the feast if she remains dressed as she is; she leaves the robes and hurries into the cottage, while Gaia wonders at the strangeness of her daughter's ways. Gaia's character is not strongly individualized, and this scene is virtually her major contribution to the opera. Perhaps because she is the personification of Nature, Strauss gives Gaia no themes of her own beyond a transformation of Nature's Ex. 1b. Gaia's outstanding characteristic is the low tessitura of her music, a *contralto profondo* like her Wagnerian counterpart Erda in *The Ring*.

The two maids engage in a transparent, mercurial duet of mock sorrow for the robes and gems that Daphne refuses. They are overheard by Leukippos, who is sitting disconsolately on a bank in the vicinity and believes the girls are laughing at him. They draw him out, discover what ails him, and suggest a remedy. Their plot is musically represented in not so much a theme as the prefix to any number of other themes. It is given here as it first appears, attached to a version of Ex. 2.

10

The girls pretend to Leukippos that they are not maidens but dream-manifestations who bring him these girl's clothes so that he may draw near to Daphne. Leukippos at first regards this as mockery, but is soon persuaded to take advantage of his girlish features which he knows have attracted Daphne. He disappears into the dusk with the girls. Ex. 10 and Ex. 1 follow them off stage. A new, solemn theme rises from the orchestra, pregnant with dignity and hieratic moment.

11

It accompanies the entry of Daphne's father Peneios (who blew the summons on the horn at the start of the opera), but Ex. 11 represents, as usual with Strauss, not the person but what he represents. Peneios here stands for godhead in the midst of mankind (he was once god of the river that bears his name). Peneios is with Gaia and a group of shepherds who have arrived for the feast. The old fisherman is struck by the unusual radiance that hinges on the summit of Olympus. It fills him with premonitions of a godly visitation, divine beings who are coming to share the feast with men (*Herrliche Gesichte!*).

Gaia is faintly scornful of her husband's visions but he declares that, as a sometime divinity, he knows the behaviour of the gods. The meal must be made ready for none other than Phoebus Apollo, the sun-god.

An ensemble is built up for Peneios, Gaia and the shepherds. Peneios is transported by this vision of the union of men and gods at their festive celebration; Gaia attempts to return her husband to reality. The shepherds in chorus are at first bewildered, then convinced, by the fisherman's prophecy. When he speaks of their imminent visitor's divine laughter, his guffaws are echoed throughout the valley; the shepherds grow anxious, and the music recapitulates the heat-haze passage (Exs. 4 and 5) from the opening scene. A red light glows, Ex. 13 resounds everywhere, and a stranger in peasant garb strides through the gloom to join them. The shepherds shrink back, supposing him to be some demon or god. They are correct for it is Apollo himself in disguise (Ex. 12) who hails Peneios and Gaia. He pretends to be a cowherd from the slopes of Olympus who was preparing to go home when the smell of the feast here roused one of the bulls (Ex. 7) to chase the cows across the river and over the thicket, until they fell asleep exhausted and he, their keeper (Ex. 12—almost ironical), came to seek shelter. Gaia and the shepherds laugh at Peneios's vision of the divine guest who turned out to be—a cowherd no better than themselves. But Peneios greets the stranger solemnly (Ex. 11) and sends for Daphne to tend their latest guest. Gaia goes to the hut, Peneios towards the river bank with the shepherds, who sing a cheerful chorus of the gods who sent as guest to their feast a farmer like themselves and a beast on heat. Apollo hears their song and, left alone, resumes his godlike form to a new harmonic complex, melodically related to the plot of Ex. 10, since he too is here to woo Daphne.

14

Apollo chides himself for demeaning his godhead (Ex. 18) and becoming a beast on heat. A suggestion of Ex. 1a rises from the depths; there is darkness on earth, but bright moonlight now in the sky, and Daphne, with her attendant maidens, approaches, like a miraculous vision.

15

When they reach Apollo (Exs. 1a and 1b together) the maidens bow and depart. Daphne remains, and as Apollo voices amazement at her beauty Ex. 15 alternates with Ex. 1 and Ex. 12, the vision with the primeval reality and the visitant god. He greets her as Artemis, his sister, come from a fisherman's hut (Ex. 11) to scold him. Daphne clings gladly to this name of sister, and Apollo begs her in this very hour to be his sister and wash his travel stains from him. Gently she pours water over his hands, lays aside his bow and arrows, and wraps a fresh blue cloak round him; but as she does this she is astonished to see him grow visibly before her eyes—Ex. 13 brings him to full sunny stature and reminds her that in all her tasks around the neighbourhood she never saw him before. Ex. 15 intercedes, as though to hint that he, not she, must be the vision. How, he asks in answer, can man's eyes measure distance, and the music surges into Don Juan's E major as he tells how the sun circles at daytime round her house (Ex. 1b), sees Daphne, lingers and is unwilling to set. So, this evening, he saw her pleading and radiant, and was drawn towards her presence. He reminds her of her prayer to the sun (*O bleib, geliebter Tag*), to her surprise and astonishment. She asks who he might be; Ex. 13 answers and though she still does not understand, she promises, rather curiously, to hide nothing from him. She has given herself to this unknown brother with the abandonment that such a creature could only permit herself in the presence of a natural, not a human, force. At this moment (*So wenig wie der Kiesel*) Strauss impacts two themes that will later become independent.

16

Ex. 16a is a musical image of self-abandonment, of yielding to a mightier force (cf. the Marschallin's Ex. 3 in *Der Rosenkavalier* and, in *Die Frau ohne Schatten*, Ex. 19 which is not only indicative of Barak's unselfishness but of the Empress's realization that she must not impede this goodness), Ex. 16b an image of hesitant aspiration (cf. Zdenka's Ex. 12 in *Arabella*).

Apollo offers her an eternity of day, no more sadness by night, but the prospect of riding for ever with the Sun in the fiery chariot. Metamorphosis, in fact, and the rising scale figure accompanying his offer—

17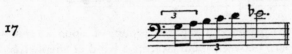

—links up with the *Ariadne* metamorphosis of a precisely similar nature, quoted in *Ariadne* as Ex. 5. This central moment of apparent dramatic resolution is pointed by a short duet in which Daphne seems to accept what Apollo offers, a situation underlined by the symphonic development of Ex. 16, Ex. 17, Ex. 1a, and the germ of Ex. 18. Apollo now brings out this solemn uplifted theme (so close to Helena's *Schön glänzt der Saal*) to signify Daphne's place among the most admired and loved of women.

18

Daphne accepts Apollo's offer, since she knows him for her brother the sun (Ex. 1b and Ex. 13 simultaneously emphasize the moment). He envelops her in his symbolic mantle of blue; Ex. 18 is momentously enshrined in a chord of E flat minor, from which Ex. 1a, Ex. 12, Ex. 14, and the inversion (hesitantly anxious) of Ex. 16b emerge, followed by the intoxicating haze of Ex. 5, and the feast motif of Ex. 7, chromatically altered since this is Daphne's initiation into a special manifestation of the fertility ritual. But the vision (Ex. 15) and the metamorphosis (Ex. 17) are too close for her to the human wooing tactics of Ex. 14, and Daphne tears herself from Apollo's embrace—the moment is significantly close to the Parsifal–Kundry kiss in Act 2 of Wagner's last opera. Apollo urges his love upon her, and Ex. 5, which he proposes to turn from dreams into reality, is taken up and heightened dramatically by the shepherds off stage as they pray for divine, spiritual visitation by Dionysos and Aphrodite. The moon has disappeared. Apollo draws Daphne's attention to the hymn (Ex. 7 is mated with Ex. 16b), and reminds her of the feast which she cannot now ignore. For Daphne the feast is still strange and unwelcome, particularly when Apollo is there, and even though he reminds her that his light is the guiding star for which, most of all, she has always longed.

The sounds of the feast, Ex. 7, and the divine visitor, Ex. 12, are surging through the music as escape comes to Daphne's aid with the return of the men and women for the great Dionysiac ritual by torchlight. Daphne joins the women, Apollo the herdsmen. Peneios announces majestically the divine spiritual presence and, through his wine, fruitful influence of Dionysos. This solemn hymn is taken up by the chorus.

19

The men and women are gathered in separate groups on opposite sides of the grove. Into the space between them swarms a band of shepherds, wearing fleeces and ram-masks, who perform a stamping dance, cunningly derived from elements of Ex. 7; the chorus warns all women to beware of Ex. 5, Ex. 19 and Ex. 7. When this masculine display is over, the women of the community enter, some almost naked and bearing flower-twined staffs, some heavily veiled and jewelled carrying drinking goblets— among these last is Leukippos in female disguise, as Ex. 10 emphasizes.

Now the ram-men reappear and importune the girls. Gaia brings Leukippos forward to make Daphne drink her libation (Ex. 5) from his/ her cup (Ex. 8). The girls laugh happily at Leukippos's convincing disguise, and he persuades Daphne to dance with him.

The enraged Apollo interrupts them, declaring that the god has been insulted. The shepherds, furious at this interruption by a stranger, threaten him and call for some sign of his superior wisdom. Ex. 13 is inadequate, so he shoots an arrow skywards, and conjures up thunder, at which the shepherds disperse to see to their flocks. Apollo is left alone with Daphne and Leukippos.

Apollo knows the identity of the masked shepherd and announces as much. Leukippos confesses quite proudly who he is, that he has served at the feast in all humility, and now comes to win Daphne's love from this bullying foreigner. Daphne longs to accept his love, but is shocked by the subterfuge. Leukippos in turn charges Apollo with appearing in disguise. Apollo defends his function as bringer of truth (Ex. 13), and plunges into a grand rhapsodic solo (*Jeden heiligen Morgen*) about the glorious course of the sun, which men and gods alike recognize in himself. Daphne admits her fascination for Apollo's songs and her undiminished antipathy towards his embrace. Leukippos takes up Ex. 14 which has referred to Apollo as suitor, and challenges Apollo, point-blank, as a liar. Daphne, on her knees, begs Apollo to put aside his desires. She recognizes him as the sun-god (Ex. 13, Ex. 14) but refuses to follow his amorous beams. Leukippos, in gratitude for what he still supposes to be her faithfulness, curses Apollo, who fits an arrow to his bow and shoots.

Amid thunder and lightning, Leukippos slumps to the ground. Daphne is blinded by the sudden brilliance of the light (a sort of Silver Rose effect in A major with Ex. 2 underneath). She recovers her senses and realizes that her playmate has been torn from her, not by the sun but by cruel lightning. She falls upon Leukippos's body, and now follows the section which Strauss demanded as Daphne's *Liebestod*. Leukippos recognizes that he was killed by a god for daring to love her; he dies. She sings a threnody for his flute (Ex. 9), for the heart that inspired it (Ex. 16b), for her own guilt in following the god instead of entreating him to leave mankind with mankind, but most of all for her weakness in not protecting her beloved playmate. She promises the body of Leukippos (a solemn version of Ex. 8) that she will sacrifice all most dear to her, all nature to honour his death (Ex. 19, a funeral instead of a birth). Ex. 13 shows that Apollo is greatly struck by her grief, and her declared intention to wait, cowering, until the proud gods call her to themselves.

For Apollo her extended lament, one of three fine solos allotted to Daphne in this opera, is the utterance of the same magical vision (Ex. 15) which he had lately encountered. Ex. 16, in its original form, flows back as he asks if the gods have not been overshadowed by the purity of one human heart. He invokes his fellow-gods on Olympus. May Dionysos receive the shepherd with his flute-playing and dances which were inspired by the wine-god's spirit. And may father Zeus pardon Apollo's daring, and restore Daphne to him, not as a woman, but as the eternal blossoming companion of her beloved friends the trees; let Zeus give Daphne to Apollo as a sacred laurel tree.

This curiously haunting phrase wonderfully suggests the transformation of unformed Ex. 2 into the different, strongly shaped new existence which is Daphne's destiny.

It grows dark as Apollo, grandly supported by his Ex. 13, calls on Daphne to serve Phoebus Apollo as his priestess in eternity. Ex. 20, the symbol of her metamorphosis, begins to unwind. The godly visitant disappears (he has grown very close to a tenor facsimile of Wotan at the end of *Die Walküre*). Ex. 7 joins Ex. 20 and Ex. 1a to remind us that this, for Daphne, is the moment of dionysiac fertilization which Gaia has promised her.

Daphne finds herself alone, unaware of Apollo's prayer, and hurries away, but is suddenly halted by a divine spell. Time seems to cease. Out of a low dominant pedal-note, Ex. 16b emerges to suggest the moment of uncertain limbo. Then she realizes her happy fate and greets her verdant brothers, the trees, whose sap, drawn from the earth, begins to permeate her form. Ex. 12 takes shape and she cries to her brother Apollo, to the wind, to the birds, to her human friends, for whom she will now and forever be a symbol of immortal love.

With immense serenity a melody, derived from Ex. 1, stirs slowly from the stillness; it includes Ex. 1b and Ex. 20, and it grows gently, tenderly, even as the bark, the leaves, grow out of Daphne's once human body. Ex. 2 enters with an implication of contented finality, Ex. 12 delicately, outlined by harps, proclaims the laurel tree's tutelary god, and from within the branches Ex. 20 and Ex. 1a call, wordless, from the soul of the tree that once was Daphne. The branches are still unfolding, the laurel leaves springing, and Ex. 1a is merging almost imperceptibly into the chord of F sharp major as the scene fades from view, and the opera is over.

3

Less controversial than *Friedenstag*, more vocally gratifying, gentle in tone of voice and audibly homogeneous in invention—an enormous quantity of this euphonious music rhapsodizes on the pentatonic *melos* of Ex. 1—*Daphne* has the positive virtues of a meaningful, attractive story that does not tax the intellect too highly, set for a nice variety of basically lyrical voices. Even the musically well-moulded title-role can be given to sopranos of diverse tonal weight, and even the stronger of the two tenors, Apollo, is given a part as lyrical, almost, as Bacchus in *Ariadne auf Naxos*. *Daphne* is an enjoyable opera to listen to, rather more tedious to watch; though when the production and lighting and music are carefully realized and controlled, the closing scene at least can prove quite captivating. In itself the work suffers from an inescapable hiatus between the muscular harmonic world of Apollo and the octogenarian easy melody that flows wonderfully but leaves little behind. The choral music, undemanding though certainly atmospheric, stands unpretentiously in favour of *Daphne* as does the presage of Strauss's musical style in his last years, and in the finale Strauss works a stunning conjuror's trick. The dramatic flow and diction still, even after much rewriting, leave something to be desired, and for much of the time we may think to hear Strauss playing amiably with the utmost expertise on pentatonic and diatonic ideas that do not leave much impress on the mind after a performance. Perhaps that is why he spent such a long time on *Daphne*, but the fault is largely Gregor's, who voiced his characters through a literary basis of cliché that leaves Leukippos and the other shepherds no different in essential weight from Peneios or Apollo. *Daphne* can pass an evening well enough but it never tempts the hesitant or anti-music-drama listener to admire Strauss's new musical development as strongly as Strauss must have intended. This pastoral style is more vividly deployed in the oboe concerto, just as the girls' *scherzando* interlude and the imperious passages for Apollo seem like preparatory sketches for things in *Die Liebe der Danae*. *Daphne* holds a certain place in the German repertory, a hundred years after Strauss's birth, but chiefly one suspects because it is a singer's opera with some marvellously scored orchestral music, and a scenario which challenges the imagination and practical cunning of the most expert producer.

Die Liebe der Danae

OPUS 83

Cheerful Mythology in Three Acts

LIBRETTO BY JOSEPH GREGOR

Jupiter	BARITONE
Mercury	TENOR
Pollux, King of Eos	TENOR
Danae, his Daughter	SOPRANO
Xanthe, her Servant	SOPRANO
Midas, King of Lydia	TENOR
Four Kings, Nephews to Pollux	TWO TENORS, TWO BASSES
Semele	SOPRANO
Europa *Their Wives*	SOPRANO
Alcmene	MEZZO-SOPRANO
Leda	CONTRALTO
Four Watchmen	FOUR BASSES

I

When Strauss and Gregor first met on that misty uncertain day in the Alps at Berchtesgaden, one of the three librettos proposed by Gregor was a treatment of the Danae legend. Strauss approved it, along with *Friedenstag* and *Daphne*, and in due course it appeared as the third of their joint creations. What neither Strauss nor Gregor realized at the time was that the idea of the selfsame opera had been worked out many years earlier for Strauss by none other than Hugo von Hofmannsthal. Both authors had independently hit on the idea of linking the myth about Midas with the Golden Touch to the other myth of Danae visited by Zeus in the likeness of a golden rain-shower.

During their correspondence about an operatic successor to *Friedenstag* and *Daphne*, Strauss and Gregor concentrated for a time on the long-mooted plans for *Semiramis* and *Celestina*. Strauss seemed to have forgotten both sketches for operas about Danae. In the summer of 1936 Willi Schuh drew Strauss's attention to the one made in December 1919 by Hofmannsthal for a comic opera called *Danae or the Marriage of Convenience* (*Danae oder die Vernunftsheirat*) and this corresponded with the composer's expressed desire for a cheerful piece, ironical, light and in the manner of operetta, to contrast with the two serious operas that he had already made with Gregor. Hofmannsthal's scenario, the sketches for which* are exactly contemporary with those of *Die Ägyptische Helena*, is in three acts, two of which are very fully elaborated. Here is a summary of it.

The old King of a little island longs for pomp and splendour, but cannot afford it since his kingdom is penniless. His hopes are entirely set on arranging a rich marriage for his daughter Danae and he has therefore sent her portrait to Midas, King of Lydia, the richest monarch on earth, who turns whatever he touches to gold. Danae's father hopes that Midas will fall in love with the portrait (cf. *Zauberflöte* and *Arabella*), which he does, and proposes marriage. At court Danae has four cousins by marriage, Io, Leda, Alcmene and Europa, each of whom has been visited by Zeus in a different disguise—as has Danae; Zeus is to be felt as an unseen but dominating presence, like Keikobad in *Die Frau ohne Schatten*, says Hofmannsthal.

Danae, who ranks gold above all things, like her father, is enchanted by the portrait which Midas sends her: it is so brilliantly golden that the features cannot be distinguished. A ship arrives bringing Midas's tailor who is to attire Danae in the latest Lydian fashion for her wedding. The

* Republished with preface and notes by Willi Schuh, Frankfurt, 1952.

tailor (Midas in disguise, who has come to investigate his prospective bride) explains that his employer, formerly a poor king, was gifted with his golden touch by an old man (Zeus in disguise) who warned that the gift might be removed at any time by the warning signal of a horn-call— or some such instrument to be decided by Strauss (Hofmannsthal borrowed the horn-call from the Victor Hugo–Verdi *Ernani*, as he admitted in a note). The tailor tells also of Zeus's amorous metamorphoses; in the tale of the Golden Shower Danae recognizes her own visitation. Her infatuation with this uncommon tradesman increases when she puts on the dress he has designed; for it looks and feels and even sounds like her dream of the golden rain.

At the wedding banquet Midas has still not made his appearance. He sends Danae a letter, however, asking her to meet him at a cave in the garden of her father's palace, and he encloses a veil of pure gold which she recognizes from her dream. She reads the letter aloud to the assembled guests (an excuse for an aria, but otherwise absurd) and leaves the banquet. In the garden grotto she meets Midas and is overjoyed to recognize in him the fascinating tailor. His person charms her as much as his wealth, and although she warns him that she can receive but not give anything, he gladly conjures up a magic palace of gold in which they will pass their bridal night. Horn-calls warn Midas that his Golden Touch will soon be taken from him.

The next morning Midas wakes before Danae, and is aghast to hear the horn-call warning of Zeus. He assumes that Danae will forsake him as soon as he loses his wealth. She awakes as the magic palace turns to rubble, and their golden robes to rags, but she is content, for the gold-hungry girl has been transformed into the love-contented wife. They find a stray donkey and ride away.

2

Joseph Gregor, who made his own sketch in 1935, could have seen Hofmannsthal's which was published two years earlier, and might well have discussed it with the author who was his friend, or heard about it from others. But, extraordinary as the coincidence must seem, he vowed that he had done none of these things. His own *Danae* differed from Hofmannsthal's in making Midas a donkey-driver, and in introducing Zeus on stage as a cheerful, slightly cynical, amorist. Hofmannsthal had been aiming at a French operetta style (there are distinct undertones of *La Belle Hélène* in his scenario), Gregor at a mythological opera—and therefore his original Danae was more serious and astringent, he thought, when he came to read Hofmannsthal's treatment. Gregor wanted Strauss to present Danae as she had been portrayed by another septuagenarian,

Titian. Strauss, on the other hand, favoured the cheerful qualities of Hofmannsthal's draft, and asked Gregor to discuss the subject with Zweig, then rework a scenario himself on the basis of Hofmannsthal's, in a preciously ironical manner that would soften the banality of the ending as it stood. Gregor found much of Hofmannsthal's detail frankly embarrassing—the episode of the tailor, the letter which calls Danae away from the feast 'as if to the telephone'—and he believed that Hofmannsthal had been unable to work out the third act properly because the basis of the action had not been logically thought to its natural dénouement.

Although Gregor's energies were chiefly occupied with the assembly and organization of his famous theatrical history exhibition which was due to open in Vienna at the beginning of September 1936, he found time during late June and July to elaborate a new scenario for Strauss. Bearing in mind his own objections to the Hofmannsthal (and these would be the stronger and more possessive since Gregor had already made his own treatment of virtually the same theme), he cast it in two acts, and heightened the comedy by including a magician as well as the celebrated Asses' Ears for Midas. Strauss disliked these features, and found the whole scenario too heavy and self-consciously profound. Gregor threw out red herrings in the shape of a pantomime *Danae* (and at one stage a modernized *Danae* with Zeus as an operatic impresario in Paris—Strauss refused to bite, but was attracted by Gregor's ideas on modern drama and characteristically asked for an original scenario in due course, set in the present day), and a return to *Celestina*. *Danae* does not seem to have been discussed at all during Gregor's visit to Garmisch in December, for two months later Strauss reverted to it as a new idea, repeating his earlier objections to Gregor's earlier scenarios, and recommending strict adherence to Hofmannsthal—the spirit, presumably, rather than the letter. Gregor therefore made a third draft, sent it scene by scene to Strauss, paid another visit to Garmisch in April 1937 and completed this recension, which includes Jupiter's farewell picnic with his four Queens, by 27 April. After further complaints and suggestions from Strauss, Gregor made his fourth draft before 15 June, perhaps in consultation with Lothar Wallerstein (to whom Strauss sent pointed greetings and who later declared that *Danae* should have been treated wholly seriously), and this time Strauss expressed approval and asked for a libretto. By 26 August Gregor had delivered this, one act at a time, sending a copy to Clemens Krauss; the work had been delayed by Gregor's illness for some weeks in July. Gregor had now made three acts of *Danae*, but Strauss referred to it in his letters as if it were still a two-act piece; he found Gregor's second act unsuitably didactic and boring, and so Gregor sent a revised version in November, and visited Strauss who was in Italy (unlike Hofmannsthal he found that he always worked better after personal consultation with Strauss—perhaps this is why the Strauss–Gregor corre-spondence is so much less illuminating than the Strauss–Hofmannsthal).

At this stage the Midas–Danae duet *So führ ich dich* seems to have come into being, as a final number after, it appears, the picnic of Jupiter and his lady-loves (the positions are reversed in the final version). But by January 1938 Jupiter's farewell was the end of the opera. The text of Act 1 was now agreed and Strauss, in Taormina, was composing it. Act 2 was under constant discussion until Whitsun when Gregor and Strauss finally thrashed it out to satisfaction at the composer's Garmisch home: Strauss had been deeply discontented by the later entries of Jupiter— What (he echoed a question asked by Clemens Krauss) was Jupiter doing in this play at all? How could the Midas–Danae love scene be carried out without him touching her and so turning her to gold (as of course happens in the final version)? The diction was too lofty; please could Gregor keep away from the word *Geliebter* ('Beloved')—Strauss said he never wished to read it again! Gregor was so much offended and discouraged by this brusque condemnation that he was unable to do any work for several months. The troubles were eventually smoothed over, and Clemens Krauss, who was anxious that Danae (his wife Ursuleac) should be given an aria, found the solution to the third-act problem in the closing scene as we now have it except that Midas was at first to have been on stage— the scene includes Jupiter's Maia monologue which Gregor had written for his very first draft. Krauss also suggested the comic scene with Mercury in Act 3, Scene 2. Final arrangements were made in December 1938 when poet and composer drove by car to Salzburg together; in mid-January 1939 Strauss received the definitive version of the text, and he set Act 3 to music during February and March, discussing it with Krauss as he progressed. The scoring of the first act was completed on 7 September 1939, that of the whole opera on 28 June 1940.

3

War had by now broken out and Strauss, bearing in mind his unhappy experiences over the first productions of *Die Frau ohne Schatten* in 1919, insisted that *Die Liebe der Danae*, an opera almost as difficult to stage, must not be produced until at least two years after the armistice had been declared—and that, he added, would mean after his own death. He had already, as early as October 1938, begun referring to *Danae* as an *œuvre posthume*, and none of his friends and colleagues could, for the time being, persuade him to change his mind. In September 1941 Clemens Krauss was appointed chief artistic director of the Salzburg Festival and at once he asked Strauss to release *Die Liebe der Danae* for a première there.

Karl Böhm had already made similar requests for Dresden, but Krauss as collaborator in the libretto could and did stake a prior claim. Strauss promised the opera to Salzburg—but on his already expressed terms, at least two years after the end of the war. However, in October 1942, at the time of the *Capriccio* première in Munich, Krauss did at last get the composer's consent to a première of *Die Liebe der Danae* at the 1944 Salzburg Festival in honour of Strauss's eightieth birthday. It was after all not to be an *Opus Posthumum*; Strauss gave it the number Opus 83, and the scores were printed in Leipzig for publication by Johannes Oertel who had succeeded Fürstner as Strauss's publisher after *Die schweigsame Frau*. In January 1943 all fifteen hundred printed copies were destroyed in an air raid on Leipzig (Strauss had received his own copies in 1941), but fortunately this setback did not jeopardize plans for the Salzburg production which was to be provided by forces from Munich led by Krauss as conductor, Rudolf Hartmann as producer, Emil Preetorius as designer, and with Ursuleac as Danae, Hans Hotter as Jupiter, and Horst Taubmann as Midas. *Die Liebe der Danae* would open the Festival on 5 August 1944 (dress rehearsal two days earlier) and be given six performances.

Earlier in the year there had been some doubt whether any Strauss birthday celebrations would take place at all. Strauss had expressed himself with pointed outspokenness on the conduct of the war and the way the country was being run. These duly reached the ears and inflamed the wrath of Hitler, who refused to allow public birthday celebrations for Strauss's eightieth anniversary, and also forbade Nazi party members to have personal social contact with Strauss. At the intervention of Wilhelm Furtwängler and of the Gauleiter Baldur von Schirach in Vienna, Hitler relented sufficiently to permit honour to be given to the music, 'but not the man'. Dr Goebbels sent Strauss a bust of Gluck as a birthday present. A miniature festival of Strauss's works was given in Vienna, and the Salzburg *Danae* was permitted to proceed. When, on 20 July, the day of the unsuccessful attempt by a group of generals to assassinate Hitler, Dr Goebbels decreed Total War and the suspension of all festivals, the Salzburg arrangements were still allowed to continue—though the Festival would now consist only of a concert by Furtwängler with the Vienna Philharmonic (Bruckner's Eighth Symphony) on 14 August and *Die Liebe der Danae*.* Strauss did not find out about the change of plan until 29 July when he received news from Clemens Krauss† that it had proved impossible to find means beforehand to assemble scenic properties and other decorative material being made in Munich and Prague and transport them to Salzburg. The *Danae* première would now take place on

* Information about the Salzburg Festival of 1944 has been greatly increased as a result of the researches of Alan Jefferson, cf. *Opera*, January 1964, Vol. 15, No. 1.

† The recently published correspondence shows that this letter was not sent off until 31 July, whereas Strauss gave the news to Gregor on 29 July, so that he must already have discovered the change of date from some other source.

15 August. The success of the Allies' Second Front campaign plunged transport facilities in Germany and Austria into chaos, with consequent difficulty in assembling artists for Salzburg. Goebbels cancelled the official festival in a decree of 10 August, but *Danae* was permitted to proceed as far as the final dress rehearsal, which now took place on 16 August. Gregor, who was at Konstanz, was informed by telegram that the *Danae* performances were cancelled; it was not suggested that he attend the final dress rehearsal and so he did not make the journey, since telephones were out of action and telegrams sent by ordinary letter post. Strauss had arrived in Salzburg on 9 August. Rudolf Hartmann* has given a vivid description of the powerful emotion with which the rehearsals affected Strauss, one in particular, apparently on 11 August, just after Goebbels's decree had made it plain to all concerned in this *Danae* première that their labours could never be crowned with the final achievement of a first night: Hartmann, sitting in the stalls as producer, was vividly reminded of a day in 1919 during the political skirmishes in Munich when he came upon a group of children playing absorbedly on a sandheap, completely indifferent to the noise of battle around them. He had often seen Strauss at rehearsal, and recognized at once that the composer was unprecedentedly attentive and serious in frame of mind. Towards the end of Act 3, Scene 2, Strauss rose and walked to the front of the stalls so that he could observe his beloved Vienna Philharmonic Orchestra as well as the singers on stage: and this, we infer, was in order that he might see as well as hear the orchestral interlude before the final scene, a piece for which he held special affection and which (who knew in those disturbed times?) he might never hear again. His frame of mind communicated itself to everybody else present, and in the duet of Danae and Jupiter, Hartmann recalls, they all suddenly felt themselves in the physical, tangible presence of the divine power called Art. At the end of the work Strauss raised his hands in gratitude, his voice choked with tears; and he called to the orchestra: 'Perhaps we shall see one another again in a better world!'

A few days later the final dress rehearsal was given before a packed audience of invited guests. Strauss took numerous curtain-calls, and then disappeared. He was found, alone in one of the dressing-rooms, gazing at the score of *Die Liebe der Danae* in his hands. He lifted his gaze to his friends and muttered: 'I shall be on my way there soon, and I hope they'll forgive me if I take this as well.'

Strauss had at least been permitted by a kindly Chronos to see all fifteen of his operas in staged performance. Later he wrote to Hartmann that with the closure of all theatres on 1 September his life was finished, and he wished that he had been summoned by the gods of Olympus on the day following the *Danae* rehearsal. Plans that the Salzburg production

* *Schweizerische Musikzeitung*, Zürich, 1952, Vol. 92, No. 6.

should be exported *in toto* to Zürich in 1945 came to nothing. In 1946 there was a plan for three simultaneous premières of *Danae* in Stockholm, Zürich, and Covent Garden (which soon fell out of the running and was replaced by Amsterdam). Strauss would only consent on condition that a fourth, simultaneous première took place in Vienna, with the 1944 Salzburg cast conducted by Clemens Krauss. But Krauss who had done much for the cause of humanity during the Nazi years had not yet been officially de-Nazified; he was sitting unemployed in Salzburg. By September Strauss had decided that a *Danae* première must under the circumstances be postponed *ad calendas Graecas*. Sad as this was, one must be sensible; he hoped that *Danae* might re-open the new Vienna Opera House—and if he was no longer able to attend, Mercury would deliver his greetings telegram!

In the event *Die Liebe der Danae* was given its world première at the 1952 Salzburg Festival on 14 August. Conductor, producer and designer were those of 1944; Annelies Kupper sang Danae, Paul Schoeffler took Jupiter, and Josef Gostic sang Midas. It was a great occasion, but one could not help feeling that the real première had taken place eight years earlier.* Local premières followed in Vienna and Berlin, Milan and Dresden, before the end of 1952. Rudolf Kempe brought the 1953 Munich production (fairly heavily abbreviated) to Zürich and London in the same year.

4

Jupiter, the Lord of the gods, came down to earth from time to time in search of amorous conquest. The jealousy of his consort, Juno, forced him to take sundry disguises when he wished to make love: thus to Semele he appeared as a cloud, to Europa as a bull, to Alcmene in the likeness of her husband Amphitryon, to Leda as a swan.

His latest prey is a difficult one. Danae, daughter of Pollux, the King of Eos, is both indifferent to the male sex and passionately hungry for the glitter of gold, a passion hard to requite in bankrupt Eos. Jupiter appeared to her as a shower of gold, but success did not blind him to the realization that Danae was more interested in the precious metal than in the masculine force that propelled it. He therefore adopted another ruse. He endowed a penniless donkey-man, Midas, with the gift of transmuting whatever he touched to gold, and set this protégé on the throne of Lydia. In return for this, Midas was to change places with Jupiter whenever the god so wished; thus Jupiter hoped to be received by Danae as a human lover.

---

* The spirit of Jupiter had forsaken the town, leaving it for the moment over-populated by the Mammon-descendants of Pollux, Danae and the Creditors!

A very short and business-like Prelude precedes the rise of the curtain.
It deals with the nagging of the horde of creditors into whose hands King
Pollux has delivered himself by his passion for regal luxury. They are
obviously insistent and voluble, as Exs. 1¹ and 1² imply.

Ex. 1³, very closely related in contents, represents these creditors' debtor
Pollux and his court.

The curtain rises to Ex. 1², revealing a decrepit throne-room, stripped
of its pomp save only for a partly gilded throne. Angry creditors from
Cyprus, Persia and other places far and near are calling for the king (Ex. 1³),
and being held at bay by the servants and guards who insist that Pollux
is not in residence. Their loyal protestations are belied by the sudden
appearance of this shabby monarch, physically defending his tottering
throne from plunder and assuring the tradesmen that he has already
handed over everything in his possession. To each of his suggestions for
temporary security they answer that the contents of the palace are already
pawned down to the last fixture and fitting, even the last nail. Where has
all the money gone to?

O Kö-nig Pol-lux   sag uns an, Wo hast du al-les hin-getan?

Gregor points their protest with the first of many absurdly comic
couplets in the text:

> *Nimm unsern Fluch, nimm unsern Spott,*
> *die ganze Insel ist bankrott!*
> (For we may curse, and we may joke;
> the island is completely broke!)

Never fear, the king assures them, hope is on its way. He has sent off his four nephews, the kings of the islands who are married to his four nieces, Alcmene, Semele, Europa and Leda, the four most beautiful women in the world.* The nephews are identified by a fragment of what will later become Ex. 11, though at present it is still incompletely formulated. Similarly there is not as yet any indication of the characteristic themes for the four Queens quoted below as Ex. 18—unless of Ex. 18³ whose descending arpeggio is vaguely traced at mention of her name. The brisk tempo and passage of words give Strauss no time to establish their themes.

The nephews have, we learn, sailed off round the vicinity taking the portrait of Pollux's lovely daughter Danae. The creditors, aware of her fanatical androphobia, expect little from this expedition (Danae is a spiritual relation of Gregor's Daphne; the two subjects were not well juxtaposed). But, says Pollux, there has nevertheless been a response from no less a person than the fabulously wealthy Midas, King of Lydia, the man with the Golden Touch.

3

Mi — das von Ly-dien

Another day will clear the problems of finance, Pollux gives his promise. But the creditors prefer a bird in the hand, and they seize the opportunity to remove the last relics of gold from Pollux's throne and his crown. We lose sight of them, though Exs. 1², 3, 1³ and 1¹, in that order, linger behind.

A tiny pause, and the first orchestral Interlude begins to describe the Golden Rain in which Jupiter visited Danae. The theme of the opera first appears as an orchestral fugato on this subject, Ex. 4¹.

4

* We notice that Hofmannsthal's Io has been replaced by Semele (though Io gets a mention from Jupiter later on, in one of Gregor's meticulous half-hours with the classical dictionary).

4

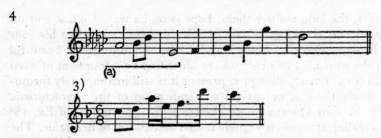

The descending scales in Ex. 4¹ may well recall the toboggan run in *Intermezzo*. Ex. 4² shows the melodic form which expresses Danae's delight at this visitation. Ex. 4³ gives the inversion of the theme heard later. But before either of these, before the second scene begins, we hear the bar-by-bar retrograde of Ex. 4¹, which probes deeper into Danae's heart.

5

Part of Ex. 5 reappears in Ex. 4², and the opening will be transformed finally into Ex. 29, when gold is no longer Danae's chief joy. A richer, more serene theme represents the god Jupiter at the heart of the Golden Rain.

6

The magical, enriching climate of G flat major soon slips into its exact antipole, bland C major; this key-contrast, equated with god-man relationship, is particularly associated with the four Queens who, like Daphne, are Jupiter's human conquests in love; and with the theme of the Golden Touch, Ex. 12.

The Interlude returns to fantastic G flat major with continued deployment of these last three themes. The form of Jupiter becomes more recognizable in two further phrases, the first related rhythmically to Ex. 6, the second melodically to Ex. 5a of which it is a more potent form (it also has connexions with Ex. 3).

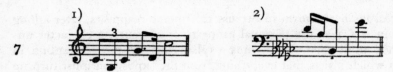

7

Exs. 7¹ and 7² are resounding strongly when the curtain rises to disclose
Danae's bedroom, or such of it as becomes visible through a darkness
blindingly pierced by Jupiter's Golden Rain. This visitation (not the first
for Danae) gradually disappears by the time she stirs from sleep and tries
to recall it. Her servant Xanthe hears her call for gold and remarks that
here is another one looking for the impossible in bankrupt Eos (Ex. 1¹).
Danae is not interested in the spending properties of cash, but in its
erotic attraction (Ex. 7²), its kiss (a foretaste of Ex. 11), its all-pervading
light in the midst of darkness—an extremely physical theme, taken up in
imitation by ascending tonal steps.

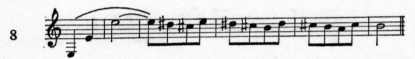

8

Danae attempts to describe her vision, but Xanthe can only understand its contents in terms of bankrupt Ex. 1³, a dream in time of
penury. Not a dream, answers her mistress, but a shining reality from the
visitant that embraced her—another virile theme, of Jupiter her lover.

9

(The second phrase is related to Ex. 5b.) Xanthe's imagination is
fettered to Ex. 1¹, but Danae feels its reality in the radiant shape of Ex.
4², which blossoms into a glorious duet for two sopranos. Here Strauss
works his *Arabella* trick by taking Xanthe to the D flat above Danae's top
B flat, and down the arpeggio for the finish of cadence. But this time he
plays a fresh trump-card, since the duet is hardly ended before Danae too
leaps to a top D flat, while she gives further details of her marvellous
dream. Xanthe may scold her for thinking more of dreams than of rich
suitors to help the country, but Danae is confident that this golden dream
can end Eos's poverty.

In the distance a curious march in quintuple time is heard.

10

For reasons best known to Strauss this theme reappears, after a long silence, in Act 3 as the personal property of Mercury, a character unmentioned until then. I can only explain this by the convention in operetta which insists that everything from the exposition must turn up in the last act, however improbable or nonsensical (and in Act 3, Scene 2 of *Danae* it does). Ex. 10 launches the most extended and persistent example of an unchanged peculiar metre in all the works of Strauss; it gives a strong flavour of caricature to the music. Danae recognizes the joyful sound as a signal of her princely cousins' return home, but she vows to accept no new suitor unless he is as strong and gold-laden as her visitant in sleep. The music ought to reassure her, since it insists on Golden Midas, Ex. 3.

A solemn, triumphant, heroic theme, still in 5/4, changes the scene to a palace courtyard overlooking the sea, thronged with the inhabitants of Eos, including the creditors from Scene 1.*

11
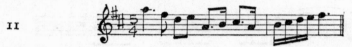

Later stages of the march bring back Ex. 10 and the various segments of Ex. 1, as the creditors turn coats and praise Pollux's sagacity—though when his nephews and nieces solemnly announce the arrival of a rich suitor, the creditors at once reply that this is where they came in. The beginning of Ex. 4 as a proud fanfare means that the singer is Danae's dream-visitor, Jupiter himself, but it signifies nothing to the creditors who look no further than the figure at the foot of the bill. He will marry Danae? What good is that? He will take her away from them to his own kingdom! Undeterred, the nephews and nieces, *a cappella* (Strauss recognized the difficulties, which is one reason why he postponed the première), rehearse the story of their voyage, accompanied by a mimetic ballet, explaining how they reached their El Dorado and met its ruler. Ex. 17 is suggested by the Queens' delighted recollections; each in turn remembers how Midas reminded her of Jupiter (Ex. 8 and Ex. 7^2 a moment later).† The vocal octet describes how Midas took the portrait and immediately turned it to gold, pausing only to send back a betrothal present for Danae—the branch of a tree in blossom, likewise turned into

---

* When the events of this act are digested, it may well be felt that the structure is uncomfortably episodic. In order to tauten it, Rudolf Hartmann and Rudolf Kempe, in the 1953 Munich production, made an ingenious reshuffle. Upon Danae's last words they cut to Midas's entry, and at the end of his duet with Danae returned to the present scene, linking it with the final scene of the first act. Cuts and rearrangements are almost always damaging to Strauss's musical fabric, and he himself would never approve of them: he told Karl Böhm 'Don't ask me to authorize a cut; if I had wanted to approve of it, I wouldn't have composed it.' Nevertheless the readjustment here described does seem beneficial to the total scheme of surrounding sections. Munich's good intentions were spoiled by several other less happy excisions.

† Leda's passion for the Swan creates a strange and comic link between Ex. 4 and the famous melody of Saint-Saëns's *Carnival of the Animals*.

gold; it is unveiled (C major switches symbolically into F sharp, the enharmonic equivalent of G flat).

This revelation is enough to stir Danae, reminding her of her dream. The delighted populace is informed of Midas's magical touch, and here the nephews and their wives sing the beginning of the theme now quoted as Ex. 12, though its completion is only heard later. For the moment the alternation of C major and G flat major is the most important element.

The creditors begin to believe, because they can see; and to see is to covet. They crowd avariciously round the golden bough. But Danae recognizes Ex. 6 in its gleam and protects her gift (Ex. 4^3). The creditors are ready to claim her as hostage. But at this moment a ship is sighted, golden from stem to stern. Ex. 5 shows that they prize the sight as much as does Danae; they call on Midas to tarry and let them serve him; and then decide to make for the port before he can escape.

Danae is left alone, obsessed with the hope that Ex. 4^2 will be realized. At this moment G flat turns into C, and Midas, finely attired, comes to greet her in heroic tones (reminiscent of Otello's *Esultate*). She greets him as Midas (Exs. 3 and 5) but he introduces himself as the Lydian King's gold-bearing friend Chrysopher, and a yearning theme conveys his inferior status.

Chrysopher has, he says, been sent ahead to woo Danae for Midas, and as with Tristan for King Mark, Chrysopher is all too successful, first of all because he brings her a resplendent dress of pure gold (borrowed from Hofmannsthal, without the same close motivation) which promises the fulfilment of her dreams.

14

Her pleasure and her charm make him bold, and she too senses a new, hesitant warmth in her heart. The musical portrait of this budding love takes shape slowly (it will provide the final climax of the opera); this is one of its more definite early forms.

15

Voices off-stage are calling greetings to Midas, and Danae asks to be led before him. Chrysopher can only obey, though he hints that his master is a transitory lover unlikely to remain long. He hints too at a secret pact (Ex. 12). They go out to the harbour and the scene changes as they go, with Ex. 8 and a pungent transformation of Ex. 4's first four notes.

Danae and Chrysopher are now amid the assembled populace who are apostrophizing their saviour Midas in full-throated C major. The golden boat arrives and Jupiter, dressed as Midas, disembarks, greeting Eos to a grand and god-like theme in D flat.

16

In due course it will be found that Jupiter thinks much about Juno; and she, his consort, has a very similar theme, given here as Ex. 16². Danae, astonished, recognizes the master of her dreams (Ex. 8), hails him as such (Ex. 4¹), questions his lordship over her heart (Exs. 13 and 15) and faints, as Jupiter releases Ex. 7², Ex. 12, and a small thunderbolt, whereupon C major ends the act.

5

After these grand solemnities Strauss was ready for something more light-hearted, and he suggested that Danae should be attended, in her nuptial chamber, by Jupiter's four lady-loves. The introduction to Act 2, allegro molto in G, chatters as volubly as they.

36 Jupiter (Constantino Ego) arrives at Eos, and greets Danae (Dorothy Dow): La Scala, Milan, 1952

37
Richard Strauss, Horst Taubmann and Clemens Krauss during a rehearsal for the Munich première of *Capriccio*

3 gr. Fl.
2 Hob
engl Horn
A Clarinett
2 B Clar.
3 Fag
4 Hörner
Celesta
I Harfe

38 The final duet from *Der Rosenkavalier*: a page from Strauss's autograph full score

39
The quarrel ensemble from
Capriccio, Berlin, 1956

17

The four Queens are occupied in twining roses round the bridal couch of Midas and Danae, jealously envying Danae's luck (Ex. 5) in winning the god (G flat major) whose favours they once enjoyed (C major). They have recognized Jupiter (Ex. 7^1) behind the form of Midas (Ex. 3), and the discovery is more than enough to set them reminiscing on their favourite, indeed only, topic of conversation—the Cloud, the Swan, the substitute-husband, and the Bull. Strauss has given vague but recognizable musical characterization to each of them. I quote their themes here, though all are not yet brought into earshot.

18

19

As they complete their vocal quartet, which floats lazily but buoyantly upon Ex. 17, the 'glorious Golden Man' himself bounces into the room, delighted with his successful disguise as a younger and more athletic suitor.

The ladies, rather to his surprise, greet him as Jupiter-Midas, to a useful conflation of Ex. 3 and Ex. 7^2. He finds it difficult enough to preserve his incognito from Juno (Ex. 16^2), without their prattle, and asks how they recognize him. Leda (Ex. 18^2), Semele (Ex. 18^1) and Alcmene (Ex. 18^3), in that order, are delighted to explain—we may notice that Leda's Ex. 18^2 is the inversion of Ex. 7^2. In their turn they ask why Jupiter is not content to woo Danae as the Golden Shower. The reason is that this disguise has failed to satisfy his hankering for human sexual love; Danae was delighted, but not stirred, by the gold. The ladies are inclined to regard this as a slight against their powers of sexual satisfaction (Europa's Ex. 18[4] raises its horns when she asks if Jupiter regrets the Bull), and find it hard to understand that what attracts Jupiter to Danae is precisely her lack of interest in men, the difficulty, and therefore the challenge, of unlocking her heart. It is easy for a god to achieve this, but more interesting if the god confines himself within human form. What then, they ask, is he doing with his *Doppelgänger*? The reason of course is the jealousy of Juno (Ex. 16[2]), and her vengeance on Jupiter's human lovers. It is true that she allowed these four to marry handsomely (Ex. 1[2]) as soon as the Swan, Cloud, etc. had vanished. But recently there was the case of the nymph Callisto whom Juno turned into a bear as a punishment for accepting Jupiter's favours (this is not the whole story, indeed not an accepted version—Diana or Jupiter made the transformation, and Juno had the bear hunted to death). And then there was Io . . . but this excursion with Gregor through a lengthy and delightful myth is cut short very abruptly. I suspect that Strauss used a blue pencil here.*

The point of inveigling Midas into the conspiracy is that he and Jupiter can change places at a moment's notice. If Juno comes to punish Danae she will find harmless Midas, Danae's legitimate husband, in bed with her. The ladies are relieved (Ex. 17), to hear this, indeed hopeful that divine visitations (specified once more in full detail) may be resumed. Jupiter is about to begin a gallant reply, but Midas joins the company (prematurely but not inappropriately to Ex. 24[x]) and this is the cue for the exit of the Queens with jocular farewells.

Strauss marks the start of the new scene with a new theme indicating the master–servant relationship of the two men.

20

Jupiter finds royal robes cumbersome, but he enjoys the easy, enviable life of a King (Ex. 3 in imitation, pursued by the talkative women of Ex. 17). Midas compliments him on his success with the personifications of Ex. 18, but Jupiter confesses to disappointment in their collapse into middle age—wrinkles, poor memory, fat. This is why he has come to woo young, desirable, difficult Danae (Ex. 5 and Ex. 8 and Ex. 4[2]a on the glockenspiel), hitherto accessible only in dreams (Ex. 9) but tonight awake for his full, human enjoyment. Midas promises him that Danae is not entirely attracted by gold (Ex. 12), and this gives Jupiter the opportunity to warn Midas that Danae is visibly paying more attention to him than to Jupiter-Midas. Midas-Chrysopher protests that he has simply been paving the way, as ordered (Ex. 13), and that Danae looks forward

* Jupiter turned Io into a sacred white cow, for safety's sake, whereupon Juno sent a swarm of gadflies to sting her and chase her round the world.

to her wedding as the fulfilment of her dreams (Ex. 14). Jupiter regards Midas's success as something like treachery, the breaking of their bond.

21

And yet we must admit that Midas has done no more than was commanded of him. Jupiter's escapade in this ambivalent form was destined to lead to jealousy; there is even a hint, in its terms of reference, of exhibitionism, though this may be condoned in a god who feels himself approaching—can we call it Change of Immortality?

Jupiter admonishes Midas nevertheless that such forward behaviour is bound, if it continues, to result in the withdrawal of the Golden Touch and Midas's reinstatement as the worthless donkey-driver from which he has magically risen. The concept of poor humble status—subsequently of importance—is signified by a characteristic chord, B flat major superimposed upon E major (in fact, riches out of rags, as the tritone relationship from Ex. 12 suggests).

22

Midas defends himself. Just as Jupiter raised him prematurely to stardom, so he seems prematurely to be giving him the sack (Ex. 21). Danae's heart is profound, a riddle to the man (Ex. 12) as it is to the god (Ex. 4); not even Jupiter can know whether she will eventually yield to the man (transformations of Ex. 13 and Ex. 15) or to the god (Ex. 7^2 and Ex. 9). One cannot pre-ordain fulfilment (Ex. 14).

Jupiter becomes, pardon the phrase, more jovial: once again the god's destiny is bound up with the independent ways of man. So it is that he has brought gold to two humans. After tonight Midas can keep the gold; for tonight Danae belongs to Jupiter (the force represented by Ex. 6). And now he repeats to Midas the charm of the Golden Touch, which we are hearing complete for the first time (Ex. 12). It inspires Jupiter to an outburst of authentic Wotanesque wrath—a not so pale reflection of the Wagnerian god's warning to Brünnhilde in Act 2, Scene 3 of *Die Walküre* (must the epigone, Strauss seems to ask, always be denied originality?). He dares Midas to cross him and risk the comfort and happiness of two humans who have been raised from insignificance. This is the moment of decision; Danae is approaching, at the god's command. Let Midas dare!

Jupiter storms from the room, like Wotan from the forest outside

Fafner's cave in *Siegfried*, Act 2, and flashes of light in the darkness here and there attend his departure. So do Ex. 21, Ex. 7^2, Ex. 6, Ex. 9, Ex. 7^1, Ex. 4, and finally Ex. 12. It is a grand Wagnerian interlude by Richard III (as Bülow called Strauss, adding: 'there is no Richard II').

Danae approaches the nuptial chamber in her golden wedding dress, followed by servants dressed as golden Cupids and by the four Queens. Strauss built this little wedding march, with solo female quartet, symphonically into the structure of the act; but it carries strong and almost conscious overtones of *Treulich geführt* in Wagner's *Lohengrin* and since it is of rather finer musical quality one might try to find for it an occasional place in wedding services. Perhaps, though, it asserts its quality only in context, since the thematic references—the Scotch Snap transformation of Ex. 4 plus Ex. 7^2, the delighted Ex. 17, the carefully allusive Ex. 3, and the slightly salacious reference to Ex. 7^2—would convey to an outside congregation either nothing or (even if the text were adapted for liturgical, i.e. meaningless use) something very improper indeed—though the Greeks would not have thought so, and nor did that good Hellenist Richard Strauss.

This delightful little piece closes with a nicely ironical coda and ends in silence. Danae and Midas are left alone. Danae feels that she has been drawn involuntarily here, to her dreamland. But Ex. 15 contradicts her as she sings, and Midas has to convey that he embodies the physical attraction of Ex. 13, the lover's power of Ex. 7^2, and the glamour of Ex. 3. His explanations remind her of her visitor in dreams, but they are not at all clear, and she sensibly asks if he is the bringer of her golden robe, or the master of her dreams. Neither, he answers; he is her lover Midas, more than the bearer of dangerous gifts (Ex. 21) and more than any god. She blissfully recalls the dream (Ex. 4^1) and the bringer of gold, and begs for a sign of Midas's power. He indicates the rosy wreath round the bed, plucks a flower—

23

and pronouncing the charm of Ex. 12, converts it into pure gold, and hands it to her. Danae is upset by this fatal alchemy, and Midas suggests that there is a higher form of love and of living. The long melody of transformation has a specifically human connotation—Hofmannsthal's theme of metamorphosis.

24

Because it refers to human transformation it has connexions with Ex. 26.

Danae may not care for the life-destructive effect of Midas's gift, but she is still charmed by the resultant product, and she entreats him to go on. Midas boldly pronounces himself not only a magician (Ex. 4^1) but even more a lover (Ex. 13). However, since suitors are expected to produce presents, he converts the entire room into solid gold (it cannot help looking very vulgar indeed, but perhaps that is part of the point). Ex. 24 obliges orchestrally, and a duet ensues, first in dialogue then, after ominous intonation of Ex. 21, splendidly in ensemble (*Herrliches Spiel!*).*

At the climax of this tremendous outpouring, scrupulously enriched with appropriate thematic references notably Ex. 24 (because this is the moment of Danae's spiritual metamorphosis, viz. growing-up), she falls into Midas's arms. The hoary, overworked, but still communicative diminished-seventh chords plunge the room in darkness, Ex. 21 thunders forth. Midas calls out, aghast, to Danae.

D flat minor and Ex. 16^1 slowly restore a wan light in which we and Midas can recognize Danae's form in the golden statue that she has become. Midas curses himself, his gift, and finally the god who bestowed it. And now it is Jupiter's turn to appear and protest (Ex. 20) that Midas is rather precipitate in complaining. Jupiter, from whom he accepted the magical gift, has kept his part of the bargain; Danae may be dead to Midas, but she will live immortally for Jupiter. Midas claims that her love was for him, not for the Golden Rain. He dares Jupiter to let the statue decide. In a solemn duet they plead their respective claims on her love. Jupiter makes the eloquent contrapuntal point that god (Ex. 16^1) and lover (Ex. 9) combine well and that Ex. 22 is no desirable suitor for a girl who has a declared interest in every sort of transformation of Ex. 4. But Midas can offer humanity and a happiness greater than gold, that of a faithful heart. As their stentorian duet ceases, Ex. 13 urgently entreating and Ex. 21 imperiously commanding trail in the wake of their voices.

From far away Ex. 15 answers, and the human voice within the golden statue calls for her beloved Midas to remain close to the love which she has begun to feel (Ex. 5). She bids farewell to her dream.

There is a flash of lightning in which the statue is seen to resume Danae's loving form. She hurries to Midas and they make their escape together. Jupiter is left alone, full of wrath and Ex. 21. Danae has chosen wretchedness and penury (Ex. 22 and Ex. 13 are now seen to contain

---

* A close study of Gregor's librettos reveals that Strauss's complaint of the excessive use of *Geliebter* was modest indeed. The word *Herrlich* is also pleonastically overworked, for every desirable object, animate or inanimate, even (in a moment or two) to Danae's *herrlich* bosom. *Herrlich* and *Geliebter* are fine words which lose their suggestive force unless sparingly applied. The musician must admit, however, that Strauss was on occasion guilty of a similar musical carelessness in his thematic diction—many of his scalic and arpeggio figures are not strong enough, because too common, to support the poetic weight placed on them. This is not, on the whole, true of the themes in *Die Liebe der Danae*, but it is certainly true of *Intermezzo*, *Die schweigsame Frau* and *Daphne*.

Ex. 15), even though Jupiter could have given her an everlasting temple —a momentous broken scale of D flat major strides upward (the Valhalla key of course!)—in which she would have been an eternal goddess. She was offered divinity; she chose mankind (Ex. 22). Jupiter has finished with her, and the second act ends in a monstrous tempest of Ex. 21, Ex. 7² and menacing F minor chords.

6

Some German opera houses have a barbarous habit of billing only one interval in an opera of several acts. The Prelude to Act 3 of *Die Liebe der Danae* suggests that this interval must fall after the second act, since we now have an extended orchestral résumé of what has occurred so far: the Golden Rain melodically idealized; the rivalry of a new genial Ex. 7¹ (Jupiter) and a newly seductive Ex. 13 (Midas), for the hand of a wiser and more profound Ex. 5 (Danae); the gorgeous transformation theme, Ex. 24; the critical diminished seventh, and the outraged Ex. 21, followed by the more sorrowful than angry D flat minor version of Ex. 16¹. Then, after so much molto allegro action, a held chord of Ex. 22, statusless penury, upon which the curtain rises, and we see Midas and Danae waking from magic sleep under a group of pine-trees, presumably somewhere in the Middle East.

Danae's first thoughts are of her *Geliebter*, Ex. 15, his answer of Ex. 13 and, just to remind her, of Ex. 24. Gold, and pomp have vanished. She asks if any magic still remains for them. He answers with the opening of Ex. 26; the world which they chose is their magic. As if to confirm this, she asks: What is that shining vision before them? It is, he answers, a stone lit by the sun—and C major blazes out of divine sumptuous G flat (I suspect that such an idea meant a lot to Strauss in the miserable conditions of wartime Nazi Germany). They remember together their fateful love scene, in the shadow of Jupiter's curse (Ex. 21), and Midas recalls how, in his earlier donkey-man days, he met an old man in a burnous who promised him wealth. The identity of the old man is made clear by Ex. 7², but it is attached to a new theme portraying a wanderer (and he is indeed the Wanderer).

25

Midas's recollection of this strange interlude is evocatively accompanied by rich low strings. Midas tells Danae the charm (Ex. 12), and the condition of personal exchange at a moment's notice, as well as the let-out clause (Ex. 21). He further recalls the wooing of Danae, and the circumstances leading up to her choice—all of which makes a good structural reprise and a reasonable solo, the only one for Midas, ending with a hint at Ex. 26. Danae assures him that her heart was won, not by the gold he brought, but by his kindly glance. He puts her on their donkey and they continue their travels, singing a unison duet indicative of their complete spiritual union.

26

Strauss had modestly said, at the time of *Die schweigsame Frau*, that he couldn't write long tunes. On the whole he did not, but in *Danae* he wrote almost half a dozen of them (Ex. 4², Ex. 24, Ex. 26, Ex. 27, Ex. 30, to quote the best ones).

Ex. 26 provides the orchestral interlude before the next scene, which materializes to Ex. 6 mated with Ex. 16² and followed by Ex. 16¹. This shows a mountainous afforested landscape to which Jupiter has betaken himself, deep in troubled thought involving all his themes of godhead and passion. The Wagnerian brooding is broken by the sudden arrival of Mercury, to Ex. 10², announcing that Jupiter can now return home to Olympus. Mercury makes pointed comments on Danae's unflattering choice of lover and, to Jupiter's astonishment, reveals that all Olympus has been laughing at the news conveyed by Jupiter's thunder (Ex. 21). Ares did a war-dance; Vulcan vomited his drink with mirth; Ganymed spilt the nectar he was pouring, all over the earth; Juno (Ex. 16²) most amused of all, laughed until she cried. In Eos, on the other hand, Jupiter's destruction and escape have had an enraging effect (Ex. 1²), and Jupiter had better escape rapidly. Already his departure is delayed, because the four amorous Queens have found his hiding place.

And here they are as voluble as ever, apprised by Mercury of Jupiter's whereabouts. Their ex-lover tries to frighten them off with threats of thunder, but they know a joke when they hear it, and proceed to say so in a delightful canonic quartet—Strauss outdoing the Mozart of his favourite *Così fan tutte*.

27

-schieden zum Stell - dich - ein!

Semele leads off with references to Ex. 18[1], Europa follows, then Alcmene and Leda. Jupiter eventually orders Mercury to conjure a banquet for them all. Juno, they remark approvingly, can hardly complain of her husband if he sits down to table with four married women. They are above suspicion—unlike Danae (Ex. 4). Each of the ladies in turn thanks Jupiter for his love in disguise, and he answers each with a word of loving farewell; he is going to retire. Their memories are happy, his are marred by the last failure with Danae; and this it is which has prompted his graceful withdrawal from promiscuous amour. He loved them all, but Danae most deeply and unsuccessfully. Jupiter bids them all good-bye.

Just at this moment of apparently serene coda, we hear the voices of Pollux, the Queens' four husbands, and the creditors, who have hunted out this welshing Midas. In true musical comedy spirit they all appear, together with their musical themes, demanding retribution or compensation. Jupiter does not dare admit that he is not Midas, and Mercury advises him to use the age-old remedy of money. So Jupiter makes a gesture and yet once more brings down a Golden Shower (transformation of Ex. 4) which has as distracting an effect on them all as Papageno's magic bells upon Monostatos and his crew in a very similar context. And by making the shower of coins travel, he sends them all away.

Lucky Jupiter, laughs Mercury. But his master is not in a laughing mood. He is still full of regret about his affair with Danae. Mercury loyally supplies the answer (actually it was Strauss's Mercury, Clemens Krauss). Poverty is never happy: Let Jupiter seek out Danae in her donkey-man's hut: she will be glad to welcome him, the bringer of gold, and now the loving god. Jupiter thanks him with a smile, and the orchestra moves into the last interlude, based on Ex. 7[2], no longer smiling or passionate, but now deeply pervaded with seriousness and solemnity. This was the piece which Strauss nicknamed 'Jupiter's Resignation' and which, at the rehearsal described by Rudolf Hartmann, moved him so strangely and profoundly that the entire audience felt emotionally transformed. In terms of thematic development it calls for no comment except that Strauss here pulls out Ex. 7[2] as though it were an infinite quantity of baker's dough, expanding with every pull; and that every key-switch is rich in emotional meaning when one remembers that Jupiter, the lord of all the gods, started from human C major.

The interlude finishes with references to Ex. 22 that take Jupiter towards B flat, in which key we find Danae alone in her large but simple hut, a sort of tent with a huge couch, and a carpet for the door. Krauss asked for an aria at the beginning of this scene and Strauss obliged Ursuleac–Danae with a revelation of lyrical simplicity, deriving from the trustful parallel sixths of Ex. 26, but alluding to earlier Danae themes as she remembers the curse which brought blessing to her life. Out of the final B flat chord grows Ex. 7^2, now gentle and spacious. Jupiter walks into the hut, dressed in the burnous which he had worn when he first met Midas. He speaks first of all as Midas's employer and, learning that the householder is away, prepares to travel further (an odd reference to Ex. 19). But Danae invites him to stay awhile for rest and refreshment. She soon links him with Midas's sometime guest, the old man in a burnous (Jupiter repeats her phrase—The Old Man: it is the end of the amorous road for him). Jupiter has already, in the preceding interlude, suffered his own metamorphosis; he is no longer a suitor, but a bringer of blessing and serenity, and it is in this mood that he prepares to unlock his heart with a spacious derivative of Ex. 5 on the viola.

This grand melody flows through Jupiter's blessing. But Danae, whenever he admits his love, answers with Ex. 15 that her love is given to Midas; the memory of Golden Rain no longer stirs her heart. Their duet is extended and marvellously dignified, full of thematic development. Jupiter, fundamentally convinced of Danae's constancy in real love, but still hopeful, tells the tale of Maia whom Jupiter loved. His narration is accompanied by another buoyant thematic figure.

Jupiter, says the old man, once loved Maia and at his side flowers sprang to life. Yet another new melody erupts.

Danae sees this story not as an invitation to physical love, but a spiritual image of Nature's blessing, something far greater than any human love. Maia's benediction is visible to all the world every spring

Jupiter, who knows when he is conquered, turns to go, but Danae holds
him back so that he may be given a guest-gift—it is the golden clasp from
her hair. To a stately D flat major string complex she stresses yet again
her happiness (*Siehe, ich liebe*). Ex. 30 floods yet again through the
orchestral texture. Jupiter knows that he can confer upon Danae nothing
more deep and inspiring than his paternal blessing (Ex. 16¹). Ex. 8 is
combined with Juno's Ex. 16² as he embraces her and leaves the hut,
followed by his Ex. 7¹ and Ex. 7². Danae turns to her household duties,
sustained by the love of Ex. 15. Out of the stillness calls Midas's Ex. 26
on six horns. She turns and with the utmost joy and inspiration, rising to
top C sharp, she calls her husband's name to Ex. 15. We do not see their
reunion, but the serene chords of B flat major close the curtains on a
drama that has already ended happily ever after.

7

Shortly after the 1944 dress rehearsal Strauss wrote an account of it to
his friend and official biographer Willi Schuh in Switzerland, and this
contains the rare phenomenon of a composer's own detailed critical
assessment of his own work. Strauss is not, to be sure, an entirely un-
biased critic of *Die Liebe der Danae*, but by vivid analysis he shows us
what it was that made him love the work. Of the first scene he mentions
the 'flexibility' and 'grey-brown' colouring of the choruses; he singles out
the trumpet and trombone statements of Ex. 7² in the Golden Rain interlude, and the 5/4 March of which he was proud that the listener hardly
noticed the oddity of the metre until the sighting of Midas's ship.
Strauss admitted to a falling-off of inspiration in the first Danae–Midas
duet: perhaps the rather dry text was to blame, but at least the scene
seemed to pass quickly, thanks to the beautiful singing of Horst Taubmann, a tenor whom even Strauss (a famous anti-tenor), found it a
pleasure to listen to. Strauss had been afraid that the end of Act 1 might
fall flat, but was relieved to notice that it came off well—he gave credit
to Hotter and Ursuleac for this. Similarly he had suspected that the
badinage of Jupiter with the four Queens (Strauss misnames them Goddesses) might be over-long; but was glad to find it amusing and a positive
contribution to the development of Jupiter's character. He noted that the
various scenes of Act 2 were well contrasted and built up uninterruptedly
to the close. The third act Strauss ranked with the best music he had ever
written; 'something for a seventy-five-year-old to be really proud of',
especially the Midas–Danae duet whose melody is taken further in the
subsequent interlude, then the second interlude, and the final Danae–
Jupiter scene 'whose effectiveness can be clearly recognized even from

the vocal score'. Finally Strauss observed that his orchestral colour glowed with pristine splendour once again (a hint perhaps that he had not been happy about some of his late scores) and that Gregor's libretto was very entertaining and abounded in the true Hellenic spirit.

A younger, less committed critic may agree with much of Strauss's critical commentary. In the first place he observes that Strauss's omissions are significant: not a word about Act 3, Scene 2 which contains the delightful canonic quartet *alla Così fan tutte*, the slightly less charming Jupiter–Mercury scenes, and the fairly feeble squabble with Pollux and the creditors; nothing about Danae's solo at the start of the last scene, a flood of soprano lyricism that fails to touch the high-spots of equivalent solos in other operas (even in Daphne's and the Countess's solo scenes); merely a blanket approval of Act 2 without special mention of the first Midas–Jupiter scene, which some of us may find rather dry and hard on the palate—but the Midas–Danae scene, perhaps lengthy for its content, goes pleasantly enough. Strauss's recognition of the weakness at Midas's first entry is significant as well; he was too close to the work to appreciate that the failure here is a structural one, that the two sandwiching choral ensembles are diplographic—only one is needed, and the Hartmann revision for Munich helps the drama in this respect, though it is a pity that Strauss was not persuaded to recognize the fault before he completed the act. The 'grey-brown' opening scene is not firmly enough based for its context, and depends on exceptionally vivacious singing and direction for the impetus needed in a comic opera's initial stages.

But is *Danae* a comic opera? Strauss, who was giving a 'factual report' on the finished product, did not feel bound to consider how the character of the work had changed. It began as a cheerful ironical piece intertwining two familiar stories so as to give a new twist to both of them. There was to be much operetta feeling about it, and some of this has remained in the quartet of Queens, and the sarcastic comments of the creditors. The humorous aspect of Jupiter was effectively damped down by the joint efforts of Wallerstein and Krauss who found it distasteful to 'send up' Jupiter—damped also by Strauss whose music suggests his own self-identification with Jupiter, an old boy glad to go out from time to time on the spree, but rather relieved to assume eventually a more passive paternally benedictory role. For Strauss–Jupiter the intermediate version, which bade farewell to him at the picnic with the Queens, would have been disappointing. What emerged from the textual reshuffling was something neither comic nor wholly serious, but a Mozartian blend of both, with the special themes of metamorphosis and leave-taking as cornerstones of the structure.

By comparison with the other late operas of Strauss we must specially admire the extraordinarily inventive and skilful thematic treatment in *Danae*, an ideal demonstration of Strauss's modest boast to Zweig (see

Die schweigsame Frau, p. 274), and also the strength of character in the themes themselves, much more clearly defined than in *Daphne* or *Die schweigsame Frau* or much of *Friedenstag*. Of the orchestral colouring, which so pleased the composer, we may remark that its glow and variety retain something of the hard bright incandescence which were noticed in *Die Ägyptische Helena* and the Apollonian scenes from *Daphne*; the generous warmth of *Der Rosenkavalier* and *Ariadne* are missing. But this is not to say that *Danae* is heartless or cold in its music; the final orchestral Interlude must effectively declare the opposite. It is simply that times change, and Strauss at seventy-five was a different artist from Strauss at fifty.

It will be noticed in performance, if not from reading the foregoing synopsis of the opera, that *Die Liebe der Danae* is much more about Jupiter than about the title-character. Danae, though she may spend more time on stage, does not establish a positive or clearly drawn personality; she is even a rather boring young lady (but not as boring as Daphne). Jupiter on the other hand is a vivid and endearing old fellow —there is an excellent moment in the last scene when, as Danae mentions 'another old man in a burnous like you', he remarks: 'Old, did she say? It is the end!' One need not try to conclude that Strauss had lost interest in women. He was even then bringing one of the loveliest and most lovable of his heroines to dramatic life, the Countess Madeleine in *Capriccio*.

Capriccio

OPUS 85

Conversation Piece for Music in One Act
LIBRETTO BY CLEMENS KRAUSS

The Countess	SOPRANO
Clairon, an Actress	CONTRALTO
Flamand, a Musician	TENOR
Olivier, a Poet	BARITONE
The Count, the Countess's Brother	BARITONE
La Roche, Director of a Theatre	BASS
Monsieur Taupe	TENOR
An Italian Singer	SOPRANO
An Italian Singer	TENOR
A Young Ballerina	
The Major-domo	BASS
Eight Servants	FOUR TENORS, FOUR BASSES
Three Musicians VIOLIN, CELLO, HARPSICHORD	

I

The genesis of Strauss's last opera is the most involved and fascinating of them all. It involves Mozart, Da Ponte, Giovanni Battista de Casti, as well as Stefan Zweig, Joseph Gregor, Hans Swarowsky, Rudolf Hartmann, and the two eventual accredited authors Clemens Krauss and Richard Strauss. It is a miracle that so many cooks did not spoil the *Kraftbrühe*.

On 7 February 1786 the Orangery at Schönbrünn near Vienna was the scene during Carnival-time of an operatic double bill produced at the command of the Emperor Josef II for the Governor-General of the Netherlands. Both operas were concerned with the actuality of making operas: one was Mozart's *Der Schauspieldirektor* which is about an impresario's difficulties with two of his leading ladies; the other was Salieri's *Prima la musica e poi le parole*, to a libretto by the Abbé Giovanni Battista de Casti (1724–1803). Salieri's comic piece included among its characters a poet who was designed as a parody of Casti's rival librettist Lorenzo da Ponte. It achieved no further fame, whereas Mozart's *Schauspieldirektor* has become a classic curtain-raiser—and the fact that it is concerned primarily with the troubles of an operatic impresario is not entirely insignificant to the contents of Strauss's *Capriccio*.

The action moves to 1932 when, during the preparation for *Arabella* at Dresden, Strauss had some theoretical discussions with Clemens Krauss, the conductor of the première, about the nature of opera, and the relative importance of words and music. This was no haphazard chatter for time-wasting. Strauss had spent his life in the opera house, had thought deeply about his work with Hofmannsthal, and was now thinking even more deeply about how he could go on writing operas after the death of the only librettist genius of the century. Krauss (who had been born on 31 March 1893, the son of Hector von Baltazzi and Clementine Krauss —Clemens took the name of his mother who was a well-known dancer and later actress) was arguably the most perceptive musician of the theatre that this century has yet seen. Far beyond his ability as an operatic conductor and vocal coach, he had a profound, because carefully nurtured, knowledge of the theatre in all its manifestations. He was an eagle-eyed connoisseur of production, décor, lighting, acting and stage-management (it was said that the costumes of a chorister mattered no less to him than the score he was conducting). Above all he cared passionately for the logic and suspension of disbelief in the theatre, so much that he was at pains to re-think unsatisfactory existing productions, and to re-translate foreign operas whenever he found the existing translations unworthy. Krauss had been one of Strauss's musical assistants at Vienna in the early 1920s, and as soon as he graduated to an opera house of his own he made it a point of honour to present Strauss's operas, and if necessary to persuade the composer to accept changes for the credible commonsense of the opera. He forced significant alterations on Strauss for *Die Frau ohne Schatten*, *Die Ägyptische Helena*, and *Arabella*; he tried in vain to persuade Strauss to make a three-act version of *Intermezzo*; he intervened positively in the creation of the librettos for *Friedenstag* and *Die Liebe der Danae*; and he coached and married Viorica Ursuleac who became Strauss's favourite soprano in the composer's later years, and therefore the inspiration of his last operas (since opera and the sound of the soprano voice were more or less identified in Strauss's mind). Clemens Krauss's intelligence and knowledge of history and literature as well as music were quite exceptional, and his correspondence with Strauss over the years is arguably the liveliest, most readable and illuminating of all the Strauss collections which have been published. Unlike Joseph Gregor, Krauss was a good letter-writer and worked well by post. Fortunate posterity can retrace the composition of *Capriccio*, almost sentence by sentence, through the letters which passed between these two collaborators, at one time almost daily, and sometimes even twice a day.

It was Stefan Zweig who first put the Abbé de Casti into Strauss's head. Towards the end of January 1934, after he had completed the *Schweigsame Frau* libretto and was being urged by Strauss to think of their next joint opera, Zweig announced that during his forthcoming stay in London he would make a point of reading, in the British Museum, all the librettos of Casti whose great charm and perfected art of comedy Pergolesi had failed to match (Pergolesi, as far as I can discover, never set a word of Casti to music!). In August of the same year, Zweig reported enthusiastically on the possibilities of Casti's *Prima la musica e poi le parole*; the piece itself was unusable apart from some details, but the title set ideas in his mind—as Strauss agreed. And in October Zweig promised Strauss a scenario elaborated from Casti's libretto.

At the risk of mystifying the newcomer to the eventual *Capriccio* we may at this point profitably summarize very briefly the contents of Casti's *Prima la musica e poi le parole*.

2

The cast of Casti's divertimento consists of the following:

Un Maestro di Cappella	(i.e. a Composer)
Un Poeta	(a Librettist)
Donna Eleonora	(a Virtuosa Seria, i.e. Prima Donna)
Tonina	(unparticularized, but clearly a Maidservant)

The action takes place in the Composer's house, the pertinent room of which is furnished with a spinet, a harpsichord, copious quantities of music, chairs, and a table supporting glasses and the wherewithal to fill them.

The unseen Master of Ceremonies is one Count Ospizio who is the amorous protector of Donna Eleonora, and also the patron of the Poet and the Composer; the Poet is carrying on a more or less serious flirtation with Tonina. Count Ospizio has demanded a new aria from his two artistic protégés, to be completed that very day. It is to be a duet scene, sung by a soprano (Donna Eleonora) and a castrato. The Poet revolts at the idea of a castrato as lover, but the Musician quickly sketches a situation, writes half the libretto himself, and persuades the Poet to complete the task. He then writes out his music, and Tonina (*vice* a castrato) rehearses it with her mistress. It consists of ten lines for Donna Eleonora (*Sequesto mio pianto*) and thirteen lines for Tonina (*Per pietà, padrona mia*). Poet and Musician express their satisfaction, and a vocal quartet concludes the whole.

Of all this nothing was transferred to *Capriccio* but the roles of Poet and Musician (and the fact that the text of Strauss's opera was eventually written by a musician!).

3

On 20 April 1935 Strauss jogged Zweig's memory of *Poet and Composer*, with a further suggestion that E. T. A. Hoffmann might provide extra ideas. Zweig was at this time trying to resign his post as Strauss's official librettist, owing to political difficulties which resolved him more and more to quit Austria and live elsewhere. He had determined that his friend Joseph Gregor was the ideal person to succeed him—not least because their relationship would not exclude Zweig's advice on everything that Gregor wrote. Strauss specifically requested Zweig on 4 April not to let Gregor touch the Casti piece, but at Whitsun the two writers met by the lake of Zürich and spent some days together; during one walk they stopped at an inn, and in a 'wild, dionysiac, poetic mood' they conceived together the ground plan for a scenario derived from Casti's title, and dealing with the contribution of words and music to opera. The scene would be a feudal castle where a poet and a musician were rivals for the hand of the lady of the castle. A troupe of strolling players arrives, led by a manager who would be a caricature of the authors' revered friend Max Reinhardt. The whole idea strongly recalls a situation in Goethe's *Wilhelm Meister*.

On 17 June Gregor sent a scenario on this theme to Richard Strauss who at once recognized that it was largely Zweig's work and wrote at once the famous letter which the Nazis intercepted (see page 279). He dropped *Prima la Musica* like a hot coal, and in the next four years prepared three other operas with Gregor.

However, on 23 March 1939 Strauss re-opened the subject of the Casti opera with Gregor. By now they had both re-christened the work *Erst die Worte dann die Musik* or *Prima le parole dopo la musica*—'First the words, then the music', which was the precise opposite of Casti's title (and the opposite of the eventual opera's implicit dénouement, as I shall in due course suggest). Strauss invited Gregor to discuss this further as an operatic theme. Gregor assured Strauss that only the title was worth preserving—the libretto only ran, he said, to a couple of pages (did he know that it occupies sixteen octavo printed pages, and had he read the contents? If he had, surely he would never have reversed *Parole* and *Musica* in his mind, or allowed Strauss to do so.). His own 1935 version he admitted meant nothing to him now, but he prepared a new scenario and sent it to Strauss in early May 1939; the one new pertinent feature of this was the appearance of Italian opera singers. Strauss responded with a series of catch-phrases designed to spur Gregor's inspiration, to impress on his collaborator the different weights that great men of the past had found in the relationship of words and music—Goethe, Mozart, Wagner, Verdi—the meaning of opera for conductor and producer, for a Mendelssohn who could write *Songs without Words*, and for a modern composer whose songs had their melodic lines more or less dictated by the words. All this, said Strauss, would need at least eight or ten singers, and the task was worthy of Beaumarchais, Scribe and Hofmannsthal all rolled into one.

Gregor made a new scenario and this was to Strauss's taste, though all depended on the quality of the dialogue, which should incorporate speech, recitative and vocal music. Gregor had intended this, but he objected to Strauss's suggestion that the action should take place at the start of the Romantic era after the composition of Weber's *Der Freischütz* (or even in modern times). Gregor was thinking quite definitely of Goethe's first years in Weimar; a contemporary setting was out of the question, since these topics were no longer discussed by anyone. Gregor made a fresh version in August—Strauss at this stage suggested a choral commentary by the servants in the castle, as representatives of the audience (and he suggested also that they should give preference to ballet as the art-form in which rhythm means more than words or music—an idea which survives in the fugue *Tanz und Musik* of the final *Capriccio*). Gregor's new scenario shocked Strauss by its allusions to Beethoven and Mozart; it was not at all what the composer wanted. Besides, it was much too poetic —a failing of all Austrians, he later explained. His own declared ideals were Molière and Oscar Wilde.

It was at this stage that Clemens Krauss began to take part in the planning of the work. After listening to Gregor's scenario which the author read aloud to him, Krauss advised him to keep the duration of the piece to within three-quarters of an hour (Strauss was planning it as a curtain-raiser for *Friedenstag* or *Daphne*), and dropped Strauss a sarcastic note comparing Gregor's work with that of the opera composer Julius Bittner. Strauss confessed to Krauss that Gregor's work was too lyrical, too poetic (typically Austrian, like Bittner—and like Krauss, he implied), whereas what Strauss wanted was intellectual theatre, dry wit. And yet Gregor was, Strauss admitted, a man of talent, ideas and great willingness. Perhaps Krauss could advise him a little? Always remembering, though, not to play too heavily the Man of the Theatre. Strauss needed more than plain theatre to inspire him. Puccini's operas, for example, were like that white sausage (*Münchner Weisswurst*) which has to be eaten two hours after it is made; Strauss preferred salami which keeps fresh for some time! 'Really I don't want to write any more operas, but with the de Casti I would like to write something exceptional, a dramatic treatment, a theatrical fugue.' To Gregor he wrote that the opera must end with a question mark, not a Happy End; he suggested that the Count and Countess should be twins, like words and music (the Composer in *Capriccio* compares these two elements to Brother and Sister, we are reminded), for whose birthday the Poet arrives with his poem, the Musician with his string quartet (eventually a sextet), and the Impresario with his two Italian singers. On 7 October Strauss sent Gregor a very detailed synopsis of the plot which he had in mind; it embraces most of the incidents familiar from the final libretto. And on 12 October he discussed his plans in detail with Clemens Krauss and the producer Rudolf Hartmann. As a result of this meeting Krauss made a closely detailed scenario of his own and submitted it with the suggestion that Strauss ought to write the text himself.

This scenario differed in some respects from the definitive one. The scene was laid in wintertime with snow visible in the garden outside. At the beginning the Composer and the Countess could be seen in an adjoining room listening to his string quintet. The Poet, Actress and Impresario arrive and are shortly met by the Count, who leads them into the theatre. The Poet, left alone, reads his poem, while the quintet is still going on (thus the two arts are audibly separated), before going into the theatre.

The Countess enters with the Composer, who declares his love. He is shortly called to rehearsal, and the Count joins the Countess; they discuss their respective love-affairs. The poet now has his love scene with the Countess, and reads his poem to her. The Italian singers arrive and go to rehearsal. Poet and Composer are now alone together; they decide to collaborate. Now follows the Quarrel Ensemble (overheard by the servants) and the Italian Duet. The Count offers to escort the Actress back to Paris. All leave, and the servants tidy the room, airing their own opinions. The Composer returns and sings his song, overheard by the Countess; he makes his rendezvous for next day and goes. The Countess reads the poem to herself, then sings the melody without words. Both leave her unmoved, but when she puts words and music together she is deeply stirred. The Butler enters and announces the Poet's request for a rendezvous next day at the time already arranged by the Composer. Greatly astonished she leaves the stage.

Strauss prepared dialogue for the first scene, and invited Gregor to do the same. Krauss was making his own version, and eventually, Strauss thought, they could collate the three scripts. Gregor's version arrived on 24 October and Strauss realized at once that his own dialogue was more precise than Gregor's and the Krauss scenario structurally the more logical and clear of the two. At first the two musicians agreed that Gregor should be kept at work in case he provided them with good ideas, and in case their own scenario proved unworkable by themselves. But Strauss must have realized the unfortunate long-term consequences of such a subterfuge, and on 28 October he told Gregor to stop work on *Parole-Musica*; as with *Intermezzo* and Hermann Bahr in the early twenties, Strauss knew that he must tackle this subject alone.

Krauss was at this stage only involved as ideas man and stern critic; he subjected Strauss's dialogue for the first three scenes to rigorous examination, cleansed them of grammatical and aesthetic impurities and pronounced them good. He undertook to find an attractive sonnet or love-poem from the period, also a piece of suitable dialogue for the scene declaimed by the Actress and the Count, and some Metastasio for the Italian opera singers' duet. He then recast the scenario into the form finally adopted; all this on 26 October. By early November Krauss was writing the text himself, perhaps because Strauss was ill and forbidden to write or smoke, perhaps already as the result of a conference at Garmisch. The hunt for a sonnet had been entrusted to Hans Swarowsky, a young conductor who had been in difficulties politically (he was suspected of spying for Britain) and whose flair for languages prompted Krauss to engage him at Munich as *Dramaturg* to supervise German translations of foreign operas. (After the war Swarowsky was, for a time, conductor of the Scottish National Orchestra.) Some research in Zürich led Swarowsky to the conclusion that love poetry in late eighteenth-century France was non-existent apart from that of André Chenier (essentially a Revolution poet) and folk poetry. He had however gone back in time to Pierre Ronsard (1515–85) and translated one of his most beautiful love sonnets, *Je ne sçaurois aimer autre que vous*, and this was at once approved ideal by Krauss and Strauss alike, and further researches proved unnecessary since Strauss set the sonnet, in its first version, on

23 November.* Swarowsky was also asked to supply the spoken dialogue recited before the sonnet.

Little by little, sometimes day by day, the final libretto came into clearer focus and was committed to the post. The Ballet Dancer was invented on 18 November, the time of the double rendezvous on the 19th. Krauss did plentiful research on the popularity of Gluck's operas in Paris, and on the historical conditions of the period, so as to establish the precise year of the action; they settled for the winter of 1776/77. Strauss was anxious, however, that the text should not be too crammed with names. Krauss discovered Mlle Clairon in history (her name was Hippolyte and she published her memoirs in 1790) and named her to Strauss on 22 November. On the following day he told Strauss details of La Roche's programme; he and Hartmann had invented the Destruction of Carthage as a fuse to explode the Quarrel ensemble—Strauss found it far-fetched but it stayed. M. Taupe was invented in mid-December—a satirical character à la Bernard Shaw, said Krauss. The Metastasio duet was found in late January 1940. But in February Strauss was still assuming that the opera in which Poet and Composer would collaborate was his own *Daphne*; the ingenious twist whereby they are challenged to write an opera on the events of that day (in fact the opera that is *Capriccio*) did not occur to Strauss until 18 June—a quotation from Strauss's *Daphne* remains in the score at an appropriate place. Much of the text was already in Strauss's hands by now. Flamand, Olivier, and La Roche (another historical character) had been named. Strauss had written parts of the text himself—including much of La Roche's dialogue—and he began composing the introduction and opening scene in July 1940. By 4 September he was able to play the first two scenes to Krauss. Later in the same month Strauss decided that A major, the key in which he had set Ronsard's sonnet, was painfully high for the singers; he rewrote it in F sharp, which was also a more suitable key for the harp accompaniment in the closing scene. The two authors now set about ensuring that every detail of the text was dramatically sound and convincing. They abandoned the snow and settled for May (1777 presumably). They discussed times of day and details of topography; and in November they had to fix a title. *Wort oder Ton* (a translation of *Parole-Musica*) was rejected; on 6 December Krauss thought of *Capriccio* and his fellow-author agreed (he had reservations eight months later, and suggested *The Sonnet* or *The Countess's Sonnet; an Enigmatic Play*, but was talked back into *Capriccio*, not before a Viennese theatrical colleague had suggested the even preferable *Extempore*).

Krauss sent the last of the libretto on 18 January 1941, and by

* The first public performance of this A major setting, with its piano accompaniment and differing rhythmic details, was given by Elisabeth Schwarzkopf and Gerald Moore at the Royal Festival Hall in London on 26 May 1961.

24 February Strauss had completed the vocal score—after only seven months during which he was also preparing the ballet music, freely based on Couperin, for *Verklungene Feste* (his new movements for this, which also included the *Couperin Suite*, were published as the *Divertimento*, Opus 86). True to his promise Strauss sent the completed text to Joseph Gregor, who wrote back rather stuffily that he did not feel competent to judge it —though he was good enough to question some of the diction. (It may be remembered that Hofmannsthal took a similar attitude to the completed *Intermezzo*.) Strauss completed the full score of the opera on 3 August. Krauss had begged permission to plan their next opera together. Strauss recommended him by all means to plan, but added, 'Do you really think that after *Capriccio* there can follow anything better or at least as good? Isn't this D flat major the best conclusion to my theatrical life-work? One can only leave one Will!'

There were in fact some small additions and corrections, notably to the ensemble on *The Birth of Pallas Athene*. And then they had to decide where *Capriccio* should be baptized. Krauss was musical director at Munich and a regular guest conductor at Berlin and Vienna. On 19 September 1941 he was also named artistic director of the Salzburg Festival. It was here that Strauss was anxious to see the première, in a small theatre, prepared under festival conditions. Krauss was anxious to give the first performance in Munich in June 1942, with his own expert troupe of Strauss interpreters; he had an almost complete set of new Strauss productions in the repertory there. Strauss pressed the advantages of Salzburg: better acoustic conditions for the intelligibility of words, a more intimate atmosphere. . . . 'Don't forget that *Capriccio* is not a piece for the public, or rather not for a public of eighteen hundred people per evening.* Perhaps a delicacy for cultural connoisseurs, musically not very important, in any case not so tasty that the music will help out if the great public fails to warm to the libretto.' Strauss continued in this all too modest tone of voice, so as to strengthen the claims for Salzburg, which of course included Clemens Krauss's début as festival director. He was unsuccessful. Munich planned a major Strauss festival for the summer of 1942 and *Capriccio* must surely, Krauss argued, be involved in this. Eventually the festival was postponed until after Salzburg because of transport shortages due to military movements (one of the few Strauss–Krauss letters in which the war is actually mentioned) and also because the indispensable Hans Hotter suffered from hay-fever every June. Strauss was the more ready to accept this plan because his real anxiety was, we read between the lines, that the cast should have sufficient time to absorb not only the notes and words but also the unconventional

---

* After the première Strauss changed his tune, and wrote to Krauss on 31 October 1942: 'Must [*Capriccio*] really be (as some papers declare) only a joy to the Connoisseur, and not "speak to the heart of the people"?'

style of *Capriccio*. Herr Hotter, for instance, famously as he delivers Wotan's semi-recitative passages in *Rheingold*, would, Strauss remarked, have to accustom himself to Olivier's freer, rhythmically more idiosyncratic music, closer to *recitativo secco*.

The Munich première was therefore fixed for 28 October 1942. The Overture for string sextet (the original quartet had been augmented by two parts in the meanwhile) had been played on 7 May 1942 by members of the Vienna Philharmonic Orchestra at a concert of contemporary music in the house of the local Gauleiter Baldur von Schirach (whose good deeds included insistence, against Hitler's wish, on public celebration of Strauss's eightieth birthday—though his bad deeds won him twenty years' imprisonment at the Nuremberg Trials in 1946). For the première the cast was a magnificent one: Ursuleac as the Countess Madeleine, Horst Taubmann as Flamand, Hans Hotter as Olivier, Georg Hann as La Roche, Walter Höfermayer as the Count, Irma Beilke and Franz Klarwein as the Italian Duettists. The part of Clairon, written for a contralto, proved difficult to cast since much of the tessitura fell uncomfortably low for clear verbal articulation even by the star contralto Elisabeth Höngen; Strauss therefore made an alternative version for soprano and the role was given to Munich's Salome and Aithra, Hildegarde Ranczak. Rudolf Hartmann, of course, produced the opera, and Krauss conducted. The décors, which had been the subject of numerous arguments by diagram between Krauss and Strauss, were eventually elaborated, to the satisfaction of both authors, by Rochus Gliese (a modified version was seen at Covent Garden in 1953). Critical acclaim, for once, was unanimous, and further performances, even with increased prices, continued to sell out until, on the night of 2 October 1943, the Munich Opera House was destroyed in an air raid. Eight days later the Darmstadt première took place. Dresden followed suit on 2 January 1944, and Vienna on 1 March. The harpsichordist at Vienna was Isolde Ahlgrimm, and at Strauss's request she took the dances from *Capriccio* into her recital repertory; Strauss expressly added a concert ending. Karl Böhm, who had hoped for the first performance, conducted *Capriccio* in its Swiss première at Zürich in June 1944. Salzburg did not see *Capriccio* until the 1950 festival, when Lisa Della Casa gave fresh radiance to the part of the Countess. The English language première was given at the Juilliard School in New York in 1954, the French version (prepared by Gustav Samazeuilh at the request of both authors—though neither lived to see it) in Paris in March 1957. For the Hamburg local première two months earlier Rudolf Hartmann and Joseph Keilberth divided the opera (which runs for some hundred and thirty minutes) into two parts with an interval, adding ten bars—or rather repeating them, since they are imported from elsewhere in the score—to the close of Scene 7 when the Countess says: 'We will take chocolate in the drawing-room.' This two-act version has since been generally adopted. Strauss made his last appearance as a conductor on 13 July 1949 when he gave the magical orchestral Intermezzo which precedes the closing scene.

Capriccio was not Strauss's last composition. He followed it with a series of instrumental works, notably the concertos for oboe, horn, and clarinet with bassoon, the string orchestral study *Metamorphosen*, and the two works for wind band, and finally the *Four Last Songs*. But when in 1946 Krauss tried again to reopen operatic collaboration Strauss replied firmly: '*Capriccio* had to be definitely the end; now as ever it is the best and worthiest conclusion, and must remain so for ever and ever Amen.'

4

The Countess Madeleine is sitting, one fine May afternoon in 1777, in a drawing-room of her rococo palace near Paris, listening to the string sextet which her admirer and protégé, the Composer Flamand, has written in honour of her birthday. Until the curtain rises we are to imagine that we are in this room too, for the sextet is being played by six members of the orchestra in the pit in front of us. Its music is as clear to us as to her, particularly when we know that Ex. 1 represents Flamand, symbolically, and the sextet is intended as a declaration of love.

It is a cool piece for such a declaration, we might think; but the eighteenth century would have found it rather forward, particularly in its agitated tremolando middle section. The purpose of this extended chamber-musical overture is primarily to waft a twentieth-century audience into a frame of mind that Richard Strauss would have us pretend is authentic 1777 French, when cultured conversation really thrived every day on such topics as the artistic value of opera compared with the spoken drama and absolute music; and also a frame of mind where this sextet appears as ardent and as timely as any love poem we might think of writing a few minutes from now.

The sextet reaches its final close in F major. The curtain is lifted, and now we are to put back the clock a minute or two and hear part of the music again, but from another listening point. We have moved into the adjoining garden-room where it is being heard, through open doors, by Flamand and the Poet Olivier who is his rival in love. There is a third party present, the theatrical Impresario, La Roche. But he is asleep.

Between the Countess's drawing-room and the french windows over-looking the park is the door to the dining-room. On our right is the entrance to the Orangery and, farther away, to the theatre.

Flamand and Olivier are both watching the Countess as she listens; might a glance or a flicker of the eyelids give a clue to her feelings? No, her eyes are closed, and if that suggests enchantment, it is also the unflattering identical reaction of La Roche, as Olivier points out. The two young men are bound to declare themselves enemies in love, friendly rivals. The Countess will have to proclaim her preference: words or music? They misquote de Casti's opera title: *Prima le parole dopo la musica* . . . or is it *prima la musica*? Music and words, Flamand thinks, are like sister and brother—Olivier finds it a daring comparison; but here, within vision, are two such, a brother fascinated by the drama, his sister a tremendous music-lover.

The sextet is now over and La Roche awakes, having enjoyed the soft music for its soporific qualities. Even Olivier finds this a cynical attitude in the guardian of every artist's destiny. La Roche assures them both that without his scenic splendours their works would be nothing; his theatrical vocation, not to say egoism, is suggested by a hint or two of Ex. 4^1. How, they ask, can he maintain this in the face of Gluck's work? The orchestra helpfully recalls the overture to *Iphigénie en Aulide*.

2

Between the two halves comes a mysterious but not quite meaningless forward reference to Ex. 16; incidentally we may remark that Strauss's accentuation of *Iphigénie* on the third syllable was corrected punctually by the more scrupulous Clemens Krauss (we shall encounter further examples of Krauss's watchful eye later).

The two creative artists point enthusiastically to the excitement, the partisanship, full houses which Gluck has provoked. La Roche dismisses them as tedious fashion, unaccepted by the real élite which still waits, frustrated, for the top notes. And for these one has still to go back to Italian opera. Strauss refers here to two themes, supposedly by Piccini, Gluck's major rival in the so-called *Guerre des bouffons*. Both are recalled later in reference to the idea of eighteenth-century Italian opera.

3

La Roche brings Goldoni's evidence in his favour. The old man told him only yesterday that these modern operas might be paradise for the eye (Ex. 4[1]) but they are hell to the ear. How, La Roche adds, can antique Druids, Orientals, Biblical persons move the public which wants flesh-and-blood characters (Ex. 4[2]). Here are these two La Roche themes, the one proud, the other rather self-pitying.

Poet and musician disparage La Roche for pandering to the frivolous museum-taste of the public, Ex. 3 (a charge very near home for British opera in 1964). The Impresario insists that his repertory is good, his female performers attractive. The orchestra cites one of them, the actress Clairon—

whom Olivier has not disdained, and with whom the Count himself, inspired by Olivier's play, proposes to share the stage.

But look—the Countess is approaching.

She is still under the spell of Flamand's sextet (strains from which twine with Ex. 6): beautiful, intelligent, and an eligible widow. La Roche calls his colleagues into the theatre to prepare for rehearsal. Now he can assume his true *métier*: production—Strauss suggests the authority and the rococo pomp of his technique.

The three leave the room free for the young Count and Countess. She is still spellbound by Flamand's sextet. Her brother was left cold by it; three tiny phrases emphasize his characteristic attitude to music, and life in general.

The Count teases his sister for judging music by the personality of the Composer (Strauss offers some sharply etched character-portraits of

Couperin and Rameau). He reminds her that she can at least admire Olivier whole-heartedly, since his play is as excellent as himself: we can judge his vibrant poetic cadences from the Olivier-poetry theme (Ex. 9^1) and his personal ardour from Ex. 9^2.

9

The Countess turns the tables on her brother with a reminder of Clairon's attractions, and they tease one another with appropriate motifs. Their duet brings forward the Count's theme of carefree amorous adventure—

10

—but for the Countess it cannot be quite carefree, since Flamand's Ex. 15 is just round the corner.

Into their cheerful mood come La Roche and his two authors, ready for the rehearsal of an admirably varied programme: Flamand's symphony, Olivier's play, and one of La Roche's operas (dogged Alberti accompaniment here)—no empty vocalizing but a grand *Azione teatrale* whose theme will be disclosed later. Already it is musically described.

11

In it the Countess will hear marvellous Italian singers (Exs. 3^1 and 3^2). Uninteresting the text may be (Ex. 9^1) nevertheless. . . . But here is Clairon (Ex. 5). They are all thrilled to see her (Flamand wishes only that she were a singer as well) and compliments are piled high, though the Countess's genuine praise eases her embarrassment such as it is. Clairon's first concern is a professional one, for the continuation of Olivier's play which has stopped short of the love scene, but for which he has now found the inspiration. Clairon and the Count are given their parts. And now they run through their new spoken dialogue, a scene of parting that ends with a love sonnet, passionately declaimed by the Count. Eleven of his lines are enough to warm Clairon's enthusiasm for her patron-partner's acting ability, and in tones of not quite natural emotion to make her ask La Roche for an immediate rehearsal (Ex. 7). He assents, and leads them equally solemnly into the theatre, telling Olivier to remain outside for a while. The poet admits to the Countess that the Count spoke his lines well; only he addressed the sonnet to the wrong person. He begs leave to repair this miscalculation (a bland but striking harmonization of Ex. 8^2), which by a Freudian thought-connexion will eventually find itself attached to Flamand as the Countess's beloved.

Olivier starts the sonnet, interrupted after four lines by the Countess's comment that it is somewhat unworthy to change the address of such a poem's recipient according to whim. When Olivier reaches the ninth line Flamand, now seated at the keyboard, begins to furnish it with accompaniment. The Countess praises the warm expression of the poem (Ex. 9^2) as well as its vibrant diction (Ex. 9^1). Flamand seizes the page and hurries into the next room to set down his just inspired setting of it.

Olivier, though delighted by this chance of a solo interview, is at first appalled by the fated prospects of his beautiful sonnet; music, he knows, always ruins a poem, and here is Flamand 'composing' Olivier—in fact applying Ex. 1 to Ex. 9^1. The Countess suggests that he might for a moment forget poetry and talk prose to her. He insists that he cannot manage prose. His heart is full of grand thoughts—

12

—and they are close to Ex. 9^2, but they make him stammer. The Countess is rather thankful for a modicum of hesitation.

13

This suggestion is enough to unlock Olivier's lips and let them pour out love. He tells us, among much else, her name—Madeleine. She, the Muse of two arts, reminds him that Flamand is also wooing her with his composition in the next room, and that poetry, much as she loves it, cannot say all that she seeks to hear revealed. Every plea of his she turns to include Flamand as well. In desperation Olivier entreats her to crown the victor. Here he is, cries Flamand, re-entering with his completed composition. Amid a flurry of semiquavers associated with Ex. 1 he sits down at the harpsichord (or should it be square piano in 1777?) and sings his setting of the sonnet. It begins as follows:

14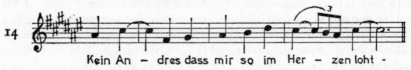

Kein An – dres dass mir so im Her – zen loht -

As soon as Flamand has finished the song, the Countess and Olivier give their conflicting verdicts—she finds that the music has given clarity and added weight to the words; Olivier can only lament the cavalier distortion of his carefully plotted prosody; Flamand meanwhile plays his composition again, singing a phrase here and there, so that a trio arises. The tempo becomes more conversational, less reflective, and Ex. 1 flits along in semiquavers, interrupted by the Countess's Ex. 6 and the words theme Ex. 9^1; the Countess again remarks on the greater force that Olivier's poem has acquired. She notices his absence of enthusiasm and he explains that he no longer knows to whom the sonnet belongs, to himself or to Flamand. The Countess begs leave to appropriate it to herself as a souvenir of this day; it has for ever united the two in her mind.

United they may be, but at this moment La Roche appears to part them since Olivier has to approve a 'genial cut' in his play (Ex. 12 is subjected to analytical surgery). He is led into the theatre, and Flamand is alone with the Countess. His passionate delight is at first expressed in a transformation of Ex. 10 (helped along with Olivier's Ex. 12 and Ex. 9 and his own Ex. 1 and Ex. 14) and this is because the Count's *Heiter entscheiden* is about to become a serious symbol of Flamand, the lover in Ex. 15, one of the two between whom the Countess is now asked to choose (*entscheiden*). She herself is the cause of this confusion in her mind, Flamand suggests: she has made them both love her—though Flamand speaks only of his own love. His love theme bursts out in full ardour, and it is close to the theme of that other Composer in *Ariadne II*.

15

Flamand tells the Countess how his love was born one afternoon in her library when he was working (on his sextet, the orchestra implies). She entered, took a book and, without seeing him, sat down and read for several hours while Flamand gazed and gazed at her loveliness. Music surged within him—he had to close his eyes. When he opened them she had gone, leaving the book open on the table. He picked up the book, Pascal's *Pensées*, and read 'Silence speaks more eloquently than words when one is in love.' That afternoon changed Flamand's whole being, he admits. The Countess observes with surprise his flow of eloquence; has he changed roles with his friend the Poet (Ex. 12)? Flamand sensed that his sextet had not told all his thoughts to her who inspired it; was he wrong then to declare his love verbally? She answers him with another *Pensée*: 'the happiness of an undeclared love is thorny but sweet'. Ex. 15 grows more and more insistent as Flamand demands an answer. She promises it to him, in the library, tomorrow morning at eleven o'clock. He calls her name, 'Madeleine!', presses a kiss upon her arm and hurries away while the orchestra allows Ex. 12, Ex. 1, Ex. 15, and Ex. 14 to whirl through her mind, calming down to further reminiscences of the sextet. Sounds of rehearsal penetrate from the theatre and arouse Madeleine from her reverie. She rings a bell and orders chocolate to be served here in the drawing-room.

When the opera is given in two acts, her order is followed by five bars from Flamand's love scene and the last bars of the sonnet, as a curtain-lowerer.

5

These same bars begin the second half, and disclose the same scene on to which the Count runs impetuously from the theatre, singing Clairon's praises (Ex. 8² and Ex. 5) not least because she has praised him. Madeleine suggests that flattery is the food of love (and Ex. 1 answers her back). The Countess reveals to her brother the difficult situation in which both artists have put her; she explains the circumstances of the sonnet's musical setting, and its effect on her. What will come of it? Perhaps an opera! Woodwind introduce a pompous, harmonically ambiguous phrase, concerned with opera.

16

If he were to decide, his choice would be for the Word, since Clairon is for him Venus and Minerva in one body.

And here she comes with La Roche and Olivier, praising the Count's dramatic talent to his sister; why, he did not forget his lines even when the Prompter dozed off. The Count invites Clairon to remain in the Château for the evening, but she pleads preparation for a gala performance of Voltaire's *Tancred* next day. The Countess offers them all a cup of chocolate as refreshment (the fashionable drink of the 1770s in France). Flamand has silently returned to the company. La Roche proposes a small entertainment while they drink their chocolate: a Dancer and two Italian Singers. The Countess gladly gives approval, and to an accompaniment on stage of violin, cello and harpsichord a Dancer shows her skill in a passepied, a gigue and a gavotte.* During the first of these La Roche explains to the Count how he found this slip of a girl, so balletically gifted, under an old Viscount's protection. In the gigue Olivier attempts to resume his liaison with Clairon; she declares their affair firmly and

---

* At Glyndebourne in 1963 she was given a male partner, whose presence is not properly justifiable.

definitely closed, and goes to sit by the Countess. La Roche prophesies
that Olivier will not figure largely in Clairon's memoirs. At the end of the
gavotte the Count pays nice compliments to the Ballerina, and suggests
to Flamand that, in this art at least, music's role is purely subsidiary.
Flamand dissents; nobody would move a step without music.

Olivier puts a different view: dancing and music alike are the vassals of
rhythm.

Tanz und Mu-sik stehn im   Bann des Rhy - thmus, ihm un - ter-

-worf-en   seit   e - wig - er   Zeit.

This is made the subject of a fugal 'discussion on the theme Words or
Music'. The fugue subject remains melodically prominent throughout,
while the various parties put forward their divergent views. When
Flamand maintains that sublime music is an unwilling accomplice of the
theatre, the Countess disagrees since the stage is a secret mirror of
reality; and her point is underlined by a melody here symbolizing Opera
as an ideal.

18

Strauss borrowed this tune from his satirical song-cycle *Krämerspiegel*
(Tradesmen's Mirror) where it represented the pure inspiration that
music publishers prostituted for their own financial gain. The melody
appears in two of these delightful songs, and later in *Capriccio* Strauss
conflates elements of both manifestations. For the moment it is just a
snatch, and the fugue is resumed with Ex. 12 and Ex. 1 as countersubjects, and with numerous stretti. The Countess reminds the contenders
(Ex. 6) that while they dispute, the proof of musical tragedy is being
provided by Gluck. The Count recalls her to commonsense; she means
Opera, an absurd phenomenon (a longer version of Ex. 18). Clairon
admits the good qualities of operatic convention, but objects to the bad
texts. The Countess champions Gluck's new, more broad-minded treatment, and is seconded by Flamand—all this while the *Krämerspiegel* tune
flows forward. La Roche returns to the argument and the fugue: his
objection is to dreary recitative, but Flamand cites Gluck's pointful,
revealing orchestral recitative as evidence to the contrary. La Roche sees
this as mere hullabaloo to drown *bel canto* (Ex. 3) which is dying. This

gives the Countess her cue to ask, before Song dies, for La Roche's Italian Singers. The Impresario announces that they will offer a duet to a text by Metastasio.

The tenor and soprano pour out their voices in an A flat major *Andante con moto, Addio mia vita*, much more cheerful than Metastasio's words suggest, but less ebullient than their jog-trot cabaletta of tearful farewell. The opening phrase of each section is quoted here.

19

While the Count offers to escort Clairon back to Paris, the Countess thanks the Singers for their duet and orders refreshments for them, of which both partake heartily. That they should eat and drink with the gentry was impossible in the period, but their continued presence and contrasting vocal characteristics were necessary to the authors for the next ensemble.

The Countess asks after La Roche's entertainment for her birthday. He demurs shyly (Ex. 4¹) but when pressed announces that it has two parts. The first is an Allegory, 'The Birth of Pallas Athene' (Ex. 11). The startling mythological details of the story—she sprang fully armed from Jupiter's head, he having swallowed her Mother—rouse the mirth of all present, and inspire a gently swinging, texturally transparent vocal octet, the so-called Laughing Ensemble. This is dominated by a theme first presented, rather anxiously, by the Countess, who has no wish that La Roche should be mocked.

20

Sie la- chen ihn aus   und er meint es so   ernst.

The six members of the party contribute in character, while the two Italian Singers comment excitedly on the quality of their meal (the tenor fears his colleague is looking too enthusiastically on the wine when it is red). Ex. 11 resumes prominence and the Countess apologizes to La Roche for the questioning surprise that his opera synopsis has aroused—it seems impossible of theatrical realization. Politely she asks what will be the second half of his *azione teatrale*. This, says La Roche, is a grand heroic drama (Ex. 7) on *The Destruction of Carthage*, a miracle of stage machinery. And it too evokes protests from Flamand and Olivier, who ruthlessly expose its absurdities and artistic invalidity. Now the second half of the octet, a quarrel ensemble, begins; and this is dominated by a briskly animated idea.

21

The texture here is more dense, but it carefully allows the gist of the quarrel to be followed. In the interests of tension and structure (but much against Clemens Krauss's will) the Italian Singers, now thoroughly merry, revert to their *Addio* duet. Olivier and Flamand are united in their scorn for La Roche's antiquated ideas, singing together in thirds and sixths like any of his Italians. The Countess is seriously alarmed (she mis-accentuates the Poet's name, as Krauss pointed out, but Strauss failed to correct his error), for the uproar increases in pace, and her Ex. 6 comes anxiously to the fore.

But La Roche is authoritative enough to silence the uproar and defend himself in a grand monologue of Apologia (*Holà! Ihr Streiter in Apoll!*).* La Roche rebukes Flamand and Olivier for jeering before they have created works for the theatre. Olivier's verses (Ex. 12) command respect when Clairon (Ex. 5) speaks them, but they need assistance from the scenic workshop. Flamand's dainty string sextet (echoes of the overture) sent La Roche to sleep. They know nothing of his troubles (Ex. 7). The public admires only the lowest manifestations of art, farces, charades; but the artists, who could replace these low tastes with finer workmanship, condone them by their abstention. They condemn traditional rules, but make no new ones. The subjects of operatic novelties are still fusty priests and Grecian Kings (a strong suggestion of *Elektra*!). La Roche wants to people his stage with real people. Let these two creators make such works for him, or keep quiet. La Roche has given his life to beauty and nobility in art: *sic itur ad astra*; he is not ashamed to dictate the inscription for his tombstone—'the gods loved him, mankind admired him. Amen'. All of which rouses the Italian soprano to noisy sobs, so that the tenor has to lead her away.

Ex. 6 takes over and the Countess solemnly adjures Flamand and Olivier to accept La Roche's invitation, and collaborate in an opera for her birthday, collaborate with her inspiration (Ex. 18) to give the arts a new home. Clairon makes the most of this pretentious moment to lead both authors by the hand to the Countess, who addresses them severally. Flamand and Olivier are joined by Clairon and La Roche in a solemn Homage Quartet that would be ludicrous if Ex. 5 and Ex. 18 were not so nobly matched in it. Even the Count senses the philosophical value of this new armistice between words and music (Ex. 17, the meeting point of both parties), though its result may be an opera (Ex. 16). La Roche gives helpful instructions: let Flamand give Aria its due, subdue the orchestra

---

* This line is a hangover from an earlier version of the libretto connected closely with *Daphne* as the end-product of the discussion.

to the singers; let Olivier keep the Prima Donna's solo until later in the piece, and keep his text simple so that, upon frequent repetition, it will be understood. The two authors are not much impressed; after all, they have been told to create the new rules. The subject? Olivier, not much of an innovator, suggests *Ariadne auf Naxos* and Strauss answers with Ex. 20 from his own setting. Flamand proposes *Daphne* (Ex. 1 of the Strauss setting, then the transformation theme). Fortunately La Roche condemns these old-fashioned suggestions. The Count has a much more novel idea: portray the conflicts of this day, the characters here in this room, make them into an opera (Ex. 8², Ex. 4¹, Ex. 15, Ex. 12, Ex. 5, Ex. 1, fall on one another in excitement). What an inspiration! Flamand acclaims it, and an anagram of Ex. 1 arrives to suggest the Opera in question—and later specifically its dénouement.

22

The others are delighted as well, though Olivier fears the action may be uneventful. They comment with ironic relish on their roles, and Clairon remarks that lovers will not be wanting. Olivier nicely asks Flamand who will be the tenor. La Roche is slightly apprehensive (Ex. 7 is turned upside down) of the indiscretion involved, but Clairon assures him that if so, it will be all the more popular.

They all prepare to return to Paris and take their several leaves; Flamand's is the most ardent, to Ex. 18. He and Olivier depart murmuring *Prima le parole, Prima la musica* as they show each other the door, in the manner of Falstaff and Ford. (Krauss had just conducted a new production of Verdi's last opera in Munich and Vienna.) La Roche draws them away with copious suggestions for his own role, especially about good exits and exit-lines—but he is gone before he can give us one.

The stage is empty, and eight servants come to tidy the room. They move quietly, discreetly.

23

As they clear up, the servants discuss the quarrel, the gluttonous Italians, the Impresario's lengthy speech, the idea of including servants in operas; La Roche's Ex. 4² is prominent, and there is a telling new version of Flamand's Ex. 15. The whole world, they conclude, is mad (Ex. 22), though from the wings a servant sees more clearly the predicaments of the Count and Countess. Opera and Ballet are discussed, and they plan a harlequinade of their own for the Countess's birthday (the orchestra plays *Die Dame gibt mit trübem Sinn* from *Ariadne*). The discussion is interrupted by the Major-domo who orders them to prepare for supper—

24

—after which they will have a free evening.

The servants greet this news enthusiastically but as ever in respectful whispers. They disappear exchanging the household gossip.

The Major-domo is lighting the candles when a voice from the theatre is heard calling for *Herr Direktor* (Ex. 7). A small, short-sighted man with a large book under his arm runs in. But instead of La Roche he finds the Major-domo.

25

The strange apparition, accompanied by extremely shadowy music, calms the Major-domo by explaining that he seldom appears above the earth's surface, since he is the invisible ruler of a magic world. By ill-luck he fell asleep and was forgotten when everybody else left the theatre. He identifies himself as Monsieur Taupe, the Prompter, who sets the magic of the theatre in motion with his continual hieratic whispers. How is he to get back to Paris? The Major-domo promises him a coach, and meanwhile some comestible fortification. The whole scene, growing out of the servants' pianissimo chorus, has an extravagant, fantastic character like a caricature of the foregoing realism. Monsieur Taupe and the Major-domo move away into some welcoming pantry. A solo horn reiterates the opening notes of—what? for shadowy Taupe-like harmonies keep intervening.

At length, to a deserted, darkened room, the horn enlarges those repeated notes into the full version of Ex. 18's beginning, the exquisite nocturne that flowered from *Krämerspiegel*. Glowing, dignified and exhaling romantic mystery, the glorious tune unfolds. A flat shifts into A major, the moon rises and beams through the french windows; the Countess, dressed for dinner, wafts into the room and stares out into the garden, her being transfixed by moonlight; we see her as the eternal Muse that she represents. The Major-domo enters and lights the candles. She turns and asks after her brother who has left her to dine alone (without Flamand or Olivier, the orchestra reminds her). She recalls, amusedly, his superficial advice on love. The Major-domo retails his next message: Olivier (Ex. 9) will attend upon her next day to learn how the opera is to end (Ex. 22). He will meet her in the library at eleven o'clock. The Major-domo withdraws.

Ex. 22 explodes, carrying Flamand and Olivier themes with it, and the Count's Ex. 8^2. The Countess is bewildered. Here is further material proof of the identity which Poet and Composer have assumed for her since the composition of the sonnet. Certainly the two men will be disappointed when they find one another. But she, how can she know whether the Word or the Music means most to her? To test her reactions she picks up Flamand's composition, sits at the harp and sings the sonnet to herself, pausing after the octet only to admit the impossibility of separating the two suitors. She finishes the song, gets up and paces round the room. The thread cannot be snapped; she herself is part of it. Each of the two is attractive. Suddenly she sees her reflection in a long mirror, and Ex. 18 comes back to her. It is, she knows, her heart which must decide. The last new theme of the opera, perhaps most magnanimous and moving of all, floods out.

26

And in response the feelings of Madeleine also spring irresistibly with it. Her weakness, her pact with love, has set her unredeemably between the two fires. Choice must mean loss; can one win without also losing? Give me an answer, she demands of her mirror-self. The reflection is silent, but from the orchestra, her inner being, we hear Ex. 15 which belongs to Flamand. A great calmness descends upon her. She looks again into the glass. Olivier as well as Flamand is reflected in the music, but the mirror image below Ex. 26 is the retrograde of her brother's *Heiter entscheiden* which is also Flamand's Ex. 15. She tells herself that any conclusion for this opera must be trivial, must it not? Ex. 1 is indissolubly entwined with the end of Ex. 12.

The Major-domo interrupts to say that supper is served (Ex. 24). To his surprise she smiles and waves her fan at her reflection, curtsies to it, and walks in to supper highly delighted, as the music plays gently with themes belonging to her and her brother and her two suitors.

'We must end with a question mark,' said Strauss. The horn twice muses on Ex. 22, the ending of the opera, and the full orchestra slices each phrase with a razor-sharp chord of questioning. But the Composer rhythm of Ex. 15 was last to be heard. It sounds, when you consider, like a probable answer to the concluding query.

6

In one sense *Capriccio* is the *finis quae coronat opus*, a master's last and most delightfully, practically instructive words on the major pre-occupation of his life. In a stricter sense it is not part of the Strauss operatic canon at all. He had already decided that *Die Liebe der Danae* was to be his last opera, and as soon as the Hitler War began he knew that he would not live to attend the première. *Capriccio* was to be a private entertainment for his own pleasure—he is supposed to have justified his later instrumental works with the self-depreciating admission that One can't play Skat all the time; it was his personal translation of Verdi's *Mi diverto* in connexion with *Falstaff*. The subject of textual audibility in operatic performance had obsessed Strauss for most of his working life, certainly from *Der Rosenkavalier* onwards; it was the subject of his forewords to *Intermezzo*, and of his preface to *Capriccio* as well. It played one part, if no more, in the resort to a chamber orchestra for *Ariadne auf Naxos*; another in the, so to say, terraced orchestration of *Die Frau ohne Schatten*. It was fundamental to the credo of an opera composer who even in the years of his high maturity was not too proud to alter vocal tessitura (for the first Clairon, and the first Da-ud) and orchestral nuances during rehearsals so that everything would be audible. He ended the preface to *Capriccio* with some reflections on the need to recognize that music does not sound the same from one place to another; that his first piano teacher, the harpist Auguste Tombo, had been told by Wagner to alter the 'unplayable' harp part in the Magic Fire Music of *Die Walküre* so that the obvious intentions were practically realized; and that 'loyal interpretation and congenial improvisation are brother and sister—like Words and Music'.

In the Conversation Piece *Capriccio* music may be the winner, but words are the subject of the thesis and total audibility was the challenge that Strauss set himself—with the *datum* that here, for the third time in his fifteen operas, he could be certain that his music would reflect everything contained in the text, simply because he had been in charge of every word, even if he had not, as in *Guntram* and *Intermezzo*, written the whole text himself. Though he might not admit it, his professional instinct gave him the further challenge (gave it also to Clemens Krauss who, as a Straussian conductor, had a vested interest in the successful qualities of any Strauss opera) of turning a theoretical discussion into a worthwhile theatrical experience for an audience. The acknowledged master of operatic effect was, finally, to investigate in public the causes of his effects. Intractable philosophizing (such as Strauss had frequently been asked by Hofmannsthal and Gregor to transform into music) must, for the gratification of his own self-respect, be realized in terms of credible, lively, interesting human beings such as he had, all his life, demanded of his other librettists. Yet the discussion must have a musical as well as rhetorical and dramatic shape. All this, if scrupulously calculated, would condition the nature of the musical invention, the least of Strauss's problems by this stage, granted his facility's requirements of interesting text and challenging situation—the challenge was not a dramatic one, this time, but a challenge to the virtuoso opera composer.

The foregoing chapter, in its initial pages, has shown how *Capriccio* gradually attained its final shape; but, if considered as a complete integer, it seems to have grown from the centre outwards in both directions. The two large ensembles with their trailing aftermath (including La Roche's monologue) form the centrepiece, flanked on one side by the ballet, on the other by the servants' chorus; Monsieur Taupe's curious scene is paralleled by the otherwise prominent reading from Olivier's play; the opening sextet is reflected in the likewise purely instrumental Intermezzo, and the two love duets by the closing monologue which discusses them, as the presence of the composed sonnet in both asks us to appreciate. Everything in *Capriccio* goes by pairs, like words and music, brother and sister, Flamand and Olivier—the Ballet Dancer's *divertissement* is the exception, and she too may find her pair in La Roche's monologue if one regards the construction through another turn of the prism.

One may carry these pairs a stage further into the musical style which uses a sizeable orchestra very largely for chamber-musical purposes. Strauss needed the number of players not for emphasis so much as for variety, and as a result *Capriccio* is one of his most richly diversified and intriguing operatic scores, a grander *Ariadne* as *Intermezzo* is a fined-down *Rosenkavalier* (theatrical experience may confirm the justice of these perhaps curiously paradoxical comparisons). The large available force of orchestral musicians also encouraged Strauss to chance his arm in the juxtaposition of singing voices (sung words which must be heard and understood) with symphonic orchestral polyphony, the Satanic birthright of all German composers, as Strauss had called it. And sure enough, the experiment succeeds in the master orchestrator's hands, except perhaps in the Quarrel Octet where under no circumstances could all the words hope to be distinguished.

The individualization of the topics under discussion is extraordinarily successful. One might wish that Clairon and the Count had become stronger characters, yet they are musically distinctive and, by their modest prominence, throw into fuller light not only the Countess and her two swains but also La Roche who is fully coloured—it is he, not Flamand, who suggests Strauss's point of identification. The natures of Flamand and Olivier are delightfully suggested, not only in their wooing interviews with the Countess—Flamand's rather the more forthcoming and musically amplified, as one expects from musician-authors (even from the one who disliked tenors)—but in their dialogue at the start of the opera. And Strauss's identifying themes have a strength and memorability which we may miss from some of his immediately preceding operas.

Most strongly characterized of all is the Countess herself, the personified spirit of the opera's theme, Opera as a compound and inspiratory muse of both words and music. She it is who lifts *Capriccio* out of the realms of theoretical argument and into the wider, more generally appealing climate of the *Ewig-Weibliche* that had, through the soprano voice, compelled Strauss to devote the best years of his composing life to opera. This identification of the soprano heroine with the spirit of Opera is, and perhaps has long been, quite natural to the unsophisticated opera-goer, the canary-fancier and the connoisseur of beautiful singing as such; but it is only incidental to the musical dramatist. Since the composer is usually a man he naturally tends to favour the object of the hero's affection, and as a result most of the great soprano heroines in opera suggest, while they are singing and we are caught up in the spell, that they have in some way composed their own music, are indeed doing so on the spot as they voice their emotions. The composer had projected himself (his *anima*, disciples of Jung would say) into the personality of his heroine. But in the Countess Madeleine, and in some other of Strauss's heroines (Barak's wife in *Komm zu mir, Barak mein Mann,* Helen in *Zweite Brautnacht!,* Danae in the interview with Jupiter) I have experienced the unnerving sensation that, on the contrary, the heroine is projecting her *animus* into the inventive faculty of the composer, and that it is Strauss himself who is singing. Perhaps this is merely an aspect of the permissive hedonism to which Strauss increasingly submitted as he grew older with a dominating wife (and a dominating Hofmannsthal too), perhaps of the ambivalence characteristic of Strauss's heroines. The bigamous tendency implicit in Madeleine's dilemma is closer to masculine polygamous instincts than to the natural instincts of women which are essentially monogamous, as the old Higamus Hogamus rhyme tells us. This may, indeed, explain Strauss's immediate attraction to Zerbinetta rather than to Ariadne, not to mention the Marschallin with her numerous lovers, Helen with all Troy at her feet and Christine Storch who was teased for befriending Baron Lummer.

Countess Madeleine, lovely, intelligent, young, and caught between two fires, made the ideal diversion for Strauss's intended retirement. In her honour he assembled round her all the elements of operas that he loved best: the hit-tune from *Die Meistersinger* (and *Otello!*), the chamber-musical sounds of Mozart and the nostalgic re-creations of rococo, the big ensembles of conflicting sentiment, the allusive quotations (Mozart's piano concertos, and Strauss's recitative accompaniments to Mozart's operas), the dance, the age of Italian *bel canto*, the servants from *Don*

Pasquale, the laughing ensemble from *Un Ballo in Maschera*, the full-orchestral commentating intermezzo (from Wagner), yes and the wide-eyed, rather envious observation of aristocratic behaviour in a time when aristocracy really mattered (and the bourgeois artist could dream in vain of mixing freely with the aristocrats instead of the servants' chorus). The pastiches are more felicitous because completely at home, looking outside from within, in *Capriccio*. But if they continue to delight operatic audiences it will be because at their centre stands the Countess, the ideal incarnate, Strauss's Galatea sculpted to his own specification and conjured into glowing life.

Tilford 1963–Vieux Bourg de Pléherel 1964

Bibliography

Aeschylus	*Plays*, Dent 1956
Asow, Erich H. Müller von	*Richard Strauss Thematisches Verzeichnis*, Vienna 1959
ATV See Asow	
Barclay Squire & Fuller Maitland, ed.	*Fitzwilliam Virginal Book*, 2 Vols, London 1899
Beecham, Sir Thomas	*A Mingled Chime*, Hutchinson 1944
Bithell, Jethro	*Modern German Literature*, 1880–1950
Blakeney, E. H.	*Smaller Classical Dictionary*, Dent 1910
Brandl, Willy	*Richard Strauss Leben und Werk*, Wiesbaden 1949
BUE See Strauss, Richard	*Betrachtungen und Erinnerungen*
Busch, Fritz	*Pages from a Musician's Life*, trans. Marjorie Strachey, Hogarth 1953
Casti, Gian Battista de	*Opere Varie*, Paris 1821
Del Mar, Norman	*Richard Strauss, A Critical Commentary on his Life and Works*, Vol. 1, Barrie & Rockliff 1962
Erhardt, Otto	*Richard Strauss*, Breisgau 1952
Euripides	*Plays*, Dent 1956
Frazer, Sir James	*The Golden Bough, Balder the Beautiful*, Vols. 10 and 11, Macmillan 1962
Gehring, Egid, ed.	*Richard Strauss und Seine Vaterstadt*, Munich 1934
Graves, Robert	*Greek Myths*, Cassell 1958
Gregor, J.	*Clemens Krauss, Seine Musikalische Sendung*, Bad Bocklet 1953
——	*Richard Strauss, der Meister der Oper*, Munich 1939
Hammelmann, Hanns	*Hugo von Hofmannsthal*, Bowes & Bowes 1957
Hofmannsthal, Hugo von	*Die Erzählungen*, Stockholm 1949
Homer	*Opera*, Oxford 1902
——	*The Odyssey*, trans. E. V. Rieu, Penguin 1946
Jefferson, Alan	*The Operas of Richard Strauss in Great Britain 1910–1963*, Putnam 1963
Jonson, Ben	*Plays*, Dent 1953
Kapp, Julius	*Richard Strauss und die Berliner Oper*, Berlin 1934

Kende, Götz Klaus	*Richard Strauss und Clemens Krauss*, Munich 1960
Kralik, Heinrich	*The Vienna Opera House*, Vienna 1955
Krause, Ernst	*Richard Strauss Gestalt und Werk*, Leipzig 1956
Krueger, C. J.	*Hugo von Hofmannsthal und Richard Strauss*, Berlin 1935
Louvet de Couvray, J.-B.	*Amours du Chevalier de Faublas*, 3 Vols, Paris 1884
Molière, Jean-Baptiste	*Oeuvres Complètes*, Paris n.d.
Moszkowski, Moritz	*Caricatures by Moszkowski and others*, 1910
Muschler, R. C.	*Richard Strauss*, Hildesheim 1924
Natan, Alex	*Richard Strauss Opern*, Basle 1963
Newman, Ernest	*Richard Strauss*, John Lane 1908
——	*Opera Nights*, Putnam 1943
——	*More Opera Nights*, Putnam 1954
——	*Testament of Music*, Putnam 1962
	Musical Studies, John Lane 1905
OED	*Oxford English Dictionary*
Pander, Oscar Von	*Clemens Krauss in München*, Munich 1955
Petzoldt, Richard	*Richard Strauss, Sein Leben in Bildern*, Leipzig 1960
Pfister, Kurt	*Richard Strauss, Weg, Gestalt, Denkmal*, Vienna 1949
Renault, Mary	*The King Must Die*, Longmans, Green 1958
Rolland, Romain	*Richard Strauss et Romain Rolland, Fragments de Journal*, Paris 1951
——	*Souvenirs sur Richard Strauss*, Paris 1948
Röttger, H.	*Das Formproblem bei Richard Strauss*, Munich 1937
RSJB, ed Willi Schuh	*Richard Strauss Jahrbuch 1954*, Bonn 1953 1959/60, Bonn 1960
Schuch, Friedrich von	*Richard Strauss, Ernst von Schuch und die Dresden Oper*, 2nd Edition, Leipzig 1953
Schuh, Willi	*Die Entstehung des Rosenkavalier*, Zürich 1951
——	*Über Strauss Opern*, Zürich 1947
Seltsam, William H.	*Metropolitan Annals*, New York 1947

Slonimsky, Nicolas — *Music since 1900*, Dent 1938

Specht, Richard — *Richard Strauss und sein Werk*, Leipzig 1921

Steinitzer, Max — *Richard Strauss*, Berlin 1911–27

Stern, Ernest — *My Life, My Stage*, Gollancz 1952

Strauss, Richard — *Betrachtungen und Erinnerungen*
  (i) 1st Edition, Zürich 1949
  (ii) English translation by R. L. Leonard, Boosey & Hawkes 1953
  (iii) 2nd Edition, enlarged, Zürich 1957

—— *Briefe an meine Eltern* ed Schuh, Zürich 1954

—— *Briefwechsel Joseph Gregor* ed Tenschert, Salzburg 1955

—— *Briefwechsel Hugo von Hofmannsthal* ed Franz and Alice Strauss, (i) Zürich 1952 (ii) Collins 1961

—— *Briefwechsel Clemens Krauss*, selected and edited by Götz Klaus Kende and Willi Schuh, Munich 1963

—— *Briefwechsel Stefan Zweig*, Zürich 1955

—— *Correspondence Hans von Bülow* trans. A. Gishford, ed Schuh and Trenner, Boosey & Hawkes 1955

—— *Correspondence Romain Rolland* See Rolland

—— *Richard Strauss Stage Works, Documents of the first performances*, ed Ernst Roth, Boosey & Hawkes 1954

Tenschert, Roland — *Anekdoten von Richard Strauss*, Vienna 1945

—— *3 × 7 Variationen uber das Thema Richard Strauss*, Vienna 1944

—— *Richard Strauss und Wien*, Vienna 1949

Trenner, Franz — *Richard Strauss Dokumente seines Lebens und Schaffens*, Munich 1954

Walter, Bruno — *Theme and Variations*, Hamish Hamilton 1947

Wedgwood, C. V. — *The Thirty Years War*, Penguin 1957

Wilde, Oscar — *Plays*, Dent 1960

Zweig, Stefan — *World of Yesterday*, Cassell 1953

Index

Unless otherwise indicated, all works mentioned are by Richard Strauss.
Names within quotation marks (thus: 'Actress') are those of characters in operas.
Figures in bold type refer to plate illustration numbers.

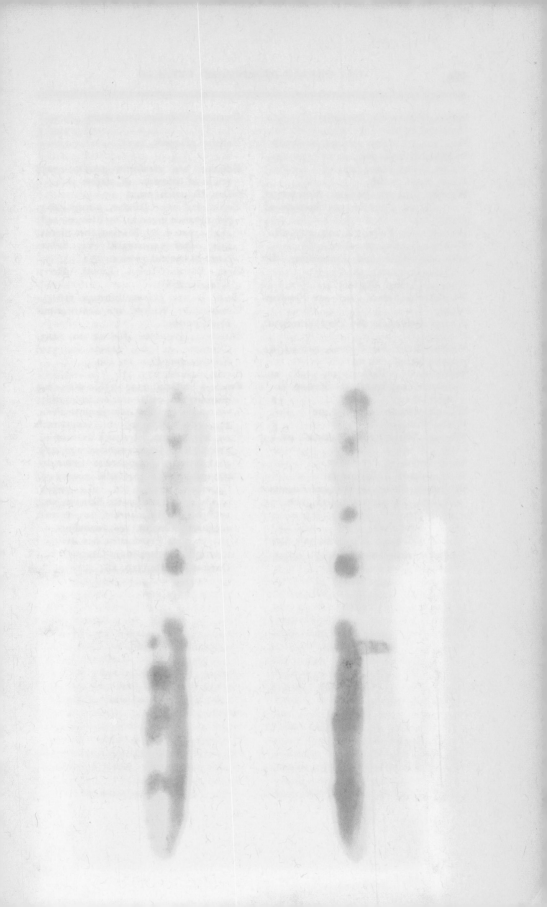

52919

MT
100
S84
M3

MANN, WILLIAM
    RICHARD STRAUSS.

DATE DUE

DEC 14 2001	

Fernald Library
Colby-Sawyer College
New London, New Hampshire

GAYLORD   PRINTED IN U.S.A.